The Colossian and
Ephesian *Haustafeln*
in Theological Context

american
university
studies

Series VII
Theology and Religion

Vol. 260

PETER LANG
New York • Washington, D.C./Baltimore • Bern
Frankfurt am Main • Berlin • Brussels • Vienna • Oxford

James P. Hering

The Colossian and Ephesian *Haustafeln* in Theological Context

An Analysis of Their Origins, Relationship, and Message

PETER LANG
New York • Washington, D.C./Baltimore • Bern
Frankfurt am Main • Berlin • Brussels • Vienna • Oxford

Library of Congress Cataloging-in-Publication Data

Hering, James P.
The Colossian and Ephesian Haustafeln
in theological context: an analysis of their origins,
relationship, and message / James P. Hering.
p. cm. — (American University studies. VII,
Theology and religion; vol. 260)
Includes bibliographical references.
1. Bible. N.T. Colossians III, 18–IV, 1—Criticism, interpretation, etc.
2. Bible. N.T. Ephesians V, 22–VI, 9—Criticism, interpretation, etc.
3. Family—Biblical teaching. 4. Ethics in the Bible. I. Title.
BS2715.6.F33H47   227'.506—dc22   2006101461
ISBN 978-0-8204-9505-7
ISSN 0740-0446

Bibliographic information published by **Die Deutsche Bibliothek**.
Die Deutsche Bibliothek lists this publication in the "Deutsche
Nationalbibliografie"; detailed bibliographic data is available
on the Internet at http://dnb.ddb.de/.

The paper in this book meets the guidelines for permanence and durability
of the Committee on Production Guidelines for Book Longevity
of the Council of Library Resources.

Printed in Germany

Meiner lieben Frau

Kerstin Maya

in Dankbarkeit

καλὴ καὶ ἀγαθή

Contents

Introduction

The New Testament *Haustafeln*: What's in a Name?

Long before Shakespeare passionately asked this question through the distraught Juliet, the nominal/phenomenal question had been debated by philosophers, employed by poets and exploited by worldly-wise politicians. A name can, when the object in question is not thoroughly familiar to the hearer, determine a great deal about the object's perceived character. This is particularly true in the case of the New Testament *Haustafeln*. The German term *Haustafel*, frequently rendered in English as "household codes," has, since the time of the reformer Martin Luther, referred to a rather broad number of New Testament texts which feature admonition directed toward particular social groupings within the church.[1] More recently, it has become a literary *terminus technicus* indicating a far smaller grouping of parenetic texts. Possessing common and recognisable characteristics, these New Testament passages evoke a sense that they stand, if nothing else, in relief to their broader letter-form contexts. This perception is not without substance; the letters of Colossians, Ephesians and 1 Peter all contain the distinctive *Haustafel* form[2] in their extended parenesis, each of which is readily recognised by its direct form of address, consistent relational pairings and reciprocal commands. In the case of the New Testament *Haustafeln*, then, the distinctive name corresponds to an equally distinctive literary phenomenon.

---

[1] Luther did not, however, attempt to locate particular NT texts in order to consign them to this modern NT category, as some maintain. His contribution was to collate a broad body of ethical teaching, wholly derived from NT texts, which he named *Haustafel*. In contrast to the technical use of the term in modern scholarship, Luther combed the entire New Testament for examples of *Mahnungen*, e.g., any exhortations which might be gathered to constitute a body of teaching on relations in the church, a "Haustafel etlicher Sprüche für allerlei heilige Orden und Stände, dadurch dieselbigen, als durch eigene Lektion, ihres Amtes und Dienstes zu ermahnen", "Der kleine Katechismus von 1529," in *Luthers Werke, Volksausgabe in acht Bänden*, ed. Kawerau, Buchwald, Köstlin, Rade and Schneider (Berlin: C.A. Schwetschke und Sohn, 1898), 103. From this large variety of texts, Luther construed the relational/ethical portion of his shorter catechism known as the *Haustafel*, which included instruction concerning bishops, pastors, evangelists, the state, finances, youth, widows, husbands, wives, parents, children, servants and the church member as an individual.

[2] *Haustafel* is now regarded as distinct from other, similar forms such as *Gemeindetafel*, *Pflichtentafel* or *Ständetafel*. See discussion in chapter one, 9f., concerning the characteristics of, and texts belonging to, the *Haustafel* form.

Having identified a recognisable literary form within several early Christian letters,[3] it was a matter of course that these should come under scholarly form-critical scrutiny, both as discrete units of instruction, as well as a potential (extra-biblical) genre. A number of questions have arisen: how should scholars identify, and ultimately understand, this neatly demarcated form which confronted them, albeit in slightly altered guise, in a number of New Testament letters? Are its admonitions simply a familiar product of the ancient Christian community (and unique to its ethic), or do they hail from another faith community, representing ancient, and perhaps pagan, provenance?

Secondly, and equally important to the understanding the origins of the *Haustafel*, is whether this identifiable form finds integration within the larger message of the letter which is acting as its "host." Does each *Haustafel* (hereafter HT), regardless of its origins, demonstrate similarities to the theology and ethical vision of the larger letter? Is it, as some have maintained, an early Christian *Lehrstück*, hastily inserted without thought of its theological integration, or perhaps merely a crude attempt to christianise an otherwise profane import? Do the tenor and content of its mandates indicate a relationship to the concerns and theology of the respective letters, or are they to be traced, in the final analysis, to situations beyond their literary purview? The questions of HT origins and theological integration are, of course, closely related, and provide the impetus for the following study. The question of origin, we hope to demonstrate, though essential to our investigation, does not *necessarily* prejudice the answer as to whether the HT form finds a degree of integration in the theology and ethics of the "host" letter.

The question regarding the literary and sociological provenance of the HT has been the subject of an extended scholarly debate, spanning nearly a century. Evidencing astonishingly varied conclusions, competing source theories have attempted to ascertain the HT's original literary form and context, as well as the manner and time of its eventual appropriation[4] within the

---

[3] The *Haustafel* was short-lived as a literary phenomenon; limited to the early Christian period, extra-biblical examples (though different in organisation and content) can be found in Didache 4:9–11; Polycarp, Phil. 4:2–6:1; Barnabas 19:5b, 7; 1 Clement 1:3, 21:6–9; Ignatius, Polycarp 4:3, 5:1–2.

[4] Though this approach suggests that the HT existed in a form which predates the immediate context, most scholars agree that the adoption took place at the time of writing. A more radical disjunction between the HT and its literary/social context has been suggested by W. Munro, "Col. 3:18–4:1 and Eph. 5:21–6:9: Evidences of a Late Literary Stratum?," *NTS* 18 (1972): 434–47, who considers the HT an interpolation. Sarah Tanzer, "Submerged Traditions of Sophia: Ephesians," in *Searching the Scriptures: A Feminist Commentary*, ed. E. Schüssler Fiorenza (New York: Crossroad Publishing Company, 1994), adopts her argument. W.O. Walker, "The "Theology of Woman's Place" and the "Paulinist" Tradition," *Semeia* 28 (1983): 101–112, represents the most radical expression of this theory, assigning

Christian community. Such analysis is critical in forming an understanding of the features and content of the HT in the broader Hellenistic context. The elements of this debate, and its prominent representatives, will be discussed in detail in the following chapter. These theories, however distinct in their observations and conclusions, share a common element: they are character-ised by an understanding of the HT as an imported, *foreign element* within the larger text of their respective letters.[5] No major investigation of HT ori-gins, whether Christian, Hellenistic or Hellenistic-Jewish, assumes that the code finds it genesis within the New Testament letters, or that the HT form emerges from the impulses of its *present* literary context. Consequently, as we shall see, the HT is ascribed to sources as diverse as the sayings of Christ to the economic theory of Aristotle. As reasonable and demonstrable as the "foreign element" assumption may be, it carries with it an attendant meth-odological feature which has coloured research throughout the century: the HT form and its particular ethical features have undergone diachronic analy-sis in isolation from its letter context. The gaze of recent scholarship has been consistently focused beyond the immediate literary context of the HT, in an attempt, oddly enough, to ascertain the present, contextual meaning of the biblical text. This analysis generally includes, as we shall see, a proposed original form, context and meaning of the HT, as well as a hypothetical so-ciological scenario, which depicts the occasion and reasoning for the HT ap-propriation into the biblical text. Both elements of the analysis, the proposed origins and the nature of the sociological occasion, promote an isolation of the HT from its theological/letter context; it remains, both in terms of origin and theological intention, a thoroughly alien element. The antidote, we be-lieve, is not to reject the important findings of previous research, but to add to this a synchronic analysis of each HT form, which takes into account the literary characteristics and theology of the HT context.

The second question posed above, as to whether the HT can be rightly understood in terms of the theology of the larger letter, has been raised, but

---

numerous texts touching upon sexual ethics to a later, "Paulinist" redactor. A. Stand-hartinger, *Studien zur Entstehungsgeschichte & Intention des Kolosserbriefs*, ed. A.J. Malherbe and D.P. Mössner, Supplements to Novum Testamentum, vol. 94 (Leiden: Brill, 1999) argues convincingly against such glosses.

[5] Karl Weidinger's sentiments are both early and typical: The HT mandates repre-sent for him "an intrusion of profane/societal phrases within Christian scripture", a "foreign body" which holds no Christian values. *Die Haustafeln, ein Stück urchris-tlicher Paränese*, ed. H. Windisch, Untersuchungen zum Neuen Testament, vol. 14 (Leipzig: J.C. Heinrichs'sche Buchhandlung, 1928), 50.

has not been the subject of a more thorough investigation.[6] It is the intention
of this study to explore the admonitions of two of the earliest examples of the
HT in the New Testament, Colossians 3:18–4:1 and Ephesians 5:22–6:9,
both in relation to their individual literary contexts, as well as comparatively.
After a careful analysis of these HT forms, a comparison will be made, in
similar manner, with selected relevant texts from ancient and contemporary
Hellenistic authors. It is hoped that a synchronic and comparative examination will provide evidence of the HT's relationship to the letters, as well as
the respective authors' theological reasoning. This approach, though by no
means displacing the helpful and necessary study of HT origins, may help in
locating the distinctively Christian elements within the HT form, and thereby
present possible models for understanding its fundamental ethic.

Climate Surrounding the HT Today: Can the *Haustafeln* Find a Contemporary Hearing?

Another aspect of the HT which further complicates its relationship to its
broader literary context is its apparent promotion of stratified social relations; in particular those between husbands and wives, as well as slaves and
masters. How might the HT regulations, given with the force of command,
be reconciled with the more egalitarian impulses seen, for example, in 1 Cor.
7, Gal. 3:27–28, or much closer at hand, Col. 3:11? Can the New Testament
HT be construed as genuinely Christian, or do their mandates promote an
essentially alien, sub-Christian ethic? This element of HT scholarship cannot
be ignored; any study of the HT must address the relationship between the
HT commands and broader Christian ethical vision. If we venture beyond the
previously mentioned form-critical and *entstehungsgeschichtliche* concerns,
we find that the *theological* and *ethical* implications of the New Testament
HT elicit historical analysis and sharp criticism.[7] Wolfgang Schrage opens
his article "Zur Ethik der Neutestamentlichen Haustafeln" with a statement
which reveals much about the tensions aroused by the ethical teaching of the
Haustafeln today, particularly the elements of obedience and submission re-

---

[6] A notable exception is John Barclay, "Ordinary but Different: Colossians and
Hidden Moral Identity," *Australian Biblical Review* 49 (2001): 34–52, 44. Though
accepting the form-critical explanation of HT origins, Barclay investigates the theology of the Colossian epistle, and finds the HT to be a "consistent attempt to apply
the Christology of the letter to the realm of the household duties."

[7] The apparent theological reasoning can, and has, been used to ill effect; see W.A.
Meeks, "The "Haustafeln" and American Slavery: The Hermeneutical Challenge," in
Theology and Ethics in Paul and his Interpreters, eds. E.H. Lovering and J.L. Sum-
ney (Nashville: Abingdon Press, 1996), 232–253.

quired of its subordinate members. The implications of paternalism and power abuse, he notes, lie close at hand. Searching for options, both theological and historical-critical, some scholars have attempted to ameliorate the negative effect of the text on modern sensitivities; yet the HT receives "bad theological marks." He writes:

> Die Haus- oder Pflichttafeln des Neuen Testaments erhalten heute in der kritischen Exegese üblicherweise schlechte theologische Zensuren. Wo man sich über die historischen und religionsgeschichtlichen Fragen hinaus theologisch mit ihnen auseinandersetzt, ist "Verbürgerlichung" noch eines der harmlosesten Urteile, das über sie gefällt wird. [8]

The theological value of the HT is, as Schrage has indicated, frequently estimated to be less than admirable, and at best, an indication of the corruption of pristine Christian thought. Indeed, the *Haustafeln* have attracted attention beyond biblical scholarship, drawing sharp criticism. Atheist Joachim Kahl castigates the HT mandates as the prime manifestation of a Christian worldview, which breeds a "Klima der Menschenverachtung."[9] The HT cannot be, logically speaking, both the antithesis and representation of Christian theology. Attempts to redress the apparent discrepancy between "genuine" Christian ethical values and the HT have characteristically relied upon two approaches. Some ascribe to the HT an extraordinary meaning not actually found in the text (a hidden and laudable Christian ethic), which is then held in contrast to the surrounding pagan ethical milieu.[10] This approach overlooks numerous and *bona fide* points of similarity, and avoids, of course, the rather embarrassing charge contained in the second approach: that the HT is simply promoting commonly held (and manifestly questionable) views of the contemporary culture. The second approach isolates the HT from its Christian context by emphasising its common origins and character. Of course, any interpretation which allows for too great a commonality between the HT and its contemporary ethos is bound to consign the HT to essentially non-

---

[8] W. Schrage, "Zur Ethik der neutestamentlichen Haustafeln," *NTS* 21 (1975): 1–22, 1.

[9] Joachim Kahl, *Das Elend des Christentums oder Plädoyer für eine Humanität ohne Gott*, Rororo aktuell, vol. 1093 (Hamburg: Rororo, 1977), 17.

[10] J.E. Crouch, *The Origin and Intention of the Colossian Haustafel*, eds. E. Käsemann and E. Würthwein, Forschungen zur Religion und Literatur des Alten und Neuen Testaments, vol. 109 (Göttingen: Vandenhoeck & Ruprecht, 1972), 31, castigates David Schroeder (*Haustafeln*, 123) for his "attempt to remove from the *Haustafel* that which offends modern sensitivities", an approach which "defies sound exegesis." Schroeder had contended that ὑποτάσσεσθαι, in contrast to its meaning in Hellenistic literature, receives a substantially new, Christian meaning in the HT.

Christian ethical norms. The genuinely Christian theological aspect is thereby revealed to be superficial,[11] and the level of relevance for the church is profoundly diminished.[12] It would not be unreasonable, in such a case, to question the HT role as Scripture.[13] Klaus Thraede sums up this hermeneutical quandary with logical precision:

> Je mehr sich der Eindruck verfestigt, daß gerade im Punkt "Gehorsam" die Haustafeln innerhalb einer schon antiken Debatte Partei ergreifen, desto mehr büßen sie leider an heutiger theologischer Verwertbarkeit ein. Der Versuch, sie vom Vorwurf des "Paternalismus" reinzuwaschen, hat infolgedessen allerlei "Eisegese" ins Kraut schießen lassen. Am weitesten gehen dabei wohl jene Gelehrten, die ihnen eine gesellschaftskritische Komponente zuschreiben und mit ihr ein christlich-erstmaliges Plädoyer gegen autoritären Ordnungsmißbrauch meinen. Das bedeutet meistens, zu Gunsten eines—oft begriffsrealistisch oder aus Äquivikation gewonnenen— "grundlegend neuen Sinnes" den Textinhalt außer Kraft zu setzen. Wer dagegen um den Literalsinn bemüht ist, muß sich auch sorgfältig um die hellenistische Ethik kümmern und z.B. der schier unausrottbaren Ansicht entgegentreten, daß die antike Eheanschauung nur ein rüdes κρατεῖν des Mannes, kein ἀγαπᾶν gekannt habe.[14]

Thraede's assessment highlights the tendency within scholarship of exaggerating the significance of pre-Christian influences, or overlooking them altogether. To assess properly the theology of the New Testament HT mandates, it seems critical to avoid the pitfalls of attempting to distance them from other, extra-biblical occurrences of the HT form (extricating or ignoring the common elements seen among Hellenistic authors or granting these a special heretofore unknown Christian sense), or to consign them to irrelevance, due

---

[11] Martin Dibelius notes that the Col. HT stemmed from a "nichtchristliche Regel" whose fixed, societal value had undergone a "leichte Verchristlichung." M. Dibelius, *An die Kolosser, Epheser, an Philemon*, ed. H. Greeven, 3 ed., Handbuch zum Neuen Testament (Tübingen: J.C.B. Mohr, 1953), 46.

[12] E. Schüssler Fiorenza, *In Memory of Her: A Feminist Theological Reconstruction of Christian Origins* (London: SCM Press, 1983), 254, notes, correctly, that a majority of scholars no longer view the HT as a uniquely Christian, but rather as an adaptation of contemporary values; as such they are to be questioned.

[13] James Dunn, "The Household Rules in the New Testament," in *The Family in Theological Perspective*, ed. S.C. Barton (Edinburgh: T.& T. Clark, 1996), 60, puts his finger on the hermeneutical gulf which separates the ancient and modern churches and their respective values. The ancient church does not "share our enlightenment", and the question must be asked, he insists, if the HT can be regarded as scripture for the church of today.

[14] Klaus Thraede, "Zum historischen Hintergrund der Haustafeln des Neuen Testaments," *Pietas* Sup. Vol. 1980, FS B. Kötting (1980): 359–368, 361. Thraede, in spite of his interest in the HT form, argues that the HT has lost its *Verwertbarkeit* for the modern church.

to their common pedigree. It is more important, it seems, to acknowledge common literary elements, while attempting to expose features which evidence genuine, Christian innovation. This approach anticipates aspects of the HT which reveal affinities with pagan literature, and, likewise, with the theology of the broader letter. If we are able to identify these latter elements and establish literary and theological common ground, we believe that it may be possible to determine, at least to some degree, the theological and ethical intention of the HT authors, and thereby the distinctive elements of their Christian ethic. It may be, then, that the HT, read in its theological context, can offer substantial insights into the ancient Christian perception of household relations, and reveal their essentially *theological* regulation, as well. Our investigation will include the following elements:

1. An assessment of previous HT scholarship. This chapter will attempt to catalogue and analyse the various approaches to understanding the meaning and social context of the New Testament HT over the last century. Particular attention will be given to the advances in understanding of the HT as various theories unfold. We hope to illustrate, as well, how scholars have, due to methodological commitments, avoided a synchronic reading of the HT text.

2. An analysis of the two earliest HT forms as found in Colossians and Ephesians. In these two chapters, we will investigate elements of each author's vocabulary, style and theological emphasis to determine the HT's affinity with the larger letter. Particular attention will be given to the unique, expanded sections of each HT as an indicator of the author's theological concerns.

3. In addition, a chapter will be devoted to investigating the literary and theological relationship between Colossians and Ephesians, with particular attention given to the Colossian-Ephesian redaction. We will attempt to ascertain both stylistic changes and theological developments, which illustrate the creativity and concerns of the Ephesian redactor. The HT form, we hope to demonstrate, undergoes similar editorial change, and serves as an example of the Ephesian redactor's transformation of the Colossian *Vorlage*.

4. A final chapter will undertake a comparison between the HT and six ancient texts, which are significant in the understanding and development of ancient household regulations. These texts, we hope to show, evidence not only common HT characteristics, but a remark-

able independence of thought, particularly in terms of their ontological assumptions and the practical regulation of the household. It is our hope that the comparison will lend understanding to the nature of ancient household regulation, as well as highlighting the uniquely Christian elements of the New Testament HT.

Chapter One
Survey and Assessment
of Scholarship

Introduction

It was the Heidelberg theologian Martin Dibelius who narrowed the field of texts which belong to the now technical term, *Haustafel*. *Haustafel* no longer denoted the catechetical teaching derived from a conglomeration of NT hortatory texts, but was seen as a type of literary/traditional stratum which could be found within the larger New Testament text. Those biblical texts designated by Dibelius as *Haustafeln* were Col. 3:18–4:1; Eph. 5:22–6:9; 1Pet. 2:18–3:7; Tit. 2:1–10; and 1 Tim. 2:8–15; 6:1–2.[1] His student, Karl Weidinger, was to follow this list in his 1928 monograph.[2] Weidinger's *Haustafeln* proved to be a definitive work on the subject, demarcating for New Testament scholarship those texts which formally belong under the broad *Haustafel* rubric. Their conclusions were eventually challenged, however, as the Dibelius-Weidinger proofs (Stoic duty lists) were shown[3] to be too loosely related in form, mode of address, subject and content to constitute a single, recognisable source which might be considered as the pre-Christian HT *Vorlage*. The perceived limitations of the Dibelius-Weidinger theory and its proposed texts have introduced a number of positive developments in HT research, particularly the identification and limitation of HT texts. On the one hand, scholars suggested more refined categories to describe the HT form; the Pastoral Epistles, for instance, were omitted from the list due to their general nature and lack of structure, finding their place in a new category which Gnilka aptly calls *Gemeindetafel*.[4] On the other hand, critical essays continued to explore potential antecedents of the HT form, broadening the field to include ancient philosophical treatises, as well as Hellenistic Jewish material. The new and growing body of source material had the dual effect of freeing the HT from its exclusive attachment to Stoic texts, while effecting a refinement of its form-critical features. Arguing from common elements found among Hellenistic and Jewish antecedents of the HT, these scholars proposed a considerably smaller and well-defined grouping of *Haustafel* texts. As with

---

[1] Dibelius, *Kolosser*, 48.

[2] Karl Weidinger, *Die Haustafeln, ein Stück urchristlicher Paränese*, ed. H. Windisch, Untersuchungen zum Neuen Testament, vol. 14 (Leipzig: J.C. Heinrichs'sche Buchhandlung, 1928).

[3] Schroeder, Crouch, Balch, Lührmann and others.

[4] J. Gnilka, *Der Epheserbrief*, eds. A. Vögtle, R. Schnackenburg and A. Wikenhauser, Herders Theologischer Kommentar zum Neuen Testament, vol. 10 (Freiburg: Herder, 1971), 207.

the Dibelius-Weidinger thesis, the assumption remained that their features might be traced to traditional sources.[5] Lillie, representing the growing consensus in contemporary scholarship, has narrowed Weidinger's original list to fit the more refined and technical *Haustafel* scheme. The texts which emerge as *Haustafel* are Colossians 3:18–4:1, Ephesians 5:22–6:9 and 1 Peter 2:18–3:7.[6] Most recent scholarship has continued to adopt the shorter list of New Testament *Haustafeln*, where the common elements are seen as defining the form. These elements, distilled over years of research concerning the elementary form of the *Haustafel*, are, according to Marlis Gielen:

1. A closed parenetic unit which stands out from its context;
2. The subjects are addressed in pairs and sequentially;
3. The relationship between the pairs is one of sub/superordination;
4. Subordination is the cohesive theme of the unit;
5. The subordinated party is addressed first;
6. Direct address is employed with definite article and nominative plural;
7. The address is followed by imperative admonition;
8. The admonition is followed by an explanation (exceptions: Col. 3:19 and Eph. 6:4).[7]

Although the HT *form* has been defined with general scholarly agreement, there remains profound disagreement regarding the traditional origins of the form, and the sociological aspects of its eventual appropriation within the Christian context. These two elements are the constituent features of HT research in the last century, and form the framework of our analysis in the present chapter. In the following pages we hope to demonstrate how the scholarly debate regarding the origins and appropriation of the HT have greatly added to our understanding of ancient and first century ethical traditions, as well as proposing numerous helpful scenarios regarding the HT role in the early Christian community. Notwithstanding these positive contributions, the HT has remained a rather isolated element within its various New Testament contexts; it has been consistently regarded as a wholesale import of traditional values (whether pagan, Jewish or Christian), which in turn represent a

---

[5] W. Schrage, "Zur Ethik der neutestamentlichen Haustafeln," *NTS* 21 (1975): 1–22, 2, notes that the particular features of three NT HT forms are not to be explained in terms of literary dependence, but through a "gemeinsame Tradition."

[6] William Lillie, "The Pauline House-Tables," *Expository Times* 86 (1974–75): 179–183.

[7] Marlis Gielen, *Tradition und Theologie neutestamentlicher Haustafelethik*, eds. Frank-Lothar Hossfeld and Helmut Merklein, Athenaeums Monografien: Bonner Biblische Beiträge, vol. 75 (Frankfurt: Anton Hain, 1990), 3f.

response to a sociological event *indifferent* (or opposed!) to the theology of the letter. It is our hope that the following analysis will substantiate our observation that the understanding of the New Testament HT can be augmented by a study of their immediate, theological literary contexts.

Form-Critical HT Analysis

The question as to the origins and appropriation of the New Testament HT form has stirred decades of scholarly debate, and in the words of Gielen, it has found "keine restlos befriedigende und von allen anerkannte Antwort."[8] This is indeed the case. The debate has taken place in the arena of form-critical assumptions, and has largely adhered to the canons of form-critical methodology, yet scholars have arrived at little agreement, as we hope to illustrate below. Nearly all scholars, irrespective of their disagreements, would agree that the HT form is an identifiable unit which can be investigated under the assumptions of the *Formgeschichte* school, and have operated, since Dibelius, under these presuppositional guidelines. Change in form-critical theory has resulted in contemporary scholars tending to rely, primarily, upon written traditions only, usually according to a well-defined list of literary markers.[9] This has helped to mark the HT form with much more clarity, avoid inappropriate literary associations, and define it more precisely in relief to Jewish and Hellenistic forms.

Though most scholars have labelled the HT as an identifiable *Gattung,* and have enumerated its distinctive characteristics under the canons of the form-critical school, discovering the relationship between forms and their historical contexts[10] has remained an unrealised goal, and a point of contention. The debate over HT origins has lacked balance, being largely limited to questions

---

[8] Ibid., 24.

[9] Klaus Berger, *Formgeschichte des Neuen Testaments* (Heidelberg: Quelle & Meyer, 1984), 11f. Berger explains in detail the refinement of the *Formgeschichte* school over the past decades, noting a departure from theories of oral tradition and preoccupation with institutional structures. Extremely important is the new emphasis on the aspect of the text, which represents the interests of those who formulated it, as well as those who may be critically implicated. Earlier studies looked at the "Entstehungsgeschichte", but overlooked the intentions of the author for the further life of the church. The two new emphases are to determine "Gemeindegeschichte", while looking for any clues to the genre's pre-Christian history. Even particular forms should be very well defined, avoiding vague categories such as Bultmann's "Gesetzesworte"; this development can be seen in the rejection of much of the rather uneven evidence in the Dibelius-Weidinger theories.

[10] Ibid., 12. Berger notes the tension between "Gattungen" and "historischen Abläufen."

of form, and with few exceptions,[11] principally German scholars. From Dibelius to Berger, the theories regarding origins, and to a lesser degree, appropriation, have been compounded. These often represent only slight modifications of earlier theories, with arguments revolving in some instances around small pieces of evidence or strikingly divergent sociological scenarios.[12] In spite of the sociological aspect of their investigation, form-critical scholars have tended to concentrate upon the particular (and often discrete) elements of the HT, searching for the definitive pre-Christian form. The strong concentration upon the pre-Christian *Vorlage* has shown itself to be one of the school's potential weak points,[13] as will be discussed below. The question as to the moment and ultimate reason for the appropriation of the HT into its new literary context, an important goal of the *Formgeschichte* school, has remained unanswered. In light of the new clarity of purpose and well-defined *Gattungen*, such as we find with Berger,[14] this may change in forthcoming research. The debate may then shed more light on the meaning of the HT in its New Testament context, and possibly lead towards more agreement among scholars. The movement of scholarship, it should be noted, has been towards increasing uncertainty regarding an *exact* or *singular* pre-Christian counterpart to the New Testament HT. This has been accompanied, perhaps not coincidentally, by a greater emphasis upon the social and reli-

---

[11] James Crouch, David Balch and David Verner have treated the HT in Colossians, 1 Peter and the Pastorals, respectively. Their analyses, treated below, bring an integration between the form and its historical context, an aspect which was given less attention in earlier, German scholarship.

[12] J. Gnilka, *Theologie des Neuen Testaments*, eds. J. Gnilka and L. Oberlinner, Herders Theologischer Kommentar zum Neuen Testament, vol. Supp. 5 (Freiburg: Herder, 1994), 347, sees the HT as a "Rückkehr zur bürgerlichen Ordnung"; he catalogues several of the prominent theories attached to explaining the occasion of the HT: i.) Fading expectancy of Christ's return; ii.) Transition from mission to established church; iii.) Influence of government (threats, pressure to conform); iv.) Accommodation to the surrounding culture; v.) A reaction to other-worldly, ascetic tendencies in the church. To this list might be added K.H. Rengstorf's theory of an intra-Christian debate, which was sparked by Paul's teaching in Gal. 3:28, *Die neutestamentlichen Mahnungen an die Frau, sich dem Manne unterzuordnen*, ed. W. Förster, Verbum Dei manet in Aeternum, FS für O. Schmitz (Witten: Luther Verlag, 1953), 144. See also Schroeder, *Haustafeln*, 89f. and Crouch, *Origin*, 124.

[13] James Dunn, *The Epistles to the Colossians and to Philemon*, eds. W.W. Gasque, I.H. Marshall and D.A. Hagner, The New International Greek Testament Commentary (Grand Rapids: Eerdmans, 1996), 51.

[14] Berger, *Formgeschichte*, 9f. Berger defines the goals, method and limits of the *Formgeschichte* school, particularly in light of its past shortcomings. He points out many failed attempts to mix methodologies, which have prevented the school from developing a distinctive character.

gious-historical context of the HT's appropriation. We believe it will be helpful, then, to consider the findings which have been generated from the form-critical research thus far, with particular attention given to Berger's above-stated purpose of *Formgeschichte*, to locate the HT form in terms of its literary *origins* and the circumstances surrounding its *appropriation* into the faith community, the "historischen Abläufe." Another aspect of our analysis will be to illustrate the form-critical methodological predisposition towards isolating the object of analysis from its immediate literary and theological context. In relation to the HT literary origins, form critical investigations assume that the incidentals of the New Testament HT are largely borrowed, perhaps from numerous sources over considerable periods of time. It is, then, a literary foreign object, in its essentials recognisable and indissoluble, surrounded by material only loosely related to its mandates and ethical vision. Similarly, the proposed circumstances surrounding the appropriation of the HT are equally distant to the purposes and theology of the host letter, and generally represent another context entirely, as illustrated below:[15]

Elements of *Haustafel* Form-Critical Analysis

Origins	Path of Adoption	Appropriation
Original HT Literary Form	→	New Testament HT Form
Original Social Context(s)	→	First c. Church Social Context

Whether regarded as a catechetical instruction, borrowed ancient economic theory, or the latest expression of contemporary household management, the original context of the HT is considered to be distant, or at least discrete, from that of the letter's composition. This, of course, is not the fault of form-critical analysis, for many of the elements of the theories may indeed be true. The question posed by this study will be: Though a number of elements within the New Testament HT are most probably related to earlier literary forms and hail from substantially different literary and sociological contexts, is there yet a theological aspect which can be extricated from its mandates? Are these elements related, then, to the immediate letter context? To answer

---

[15] See fn. 12. Interestingly, several of the theories correspond to the concept of routinisation of charisma outlined in Max Weber, *Wirtschaft und Gesellschaft: Grundriß der Verstehenden Soziologie*, 5 ed. (Tübingen: J.C.B. Mohr [Paul Siebeck], 1972). Weber outlines the development of religion in terms of charismatic personality and "extraordinary" (außeralltäglich) powers, which then give way to priests (these priests are: "Funtionäre eines regelmäßigen organisierten stetigen Betriebs", 259), organisation and a developed ethic. "*Religionssoziologie*", 245–381.

these questions, it will be necessary to first assess the scholarship which has left them unanswered. Our survey will begin with the earliest theories, which cite remarkably divergent sources, and which concentrate, primarily, upon questions of HT form. As the debate progresses, we shall investigate the introduction of sociological and economic theories, which reflect a loss of confidence in older, single-source approaches. It is our hope that this investigation will illustrate not only the complexity of the HT origins and message, but also make it clear that the HT, whatever its provenance or meaning, has not received treatment in its theological and literary letter context.

Research of HT Origins: Early Theories

Catechism Theories: The HT as Christian *Lehrstück*

Behind the various identifiable literary forms found in the New Testament, including the HT, there may have existed materials and traditions used in liturgical, credal and even catechetical exercises. These traditional Christian materials have been considered by several scholars to have informed the HT structure, particularly in terms of its use of direct address, imperative character, social groupings and theological reasoning. E.G. Selwyn, a representative of this view, modifies the use of the word catechism to describe the potential ecclesiological location of the early HT tradition:

> We mean forms or patterns, both oral and written, used in the instruction of cate-chumens and of those already baptised. The question-and-answer forms which the words suggest to us are not necessarily implied, though they are not excluded.[16]

Selwyn, Seeberg[17] and Carrington[18] have all maintained that the HT is to be seen as part of a larger body of parenetic material which was adopted by the early church, being implemented as instruction in both church and missionary settings. In this manner, they are suggesting that an undifferentiated complex of texts, strewn throughout the New Testament, were part of an earlier body of Christian instruction, which Seeberg named "die Wege." All parenetic passages found in the New Testament (as well as in early post-apostolic writings), including the HT form, can be traced to this body of teaching.[19] The sources which contributed to this instruction were several,

---

[16] E.G. Selwyn, *The First Epistle of St. Peter* (London: Macmillan & Co., Ltd., 1946), 18.

[17] A. Seeberg, *Der Katechismus der Urchristenheit* (Leipzig: A. Deichert, 1903).

[18] P. Carrington, *The Primitive Christian Catechism* (Cambridge: CUP, 1940).

[19] Seeberg, *Katechismus*, 37f.

including Jewish instruction (Acts 15; this early council gives evidence of appropriation of Jewish ethical norms), the words of Christ, John the Baptist and the early church.[20] Carrington and Selwyn, both writing considerably later than Seeberg, were aware of the tensions which their theories created with *Formgeschichte* methodology, especially the aspect of consigning so many different literary forms to one proposed source. Selwyn anticipates the friction of ideas, noting that the "scientific assumptions with which it [*Formgeschichte*] starts and the analytical methods it employs" are similar to his, yet vary radically "in the angle of approach."[21] Indeed, Weidinger (German) and Crouch (English) were to catalogue the shortcomings of the catechism theory in due time.

Weidinger recognises Seeberg's contribution in identifying "formelhafte Elemente" in the NT texts, but cites his mistake in trying to force these various elements into the single, fixed form of a catechism. That the NT authors were in possession of such a form is for Weidinger unlikely; he cautions against the extremes of attempting to determine either the exact *Sitz im Leben* of Christian parenesis, or more critically, to suggest a fixed form.[22] Seeberg, he observes, having postulated a fixed form, has to modify the nature of this catechism by means of "Abweichungen", in an attempt to harmonise the discordant elements. This casts doubt on the entire thesis of a fixed form.[23]

Crouch, after noting that the sources which Seeberg suggests (Jewish tradition, Jesus, John the Baptist and the early church) are too disparate and "too much of a construct to warrant serious attention", points to the main flaw of Seeberg's theory for the adherent of the *Formgeschichte* school: "His most serious weakness, however, lies in his failure to distinguish adequately between the larger body of ethical material and its individual units. In his haste to describe the liturgical *Sitz im Leben* of the larger collection, he bypassed the necessary preliminary examination of the individual *Gattungen*."[24] Indeed, Seeberg was extremely ambitious in his attempt to tie together, first of all, various ethical traditions into a single catechetical corpus; likewise, it is unlikely that this catechism could be the root of the numerous parenetic texts of the New Testament. Here Crouch is correct in asking where the HT form is to be found in the earlier Pauline epistles, if the catechism were extant at that time: "The burden of proof lies on those, however,

[20] Ibid., 85.
[21] Selwyn, *Epistle*, 367.
[22] Weidinger, *Haustafeln*, 3f.
[23] Ibid., 5.
[24] Crouch, *Origin*, 15.

16

who maintain that the *Haustafel* schema was an integral element of the Christian parenetic tradition from an early date. They are obliged to offer an adequate explanation for its relatively late appearance."[25] Not just an argument from silence, Crouch's criticism points to the failure of the catechism theory to explain, especially in light of the very broad nature of the catechetical material, its uneven representation (in particular the HT form) in Pauline and non-Pauline texts. This paucity and unevenness of representation, along with the undifferentiated collation of literary forms, have dislodged the catechism theory, as unproven, from serious scholarly consideration in recent years. Crouch concedes that Selwyn has amassed impressive parallels between 1 Peter and other New Testament texts, yet "...he has not convincingly demonstrated that these parallels enable us to reconstruct an early Christian catechism or that they even demand the assumption that there was such a catechism."[26]

In spite of the shortcomings of their theories, Seeberg, Carrington and Selwyn have proposed a *Sitz im Leben* for early Christian parenetic material: catechetical teaching and the mission of the early church. Not denying the presence of various literary forms, nor insisting that these forms were the exclusive invention of the church, they display a confidence in form-critical assumptions. Their theory represents the first attempt to identify the parenetic material of the New Testament, including the HT, as a phenomenon whose literary composition and original social context are distinct from its literary "host." The identification of the HT as an imported, traditional element became, hereafter, a canon of HT research. Later form-critical scholars would expand the social contexts to include Hellenistic sources; parenetic literary forms would be catalogued, moreover, according to the unique characteristics of each,[27] creating a broad diversity of source types. Among the newly differentiated forms, the HT would emerge as an object of particular attention. Hereafter, attempts to unify the various strands of parenetic mate-

---

[25] Ibid., 15.
[26] Ibid., 18.
[27] See Berger, *Formgeschichte*, 9f. for a detailed listing of the many types of *Gattungen* to be found in the NT text. The HT is located under the rubric *Symboleutische Gattungen: Haustafel und Pflichtenspiegel*. Here we see the refinement of the form-critical school, in particular the expansion of categories which possess well-defined characteristics, and are seen as representing *Gattungen* which can be traced through the literature of the period. That these *Gattungen* and their attendant characteristics have developed inductively in the wake of research, Berger testifies: "Vormeinungen darüber, was Formgeschichte sei, wurden anhand der neutestamentlichen Texte revidiert und erweitert. Das einzige maßgebliche Bestreben war, einen Aufriß zu schaffen, der für alle Texte des Neuen Testaments eine formgeschichtliche Bearbeitung erlaubte."

rial into some form of early Christian *Lehrstück*[28] were largely abandoned; the *Gattung* HT came to define the parameters of the form as well as the methodological approach for understanding the form within its larger context.[29] Identified texts, formerly isolated and (after analysis) integrated into the *Sitz im Leben* of the faith community (Selwyn, Seeberg), would now undergo a more thorough critical odyssey: isolation and extrication from the greater *Textfeld* to determine genre, a literary and social analysis to determine origins and social context, and finally, a re-introduction into the text by means of a theory of adoption. The evolving methodological sophistication would be matched by the expansion of Hellenistic source materials; an emphasis upon a distinct, pre-Christian *Vorlage* would be the next step in interpreting the HT form.

Dibelius-Weidinger: Adoption of the Hellenistic Ethic

Martin Dibelius, a contemporary of Seeberg, was to have a lasting impact on the direction of research touching upon the HT form. It was he who pointed to the Stoic list of duties as the foundation of the HT, citing its induction into the Christian *Gedankenwelt* as an attempt to come to grips with the unrealised parousia:

> Diese Sprachsammlungen [the HT forms found in the NT and early Christian literature] wollen die Pflichten der einzelnen Gruppen im Hause festlegen. Ihre Existenz in urchristlichen Schriften bezeugt das Bedürfnis des jungen Christentums, sich im Alltagsleben einzurichten. Selbstverständlich ist dieses Bedürfnis nicht; denn das Christentum, das als eschatologische Botschaft in die Welt und auch speziell in die griechische Welt eintrat s. 1 Th 1:9f., konnte scheinbar auf jede grundsätzliche Stellung zu den Kulturgemeinschaften Familie und Vaterland wie zur Kultur überhaupt verzichten vgl. die persönliche Stellung des Pls zur Ehe 1 Cor 7:29ff. Infolgedessen war das Christentum auf die Befriedigung jenes Bedürfnisses wenig vorbereitet, konnte ihm zum Mindesten nicht mit Gedanken des Evangeliums Jesu gerecht werden. Man war also auf die sittlichen Belehrungen angewiesen, wie sie in hellenistische und jüdische Propaganda ausgebildet hatten:
>
> > 1.die populäre Morallehre der Stoa hatte offenbar ein Schema ausgebildet;
> > 2.die jüdische Propaganda hat das Schema verwendet;

---

[28] Seeberg, *Katechismus*, 37. *Lehrstück* is Seeberg's general category for the collated ethical instruction found in the NT. The HT belong within this body of material.
[29] Berger, *Formgeschichte*, 10f., notes that elements of *Literaturgeschichte* and *Religionsgeschichte* combine in determining HT research.

3.mit oder ohne die Vermittlung des Judentums haben die Christen das Schema erhalten.[30]

Dibelius' theory was both new and complete; he suggested a proto-Christian context for the HT form, its possible path of adoption through Hellenistic Judaism, and a sociological impulse for its implementation. Before Dibelius, early form-critical research had taken note only of the outward forms of various parenetic texts, without suggesting a particular *Vorlage* in terms of an isolated genre. *Kolosser* located, for the first time, the HT in a popular form (Stoic lists of duties) and cultural setting (broad Hellenistic context, including Hellenistic Judaism). Dibelius' cited sources were rather limited,[31] however, and lacked the necessary characteristic markers that might connect them closely with the NT *Haustafeln*. His proposed transitional step by

---

[30] Dibelius, *Kolosser*, 48.

[31] Ibid., 48–49. Here he lists fragments from Epictetus: II 17,31, words from an eager student: θέλω δ᾽ ὡς εὐσεβὴς καὶ φιλόσοφος καὶ ἐπιμενὴς εἰδέναι τί μοι πρὸς τοὺς θεούς ἐστι καθῆκον, τί πρὸς γονεῖς, τί πρὸς ἀδελφούς, τί πρὸς πατρίδα, τί πρὸς ξένους; II 14,8, as a conclusion to a philosophical discussion (besides the Stoic avoidance of passion), the following is proposed: μετὰ τῶν κοινωνῶν τηροῦντα τὰς σχέσεις τάς τε φυσικὰς καὶ ἐπιθέτους, τὸν υἱόν, τὸν πατέρα, τὸν ἀδελφόν, τὸν πολίτην, τὸν ἄνδρα, τὴν γυναῖκα, τὸν γείτονα, τὸν σύνοδον, τὸν ἄρχοντα, τὸν ἀρχόμενον; and II 10, where Dibelius finds the heading τῶς ἀπὸ τῶν ὀνομάτων τὰ καθήκοντα ἔστιν εὑρίσκειν, which for him reads like a delineation of the above program. Interesting to note here is that Weidinger, *Haustafeln*, 36, adds an important quote regarding Epictetus' answer to this student, ἔρχου καὶ ἐπὶ τὸν δεύτερον τόπον, which became the topos ὁ περὶ τὸ καθῆκον, the uniting thread between the Dibelius-Weidinger proofs, the καθῆκον-Schema. The following passage opens with the query, σκέψαι τίς εἶ, with the listed options following: ἄνθρωπος, πολίτης τοῦ κόσμου, υἱός, ἀδελφός, βουλευτής, πατήρ. Diogenes Laertius defines the καθήκοντα in this manner, VII 108: καθήκοντα μὲν οὖν εἶναι ὅσα λόγος αἱρεῖ ποιεῖν, ὡς ἔχει τὸ γονεῖς τιμᾶν, αδελφούς, πατρίδα, συμφέρεσθαι φίλοις. Hierocles' epitomes (second c. A.D.), preserved for us by Stobaeus (fifth c. A.D.), summarise Stoic thought and represent the closest affinities to the HT form in Dibelius' list. In his list of duties we find the following topoi: the gods, country, parents, brother, and relatives. In separate sections he treats the household (περὶ οἴκων) and marriage (περὶ γάμου). Dibelius relied on the collection of Karl Praechter, *Hierokles der Stoiker* for these evidences. These particular texts can be found in their entirety in Malherbe, *Moral Exhortation*, 86–104. Dibelius' final citations are from Pseudo-Phocylides, didactic verses 175–228, Flavius Josephus, *Contra Apionem* 2,198–208, and Philo, *De Decalogo*, 165–67 (all representing the Hellenistic Jewish transition). These show a familiarity with the Greek categories, including relations towards parents, friends, children, foreigners, God, slaves and masters. This material, he admits, has particular Jewish elements, but is primarily determined by the "Allgemein-menschliche" which has been received from Hellenistic sources. In all these above examples, Dibelius is concerned to show that lists were extant in both the Hellenistic and Hellenistic Jewish worlds, which anticipated, and perhaps even helped form, the HT.

means of Hellenistic Judaism was also without convincing supportive evidence, particularly in light of the more exacting genre analysis which would develop among form-critical scholars.

Dibelius' research, in particular his proposed Hellenistic *Vorlagen*, was expanded by his student, Karl Weidinger, who published the first monograph, *Haustafeln*, in 1928. Following Dibelius, he includes a much longer list of HT forms than would be recognised today, including examples from the early Church Fathers. Weidinger locates the roots of the HT form in the popular philosophy circulating at the time of the church's founding; these roots can be documented and traced over a number of centuries:

> "Man kann es wagen, die ganze Zeitspanne vom 3. Vorchristlichen bis zum 4. Nachchristlichen Jahrhundert für Parallelen mit dem Christentum in Betracht zu ziehen; denn die Durchschnittsmoral der griechischen Gesellschaft ist in der ganzen Zeit wesentlichen Veränderungen nicht ausgesetzt gewesen."[32]

The Hellenistic world view functioned as "philosophische Propaganda", whose sphere of influence touched all educated citizens of the day. Their philosophical categories, ethical teachings and didactic turns of phrase became part of the common parlance of the era.[33] Weidinger expands the list of evidences which Dibelius had collected, but adds no new citations which might be more closely linked with the HT form of the New Testament. It is this lack of new forms, especially those that more closely resemble the HT form, that would soon draw criticism.[34] The evidence consists primarily of lists of duties which the philosophers considered critical to the exercise of the good, "eine Aufreihung der Pflichten gegenüber den Göttern und den verschiedenen Ständen", which in the Stoic system received the appellation καθῆκον.[35] Weidinger also cites the term νόμμα ἄγραφα, taken primarily from judicial pronouncements and tragic plays, as another category which was known, and which would have appealed to the "sittliche Bewußtsein des

---

[32] Ibid., 19f.

[33] Ibid., 19.

[34] David Schroeder would be the first to embark on a full study of the HT form in his 1959 dissertation, *Die Haustafeln des Neuen Testaments*, building on Rengstorf's broad observations regarding the form of the HT. Already in 1919, Alfred Juncker had pointed out differences between the HT and their Jewish and Hellenistic counterparts, *Die Ethik des Apostels Paulus*, Vol. 2, Halle: 1919, 205. Speaking from a vantage point of over fifty years of further HT research, Gielen sums up the criticism very well: "Nirgendwo findet sich auch nur ein einziger, konsequent durchgeführter Vergleich zwischen diesen 'HTT' und denen des NT, weder sprachlich-stilistisch noch inhaltlicher Art." *Tradition*, 26.

[35] Weidinger, *Haustafeln*, 42f.

20

Volkes."[36] These laws, containing nearly the same list of relations in society, are to be identified with the καθῆκον of the Stoics, and probably antedate it. The two strands of thought represented in these terms were conflated with time into an "altes Stück griechischer Volksethik" that had the tenacity to survive and even influence the ethics of a number of centuries.[37] Weidinger does not attempt to locate the exact point of introduction of the HT into the Christian community, whether directly from Hellenistic sources or mediated through Hellenistic Judaism. The answer to this question is, first of all, "impossible to determine", and furthermore "irrelevant", for the integration of the "Volksethik" was a simple matter of borrowing common concepts.[38]

That Weidinger considered the HT to be a profane import becomes quite obvious. Phrases such as "Das Eindringen solcher profan-gesellschaftlicher Wendungen in christliches Schrifttum" or "Fremdkörper im neutestamentlichen Gedankenkreis" indicate with unmistakable clarity the lack of integration he senses between the HT form and its letter context. The HT values are, he writes, clearly "keine christlichen", and show an obvious pagan pedigree. Only the superficial appendage of ἐν κυρίῳ, "einen angehängten Zusatz", creates a Christian emphasis in the Colossian HT: "Löst man das ἐν κυρίῳ aber ab, so bleibt nichts übrig, was nicht ein Stoiker oder ein jüdischer Lehrer sagen könnte."[39] As his teacher Dibelius, Weidinger saw the HT form as a concession on the part of the church to its abandonment of earlier, more radical living. "Der heiße Atem der ersten Epoche" no longer informed the church, rather a compromised ethic: "Insofern bedeutet die Haustafel einen Rückschritt: sie ist moralisch und arbeitet mit schwachen, geläufigen Motiven."[40] Dibelius and Weidinger set upon new territory in terms of research of the HT form. They introduced an entirely new grouping of source texts which would influence scholarly opinion for several decades. In terms of understanding the HT message, these texts (and the proposed sociological context which prompted their adoption), suggested a profound isolation between the HT, its host letter, and Christian ethical instruction.

Ernst Lohmeyer: Jewish Source Theory

As commentaries were being written to include the latest form-critical theories concerning HT origins, Ernst Lohmeyer was formulating what would be

[36] Ibid., 46.
[37] Ibid., 48.
[38] Ibid., 50.
[39] Ibid., 51.
[40] Ibid., 52.

the first thesis to contradict the Hellenistic source theory.[41] As a contemporary of Dibelius, he was aware of the new research regarding Hellenistic origins and the HT form. Yet he took another approach, finding the Hellenistic sources to be an improbable source for the Apostle.[42] He joined Dibelius in placing the HT in a pre-Christian context, but fundamentally departed from the Dibelius-Weidinger thesis in his search for origins, becoming the first to place the HT form within exclusively Jewish traditional instruction. In support of his theory, he notes that women, children and slaves are the primary addressees of the HT, the exhortations to the husbands, fathers and masters being only a "Nachtrage."[43] These primary addressees were, he notes, disadvantaged in terms of participation in many aspects of deuteronomic law, and were therefore treated with special attention in the form of the HT:

> Sie [women, children, slaves] bilden aber seit dem Deuteronomium nur deshalb eine Einheit, weil sie gegenüber den Männern in Kultus und Recht, in Glaube und Sitte die minder Berechtigten sind; sie können weder zur Erfüllung des Gesetzes noch zur Ausübung kultischer Pflichten in gleichem Maße wie die Männer herangezogen werden. Aber dennoch gehören sie zu dem Volk; es ist deshalb auch notwendig, die leichtere Bürde ihrer Pflichten auf einer besonderen Tafel zu formulieren, wie schon das Deuteronomium begonnen hat und bis in die rabbinische Zeit fortgesetzt ist...So gibt Paulus auch hier jüdische Katechismustradition weiter.[44]

The deuteronomic regulation, then, was preserved in a broader regulatory form, akin to the HT. Lohmeyer's contention that Paul was writing directly from a "paränetischen Tradition des Judentums" (perhaps even a catechism), the contents of which he never attempted to, nor could, transcend,[45] may be a bit exaggerated, especially in light of the newness of the Gospel and the unique needs of the Pauline Gentile mission. As Crouch has observed, Lohmeyer's theory of a pre-Christian Jewish code remains unsupported in terms of literary evidence, making it no more than a "theoretical construction."[46] In spite of this, Lohmeyer has drawn attention to Jewish traditional teaching and the Old Testament as possible sources for the New Testament HT form

---

[41] Ernst Lohmeyer, *Die Briefe an die Philipper, an die Kolosser und an Philemon*, ed. H.A.W. Meyer, 13 ed., Kritisch-exegetischer Kommentar über das Neue Testament, vol. 9 (Göttingen: Vandenhoeck & Ruprecht, 1964).

[42] Ibid., 155.

[43] Ibid., 155.

[44] Ibid., 155. It is questionable whether the HT duties of women, children and slaves represent "die leichtere Bürde"!

[45] Ibid., 156.

[46] Crouch, *Origin*, 24.

and content. This was not without value, and he was certainly not alone in his observations.[47] Additionally, he was correct to point out the emphasis upon the condition of the subordinated members. Lohmeyer represents an early scholar, familiar with the form-critical options, who attempts to locate HT origins within the Jewish community of faith. Later research into the HT origins would invariably consider Jewish sources. With Lohmeyer, however, the HT remains, ultimately, an import whose features reflect Jewish ethical tradition. We should not expect significant integration between the Christian theology of the host letter and the HT form. Furthermore, the commands to the superordinated members find no integration within the HT itself, so that by extension, the HT *could* not be fully integrated into the broader letter context. The HT cannot provide, then, either a reciprocal ethic, or one based in Christian theology.

K. H. Rengstorf: The HT and the Social Context οἶκος

K.H. Rengstorf represents an especially interesting development in HT research, his theories combining both old and new impulses. He would, first of all, issue a direct challenge to the findings of the Dibelius-Weidinger thesis; secondly, he would adopt Seeberg's view that the HT is a Christian creation; lastly, and most importantly, he would be the first scholar to put primary emphasis upon the social context of the HT, the οἶκος.

Employing the same form-critical arguments used to criticise Seeberg, Rengstorf showed that the Hellenistic and Jewish material presented in the Dibelius-Weidinger thesis was too diverse and unlike the form of the New Testament HT to be convincing, concluding that "Die Ableitung der Haustafeln aus der nichtchristlichen Paränese der Zeit erweist sich zum Mindesten als schwierig."[48] Although he notes common themes between the HT form and the Hellenistic lists of duties, these are couched in lists which include a larger spectrum of the populace, and that the primary relationships of the household (husband/wife, parents/children, masters/slaves) are treated in

---

[47] David Daube, in an appended note to Selwyn's commentary on 1 Peter, "Participle and Imperative in 1 Peter" (467–488), shows how a number of present participles found in the New Testament (particularly those found in the HT of 1 Peter, Colossians and Ephesians) express the imperative mood. This usage, he argues, is a Semitic use of the participial form, not to be traced to Hellenistic usage. It is found only when used as a rule, and "occurs only in the Haustafeln and similar rules" (471). This argument, along with Lohmeyer's observations, would become part of later argumentation of Schroeder and others supporting a traditional Jewish *Vorlage*. This is also discussed in Schroeder, *Haustafeln*, 102f.

[48] Rengstorf, *Mahnungen*, 134.

only the most indirect manner, "unter anderem."[49] The Christian HT form, in contrast, has particular features which find no equivalents in either Hellenistic or Jewish sources; he draws attention to the concept of submission,[50] the call to love,[51] the element of reciprocity,[52] and, as we shall see, an emphasis upon the household.

Rengstorf rejected any notion that the HT represented a "Verbürgerlichung" of genuine Christian values; instead, he postulated an intra-Christian crisis theory of his own, which emphasised continuity with the message of the faith community.[53] The "radikale Sätze wie Gal. 3,28" had, as he suggests, created social expectations which could not be realised before the parousia, with the concomitant relaxation of relational boundaries (an idea which found circulation in later theses). The HT, he believes, served to counter such radical tendencies, while establishing the household as the "Ordnung Gottes."[54] The HT is, then, an expression of the will of God for the church, and not a compromise of the genuine Christian world-view.[55] As a result of this view, Rengstorf did not undertake a comprehensive critique of Weidinger's Hellenistic proofs, but introduced instead a new and much more

---

[49] Ibid., 134.

[50] Ibid., 132.

[51] Ibid., 137.

[52] Ibid., 139.

[53] Rengstorf's concern to see integration between the HT, the epistle and the larger Christian faith is at odds with the crisis theories of the day. He is convinced that each HT is a form of applied kerygma, a message which is uniquely Christian, and inseparable from early Christian proclamation. "Die Haustafeln wollen somit 'Kerygma' sein, und zwar in der Weise, daß sie den οἶκος in seiner der Zeit geläufigen Erscheinungsform in den Wirkungsbereich des Evangeliums rücken. Sie befassen sich in ihm mit einer Lebensform und –ordnung, die in ihrem Dasein und ihrer Form von einer individuellen Stellungnahme zu ihm ganz unabhängig ist. Das gilt ebenso von allem, was der οἶκος einschließt, sowohl von der Ehe und dem Miteinander von Eltern und Kindern wie auch von dem Miteinander von Herren und Sklaven." This order, so closely linked to the Gospel, cannot represent "den Einbruch bürgerlichen Denkens in die Welt der eschatologischen Verkündigung Jesu und der Apostel und damit den Anfang eines bürgerlich gewordenen Christentums…genau das Gegenteil ist richtig." (*Mahnungen*, 141). Wolfgang Schrage, writing in 1975, questions the crisis theories which intimate a defensive posture on the part of the church, especially as seen in the HT form. He suggests that the HT is a "offensives Moment", free from the concern to battle "emanzipatorische Gelüste" or "schwärmerischen Enthusiasmus." Speaking of the HT in Colossians, he describes the tone and message of the HT as "…den Sieg des Kyrios Jesus Christus über die elementaren Kräfte und Mächte", which has as its goal to make the lordship of Christ a reality in the οἶκος (*Zur Ethik der neutestamentlichen Haustafeln*, NTS 21, 5f.). These sentiments are remarkably close to Rengstorf's.

[54] Rengstorf, *Mahnungen*, 144.

[55] Ibid., 144.

24

defined method of approaching the HT form, which emphasised the *sociological* context of the household. The HT of the New Testament has as its focus the members and the concerns of the οἶκος:

> Unter ihnen [characteristics of the NT *Haustafel*] ist zuerst zu nennen, daß es sich in den Haustafeln um Mahnungen handelt, die es tatsächlich mit dem οἶκος bzw. mit der familia und ihren Gliedern zu tun haben. Es ist ja so, daß Mann und Frau als Eheleute und Eltern zusammen mit ihren Kindern und gegebenenfalls auch dem Gesinde (δοῦλοι) den οἶκος bilden. Jedesmal in den Haustafeln geht es um das richtige Verhalten dieser Glieder des οἶκος und nur um dieses. Das muß deshalb betont werden, weil das ein Zug an den Haustafeln ist, der den angeblichen Parallelen zu ihnen aus der hellenistischen Umwelt des Neuen Testaments gerade fehlt.[56]

The fact that the HT is concerned with members of the household, and in particular, their behaviour, calls for a new scholarly approach. For Rengstorf, interpretation of the HT depends upon an accurate understanding of the social context; form-critical scholarship had, up to this point, overlooked this element. Rengstorf allows for various (Christian and pagan) HT contexts, but insists upon an understanding which includes the sociological aspect:

> Die Haustafeln, in denen die hier zu besprechenden Mahnungen mit Ausnahme von 1. Kor. 14,34 stehen, werden heute im allgemeinen als Stück urchristlicher Paränese begriffen und als solches wieder in den größeren Rahmen der außer- und vorchristlichen Paränese ihrer Zeit eingeordnet. Das macht es unerläßlich, von vornherein in dieser Hinsicht Klarheit zu schaffen. Für das richtige Verständnis der Mahnungen hängt so gut wie alles davon ab, ob es möglich ist, so oder so zu einem zuverlässigen Bilde ihrer geschichtlichen Zusammenhänge zu kommen.[57]

His emphasis upon the sociological framework of the household would remain largely overlooked. Criticism of Rengstorf's theory was levelled primarily against his assertion that the οἶκος could be understood as a "festen Trias von Mahnungen", a "genuin christliche Konzeption" whose reciprocal roles were determined in relation to the household.[58] Schroeder notes, for instance, that husband/father/master combination is not precise enough to be the organising principle of the HT address, but rather the individuals in their various roles. A slave, he reasons, could also assume the role of husband and father. The two categories of submission and love he finds to be more unevenly distributed than Rengstorf contends. In the end it is not the οἶκος which determines the organisation and form of address, rather "Es wird im-

---

[56] Ibid., 136.
[57] Ibid., 133.
[58] Ibid, 139.

mer der Stand angesprochen."[59] Nearly two decades later, Crouch was to dismiss Rengstorf's thesis, stating that "...the Haustafel itself reveals no explicit concerns with the οἶκος concept."[60] Rengstorf's observations regarding the members of the household would remain largely overlooked until much later scholarship would adopt the οἶκος as the definitive category for understanding the HT, and limit HT texts to those which demonstrate adherence to household concerns. His contribution would be, at least at this point in time, to reopen the discussion regarding the origins of the HT form, which had lain fallow for over two decades. More importantly, however, Rengstorf reflects an attempt to integrate the message of the HT form with its sociological setting, the οἶκος. His concern to see the HT closely tied to concerns of the immediate social context was ahead of its time, and anticipated the distancing effect which would result form the "foreign body" element of form-critical theories.[61] Though Rengstorf attempted to counter this trend, his focus upon the household as the unique concern of the HT introduces another potentially foreign element: the sociological grid οἶκος. It is impossible to verify his estimation of the household's importance to the early church community; Rengstorf made no attempt to establish his view from the theological context of the host letters. Rengstorf's contributions, however

---

[59] Schroeder, *Haustafeln*, 88f.

[60] Crouch, *Origin*, 25.

[61] Weidinger, *Haustafeln*, 4f., had already warned of the danger of interpreting parenetic material in terms of the context of the letter, which "überschätzt also die aktuellen Momente." He was reacting to the thesis of Seeberg, which he called an "exegetical extreme." "Rückschlüsse auf die Verhältnisse in den Gemeinden" would constitute a mistake in interpreting the HT. He allows, however, when carefully formulated, a possible connection between the advice given in Col. concerning slaves and the case of Onesimus. Here Weidinger is cautious, yet open to the possibility of a contextual interpretation. Rengstorf anticipated the next logical step of totally isolating the HT, as seen in Schroeder. Schroeder was enthusiastic regarding the apparent traditional nature of the HT form, to the degree that it was completely loosed from its immediate historical moorings. A longer citation is helpful to see how he extricates (*Herausstellung*) the HT from the historical context: "In der Auslegung der Haustafeln, sowie in der Auslegung der paränetischen Teile der Schrift, ist vielfach nicht berücksichtigt worden, daß sie traditionelles Gut sind. Die älteren Exegeten machten keinen Unterschied zwischen den verschiedensten Arten von sittlichen Ermahnungen. Paränetische Abschnitte wurden genauso behandelt wie die ethischen Ermahnungen, die auf eine bestimmte Situation in der Gemeinde bezogen sind. In den paränetischen Stücken sind die Regeln und Weisungen aber nicht für eine bestimmte Gemeinde oder einen konkreten Fall formuliert, sondern für die allgemeinen Bedürfnisse der ältesten Christenheit. Weil sie traditionelles Gut sind, lassen sie nicht zu, daß man direkt von diesen Abschnitten auf den Zustand in der Gemeinde schließt. Aus dem, was in Kol, 3,22 über die Sklaven geredet wird, kann man nicht Rückschlüsse auf die Sklaverei in Kolossae machen. Mit *Herausstellung* dieser Abschnitte als Paränese ist diese Gefahr weithin vermieden worden." (Schroeder, *Haustafeln*, 5).

innovative, would be largely overshadowed by the prevailing adoption of Hellenistic sources within the form-critical debate. It would be David Schroeder's critical analysis of the Hellenistic proofs which would bring the source question, with all its attendant issues, into a common orbit.

David Schroeder: The Debate Concerning HT Form

By the time Lohmeyer had published his commentary, and Rengstorf his article concerning the HT, it had become clear that scholarship was not united regarding the origins, purpose and form of the New Testament HT. Up to this point, however, only passing observations had been made regarding the dissimilarity of form between the Hellenistic and Jewish lists of duties and the HT. The two poles of thought, characterised by either Hellenistic or faith community origins for the HT form, had remained discrete. It would be David Schroeder's 1959 dissertation, *Die Haustafeln des Neuen Testaments*,[62] which would permanently change the form-critical landscape, drawing for the first time sharp lines of distinction which could be used in marking the unique form of the HT - and this from sources taken from *both* schools of thought.

Schroeder rejected Seeberg and Carrington's theories of a catechism on the grounds that such a catechism would have developed at a much later point in the church's history.[63] Lohmeyer, suggesting uniquely Jewish sources, was no more appealing to this young scholar, who points out that his proposed sources did not include all the addressees, an essential part of the HT, so that he concludes, "...hier können wir nicht mit Lohmeyer gehen."[64] He rejects Rengstorf's organisation of the οἶκος with the observation that the "Stände", not only the head of the household, are addressed.[65] It becomes clear that Schroeder was seeking a less approximate definition for the HT form. His enthusiasm for treating the HT form as a piece of traditional, early Christian parenesis is apparent in the first pages of his thesis, where he points out that traditional interpretation of the HT has been hindered by the absence of such an understanding.[66] As with the scholars before him, Schroeder identified the HT form, and assumed the form-critical approach.

Though firmly operating from the form-critical perspective, Schroeder's observations departed decidedly from the contemporary assumptions of that

---

[62] Unfortunately never published.
[63] Schroeder, *Haustafeln*, 26.
[64] Ibid., 87.
[65] Ibid., 88.
[66] Ibid., 5.

school. He asserted that the HT form, as it is found in the New Testament texts, cannot possibly have been taken from the Stoic lists,[67] but find their form imbedded in Old Testament apodictic law.[68] His challenge to the form-critics was direct as it was iconoclastic:

> Es muß von neuem geprüft werden, ob und wie weit das Haustafelschema aus der Stoa übernommen worden ist. Es ist m. E. nicht so einwandfrei festgestellt worden, wie allgemein angenommen wird...Wichtiger ist, daß Dibelius und Weidinger gar nicht dazu gekommen sind, die eigentliche Form der stoischen Pflichtenlehre und der ntl. Haustafeln zu untersuchen...Will man aber von einer Übernahme [of the Stoic lists into the Christian community] sprechen, so muß notwendigerweise auch der Inhalt [including structure and content] berücksichtigt werden."[69]

With these words, Schroeder marked his point of departure from received scholarship; a determined course of analysis of the Dibelius-Weidinger texts would show the inadequacy of these proposed evidences. His insistence that the sources resemble the HT in form *and* content was seen by some to be too methodologically restrictive,[70] yet his catalogue of HT characteristics would find their way into later research. These characteristics were cited in *contrast* to those which he enumerated as being typical of the lists of duties found in both Hellenistic and Jewish sources, or, conversely, to illustrate their absence in these same lists. A number of these characteristics (but not all) which Schroeder enumerates in his thesis are summarised by Gielen:

---

[67] Ibid., 151.

[68] Ibid., 93.

[69] Ibid., 28. His words are quite direct, and constitute a "throwing down of the gauntlet": "Es muß aber schon vornherein auffallen, daß Dibelius und Weidinger nur von dem Haustafel-schema ausgehen und alle inhaltlichen Beziehungen in ihren Untersuchungen bei Seite lassen. Ihre Schlußfolgerungen gehen aber weit über diesen gesetzten Rahmen hinaus, denn sie beschränken ihre Aussagen nicht auf das "Schema", sondern glauben den Nachweis geführt zu haben, daß die sittlichen Ermahnungen des NT bzw. der Haustafeln selbst aus der Stoa oder aus dem hellenistischen Judentum übernommen worden sind."

[70] Crouch, *Origin*, 102f. Crouch believes that Schroeder is "oversimplifying" when he points out the failure of some proofs (in this case Philo, *De Decalogo*) to match the HT in form. Schroeder's observations that the individuals in Jewish/Hellenistic duty lists are not directly addressed, that the lists are often much more expanded, and are drawn, in the case of Philo, from the Decalogue and Hellenistic sources, seem to be fair observations in terms of determining the characteristics of a traditional form (*Haustafeln*, 68f.). Interestingly, Schroeder's arguments have not been seen as being too narrow by later scholarship. Direct address, for example, is now an identifying marker of the HT form (see Gielen, *Tradition*, 3f.).

1. Fixed Order. Whereas the Stoic lists have no determined order, but are organised according to the particular situation or logical sequence, the New Testament HT is found to have a fixed order;

2. Reciprocity and Direct Address. In the New Testament HT, the addressees are spoken to in pairs; reciprocity is completely absent in the Stoic lists; only the example of Philo, *De Decalogo* 165–167, offers an example from Hellenistic Judaism in which the addressees are spoken to in pairs and in the order of subordinate/superordinate. Yet these are not directly addressed, nor are the groups addressed here identical to the New Testament HT;

3. Responsibility in Address. The Stoic lists of duties feature the free man as the understood addressee, where an individual reader is assumed; all other groups are addressed in indirect terms according to their relation to him. The New Testament HT addresses complete groups, each having its own responsibility in terms of another group;

4. Diverse Elements. Stoic lists generally contain the groups ἀδελφός, πατρίς and πολίτης, all missing in the New Testament HT; the HT contains, on the other hand, κύριοι as the appellation for the master, a name not found in the Stoic lists;

5. Imperative Usage. The usage of the imperative in the Stoic literature is a means of argumentation, whereas the New Testament HT uses the imperative to direct ethical behaviour.[71]

Schroeder's observations regarding the various differences between the HT form and the Stoic lists of duties were helpful in defining the HT form in negative terms, and critics saw this as a weakness in his argumentation. Dieter Lührmann, after acknowledging some of Schroeder's positive contributions in identifying the HT form, questions his negative approach. In his assessment of Schroeder's conclusions, he declares the Dibelius-Weidinger proofs to remain very much intact, in spite of Schroeder's observations to the contrary. The reason for this is that the detractors (Rengstorf, Schroeder, Crouch) have brought only "destructive" criticism, and have offered no new, alternative sources. Furthermore, the approach of Schroeder (and Goppelt), which acknowledges the influence of the Stoics, yet gives room for the parallel influences of the OT and the teachings of Christ, is seen as a "merkwürdiges Kompromißergebnis."[72] Here Lührmann dismisses Schroeder's proposed

---

[71] Gielen, *Tradition*, 38f.

[72] Dieter Lührmann, "Neutestamentliche Haustafeln und Antike Ökonomie," *New Testament Studies* 27 (1981): 83–97.

sources, which share no etymological roots with the form-critical sources of that time. That Lührmann could ignore Schroeder's sources is almost understandable in light of the radical departure in methodology found in Schroeder's thesis. In this regard, Schroeder was anticipating later scholarship, which would allow for the tension of several possible (and etymologically dissimilar) sources. Lührmann's remark that Schroeder and others were advancing hybrid theories, though intended to cast doubt on their methodology and sources, is actually an acute observation. Schroeder had, in his assessment of the Hellenistic material, found its shortcomings in terms of form and content. It was surprising, then, that Schroeder also acknowledged a *positive* relationship between the HT and the Hellenistic material in terms of the HT *Schema*, and incorporates these sources as the skeletal *Vorlage* in his thesis:

> Wir stellen fest, daß die Mahnungen der Haustafel, zumindest in ihrer jetzigen Gestalt, d.h., daß die Stände gegenseitig ermahnt werden, und auch weithin schon in der Wortwahl sich auf christlichem Boden befinden. Nehmen wir diese Mahnungen aus diesem Schema heraus, so zeigen sich Parallelen im Judentum und im hellenistischen Raum.[73]

Perhaps the clearest instance of criticism was levelled by Crouch, whose study took on remarkably similar contours to that of Schroeder. Because of the almost identical approach of analysing the Hellenistic sources in terms of form and content, Crouch was practically obliged to interact with Schroeder, as well as operating, to a degree, within his methodology. Yet Crouch shows little appreciation for Schroeder's scholarly contributions, in particular, his organisational method: "…Schroeder's entire approach to the subject is so unsatisfactory that any contribution which he might have made is for all practical purposes negated."[74] Schroeder's attempts to construe an original form of the HT (leaning on earlier ideas from Rengstorf and Lohmeyer which noted the primary addressees as those called to subordination) were abruptly rejected by Crouch: "Equally weak is Schroeder's attempt to reconstruct the 'original' Haustafel. Indeed, a procedure which so easily permits him to eliminate those features from the Haustafeln which are embarrassing for his thesis is suspect immediately."[75] Crouch's comments regarding Schroeder's work, as with those of Lührmann, may be a reaction to his (at

---

[73] Schroeder, *Haustafeln*, 131.
[74] Crouch, *Origin*, 28.
[75] Ibid., 30. Fortunately, Crouch exaggerates the importance of Schroeder's proposed HT to his thesis. His criticism is fair in that Schroeder's proposed "original" HT is only a construct, built by the logic of his argument. As with any unsubstantiated construct, it cannot possibly carry the thesis.

least at this point in scholarship) unorthodox proposed sources, which were indeed a departure from the norm. His thesis was difficult to integrate into either of the prevailing views, which tended to locate HT origins at opposite ends of the spectrum, either in Hellenistic *Vorlagen*, or as a creation of the Christian community. The fact that Schroeder joined both views into a tenuously integrated whole appeared to be a methodological dodge of scholarly engagement. His critics could not have anticipated the shift in methodology that was on the horizon.

Schroeder insists that the lists of duties found in the Hellenistic and Jewish-Hellenistic world, though potentially responsible for elements of the HT form, could not explain the decidedly unique form of the New Testament HT. Schroeder's second (and positive) step, his proposal of origins, would bring out further helpful contributions. It was his careful analysis of the HT in terms of the structure and content of the OT apodictic law that identified a number of organisational characteristics of the HT form. In particular, Schroeder located the four-fold nature of the HT admonition, *Anrede, Ermahnung, Verbindungswort* and *Begründungssatz* in a number of prophetic passages, as well as in the form of the law given in Exodus 20 and Deuteronomy 5.[76] These four elements in the HT form were overlooked for a number of years, yet found their way into later treatments of the HT as a parenetic unit. Gielen, writing over a quarter of a century later, demonstrates changes which had taken place in form-critical scholarship. In her discussion of the HT form, she sums up Schroeder's contributions in terms of form-critical concerns, as well as the questions of the *Religionsgeschichte* school:

> Zusammenfassend läßt sich zur Arbeit Schroeders sagen, daß es ihm überzeugend gelungen ist nachzuweisen, daß die ntl. HTT [*Haustafeltradition*] nicht in einer religionsgeschichtlichen Verbindung zu den stoischen Pflichtenreihen stehen. Darüberhinaus hat er auch die sprachliche Gestaltung der einzelnen HT-Weisungen als Anlehnung an die Form apodiktischer Rechtsätze des AT befriedigend erklären können.[77]

Although Schroeder's form-critical observations have met with some acceptance, his proposals for potential HT *Vorlagen* garnered little recognition. As might be expected, he did not represent any previous view in terms of his location of the *Sitz im Leben* of the HT, though there are similarities to Rengstorf's understanding of the HT as proclamation.[78] The ancient church had,

---

[76] Ibid., 92.
[77] Gielen, *Tradition*, 44.
[78] Rengstorf, *Mahnungen*, 141.

he points out, a number of activities which communicated the Word of God, including teaching, preaching, exhorting, and evangelism. These activities were all part of the mission of the church, which included a pronounced ethical element. The HT form belongs to the ethical side of the church's testimony, and has its place in the "didactic activity of the apostles."[79] Schroeder proposed several sources which informed these four ministries, all of which played a role in forming elements of this apostolic teaching. These sources were received with mixed criticism.[80] The occasion for the HT was not unlike Dibelius and Weidinger's thesis (transition from dynamic to more static church life), for it assumed a situation that needed attention. Schroeder finds, in agreement with Rengstorf, the root of the problem in the dissolution of roles emerging from a misunderstanding of the words of Paul in Gal. 3:27–28. Schroeder notes evidence of this in 1 Cor. 7, where the question of relationships in the expectant age are discussed. How much more, he argues, would the question be asked in terms of the radical words of Galatians? Paul answers in both 1 Corinthians and in the *Haustafeln*: "Ganz entschieden wendet sich Paulus gegen diese 'fromme' Form des Ungehorsams…Hier [in the world] gilt die Unterordnung; denn die Gemeinde lebt immer noch in dieser Welt."[81] Schroeder's suggestions for the social context of the HT, though well argued, offer no new information to the debate. His introduction of the hybrid origins of the HT in terms of form and content did, however, give the question a certain nuance that it had previously lacked. Only Schroeder, in his eclectic manner, could have formulated the following statement regarding the existential climate surrounding the formation of the HT: "Die Frage, die hinter der ntl. Haustafel und den stoischen Pflichtenreihen steht, scheint dieselbe zu sein, nämlich: 'Wie habe ich mich anderen Ständen gegenüber zu verhalten?'"[82]

The willingness to blend the sources as well as the social context of the HT and its Hellenistic counterparts was remarkable, to say the least. This apparent contradiction, along with his departure from long-accepted theories,

---

[79] Schroeder, *Haustafeln*, 26.

[80] As noted above, he saw the apodictic law as influencing the form of the HT, which was to be recognised by later scholars as a valuable contribution (Gielen, *Tradition*, 44). The content reflects the teaching of Christ, in particular the call to love (*Haustafeln*, 132). His citation of the teachings of Christ ("Es liegt nichts im Wege, sie [HT] als eine 'Überlieferung vom Herrn' selbst zu sehen." *Haustafeln*, 152) were considered to be the weakest part of his argument concerning origins, as it remained unsubstantiated. Crouch points this out clearly in his monograph (*Origins*, 30), as does Gielen (*Tradition*, 41f.).

[81] Schroeder, *Haustafeln*, 89f.

[82] Ibid., 83.

brought criticism to his thesis. In spite of this criticism, most scholars would
certainly give Schroeder credit for loosening the monopoly which the
Dibelius-Weidinger source materials enjoyed in critical scholarship, as general acceptance of his HT characteristics attest. He also opened the way for
further consideration of HT origins by drawing the two source extremes (external Hellenistic/internal Christian), however tenuously, together. From this
point on, these contexts would no longer enjoy a parallel existence; the time
was approaching when a hybrid thesis would no longer be considered an un-
thinkable oddity.[83] It is precisely this element of his thesis, the joining of
numerous literary and traditional sources as well as their social contexts
which distinguishes his thought. It is in Schroeder, however, that we find the
Haustafel most radically extricated from its letter context; as an import of
hybrid nature, it lacks unity in its parts, and cannot be construed as emanat-
ing from the theology of its letter context. As a response to the church's need
to organise social relations, it differs little, if at all, from its Hellenistic counterpart. James Crouch would be the next to push the inquiry into origins further, uniting a decidedly form-critical approach with a particular social context.

James Crouch: From HT Form to Sociological Concerns

James Crouch's *Origin and Intention of the Colossian Haustafel*, the published edition of his Tübingen dissertation, appeared in 1972. At this point in
HT research, there had been a hiatus from intensive work on the subject for
over twenty years. Crouch reopened the discussion with a thorough review of
the debate, with particular attention given to the question of origins, and the
sources cited up to that point. Though he was to be classified by Lührmann
as a critic of the Dibelius-Weidinger thesis,[84] Crouch was in reality the last
strong proponent of their general approach. Gielen points out that Crouch
operates in "deutlichem Anschluß an Weidinger von den ungeschriebenen
Gesetzen der Griechen aus."[85] That Crouch was also critical of the very gen-

---

[83] Gielen adopts Schroeder's approach in *Tradition*, accepting, for instance, his view of the
influence of OT apodictic law, while proposing a dependence upon contemporary economic
literature.

[84] Lührmann, "Haustafeln," 84. Lührmann cites Crouch as one of the negative detractors of
the Dibelius-Weidinger thesis, whose theories comprise an "odd hybrid." Crouch does indeed
propose a hybrid form as the origin of the NT *Haustafel*, consisting of both Jewish and Hellenistic sources, but his methodology and sources place him strongly in the form-critical school,
as well as showing him to be quite close to Weidinger.

[85] Gielen, *Tradition*, 45.

eral nature of the Dibelius-Weidinger proofs is true, and here he agrees with Rengstorf and Schroeder.[86] His disagreement with Weidinger is related primarily to the earlier emphasis given the Stoic material as the template of the HT form, which had been shown by Schroeder to be inadequate. Weidinger's broad collection of proofs had made allowance for Hellenistic Jewish codes,[87] however, and this became the focus of Crouch's study.[88] Crouch, in expanding his study into Jewish codes, reveals, in both methodology and conclusions, further similarities to Schroeder's thesis.[89] He is convinced, with earlier scholarship, that the HT form depends on a "schema which preceded the Colossian letter":

> Its formal nature remains unmistakable, and both its composition and its loose relationship to its context indicate that it is an independent unit most probably of pre-Colossian origin.[90]

Here we see nothing new. Crouch is, in terms of methodology and assumptions, closely tied to the research that preceded him, and keen to find a verifiable origin of the HT form, albeit in the more limited Hellenistic Jewish context. It would be his observations regarding the inconclusive nature of the previous sources which would set his thesis apart, drawing him to give more attention to the backgrounds and ethical concerns of the HT. We see a *methodological shift* in the pursuit of HT origins; it is a subtle yet unmistakable

---

[86] Crouch, *Origin*, 102. Here Crouch admits that Weidinger provided no "precise parallel".

[87] Weidinger, *Haustafeln*, 48f. Weidinger actually sets forth Hellenistic Jewish proofs first; after dealing with the Hellenistic material, he turns again to the place of the "schema" in Hellenistic thought, Greek ethical teaching and Hellenistic Judaism. His words open the door for Crouch's thesis: "Es besteht allerdings auch die Möglichkeit, daß das Schema erst auf einen Umweg in das Christentum gekommen ist, nämlich durch das hellenistische Judentum...Ob das Christentum seine 'Haustafeln' dem Judentum oder dem Heidentum unmittelbar verdankt, ist nicht auszumachen. Die Frage ist nebensächlich, nachdem festgestellt worden ist, wie leicht die Übernahme von beiden gehen konnte."

[88] Crouch, *Origin*, 102f.

[89] Though Crouch was intensely critical of Schroeder in terms of methodology and findings, he was nonetheless strongly influenced by him, and would be seen by later scholars as being closely akin to Schroeder and Rengstorf, probably because of his willingness to unite Hellenistic and Jewish elements in HT origins. Gielen states it clearly in her treatment of Crouch's survey of the Hellenistic material: "Bei der Durchsicht der hellenistisch-jüdischen Pflichtentafeln kommt Crouch zu Ergebnissen, die im Wesentlichen mit den Erkenntnissen Schroeders übereinstimmen. Die einschlägigen Texte—Crouch greift wie Schroeder u.a. zurück auf Ps. Phokylides 175–227 sowie auf Philo, Decal. 165–167 denn aber auch auf Philo Fug. Inv. 3 und Jos. c. Ap. 2, 190–219—zeigen bald eine recht große Übereinstimmung mit den stoischen Pflichtentafeln, bald jedoch offensichtliche Unterschiede." Gielen, *Tradition*, 46.

[90] Crouch, *Origin*, 10f.

drift from previous scholarship, where the two views of HT origins begin to conflate:

> There is, of course, no exact parallel to the Colossian *Haustafel* outside the New Testament. This fact, plus the obvious differences between the *Haustafel* and the Stoic schema force us to restate the *religionsgeschichtliche* problem. Properly understood, the question is not: From what source did the church borrow this code? Such a question permits only two kinds of response. Either the *Haustafel* is a pre-Christian code (Weidinger-Dibelius and Lohmeyer) or it is specifically Christian (Rengstorf and Schroeder). One approach emphasises the similarities between the *Haustafel* and the non-Christian parallels while the other approach emphasises the differences. Because the *religionsgeschichtliche* question is incorrectly posed, one is prevented from offering a solution which accounts for both similarities and differences. In reality, our task has been not to inquire regarding the source from which the *Haustafel* was borrowed but to ask the two-fold question: (1) From whence did the material come which went into the formation of the *Haustafel*? (2) What was the decisive impulse in the creation of the *Haustafel* as a *Christian* topos?[91]

In treating the first half of his methodological approach, Crouch leans on previous scholarship to suggest a better solution to the question of origins, as mentioned above. He rightly criticises the rigidity of looking to one source for the origins of the HT; for him, it is a blend of sources and traditions which have been "adapted" and "not merely taken over", in order to suit the needs of a particular community. Crouch never settles on one pre-Christian HT form that might explain its New Testament counterpart, *but rather on a sociological context.* Each community has, whether Hellenistic or Jewish, construed an ethic which reflects its basic values and present concerns. The most immediate community in which the pre-Christian HT might be located would be, for Crouch, Hellenistic Judaism.[92] Crouch devotes a large portion of his argument to illustrate how the various elements of Greek philosophy, popular Roman philosophy and Hellenistic Jewish duty lists were melded to form a distinctly Jewish schema, which had its *Sitz im Leben* in the Jewish mission activity of the Roman period. The "Jewish propagandists" made use of Hellenistic and traditional Jewish sources to promote monotheism, and form instruction for God-fearers and proselytes:

> The development of a body of ethical material for use in Jewish propaganda, however, did not cease with the selection of a number of laws from the Torah which had universal application. Clearly there was a similarity between the Noachian laws on the one hand and the unwritten laws of the Greek ethic. Both were regarded as ex-

---

[91] Ibid., 146f.
[92] Ibid., 148.

pressions of a primitive code of ethics which was valid for the entire human race. It was natural, therefore, that the Jewish propagandists as they went out into the Hellenistic world borrowed freely from the Hellenistic tradition. They felt free to make use of anything which was morally superior and could be counted on to win a sympathetic hearing for the message of ethical monotheism.[93]

Crouch's answer to the first part of his approach is decidedly sociological. A proposed social context is critical to his argument, an element which had played a less prominent role in previous theses. For Crouch, origin and function of the HT are integrally related, and can be located in terms of a particular sociological occasion. His arguments reveal a tendency to understand the parenesis, so often fully extricated from the literary context, in terms of some "impulse": "Even though it has become a dogma of scholarship that no relationship exists between the situation of the letter and the parenesis it contains, it is difficult to resist asking why the Haustafel was included in Colossians."[94] Here Crouch makes a contribution which would influence later scholarship. Engagement with the source material would diminish in the face of growing interest in the HT as an expression of sociological and ethical concerns.

In finding the impulse for the Colossian HT, Crouch is no less sociological in his approach. The implementation of the HT in a Hellenistic Jewish mission context makes its proximity to the Christian community (and mission) fairly immediate. This relatively small cultural gap between the faith communities, though by no means insignificant, represents a departure from previous form-critical theories which advocated adoption of the Hellenistic lists in a significantly different form, and from a considerably distanced cultural context. Locating the HT as a later (not catechism) development within the Hellenistic church, Crouch argues that:

…there was a general situation within the Hellenistic churches which gave rise to the specifically Christian form of the Haustafel…the existence of a definite problem in the church and the way in which the problem was met can be deduced from parenetic material, and it is legitimate to speak in this sense of an 'occasion' for the formulation of specifically Christian adaptations of non-Christian ethical material.[95]

Interestingly, he rejects the theory that the HT represented a "Verbürgerlichung" of the early church, as it grappled with the protracted delay of the return of Christ. His analysis looks closely at the elements of the HT in Co-

---

[93] Ibid., 96f.
[94] Ibid., 151.
[95] Ibid., 120.

lossians, and attempts to construe another possible social context and occasion. Crouch suggests that the HT had been formed at an early stage as a tool to combat "enthusiastic and heretical threats to the stability of both the church and the social order", the likes of which can be seen in 1 Cor. 7. The HT, reflecting the "nomistic tendency of Pauline Christianity", was recognised by the author of Colossians as a "weapon created for use by 'orthodox' (i.e., Pauline) Christianity in its struggle with enthusiastic heresies and that he included it for this reason in his letter."[96] Crouch's attempt to integrate all elements of the HT and to understand the occasion resembles earlier attempts in terms of an assumption that a crisis (heresy) precipitated the use of the form. It was his careful study of the possible social context, however, that set him apart from earlier scholars. Of the tasks involved in form-critical analysis, *Religionsgeschichte* was to take a prominent role in Crouch's analysis, and set the stage for later investigations.

Not to be overlooked in Crouch is the clear desire to communicate the *intention* of the Colossian HT, for both the original readers as well as the modern church. Here he raises the issues of slavery and women's roles as a matter of social ethics, unearthing the "tension between two demands" that faced the church then and now. How can the commands found in the HT be integrated into our situation? His answer is tentative; we live in tension between the social order and the call to love our neighbour.[97] Crouch identified the ethical component of HT interpretation, an emphasis that would accompany later HT research.

In both elements of his methodological approach, Crouch stands as a bridge between previous research and the later attention to sociological and ethical issues surrounding the HT. The waning confidence which Crouch invested in finding the HT *Vorlage* reflects later trends in HT scholarship fully to abandon such quests. His strong emphasis on the social milieu was equally forward-looking. Yet, as Müller points out, Crouch's observations were to be largely overlooked, due to the inertia generated by decades of form-critical work under the Dibelius-Weidinger assumptions, and the ignorance of superior evidence:

Die ernüchternden Ergebnisse seiner [Crouch's] Untersuchung drangen jedoch nicht durch oder wurden bagatellisiert. Zu stark war die Faszination durch das Erklärungsmodell der alten "stoischen Haustafel", die ihrer "Verchristlichung" harrte, als daß man mit Ernst zur Kenntnis genommen hätte, was J.E. Crouch mit seiner methodisch ungewöhnlich bewußten Studie herausfand. Nicht mehr und nicht weni-

---

[96] Ibid., 150f.
[97] Ibid., 160f.

ger nämlich, als daß die seit M. Dibelius und K. Weidinger immer wieder un-
bekümmert in Anspruch genommene "stoische Pflichtentafel" keines der wesentlichen, die Form der Haustafel in Kol. 3,18–4,1 unverzichtbar festlegenden
Elemente aufweist. Daß ungeachtet dieses offen zutage liegenden Defizits die
stoischen "Pflichtenschemata" nach wie vor als Bezugspunkt neutestamentlicher
Sozialethik ein nahezu unwidersprochenes Monopol haben, hat damit zu tun, daß
J.E. Crouch nicht in der Lage war, die Haustafel aus Kol. 3,18–4,1 anderen Texten
zuzuordnen, die von den gegenseitigen Beziehungen zwischen Mann und Frau,
zwischen Eltern und Kindern, zwischen Herren und Sklaven handeln, und allein von
diesen Beziehungen.[98]

Here Müller underestimates the positive reception of Crouch's ideas in the
ten years between their respective publications; Crouch had his finger on the
pulse of scholarship, as would be revealed in articles published soon after
1972.[99] The "monopoly" enjoyed by the form-critical school, in particular
the Dibelius-Weidinger thesis, was to be a thing of the past, as Crouch had
played a decisive role in dislodging confidence in their proofs, as well as
opening the methodology to include a strong sociological component. This is
perhaps his most important contribution; this combination would help direct
scholarly attention to the new *Gattung* of economic literature, thus focusing
attention, as Rengstorf had years before, on the οἶκος. The new emphasis
upon the social context, however helpful in determining the impulse for the
incorporation of the HT in Colossians, did little to change its status as an
imported and foreign element. Crouch's theory of appropriation, as well as
his proposed sources, do not anticipate a close relationship between the HT
and its host letter. Finally, Müller's cryptic reference to "other texts" cited
above refers to those found in more recent research; it would be the next it-
eration of the critical discussion that would expand the research in terms of
these "new" economic texts, and their sociological significance.

---

[98] Karl-Heinz Müller, *Die Haustafel des Kolosserbriefs und das antike Frauenthema*, eds. K.
Rahner and H. Schlier, Quaestiones Disputatae: Die Frau im Urchristentum, vol. 95 (Freiburg:
Herder, 1983), 283.
[99] Several articles demonstrate a departure from the Dibelius-Weidinger thesis, and include
altogether new approaches, including Schrage (1975), Strecker (1979), Thraede (1980),
Lührmann (1980), Balch (1981), Laub (1982) and Müller (1983). Schrage, *Ethik*, 1, leads the
way by rejecting the criticisms of the HT found in earlier, form-critical treatments as "Urteile
von pamphlethafter Literatur." Rejecting as inadequate the primary reliance upon ancient
sources, he calls for a more differentiated and precise method of assessing the HT ethic, which
focuses upon the moment of reception; in particular its sociological and theological concerns.

Economic Theories and the HT Form

David Balch: Attention to Broad Literary Context

It was David Balch who set out to trace the origins of the New Testament HT as found in 1 Peter (and in Colossians and Ephesians as well), with particular attention to the concept of submission. His thesis, *Let Wives be Submissive: The Domestic Code in 1 Peter,* became available to scholarship as a Yale dissertation in 1975, and later in an expanded monograph form.[100] It was his decidedly sociological aim to find the "culture which first used this balanced pattern of submissiveness" found in the reciprocal admonitions of the New Testament HT.[101] His brief survey of previous scholarship on HT origins is not uncritical of previous findings,[102] and betrays a desire to investigate the origins in a more circumspect manner. The question regarding the origins of the HT is for him "at this point still open."[103] Balch offers a "different approach" which would bring the discussion into the larger sphere of political theory and ethics as derived from Plato and Aristotle. He introduces a long-forgotten scholar, Friedrich Wilhelm,[104] who observed that these philosophers, as well as other political thinkers, had developed a number of categories in discussing politics and ethics, three of which he identified as closely-linked topoi: "concerning the constitution" (περὶ πολιτείας), "concerning household management" (περὶ οἰκονομίας) and "concerning marriage" (περὶ γάμου). Of these three topoi Balch writes: "I observe that the second of these topoi is nearly identical with the topos which often is referred to by the German word *Haustafel,* the NT pattern of household submissiveness."[105] According to Balch, it is this broader category of political and ethical discussion which informs the Stoics as well as the Hellenistic Jews, and acts as a conceptual umbrella for much of the material that has been cited in HT research. The primacy of the Platonic and Aristotelian categories is unmistak-

---

[100] D.L. Balch, *Let Wives Be Submissive: The Domestic Code in 1 Peter,* ed. James Crenshaw, SBL Monograph Series, vol. 26 (Chico: Scholars Press, 1981).

[101] Ibid., 1.

[102] Ibid., 6f. Balch agrees with Schroeder's basic observations regarding the inadequacy of the Stoic proofs, but is not as concerned with finding a particular order in the HT schema. Balch is further unconvinced that the "Jewish-Oriental" proofs of Crouch explain the HT adequately; texts from Philo, a keystone in Crouch's argument, are not considered by Balch to be an adequate explanation for the reciprocity of the NT codes.

[103] Ibid., 10.

[104] Friedrich Wilhelm, "Die Oeconomica der Neupythagoreer Bryson, Kallikratidas, Periktione, Phintys," *RhM* 70 (1915): 161–223.

[105] Balch, *Wives,* 14.

able in his analysis, as he insists that these topoi were equally "available in the Roman age." The currency of the topoi can be seen, for example, in his treatment of the Hellenistic Jewish sources, of which he claims that "Philo was interpreting the Decalogue in light of Platonic and Aristotelian political ethics", and that both Philo and Josephus "were reading Aristotle (or Plato) into the Pentateuch."[106] Balch had turned the funnel of evidences on its head, and exchanged microanalysis of form for a historical panorama of sources. This development represents a significant departure from the stream of scholarship which had preceded it; Balch attempts to locate the HT form in a considerably *broader* literary field and social context, gleaning the sociological impulses in each (be it the Stoics, Hellenistic Jews or the Peripatetics). His interest in showing the relationship between the topoi and the HT form (reciprocity, three pairs, dominant/submissive relations) is not in order to determine the nearest HT antecedent, as others before him; his gaze is directed towards the recognition of these basic characteristics in a number of rather diverse social-political contexts, and thereby finding a common ethic that might inform the *function* of the HT in the New Testament. His analysis, then, is not designed to discover an *Urtafel*, but to demonstrate how the New Testament HT (and thereby its ethic) is etymologically connected to a generally known tradition.[107] After observing that "a similar ethic" is to be found among pagan and Christian documents, he concludes: "The ultimate origin of the ethic is to be found in Greek political thought, but I cannot draw firm conclusions about the immediate source of the code in 1 Peter."[108]

---

[106] Ibid., 54f.

[107] Balch's thesis intimates that each HT form might, theoretically, develop independently as a result of contact with pagan literature and its extra-ecclesiastical debates, thus circumventing the assumption of a linear evolution. This was later argued by Ulrike Wagener, *Die Ordnung des "Hauses Gottes"*, eds. Martin Hengel and Otfried Hofius, 2 ed., WUNT, vol. 65 (Tübingen: J.C.B. Mohr, 1994), who called this process a continuous "Neu-Rezeption paganer Literatur". She summarises, *Ordnung*, 62: "Der Befund, daß die verschiedenen frühchristlichen Texte nicht auf einer kontinuierlichen traditionsgeschichtliche Entwicklungslinie angesiedelt werden können, führt zu einer grundsätzlichen methodischen Kritik an den bisherigen Rekonstruktionen der Formgeschichte der Haus- und Ständetafeln, die häufig einer unreflektierten traditionsgeschichtlichen Hypothese folgen: Während sie für die frühesten Texte einen entscheidenen Impuls aus paganem Schrifttum annehmen, setzen sie für die weitere Entwicklung primär eine innerchristliche Traditionsgeschichte voraus. Diese Kritik trifft nicht nur die sehr stark kontinuitätsorientierten Sichtsweisen von Lührmann und Laub, sondern auch die Ansätze von Thraede und Gielen. Durch diese traditionsgeschichtliche Vorannahme wird aber der Blick für die Möglichkeit außerchristlicher Traditionslinien verdunkelt."

[108] Balch, *Wives*, 120.

40

Balch finds the social context and function of the HT instruction in 1 Peter to be identical to that which the exhortations constituted in the ambient culture: a code of conduct. Here no distinction is made between the function of the code in the two cultural settings: "The author of 1 Peter exhorted the recipients of his letter to the behavior outlined in the code with the intention of encouraging conduct which would contradict the Roman slanders."[109] The occasion, intimated in the use of this common code, was the "reality of the Roman world" which included a distrust of new and foreign cults.[110] These cults would receive "stereotyped criticisms", regardless of their intentions or actual behaviour. In this tense religious climate, where cults were perceived to "upset household management", Balch concludes that "...it was inevitable that Judaism and Christianity would be charged with sedition, with murder, and with practicing rites which corrupted the morality of Roman women."[111] The Christian community adopted the code for its "apologetic possibilities", modifying it only slightly (as in the case of the advice to the wives in 1 Peter 3:1).[112]

Balch's theory of origins for the New Testament HT, shown in his treatment of 1 Peter, is by far the most remote in terms of source from the faith community, and doubtless the most undifferentiated in terms of its social

---

[109] Ibid., 119.

[110] Angela Standhartinger, *Studien zur Entstehungsgeschichte & Intention des Kolosserbriefs*, eds. A.J. Malherbe and D.P. Moessner, Supplements to Novum Testamentum, vol. 94 (Leiden: Brill, 1999), follows Balch's position closely, with particular attention given to the law codes of the legendary rulers Zaleucus and Charondas (cited in Stobaeus, *Anth.* IV, 2.19 and IV, 2.24 respectively; see Balch's article, *ANRW* II 26.1, "Neopythagorean Moralists", 389–404). Positing that Colossians is a late, non-Pauline writing of fictitious nature [Absenderangabe...und auch die Adresse fiktiv, 281], the HT adopts an apologetic function similar to that found in 1 Pet. and paralleled in the cult inscription of Philadelphia (trans. 266). The HT, then, assures the suspicious outsider that the hierarchical social order is not being threatened by the Christian community. Simultaneously, however, the larger letter and the HT itself contain an embedded message of radical equality (vv. 3:10f., Paul's references to servanthood, the reading of ἰσότης in 4:1 as meaning "equality") which reflects the *reality* and self-understanding of the letter's writer. This tactical use of the HT seems to us unlikely, particularly since the hidden meaning might have missed its intended effect, leaving room for the false appropriation of the HT mandates, or even worse, the outsiders' discovery of the church's true egalitarian nature. Standhartinger, 289, admits that the strategy had less-than desired results, the HT inaugurating two millennia of "Frauen-, Mädchen-, Sklaven- und Sklavinnenunterdrückung. Mag sein, daß sie den kritischen Verstand ihrer Hörer und Leserinnen überschätzten."

[111] Balch, *Wives*, 118.

[112] Ibid., 120f. Here Balch agrees with Schroeder that the advice to wives is a change in the traditional submission scheme. The behaviour required of the believing wife is clearly missionary in intent.

context. The immediate occasion for its adoption, placed in the ambient culture, makes it strikingly immediate and sociological in its impulse. The recognition of a generally accepted code of ethics allows for a much freer hand in interpretation, since it is not tied to a moment of reception from any single tradition. The tensions involved in explaining the difficult elements such as slavery or submission in terms of *theology* are ameliorated by the almost singular apologetic concern of the early Christian community: pragmatism, not theology, is the explanation for this clearly pagan import. The tension between Christian theology and the HT mandates has been effectively removed. The HT, defined in terms of broad origins, current sociological *Sitz im Leben* and thoroughly pragmatic occasion, reaches, in Balch, its most distanced mark from the surrounding NT text.

Klaus Thraede: Economic Theory in Colossians, Ephesians and 1 Peter

Klaus Thraede, aware of the contributions of Crouch and Balch, recognised that the debate had been dominated by the question of origins, in particular the degree of influence on the form by pagan and/or faith community contexts. He called for the expansion of the comparative source material, both pagan and biblical, which had been offered up to that point, since the category *Haustafel* "nicht mehr so starr gebraucht wird" and the "nichtchristliche 'Pflichtentafel' an Bedeutung verliert."[113] In particular, he was concerned that the standard texts offered up to this point in the HT debate tended to direct the discussion in terms of obedience, a term which makes the HT rather unpalatable to modern sensibilities. Here he does not remain detached[114] in his assessment of the ethical question; he accuses scholars of ignoring the literal meaning of the text, while indulging in all manner of "Eisegese" in an attempt to "whitewash" the HT from the charge of paternalism. Additionally, he observes, scholars have deliberately depicted the Hellenistic sources as cruder, less enlightened parallels to the Christian HT.[115] For those scholars who want to avoid the interpretative pitfalls of either admitting the literal meaning on the one hand, or some sort of "Eisegese" on the other, Thraede offers the new research regarding economic literature as a heretofore un-

---

[113] Thraede, "Hintergrund", 361.
[114] Wagener, *Ordnung*, 27f. Wagener observes that Thraede takes a decidedly polemical tone in his analysis. He accuses exegetes of overlooking the true nature of the ancient debate by "painting the ancient culture black" in a one-sided manner to create a foil; they have not grasped ancient social ethics; they miss the sense of the NT text; finally, he does not allow as legitimate a differentiation between content and motivation in the HT.
[115] Thraede, "Hintergrund", 362.

known solution.[116] The texts found under the ancient rubric περὶ οἰκονομίας offer similarities to the New Testament HT form and concerns:

> Wie man sieht, geht es auch hier, Nuancen einmal vernachlässigt,
> a) um ein Dreierschema,
> b) um Gegenseitigkeit der Beziehungen,
> c) um den Versuch, bloße "Herrschaft" (Unterordnung) zu mildern. Schließlich klingen Leitmotive wie "Furcht" oder "Furcht und Liebe" (d.h. Respekt) an, die im NT wiederkehren.[117]

The texts which Thraede cites are, as with Balch, quite extensive.[118] The addition of a number of later texts, including some Latin sources, substantially expands those by which the HT may have been influenced. These texts, like the Stoic lists, treat the relations in the household, and, according to Thraede, show a new humanising impulse:

> Läßt sich wohl über die Stoßrichtung dieser Texte etwas ausmachen? Sie selbst, in ihrem nichtchristlichen Zweig, bekunden klar genug die Absicht, das Grundmuster des Herrschens und Dienens im Bereich des Hauses auszuarbeiten, ja angesichts der Bestrebungen, Rechte des Individuums zu gewährleisten, darf man wohl sagen: sie versuchen, jene Grundordnung aufrechtzuerhalten. Das geschieht zugleich so, daß sie, und zwar in erkennbar verschiedener Akzentuierung, Oben und Unten "humanisierend" aufeinander beziehen.[119]

The "humanising" elements of the economic literature, which demonstrates a protracted interest in the balance between the "Extremen des stoischen Gleichheitssatzes bzw. griechischer Liberalität und des harten Postulats unbedingter Fügsamkeit", forms the mediating impulse which stands behind the

---

[116] Ibid., 363. At this point, only a few had read Balch's work, and the newness of the theory, though using texts cited by Wilhelm, was genuine. Wilhelm's work, sixty years old at the time of this article, had somehow been overlooked, so Thraede, by *Neutestamentler*.

[117] Ibid., 363f.

[118] Thraede assumes a familiarity with the Stoic texts, as well as those cited by Balch. He notes that the sources found under the heading Οἰκονομικός are quite fragmentary. There are three strands of evidence which he cites: "Relativ günstig steht es noch mit dem pseudoaristotelischen Werkchen; hingegen zu den betreffenden Opera aus dem Bestand der sog. Neupythagoreischen Stücke fehlen uns wichtige Informationen. Ein dritter Überlieferungsstrang ist die Wirkungsgeschichte des xenophontischen Oikonomikos, die wir für die Zeit zwischen Cicero und Columella einbeziehen sollen." See K.H. Müller, *Haustafel*, 286–288, for a lengthy discussion of the Columella passage, which illustrates how the theories of Xenophon were applied to the then current problem of wealthy, idle women.

[119] Ibid., 365.

New Testament HT. The former thesis, which assumed that Christian freedom and love stood over against a strict Hellenistic code of order, can no longer be maintained: "…'christlich' war in jenem frühen Moment [the writing of the Colossian HT] die Entscheidung für die damalige realistisch-humane Mittelposition, die, wie gezeigt, Kritik an zu viel Liberalität enthielt, aber auch nicht einfach 'Herrschaft' als solche restituieren wollte."[120] Hence the early church cannot be confused with strident social criticism in the name of Christ; the HT texts do not support this position. Nor can one suggest that some sort of Christian motivation inherent in the HT allows a distancing from its historical backgrounds. The Christian church had avoided either extreme by adopting the *via media* known to them through the economic texts, and the ethical debate which they reflected. For this reason the HT should remain, according to Thraede, a phenomenon of that age, one that receives "kein schlechtes Zeugnis", but which cannot serve as a "Vorbild für das gegenwärtig erwünschte theologische Modell 'Christus und die Institutionen'."[121]

Thraede's aggressive approach to previous scholarship may put some off, yet it is refreshing in its honesty, and contains a number of insights.[122] His postulation of a "middle way" which was adopted from a first century contemporary debate concerning order and authority advances Balch's thesis with new vigour, and contains a more specific component, e.g., the contemporary debate over authority. The numerous citations from late Hellenistic economic treatises, whether accepted or not, suggest a possible social context of a popular debate, and the church's adoption of a mediating position; unfortunately, however, they have done little to integrate the HT into the broader text or theology of the epistle(s). On the contrary; the HT, consisting

---

[120] Ibid., 367.

[121] Ibid., 368. Here Thraede admits that he does not allow the HT material found in Col. and later texts into the Pauline corpus. He sees, as with Lührmann, a steady progression (*Entwicklungsstufen*) of these HT (or similar) texts in the direction of institutionalisation, in particular an "allmähliche Entwicklung zur "Ständetafel" which reveals a "Zunahme des authoritären Elements" as well as a "Zuwachs an hierarchischem Denken." This development shows that conservative elements had gained the "upper hand", which he notes is "gekoppelt an theologisch bedenkliche Legitimationsmuster", probably a reference to the more extended theological underpinnings found in Eph. and 1 Peter. The clearly derivative and "questionable" character of the texts makes them unsuitable for contemporary consideration.

[122] He is quite accurate in depicting the state of scholarship as being "overshadowed" by previous concerns and a limited number of texts; he also criticises the tendency to set the faith community in stark opposition to the pagan world (a criticism of Schrage?); he observes that there was little room given for development/differentiation among the New Testament HT; finally, he raises the ethical dimension of HT studies to a primary level.

44

nearly exclusively of (progressively) pagan borrowings,[123] have become
marginalised in terms of their theological impulse, in both their present *and*
New Testament contexts. This lack of integration and concomitant theological irrelevance explains Thraede's rejection of the HT material for contemporary debate. His parting remark discourages readers from any theological
engagement with the HT texts whatsoever; one should look for a theological
model, he suggests, in the "Pauline letters".[124] The realisation of some "Verwertbarkeit" of the HT is, in the final analysis, an impossible task. Wagener
sums it up well: "Für die Formulierung einer heutigen christlichen Sozialethik sind die Haus- und Ständetafeln für Thraede als Ganzes unbrauchbar."[125]

Dieter Lührmann: An Integrated Sociological Approach

Dieter Lührmann would be the first (since Luther!) to weave the HT tradition, including the *Ständetafel* and related, early Christian formulations such
as Galatians 3:28, into an integrated whole. His approach is intentionally
positive, bringing the new economic material to the HT debate (and early
church history, as well), and then construing a sociological context in which
these texts and the HT form found expression. Though in agreement with
Schroeder, Crouch and Rengstorf regarding the Dibelius-Weidinger proofs,
he is critical of these authors' "destructive" approach, which had the fundamental weakness of not being able to bring new, more plausible texts to light.
He points out that even though Crouch and others had cited some of the economic texts, they had not been rightly understood as a "tradition which stood
in opposition to the Stoic duty lists".[126] A new integration of the texts "concerning economics" would correct this weakness, and offer a new approach
to the HT tradition in the New Testament.[127] These new texts lead us to what

---

[123] Ibid., 367. Thraede sees the pagan influence increase in the later HT and "Ständetafel", yet
holds the earlier HT in Col. to be pagan in message (a mild patriarchal scheme) as well as
provenance.

[124] Ibid., 368.

[125] Wagener, *Ordnung*, 28. It is notable that Müller comes to the same conclusion, particularly in light of women's issues. Colossians represents "...die älteste Haustafel des Neuen
Testaments *an der Seite* der zeitgenössischen Textsorten zur Ökonomik—und *nur* dort—eine
höchst respektable urchristliche Entscheidung..." Only by seeing the HT in terms of its borrowing from the economic literature, and thereby offering a "Mittelweg", can it be freed from
paternalism and its theological "horrors", *Haustafel*, 290f.

[126] Lührmann, "Haustafeln", 85.

[127] The texts which Lührmann cites, "Haustafeln", 85f., are briefly expained: Firstly, he mentions the Seneca text which, though not part of the economic texts themselves, gives witness
to them. His translation reads as follows: "...der Teil der Philosophie, der für jede Lebensrolle

Lührmann sees as the centre of the HT concern: "Die Schriften 'Über die Ökonomie' wie die neutestamentlichen Haustafeln führen sozialgeschichtlich zu 'Haus' als sozialen und wirtschaflichen Begriff." The term household, he adds, constituted the basic (and sole!) socio-economic unit in ancient times, presumably until the eve of the industrial revolution.[128] The socio-economic elements which Lührmann is emphasising take place, then, exclusively within the framework of such household relationships. If his thesis is true, the establishment of a connection between the economic texts and the HT will lend new significance to the texts themselves as well as offering a view into the social, economic and historical contexts of the time. This, he hopes, will result in a clearer interpretation and assessment of the HT ethic.[129]

Lührmann distances himself from previous scholarship which posited a crisis as the occasion for the HT form on the one hand, while rejecting the notion of *Verbürgerlichung* on the other. The HT shows, rather, that the early church was in vital relation to the political and economic forces of the time, and that these forces were taking note of the church, as well.[130] Lührmann proposes a change in perspective from the *church* context to *culture*, allowing only a single social context for the HT in the common, public forum.[131]

---

besondere Vorschriften gibt...dem Ehemann Rat erteilt, wie er sich gegen seine Gattin verhalten, dem Vater, wie er seine Kinder erziehen, dem Herrn, wie er seine Sklaven regieren soll. Die Texte: 1) Der älteste erhaltene Text dieser Tradition ist Xenophons Oikonomikos. Erörtert wird das Verhältnis von Mann und Frau und das Verhältnis zu den Sklaven, es fehlt das Verhältnis Eltern/Kinder; es geht um die Probleme der Führung eines Landgutes. 2) Aristoteles' Buch I der Politik ist sehr viel theoretischer und gründsätzlicher. Die Grundstruktur des 'Hauses' ist Mann/Frau, Herr/Sklave bzw. die Dreiteilung mit Eltern/Kindern zusätzlich. Aristoteles ist dabei weniger als Xenophon interessiert an der praktischen Chrestomathie. Wichtiger sind seine Erörterungen über das Verhältnis vom Haus und Staat. 3) Wieder viel praktischer ist Ps-Aristoteles Oeconomica I, das Xenophon und Aristoteles voraussetzt. Hier wird nur Mann/Frau und Herr/Sklave behandelt. 4) Nur fragmentarisch erhalten ist Philodemos von Gadara; es fehlen vor allem die Teile über die gegenseitigen Beziehungen. 5) Hierokles, einer der wichtigsten Zeugen für Dibelius und Weidinger, ist auch hier zu nennen, aber nur mit den Teilen seines Werkes, die nach Stobaios zu dem Abschnitt περὶ οἴκων bzw. οἰκονομικός gehören. Erhalten sind hier nur Äußerungen zur Pflichtenverteilung zwischen Mann und Frau in der Haushaltsführung. 6) Fragmentarisch erhalten sind weiter: Dion von Prusa, Bryson, Kallikratidas, Periktione und Phuntys, wobei Brysons Werk in der islamischen Tradition eine bedeutende Nachgeschichte gehabt hat. Verloren sind die Schriften des Antisthenes und des Xenokrates."

[128] Ibid., 87.
[129] Ibid., 83.
[130] Lührmann, "Haustafeln", 97, alludes to the third phase of his historical construct, where the church has come to the attention of the ambient culture as an economic and political force.
[131] Ibid., 86. In an extensive footnote, Lührmann surveys the approach of scholarship in evaluating the message of the NT codes. In general, the HT has been seen in terms of its *Sitz*

46

This particular aspect of his approach strikes a common chord with Balch and Thraede, yet he refines the new social context with a detailed social-historical construct.

The household, Lührmann insists, should be considered an autarchy, concerned with the creation and maintenance of a common livelihood. It constituted the centre of supply and demand, the basic economic unit of the city-state. The writings "concerning economics" were, however, primarily ethical in nature, as they were reflections on how this autarchy could flourish, thus securing the good of the interdependent city-culture (which Lührmann sees as an "Ackerbürgerkultur").[132] Lührmann concludes that the early Christian community was firmly rooted in the social and economic realities of the *oikos*, and did not consciously attempt social or economic change.[133] Since the Christian community did not represent an intentionally counter-cultural development, the HT and related texts can function as a socio-economic barometer, revealing three phases of development which reflect the church's own socio-economic status, as well as its relationship to the surrounding culture. Lührmann traces these developments through the subtly changing form of the HT.[134]

Dieter Lührmann's analysis of the HT form in terms of its political and economic function suggests a broad and pragmatic usage, notably absent of theological concern (certain aspects of Ephesians are seen as a leaning on the "Israel Traditon", which was regarded as a parallel model to the οἶκος tradition).[135] The integration of all the HT forms in his sociological construct significantly widens the field of texts to be considered, and places questions of

im Leben in the church, be it teaching, worship, baptism, mission, etc. The form-critical categories have, to a certain degree, determined the approach and results of the research thus far (as well as the content of the NT codes themselves). Though not advocating a sheer "Rückkehr zu einer reinen Literaturkritik", he is suggesting the introduction of sociological and historical considerations to round off the perspective: "Will man sozialgeschichtlich neutestamentliche Texte interpretieren, kann man sich demnach nicht beschränken auf Ansätze in der Formgeschichte selber…sondern muß darüber hinaus ansetzen bei der *historischen* Frage, die durch die Formgeschichte, trotz aller Wortbildungen auf 'geschichtlich', weitgehend domestiziert worden war."

[132] Ibid., 88f.
[133] Ibid., 91.
[134] The three phases include mission (Gal. 3:28, 1 Cor. 7), the implementation of the οἶκος (Col. 3:18–4:1, Eph. 5:22–6:9, 1 Peter 3) and the implementation of political-economic visibility (the Pastorals). Interestingly, the church mirrors the development and structures of other social entities, including the acquisition of political power: "Da sich Christentum von Anfang an als eigenes soziales Gebilde nach der οἶκος-Struktur realisiert, ist von Anfang an auch ein latenter politischer Anspruch vorhanden", "Haustafeln", 97.
[135] Ibid., 93.

form and content solely in relation to historical developments. The HT form, then, follows historical function. Its adaptation in the NT contexts illustrates political and economic developments, which make the HT form neither the only possibility nor a logical necessity:

> Diese Entwicklungslinie ist, wie gesagt, nur eine der im frühen Christentum möglichen, aber doch die in Zukunft bestimmende. Wie ich sie dargestellt habe, macht sie vielleicht den Eindruck zu großer Kontinuität: Es wird jeweils das festgehalten, was in der vorigen Phase erarbeitet war, und auf neue Probleme bezogen.[136]

Lührmann's model, which offered historical continuity and an integrated (and progressive) view of the HT origins and function, would not be largely adopted by later scholars.[137] Here, as Wagener points out, he reveals a clear break with the received scholarship, offering neither a single source, nor a strong occasion:

> Lührmanns Rezeption der antiken Ökonomik für die Interpretation der neutestamentlichen Haustafeln steht im Zusammenhang einer an Kontinuität orientierten Konzeption der Geschichte des Urchristentums (und der Alten Kirche), die einen Gegenentwurf zu dem in der deutschen neutestamentlichen Forschung lange vorherrschenden Schema der Krise beim Übergang zur zweiten urchristlichen Generation darstellt. Innerhalb dieser Konzeption Lührmanns stellt die von der ökonomischen Literatur hergeleitete Haustafeltradition nur einen – den mittleren – Pfeiler dar. Der eigentliche umfassende Bezugspunkt ist mit dem antiken οἶκος eine soziale Struktur, nicht eine literarische Gattung.[138]

Wagener was correct in her assessment. Lührmann had departed from the mainstream of scholarship by emphasising continuous reception, with little attention to literary forms. The crisis theories, relying on some form of adopted literary tradition, would prove, at least at this point in the debate, to be a more plausible explanation for the original adoption of the HT. This is primarily due to the perception that the church offered a distinct and theologically differentiated point of reception. Lührmann represents the steady trend to consider the historical and sociological context of the οἶκος as equally important to the question of origins and the location of a particular literary *Gattung*. He also anticipated later HT theory which would make the

---

[136] Ibid., 96.

[137] See especially Gielen, *Tradition*, 71f. She, with Lührmann, cites the *oikos* as being the common concern of the HT and contemporary culture in which both were embroiled; the HT is, then, a "Stellungnahme des Urchristentums auf einem sowohl innerchristlich wie auch außerchristlich bedeutsamen Gebiet."

[138] Wagener, *Ordnung*, 31.

48

social occasion and intention of the form's adoption identical with the contemporary culture (without any mediating effect). Any uniquely Christian elements of the HT are incidental, and not related in any intentional manner to the surrounding text, or for that matter, to the distinct values of the Christian community.

Beyond Economic Theory

Franz Laub: A Radically Sociological Approach

Where Lührmann gathered literary and religious-historical evidence to weave a plausible historical trajectory of the HT form(s), Franz Laub was to construe a similar reconstruction on a purely sociological basis.[139] This emphasis, so Laub, should enhance the former scholarly approach (limited to a "literarhistorisch-traditionsgeschichtliche Fragestellung"), whose methods are blemished by "nicht geringen Aporien und Konsequenzen."[140] Laub represents the high water mark of criticism regarding previous scholarship, which he regarded as being hamstrung by faulty theories concerning the social context, as well as an undue "fixation" of earlier scholarship with questions of form.[141] Surprising at this point, however, is his criticism of the new

---

[139] Franz Laub, "Sozialgeschichtlicher Hintergrund und ekklesiologische Relevanz der neutestamentlich-frühchristlichen Haus- und Gemeinde-Tafelparänese—ein Beitrag zur Soziologie des Frühchristentums," *Münchener Theologische Zeitschrift* 37 (1986): 249–271.

[140] Ibid., 251f. The neglect of the sociological aspects in HT research has led to a "Verzerrung der Perspektiven", leaving the uniquely Christian elements to be taken lightly or explained in terms of variations in the received HT tradition; worse than this are the tendentious arguments intended to explain the Christian elements in terms of words or concepts (κύριος or ἀγάπη motifs or obedience and submission).

[141] Ibid., 250f. Laub sees HT research as progressing in terms of slight nuances; in looking at the HT form in Col., Eph., and 1 Pet., he notes that scholarship has directed its "Hauptaugenmerk fortan immer nur auf mögliche literarische Wurzeln und Vorbilder dieser Tradition. Dabei wurde jede denkbare Zuweisung zu den unterschiedlichen Umweltbereichen durchgespielt: die hellenistische Popularphilosophie mit oder ohne Vermittlung des hellenistischen Judentums, direkte Beeinflussung durch das hellenistische Judentum, alttestamentlich-jüdische Tradition." All the proofs offered by Weidinger (Pflichtentafel), even when traced through Jewish sources, offer no foundation for the New Testament HT form. These lists have their *Sitz im Leben* as instruction concerning the position of the man in the *oikos*; the duty list is only a "splinter" of the larger Stoic popular economic philosophy. Elsewhere Laub takes the various "crisis theories" to task, as well as questioning the probability of catechetical teaching. These, he points out, which are as numerous as the theories regarding the literary form, have not been verified.

economic impulse,[142] as well as his marginalisation of the relatively new grouping of economic texts. He notes that these texts do indeed take greater note of the ancient οἶκος, as well as showing greater resemblance to the New Testament HT, yet they have not been properly understood in terms of their relationship to the HT form:

> Dennoch empfielt sich Zurückhaltung, derlei Querverbindungen wiederum primär auf der literarhistorischen Ebene zu diskutieren. Die Indizien für literarhistorische Zusammenhänge sind im Grunde genommen auch hier nicht weniger problematisch als diejenigen, die man zuvor für einen Traditionszusammenhang zwischen hellenistischer Pflichtentafel und neutestamentlicher Haustafel beizubringen bemüht war. Denn Dreierschema und Gegenseitigkeit der Beziehungen sind zunächst einfach die Realitäten des antiken Sozialgebildes Oikos, auf das Oikonomik und Haustafel gleichermaßen verweisen. Darüber hinaus haben wir es beim oikonomischen Schrifttum im Vergleich zu den Haustafeln mit verhältnismäßig umfangreichen moralphilosophischen und sozialethischen Erörterungen zu tun, die die zwischenmenschlichen Beziehungen in aller Regel vom Hausherrn aus geordnet wissen wollen, sich aber nicht wie die Haustafeln paränetisch direkt an Frau, Kinder und Sklaven wenden. Von einer "Gegenseitigkeit der Ermahnungen", wie sie für die Haustafeln so charakteristisch ist, kann also beim oikonomischen Schrifttum keineswegs die Rede sein. Anderseits präsentiert sich die Oikonomik schon in ihrem klassischen Ursprung in ihrem Selbstverständnis nicht in einer strikten Bindung an den engeren Personenkreis des Oikos.[143]

Laub's criticism of recent scholarship does not rest solely upon the fact that the pre-Christian HT proofs are lacking at several points; he is convinced that the marshalling of any number of texts from antiquity results in a wide "variability" of scholarly results, each having some merit, but producing in the end conclusions which are "merkwürdig diffus und widersprüchlich."[144] The original goal of form criticism, to find the social context of the text, a decidedly sociological orientation, has been neglected. Only a strictly sociological approach can remedy the past failings, and provide a better under-

---

[142] Franz Laub, *Die Begegnung des frühen Christentums mit der antiken Sklaverei*, eds. H. Merklein and E. Zenger, Stuttgarter Bibelstudien, vol. 107 (Stuttgart: Verlag Katholisches Bibelwerk, 1982), 85. Here Laub criticises those who quote economic literature for missing the sociological thrust of these texts. To illustrate his point, he notes that they ignore a critical text from Aristotle (Pol. I, 1253, 1–8, full text in footnote) which shows the sociological relations between the members of the *oikos*. The reason why this text does not receive mention is "...weil der Oikos als sozialgeschichtliche Realität hinter der Haustafeltradition nie ernsthaft in die Überlegungen einbezogen wurde."

[143] Laub, "Hintergrund", 253.

[144] Laub, *Begegnung*, 86f.

50

standing of the HT texts.[145] For Laub, the contemporary social reality, not traditional literature, determines the form of, and lends understanding to, a particular text. The HT provide literary expression to the "sociological profile" of the early Christian community. Laub summarises his view of the various HT forms in the following thesis:

> Das Verbindende in diesen Texten ist der im Hintergrund stehende antike Oikos mit seinem sozialen Ordnungs- und Wertgefüge, das in den verschiedenen moralphilosophischen und religiös-geistigen Strömungen je neu reflektiert und rezipiert wird mit einem entsprechenden literarischen Niederschlag. Vermeintliche Elemente einer durchgehenden literarischen Form haben hier ihren Ursprung, sind also nicht literarisch-traditionsgeschichtlicher Natur, sondern spiegeln je auf ihrer Reflexionsebene die soziale Realität des antiken "Hauses" wider.[146]

The question which must be asked when approaching the HT is not, then, "nach einer durchgehenden literarischen Tradition" but what the HT form meant to the early Christian community. Laub does not completely dismiss the form-critical research, nor does he believe that this research can be separated from the sociological approach; it is a matter of the "Prioritäten des methodischen Einstiegs."[147] The practical outcome of this methodology is that the HT form which we find in the NT represents a genuinely Christian creation, reflecting the unique perspective and historical context of the early church.[148] Laub points out the several advantages of this approach: there is no longer a need to field theories concerning the reception of the HT form *into* the Christian community; the *Sitz im Leben* can be located in the Christian community (freed from the "Fragwürdigkeit einer literarhistorischen Herleitung der neutestamentlichen Haustafel, die nur unter Hinnahme von allerlei Aporien und traditionskritischen Künsteleien gelingen mag"); and the HT form is no longer forced into historical reconstructions which are no more than a "Wertung aus der Sicht neuzeitlicher sozialethischer und gesellschaftlicher Maßstäbe."[149]

---

[145] Laub, "Hintergrund", 249.
[146] Ibid., 255.
[147] Ibid., 255.
[148] Ibid., 262. Laub sees the relation of the New Testament HT form to the earlier Hellenistic models, but warns against suggesting an "adaptation-undertaking" from a "vorgegebenen Haustafel." We should rather "…dem Frühchristentum so viel Phantasie zutrauen, bei seiner unbestreitbar sehr tief reichenden Rezeption der antiken Oikos-Wirklichkeit so etwas wie die neutestamentliche Haustafel im Kern selber geschaffen haben zu können."
[149] Ibid., 261f.

The New Testament HT reflects, then, the unique nature and mission of the Christian community, for which there was no ancient analogy. The HT and its *oikos*-structure, being *the* definitive sociological category in the ancient world, was utilised by the church in a period of "consolidation of the early church mission" and reflects the "infrastructure of the emerging church."[150] The HT is, then, "eine Anweisung, im Rahmen der gültigen Ordnung des Oikos das Gläubigsein zu bewähren, jeder an dem Ort, an dem die soziale Struktur des 'Hauses' ihm seinen Platz vorgesehen hat."[151] The new, specifically Christian impulse of the New Testament HT is its expansion of the addressees. Earlier forms of the HT show the primary addressee to be the man; this has been relativised in its Christian form to include all members of the household. The early church was an "Oikos-Kirche" which had as its most remarkable characteristic a "soziale Integrationsfähigkeit" reflected in the HT:

> Die Art, wie hier Menschen gleich welchen Alters, Geschlechts, sozialen Standes oder nationaler Herkunft als Gemeinde Gottes angeredet werden, zeugt von einer außergewöhnlichen gemeinschaftsbildenen Dynamik, die in der Religionsgeschichte der Antike ihresgleichen nicht hat.[152]

As with Lührmann, Laub sees the form of the HT changing as the church underwent gradual social and organisational change, without the element of crisis. His perspective, however, is focused on the shift of the seat of authority from the original *oikos*-church (authority vested in the head of household as seen in Col., Eph. and 1 Pet.) to the Episcopate, reflected in their respective forms, *Haustafel* and *Gemeindetafel*.[153] In this way Laub integrates the spectrum of New Testament HT forms under the changing face of church authority and organisation. His theory, though disputed,[154] explains not only

---

[150] Ibid., 261.

[151] Laub, *Begegnung*, 88.

[152] Laub, "Hintergrund", 268f.

[153] Ibid., 262. "Die auf der Oikos-Ordnung basierende sozialethische Paränese der Haustafel des Kol, Eph und 1 Petr hat ihre kirchengeschichtliche Fortsetzung in den sogenannten Gemeinde- bzw. Ständetafeln der Pastoralbriefe und der Apostolischen Väter."

[154] Georg Schöllgen, "Hausgemeinden, οἶκος-Ekklesiologie und monarchischer Episkopat, Überlegungen zu einer neuen Forschungsrichtung," *Jahrbuch für Antike und Christentum* 31 (1988): 74–90. Schöllgen is in agreement with Laub that the HT form reflects episcopal authority in its later forms; he rejects, however, the notion that the earlier HT forms represent an ecclesiastical self-understanding based on the *oikos* model. "Für die erste und wohl auch für die zweite Generation, in der sich der zahlenmäßige Umfang der Ortsgemeinden wahrscheinlich noch in einer überschaubaren Größenordnung hielt und die regelmäßigen Zusammenkünfte in Privathäusern ein familiäres Selbstbewußtsein hätten nahelegen können, fehlt

the diversity in form, but also the rapid disappearance of the original HT form in early Christian literature.[155]

Laub pushes the sociological element of HT origins to its most radical expression, yet without totally rejecting the importance of form-critical findings. He is indicative of the growing scepticism held towards earlier theories and proofs, as well as a willingness to grant the HT a fully independent social context within the Christian community. His position signals the fact that scholarship is finding ever increasingly nuanced approaches to explaining the source, reception and development of the New Testament HT form. Particularly interesting is his contention that the HT represents an uniquely christianised version of ancient household regulation. Though he does not relate the christianised elements to the theology of their respective letters, he recognises that each HT form undergoes change, and cannot be understood apart from the immediate social context. This is a significant development over the general scholarly position that offers a single occasion for the HT adoption. The HT, then, though ultimately an import, is nonetheless more closely bound to the historical Christian community in terms of its ethic and social context. If Laub is correct, it remains to be seen if the theology contained in the various letters can be traced to the changes in the HT form, as well.

Klaus Berger: Gnomic Tradition and HT Origins

In the midst of the economic discussions concerning HT origins, Klaus Berger was to publish two works in 1984,[156] both of which would suggest new possibilities in source material, namely the gnomic sentences found in Greek wisdom tradition. In the development of parenetic material such as the HT texts, there were any number of literary influences which developed simultaneously (and symbiotically), yet in a certain tension, such as law sentences and their gnomic wisdom counterparts.[157] The gnomic literature, then, is an important, though often overlooked, influence upon the parenetic HT form. Berger introduces his discussion with a sharp critical analysis of Lührmann

---

jeder zuverlässige Beleg für eine Ekklesiologie, die vom οἶκος-Modell als Leitmetapher geprägt wäre."

[155] Laub, *Begegnung*, 88f.

[156] Klaus Berger, *Formgeschichte*, noted above, and "Hellenistische Gattungen im Neuen Testament," in *ANRW*, 25.2., eds. W. Haase and H. Temporini (Berlin: Walter de Gruyter, 1984), 1031–1432.

[157] Berger, *Formgeschichte*, 122.

and Thraede's economic theories.[158] He finds that their "Hinweis hilft nur wenig weiter".[159] Oddly, however, he incorporates their findings in *Gattungen*, with a much more positive assessment.[160] His extensive compilation of gnomic literature includes a long list of "paränetischen Mahnsprüchen" which, as he points out, can be recognised as including nearly every thematic point of the HT.[161] These pithy expressions of wisdom, though originally discrete and unorganised, would later be collected in what Berger terms as "nests." These "nests" took on independent, parenetic form, and, along with other parenetic forms, influenced the formulation of New Testament HT. Here Berger proposes not only an *additional,* but the *original* source for HT.[162] His analysis of the HT form is extremely nuanced, allowing only a reserved acknowledgement of the form as a *Gattung.* The form which we find in the New Testament passages represents an "Übergangsstadium", and is a testimony to the still-forming gnomic "nests" as a cohesive entity (the process of "Verselbstständigung").[163] The recognition of the gnomic sen-

---

[158] His observation that the economic literature lacked direct address and parenetic nature was extended by Gielen, *Tradition*, 66f. Though she adopted the economic texts as the primary HT *Vorlage*, she pointed to a continuous process of reception and modification, which would explain differences in form.

[159] Ibid., 136. Berger's criticisms are quite clear, and remind us of Schroeder: "Unter der Überschrift Oikonomikos sind uns eine Reihe von Traktaten und eine größere Anzahl von Fragmenten überliefert. Form wie auch Umfang dieser Traktate sind in keiner Weise den eindeutig paränetischen Formen der neutestamentlichen Hausafeln vergleichbar. Wer die Wichtigkeit der literarischen Form erkennt, stößt hier auf einen zumindest höchst erklärungsbedürftigen 'Graben'." Berger, a form critic in every way, takes issue with the fact that economic texts evidence only slight resemblance to the HT. Here we see the tension between the broad sociological orientation and the older emphasis on finding the nearest form.

[160] Berger writes that it was necessary to turn to the economic texts "um die Gattung Haustafel wirklich erklären zu können." Here the economic texts are specially named and placed in a schema depicting the etymology of the NT *Haustafel*. "Gattungen", 1079f. The clear naming of the HT as *Gattung* also seems to contradict his unwillingness to settle on the form in *Formgeschichte*, 138.

[161] Berger, *Formgeschichte*, 137.

[162] Berger, "Gattungen", 1085. The gnomic sentences stand behind the two *Gattungen* which Berger recognises as being primary in influencing the NT *Haustafel*, καθήκοντα and οἰκονομικός. The primacy of the gnomic collections can be seen in his graphic in *Formgeschichte*, 141.

[163] Berger, *Formgeschichte*, 138f. Berger takes this opportunity to level criticism against former attempts to locate the HT origins. The fact that they did not recognise the transitional nature of the HT doomed their findings to disappointment.

54

tences, having no *Sitz im Leben*[164] and standing in terms of HT development at the very source of later parenetic texts, repositions the time frame of HT development considerably, and places former categories such as the Stoic lists or the economic literature under its general etymological influence. Even the traditional dating of the New Testament HT receives a new face, as Berger places Col. and Eph. as the most developed, and thereby latest (!) forms:

> Das Übergangsstadium besteht darin, daß das Neue Testament ein Zeuge dafür ist, daß sich diese "Nester" aus paränetischer Tradition allmählich zu verselbständigen beginnen. Der Zusammenhang innerhalb der Thematik wird stärker. In dieser Phase werden...Mahnungen über das Haus zusammengesehen und zusammengearbeitet. In 1 Petr und Tit ist diese Abgrenzung der Stoffe noch am wenigsten vorangeschritten, in Kol und dann in Eph relativ am meisten. Aus der allgemeinen Paränese löst sich mithin der Themenkomplex "Haus" erst allmählich heraus, und das Neue Testament zeigt verschiedene Stadien dieser Entwicklung.[165]

That Berger's bold, new theories would meet with criticism was only a matter of time. Marlis Gielen, herself a later adherent to the economic approach, draws attention to the fact that the economic theory approaches the HT from a *religionsgeschichtlichen* perspective; if it is criticised from a strictly form-critical perspective, it will indeed leave certain methodological questions unanswered.[166] Berger's critical approach was not Gielen's only point of criticism, however. She points out that his list of evidences, though admittedly more parenetic in form than the economic texts, still do not have the necessary "verpflichtend-paränetischen Charakter."[167] Finally, she points out that Berger's thesis, which reverses the generally recognised order of the NT *Haustafel* tradition, brings with it too many attendant problems to constitute a serious challenge to the economic theory.[168] Wagener agrees with Gielen's criticisms, and extends them. She points out, first of all, a serious lack of precision in Berger's publications, in particular his failure to define those

---

[164] Berger, "Gattungen", 1055. Berger points out the antiquity of the gnomic sentences, as well as the absence of a *Sitz im Leben*. This frees them from any particular situation, so that they can appear almost anywhere, and serve to underscore the intended teaching.
[165] Berger, *Formgeschichte*, 139.
[166] Gielen, *Tradition*, 63. She notes that Berger criticises earlier research for its fixed approach in terms of a particular *Gattungsbegriff*, yet runs the danger of this himself; he makes the *religionsgeschichtliche* question dependent on the *formgeschichtliche*, so that the content of the economic proofs are effectively nullified by formal considerations.
[167] Ibid., 64.
[168] Ibid., 65.

texts which belong to *Haustafel*, and those belonging to *Pflichtentafel*.[169] His form-critical approach, which sees the HT form as a conflation of short sentences, makes the HT form insignificant as a textual unit: "Das Ganze darf nicht mehr sein als die Summe seiner Teile." His neglect of heretofore recognised characteristics of the HT form constitutes an "Unterbewertung der formalen Spezifika komplexer Gattungen".[170] Berger's placing of HT formation in the NT period ignores similar forms from considerably earlier periods, as well. The insistence that the HT form was derived from independent groupings of sentences, she concludes, shows the strength and weakness of his thesis. The strength is that he has identified a strand (*Rahmengattung Gnomik*) that has influenced the more complex *Gattung* of the HT. His mistake is giving the gnomic sentences the determining influence in the formation of the HT, making it no more than a dislocated parenetic collage.[171]

Berger's contribution has shown that the debate over HT origins is far from over, and certainly apt to continue in new directions. He represents an almost startling return to the strongly form-critical approach, which had been receding in the wake of more sociological concerns. The newest literature, perhaps not surprisingly, reflects an integration of the earlier schools, and a willingness to operate with the tensions of its form-critical limitations. His theory adds little to the understanding of the unifying elements within the HT structure, its motivation, theology or ethic, though it must be said that his proposed conflated nature of the HT does not preclude the element of theological reflection.

Hermann von Lips: The HT as Christian Parenetic Topos

Von Lips is perhaps the best example of newer scholarship which has been able to identify HT origins apart from earlier form-critical categories. His findings lead him to conclude, with Berger, that it is no longer possible to speak of the HT as a *Gattung*: "Für die neutestamentliche 'Haustafel' muß

---

[169] Wagener, *Ordnung*, 55f. Her discussion brings up a number of inconsistencies, including conflicting schemes of etymology in his two publications, dependence upon economic theories yet rejecting them, and, of course, his failure to define the genre.

[170] Ibid., 59. Wagener is correct in her observations. The loosely organised "nests" of gnomic thought, having no *Stiz im Leben*, afford Berger a flexibility in applying these sentences to almost any genre. This can be seen in his positive assessment of Rengstorf; Col. and Eph. reveal a particular Christian formulation built on the foundation of the gnomic sentences. Reciprocity of address, for example, is explained not in terms of an earlier form, but is seen as a localised adaptation. *Gattungen*, 1079.

[171] Ibid., 60.

die Konsquenz gezogen werden, daß die Geschichte einer 'Gattung' nicht geschrieben werden kann."[172] The *Gattung Haustafel* is informed by smaller, traditional parenetic units (topoi).[173] The earlier assumption that Col.-Eph. constitute the original form (identified as *Gattung*) of the HT, from which other NT forms atrophy or undergo evolutionary changes, is also rejected by von Lips. He illustrates how previous demarcations between HT groupings, in particular the separation of 1 Peter and Titus,[174] no longer hold. In this way, he hopes to establish a new etymological relationship between these texts and Col.-Eph. His analysis of 1 Peter and Titus shows remarkable similarities in content and structure of the parenetic material, to which he concludes, "Dieser analoge Aufbau der Paränese in 1 Petr und Tit kann kaum nur ein Zufall sein. Man muß vielmehr das Vorhandensein von Verbindungen annehmen."[175] Here von Lips suggests that the similarities are due to a common parenetic tradition, one that included three impulses: instruction concerning outsiders, instruction concerning the church, and instruction concerning the household (topoi: *Öffentlichkeit, Gemeinde, Haus*). These three emphases can be seen in any number of New Testament texts,[176] but are especially prominent in the HT forms, and offer an explanation for both similar *and* divergent elements. The common roots of all HT forms, then, from Col. to Titus, can be traced through one or more of these topoi: "Dieser Topos [concerning the house] aber hatte, den Formgesetzen der Paränese entsprechend, keine einmalig festgelegte Form, sondern ließ die Variationsmöglichkeiten offen, wie wir in Kol, Eph, 1 Petr und Titus finden."[177]

The *Sitz im Leben* of this common parenetic tradition, according to von Lips, was post-baptismal instruction, which attempted to inform both church and public life.[178] It is interesting to note the similarity of this most recent proposal to the catechetical theory of Alfred Seeberg, and how the discussion of HT origins and occasion has come full circle. Von Lips has taken the discussion in an original direction, however. His identification of the three to-

---

[172] Hermann von Lips, "Die Haustafel als 'Topos' im Rahmen der Urchristlichen Paränese, Beobachtungen anhand des 1. Petrusbriefes und des Titusbriefes," *NTS* 40 (1994): 261–280.

[173] See also D. Bradley, "The Topos as a Form in the Pauline Paraenesis", *JBL* 72 (1953): 238–246. Bradley, the first to use this nomenclature, locates a number of topoi which Paul introduced from Hellenistic parenesis.

[174] Von Lips begins with 1 Peter and Titus intentionally; he wishes to avoid analysis of these books in terms of Col.-Eph., which would lead to a treatment of perceived "deficiencies", "Haustafel", 264.

[175] Ibid., 268.

[176] Von Lips gives examples from Paul: 1 Cor. 7; 1 Thes. 3 ,4, 5; Rom. 10, 12, 13.

[177] Ibid., 280.

[178] Ibid., 279.

poi, concerning outsiders, the church and the household, establishes definite sub-categories within the HT tradition. This offers new options for understanding how the larger body of *Haustafeln, Ständetafeln* and *Gemeindetafeln* have been edited and utilised in their various contexts. Variant HT forms can no longer only be seen in terms of their dissimilarity to an accepted form-critical model, but rather in how they utilise the topoi. Terms such as "deficient" or "further developed HT" would no longer apply. The immediate occasion determines the new form. That the church generated and possessed such traditional material is not a new proposition, yet it marks a subtle departure from current scholarship. The single HT model, as well as the form-critical assumptions which it represents, become secondary to the function of the HT in the faith community.

Though von Lips denies the HT form as *Gattung*, and postulates a flexible, Christian parenetic tradition as its source, this does not sever him from previous research concerning origins. Following Strecker,[179] he sees two pre-Christian traditions, the Stoic lists of duties and the economic literature, as informing the topos "household". The Hellenistic lists of duties provide the overarching themes (including the household, relations to others, government); the economic texts, in turn, reveal such characteristics as reciprocity and direct address.[180] In von Lips we find a widening of the source material behind the Christian parenesis (a clear trend in more recent scholarship), as well as the expansion of texts which have been influenced by this tradition by means of its Christian expression. The HT, though not enjoying the almost universal purview of texts given it by Luther, has had its boundaries extended once again to include Dibelius' original list.[181] The parenesis which has been incorporated into the various New Testament HT forms is, ultimately, a Christian adaptation of Hellenistic thought. Von Lips' understanding of its appropriation is more differentiated than earlier scholars, allowing for broader source topoi (origin), the selection of which, in turn, reflect the sociological concerns of the individual letters. His position moves towards recognising a level of independence between the letters, yet does not attempt

---

[179] Georg Strecker, "Die neutestamentlichen Haustafeln," in *Neues Testament und Ethik: FS für R. Schnackenburg*, ed. H. Merklein (Freiburg: Herder, 1989), 349–375, 358. Strecker holds that the two theories are not mutually exclusive, but complementary, being "mehr ergänzend als umstürzend."

[180] Lips, "Haustafel", 277.

[181] Ibid., 261f. Von Lips conflates earlier, differentiated names for the HT form (*Ständetafel/Gemeindetafel*) into the traditional word, *Haustafel*. His inclusion of the Dibelius-Weidinger HT texts is a surprising development; the texts had, for example, diminished to include only Col.-Eph., and in some cases, 1 Peter.

to relate the mandates or theology of the adopted HT to more than the socio-logical aspect.

Conclusion

An attempt to draw conclusions from the research on the HT form, even in broad terms, is bound to be frustrated, for the various positions represent, in many cases, contradicting viewpoints which have never been resolved.[182] Additionally, earlier theories, once discounted, have undergone modification, finding integration in newer, hybrid theses. There are, however, several *tendencies* emerging in the debate, which characterise the latest contours of scholarly thought:

1. Views of origins (Hellenistic, Jewish, economic, OT influences) are conflating to include a broader spectrum of texts;
2. Emphasis has shifted from earlier concerns regarding form to include sociological and ethical aspects;
3. There is a growing lack of confidence shown towards any one postu-lated source, including a total reliance on form-critical methodology;
4. The social context of the HT has become less differentiated, allow-ing for Christian and/or pagan spheres of influence, blurring the lines of adoption and their significance, and lessening the ideological ten-sion between the two communities;
5. Earlier "crisis theories" associated with the inception of the HT have lost popularity as the social context of the HT is perceived to ap-proximate that of the ambient culture;
6. The evolutionary model of HT development, Col.-Pastorals, assum-ing a degree of literary dependence, is no longer universally accepted as an explanation of their relationship to other HT forms;
7. The inconclusive nature of the proposed HT *Vorlagen*, along with the several elements unique to the HT, suggest that the NT *Hausta-feln* represent, at least to some degree, genuine Christian composi-tion.

---

[182] David Balch, "Neopythagorean Moralists and the New Testament Household Codes," in *ANRW*, 2.26.1, eds. W. Haase and H. Temporini (Berlin: Walter De Gryter, 1992), 380–411, in one of the most recent summaries of HT research, concludes that a consensus is not forth-coming.

These tendencies reflect the gradual expansion of source materials, as well as a healthy honing of a number of insightful theories. They also reflect a conservative, if not cautious, approach to interpreting the evidence brought forth in the debate. The HT question remains current, however, as the "household code" has yet to be clearly identified beyond the New Testament documents. Lars Hartman, in his critique of the form-critical methods and findings, reflects the current scholarly tentativeness when he asks, "...did the literary convention 'household code' exist? So far nothing of the sort is known – only thought patterns that reappear in different text types, text forms, text form variants, etc."[183] His criticism is levelled primarily on the methodological level; the assumption of a *Gattung* which stands behind the New Testament HT form is confusing a "socially given thought pattern with conventionally established literary forms".[184] The fact that the research has been hampered by any number of methodological approaches (which he shows to lack proper linguistic methodology) and a "swarm of terms" which "cloud the discussion", has led him to advise caution in assessing the HT research, especially in terms of "drawing conclusions about the history and thinking of the early church from this presumed literary form."[185] The iterating and sometimes circular nature of the debate has indeed left behind it an uncertain, if not vague, picture of HT origins.

In spite of the undecided nature of the debate, we have found that the HT form, as it is represented in the New Testament, is dynamic in nature; its form is not only distinct from other ancient and contemporary regulations, it also reveals differences between its NT manifestations. These characteristics and differences have been thoroughly analysed by means of the above methodologies. Yet, the question which has been raised by Schrage regarding the theological impulses of the New Testament HT,[186] has remained largely unanswered. Every theory of origins of the New Testament HT has noted, cor-

---

[183] L. Hartman, "Some Unorthodox Thoughts on the "Household Code Form"," in *The Social World of Formative Christianity and Judaism, FS Howard Clark Kee*, ed. J. Neusner (Philadelphia: Fortress Press, 1988), 226. He answers the question by rejecting the material brought forward in the debate. The syntactic features of reciprocity, address-imperative-motivation structures "existed but not as characteristics of a text-form variant following a particular compositional pattern similar to that of a household code." He also points out that the source material, if categorised by common linguistic features, belongs to expository text type, not instructional.

[184] Ibid., 229.

[185] Ibid., 230.

[186] Schrage, *Ethik*, 1. In asking how the HT form might be better understood, Schrage argues for "eine differenziertere, angemessenere und präzisere Erfassung dessen, was mit der Rezeption des antiken Pflichtenschemas durch das Urchristentum theologisch vor sich ging."

rectly, we believe, that the HT form is to be traced, in part, to traditional sources. If, however, the New Testament HT form represents a unique Christian composition which has undergone thoughtful redaction in each of its NT expressions, it stands to reason that each form reflects intentional theological perspectives, as well. Can the HT form be shown to be more than a parenetic intrusion, having only loose semantic and theological ties to the larger body of the letter(s)? It will be the purpose of this study to discover *theological* impulses contained in each of the HT forms found in Colossians and Ephesians, and their relation to the larger letter. It is our hope that the following investigation will shed more light on these difficult and controversial passages, and perhaps in this manner extend their *Verwertbarkeit.*

Chapter Two
The Colossian *Haustafel* in Theological Context

Introduction

In the preceding chapter we found that the New Testament HT has not been conclusively assigned to traditional material, be it Hellenistic, Jewish or early Christian. HT scholarship has been principally devoted to ascertaining potential *Vorlagen*, a largely form-critical question, or, alternatively, concerned with social and religious aspects such as the occasion and function of the HT in the early church setting. The former approach has determined some similarities in a number of ancient texts; the similarities, however, cannot altogether account for the HT form. The HT contains unique characteristics which define it in contrast to the various proposed literary evidences, and tie it, we hope to demonstrate, to the theology of the letter. Presupposing a genetic literary link has not succeeded in demonstrating a clear traditional genre from which the HT has emerged, but has had the unfortunate effect of isolating it from the theological context of the larger letter, making the HT little more than an isolated (and sub-Christian) parenetic stratum within the letter. This, isolation, we believe, hinders the full understanding of this admittedly controversial parenesis, and thereby its potential theological relevance. The sociological investigations of the HT in terms of its occasion and function, though varied in their conclusions, approach the HT as an expression of pragmatic expediency. Here the theological impulses contained in the larger text, as well as those found in the form of the HT, have been largely overlooked. In both cases, then, the HT has been perceived as a phenomenon of convenience to the writer, and not primarily as an expression of genuine, Christian theological reflection.

If the HT has been extricated from critical theological attention due to its apparent traditional nature, the bifurcation of the letter to the Colossians into theology and parenesis has added to its isolation from the greater text. Following Dibelius,[1] the letter has been commonly seen in terms of a former, theological section (1:1–3:4) and its attendant and complementary parenetic extension (3:5–4:6). Although this particular method of division reflects the

---

[1] Dibelius, *Kolosser*, 40, cites 3:4 as the last of a series of theological statements found in the letter, vv. 3:1–4 being an *Übergang* into the parenetic section. Most commentators have followed his schema.

relative density of sheer theological or parenetic material contained in each respective "half" of the letter, and is helpful as a point of orientation, such a neat division is not completely possible, as can be seen in the numerous references to behaviour in 1:1–3:4.[2] The assumption of a degree of dislocation between the two portions has become the hallmark of critical research, however, and has led to a particularly notable isolation of the parenetic material in the latter section, 3:5–4:6. For this reason, parenetic elements within Colossians such as the HT have not received treatment in terms of the overarching theology of the letter.[3] Eduard Lohse, though adhering closely to the traditional division of the letter, has recognised the theological character in both the dogmatic and parenetic sections, identifying each as being "determined by the theme of the universal dominion of Christ".[4] If Lohse is correct, an investigation of this theme, as it is represented in the vocabulary and theol-

---

[2] The first section of the letter represents a strong interplay between first-person, confessional material (1:3; 7; 8; 9; 13; 14; 23; 24; 28; 29; 2:1; 4) and Paul's desire to see *particular behaviours* maintained or avoided among the Colossians, perhaps in contrast to critical or innovating opponents. See Jerry L. Sumney, *"Servants of Satan", "False Brothers" and Other Opponents of Paul*, ed. S.E. Porter, JSNT, vol. Sup. 188 (Sheffield: Sheffield Academic Press, 1999), 188f. Sumney highlights the polemical nature of the first section. The parenetic element can be seen in Paul's approval of their lives in faith, demonstrating πίστιν and ἀγάπην (1:3, 8), as the Gospel bears recognisable fruit καθὼς καὶ ἐν παντὶ τῷ κόσμῳ (1:6). Faith is rooted in the "word of truth of the Gospel" (1:5), with which they are familiar (ἠκούσατε and ἐπέγνωτε). This becomes the basis for their behaviour, 1:10: a life ἀξίως τοῦ κυρίου, again bearing fruit (this time they, not the Gospel, are to bear the fruit) ἐν παντὶ ἔργῳ ἀγαθῷ. The positive effects of the Gospel outlined in 1:21–22 are equally dependent, v. 23, upon a firm adherence to the received faith and hope of the Gospel, οὗ ἠκούσατε. 2:6, the first imperative in the section, commands the believers to live as they had received Christ, a command illustrated by a string of passive participles in v.7, which show the centrality of Christ in their instruction: ἐρριζωμένοι καὶ ἐποικοδομούμενοι ἐν αὐτῷ καὶ βεβαιούμενοι τῇ πίστει καθὼς ἐδιδάχθητε. The attendant imperatives in 2:8, 2:16 and 2:18 warn against deviant teachings and behaviours which are characterised as οὐ κατὰ Χριστόν; those who promote such behaviours demonstrate independence from Christ, 2:19, οὐ κρατῶν τὴν κεφαλήν. Behaviour, though described here in broad terms, is closely linked to the Colossians' calling and relationship to Christ.

[3] Johannes Lähnemann, *Der Kolosserbrief, Komposition, Situation und Argumentation*, eds. W. Marxsen, G. Klein and W. Schrage, Studien zum Neuen Testament, vol. 3 (Gütersloh: Gütersloher Verlagshaus Gerd Mohn, 1971), 54. The separation of the two elements is "überhaupt kennzeichnend" for the "wissenschaftliche Arbeit zu den Paränesekapiteln"; he points to the resultant gap in NT research: "Die Paränese des Kolosserbriefes hat noch keine Betrachtung unter dem Gesichtspunkt der Komposition des Gesamtbriefes erfahren." Andrew Lincoln, "The Household Code and Wisdom Modes of Colossians," *JSNT* 74 (1999): 93f., agrees.

[4] Eduard Lohse, *Colossians and Philemon*, ed. H. Koester, trans. W.R. Poehlmann and R.J. Karris, Hermeneia—A Critical and Historical Commentary on the Bible (Philadelphia: Fortress Press, 1971), 3.

ogy of Colossians, may provide a useful exegetical bridge for the theological understanding of the HT material. It is our hope, then, to illustrate the thematic centrality of Christ's lordship in both the theology and parenesis of the letter, as well this theme's bearing upon, and representation within, its early HT form.[5] Special attention will be given to the development of the vertical (divine-human) and horizontal (intra-human) aspects of Christ's lordship within the Church, and how this lordship is distilled in these relations. The rule of Christ, we hope to show, is depicted in the book of Colossians as occurring primarily along these two axes. The characterisation of the Christian life in 1:4 as τὴν πίστιν ὑμῶν ἐν Χριστῷ Ἰησοῦ καὶ τὴν ἀγάπην ἣν ἔχετε εἰς πάντας τοὺς ἁγίους corresponds to these axes, providing the theological and ethical profile of the parenetic mandates. The letter develops the contours of these axes in a number of contrasting images and events related to Christ, which illustrate and conjoin the accomplished work of Christ with the ethical life of the believer. The multifaceted work of Christ, to which the believer is intimately identified, ends in the expectation of his return, which includes a pronounced note of judgement. It is this eschatological event which directly precedes and influences the tenor of the parenetic section, particularly the HT. The HT, we hope to show, is profoundly influenced by this final aspect of Christ's work, which correspondingly represents the mediating force of its mandates. The mediation of Christ, particularly his role in judgement, can be best seen in the more extensively developed instruction found in the master-slave relationship. It is this expanded section that invites more detailed analysis of ethical behaviour expected in Christ-centred relations, and will, for that reason, receive particular exegetical attention. The master-slave relationship, we hope to show, combines the central theological themes of the letter by means of elements found in the HT form (outward nature of address), as well as its theological content.

The Christ of Colossians: Universal Dominion

The Pauline vision of a transcendent and victorious Christ, the κύριος ἐν οὐρανῷ (Col. 4:1), represents the definitive expression of divine authority.[6]

---

[5] The antecedence of the Col. HT among similar forms in the NT represents the prevailing view. Elements of this discussion will be introduced in the following chapter. See W. Munro, "Evidences", *NTS* 18, for arguments in favour of the antecedence of Ephesians. Her views have found little resonance among scholars treating the HT form. Contra Munro: Dunn, *Epistles*, 243, fn. 8; Müller, "Frauenthema", 311; Schrage, "Haustafeln", 2; Strecker, "Haustafeln", 359; Pokorný, *Brief*, 152.

[6] Werner Kramer, *Christ, Lord, Son of God*, trans. Brian Hardy, Studies in Biblical Theology, vol. 50 (London: SCM Press, 1966), 173. Kramer notes that the title κύριος always

Although the unmodified title of Lord carried with it an imposing sense of power,[7] the original hearers were left in no doubt as to the divine prerogative of Christ, as the letter develops this theme through extensive use of authoritative language. He is represented as the one in whom all fullness should dwell (1:19), even πᾶν τὸ πλήρωμα τῆς θεότητος (2:9). As the κεφαλή, Christ leads and sustains the church (1:18, 2:19), and πάσης ἀρχῆς καὶ ἐξουσίας, as well (2:10). This universal rule is underscored by the "extraordinary frequency" with which the author employs πᾶς and its cognates, reading "like a red thread drawn through every section of the letter",[8] reinforcing both the superlative nature of Christ's rule, as well as its expected influence upon the lifestyle of his followers.[9] The hymn of Christ in 1:15–18 focuses upon his superlative nature, and leaves no doubt that this κύριος[10] is peerless, the list of qualifications and relations[11] substantiating the claim of 1:18b, "that he might be first in all things."

The ethical demands found in Colossians, derived from and contingent upon Christ's authority, cast an unparalleled, almost oppressive[12] relationship of dominion and obedience, and initiate, if nothing else, a high ethical

---

carries with it ethical obligation; this title is "all-embracing in its authority", with no area of human activity beyond its purview. This is certainly the case in Colossians, where nearly every mention of *kurios* (1:3, 10; 2:6; 3:13, 17, 18, 20 22, 23, 24; 4:1, 7, 17) is joined with a call to ethical behaviour, nearly half of the occurrences appearing in the HT. *Kurios* provides the primary titular language for Christ in the letter.

[7] Ferdinand Hahn, *Christologische Hoheitstitel: Ihre Geschichte im frühen Christentum*, eds. E. Käsemann and E. Würthwein, 2 ed., FRLANT, vol. 83 (Göttingen: Vandenhoeck & Ruprecht, 1964), 74. Hahn notes that, in the Hellenistic world, "die Kyrios-Titulatur unter orientalischem Einfluß vor allem in den Mysterienreligionen und im Kaiserkult Bedeutung erlangt [hatte]. Sie bezeichnete die unbedingte Macht und Göttlichkeit ihres Trägers…"

[8] Lohse, *Colossians*, 4.

[9] πᾶς and its cognates appear 39 times throughout the letter, appearing in relation to Christ, the gospel and ethical behaviour: 1:4, 6, 9–11, 15–20, 28; 2:2–3, 9–10, 13, 19, 22; 3:8, 11, 14, 16–17, 22; 4:7, 9, 12.

[10] It is interesting to note that the hymn does not contain the title *kurios*, a title which appears to be used, not in term of Christ's relation to the universe, but rather as arbiter of human relations.

[11] Christ is depicted in terms of his relation to divinity (εἰκὼν τοῦ θεοῦ τοῦ ἀοράτου, v. 15), as well as sustaining rule (τὰ πάντα ἐν αὐτῷ συνέστηκεν, v.17). He is primarily understood in relation of pre-eminence to his own created order (πρωτότοκος πάσης κτίσεως, v. 15; ἐν αὐτῷ ἐκτίσθη τὰ πάντα, v. 16a; τὰ πάντα δι᾽ αὐτοῦ καὶ εἰς αὐτὸν ἔκτισται, v. 16b; καὶ αὐτός ἐστιν πρὸ πάντων, v. 17), which logically places him as head of the church (1:18). The image of Christ is one of undisputed dominion.

[12] C.F.D. Moule, *The Epistles of Paul the Apostle to the Colossians and to Philemon*, ed. C.F.D. Moule, Cambridge Greek Testament Commentary (Cambridge: CUP, 1968), 3. Moule characterises Christ's position of authority in relation to the universe and Church as "intolerably weighty".

benchmark. The language of dominion, combined with the HT's decided absence of modern social egalitarianism, may lead the reader to assume that Paul's vision of the ruling Christ is in some way fundamentally flawed. Is the Colossian HT not, by means of sheer divine force and the apparently pragmatic use of commonly known social regulation, Christian *Realpolitik*? Perhaps. The answer, we believe, lies not in an abstract understanding of divine authority, but in the letter's clear emphasis upon the person, power and work of the exalted Christ in *redemption*. It is the multifaceted, soteriological Christ-believer relationship which determines the nature and scope of Christ's authoritative rule within the church. The ethical mandates of the letter of Colossians, growing from the soteriological benefits effected in Christ, are not merely propositional, nor based in unmitigated power alone; they are ultimately *relational*. It is, first and foremost, the *person* of Christ who dominates both the theology and ethics of the letter, his rule portrayed as transcendent, yet his sphere of authority is as alarmingly close *in Christ* as one's spouse, child or slave. The HT mandates, though related to the exalted Christ, derive their authority not only from his position of power, but from his historical, redeeming work. It is in Christ, we hope to show, that God has initiated and transformed relationships; primarily on the divine-human level, and consequently and correlatively, upon the intra-human level. Christ's dominion, though absolute, takes on benevolent contours in both its theological and ethical dimensions, when understood in terms of redemption. The benevolent character is displayed in the initiation of relations along the divine-human axis.

Christ's Dominion in the Believer: The Divine-Human Axis

In his opening words to the Colossians, Paul expresses thanks for the recipients' lives in a manner that reveals two distinct levels of relationship, described in general terms as τὴν πίστιν ὑμῶν ἐν Χριστῷ Ἰησοῦ καὶ τὴν ἀγάπην ἣν ἔχετε εἰς πάντας τοὺς ἁγίους (1:4). The former relationship, described as faith in Christ, constitutes, as we hope to demonstrate, a vertical axis establishing a unique relationship between Christ and the believer. This axis, finding its genesis in the salvation effected by Christ, becomes the irreducible relational foundation from which the ethical mandates, including the HT, receive their impulse. "The love for all the saints" serves, similarly, as a general rubric for intra-human relations, a second, horizontal axis substantially related to the primary, vertical axis. Faith in Christ and love of the saints, we hope to show, become the programmatic concern of the epistle; these axes are ultimately expressed in ethical terms, having important implications for the understanding of the Colossian HT.

66

The divine-human relationship displays an absolute, yet benevolent character. It is God who initiates the reconciliation in Christ, δι' αὐτοῦ ἀποκαταλλάξαι τὰ πάντα εἰς αὐτόν, εἰρηνοποιήσας διὰ τοῦ αἵματος τοῦ σταυροῦ αὐτοῦ (1:20a), calling believers into the context of the church, ἐν ἑνὶ σώματι (3:15). Colossians makes it clear that this calling is tied inextricably to rescue (ῥύομαι)[13] from the dominion of powers *other* than Christ (ἐκ τῆς ἐξουσίας τοῦ σκότους, 1:13). Redemption in Christ, then, implies more than a judicial declaration or a particular change in behaviour. The effects of the cross carry with them an essential and *positive* transfer into the kingdom of the Son, in whom the hearers of the letter have redemption (ἀπολύτρωσις), v.1:14, as well as deliverance from powers of darkness, the Colossian recipients' previous masters (1:13). These malevolent forces have been stripped of power (ἀπεκδύομαι), and exposed (ἐδειγμάτισεν ἐν παρρησίᾳ) in the manner of vanquished captives (2:15). For both slaves and free citizens hearing this message, the language amounts to nothing less than a restructuring of their identity. This fundamental change is what Gielen aptly terms *Herrschaftswechsel*: the former dominion has been replaced by another.[14] The believers in Colossae are reminded that the basis for their ethical conduct is their *new* status ὡς ἐκλεκτοὶ τοῦ θεοῦ ἅγιοι καὶ ἠγαπημένοι (3:12). Ethical behaviour and moral identity are determined by, ultimately, the purposes of God in the establishment of the divine-human axis.

The nature of the sacrifice by which the new status was procured is the cross (1:20). This form of execution represents, most tellingly, the cruel punishment reserved for slaves.[15] The emphasis upon suffering, and the inclusion of the cross in Paul's theology, especially in collocation with the title of the Christ, was "an offence without analogy."[16] Believers in Colossae, regardless of social standing, discover, perhaps for the first time, a dual sense of solidarity in their common redemption from sin. Firstly, they share a common pedigree of sin, and its astonishing antidote, the cross. This constitutes the

---

[13] Compared to σῴζω (over 100 NT occurrences), usage is rare (15 instances) in NT, and absent in Eph.; 7 NT references are imbedded in LXX citations; OT use is limited to the sense of deliverance and liberation, particularly from death or enemies, and always by the working of God. Ex. 6:6, 14:30 and Ju. 6:8–9 give examples of deliverance from δουλεία. See Kasch's article in *TDNT* 6, 998–1003.

[14] Gielen, *Tradition*, 177.

[15] Martin Hengel, *Crucifixion in the Ancient World and the Folly of the Message of the Cross*, trans. J. Bowden (London: SCM Press, 1977), 62.

[16] Ibid., *Studies in Early Christology* (Edinburgh: T. & T. Clark, 1995), 363. Hengel cites the argument of Celsus (Origen, *Contra Celsum* 2.68), which insists that if Christ were divine, he would have vindicated his genuine, impassible identity by becoming *invisible* on the cross.

primary, human level of solidarity in the church, and bears implications for the intra-human relational axis. That the entire church has been rescued from this condition by the *Lord Christ* is their second point of commonality. It is Christ who reconstitutes human relations under the provisions of the divine-human axis. Christian identity implies, then, a new allegiance which defines itself negatively in terms of the past loyalties and actions, and positively in terms of Christ. Far from being a superficial, christological appendage,[17] the Colossian phrase "in the Lord" presupposes both human and divine levels of identification by means of transfer; it is a relationship involving both axes, which intersect, particularly in ethical appeals such as the HT, in Christ.[18] Christ becomes the irreducible foundation of salvation *and* ethics, the meeting point for relations, human and divine. By assuming a common salvation, the letter promotes a subtle level of egalitarianism. However diverse the social and economic status of the members of Christ's body may be, the essential and common point of *all* members is in the work of Christ, as noted above. The believers' redemption is a point of common ground κατενώπιον αὐτοῦ, which implies both allegiance *and* status. The transformation is regarded as genuine and complete, for here "There is no Greek or Jew, circumcised or uncircumcised, barbarian, Scythian, slave or free, but Christ is all, and in all." (3:11). The new and primary identity of the believer is now *in Christ*; the old self and its pedigree of sin are discarded for an identification (as we hope to demonstrate below) with Christ in the elements of his passion, as well as the coming glory (3:4). The identification is so complete, that Paul describes them as having died, receiving a new life which is hidden in Christ (3:2). Indeed, Christ *is* their life, ἡ ζωὴ ὑμῶν (2:4). This vision of complete salvation, changing the very essence of a believer's identity and creating a common fellowship, has profound implications for the understanding of Paul's ethic, particularly in terms of the HT. This transformed vertical axis, established in Christ and sustained by faith, is never suspended in the letter's ethic, and is ultimately applied in the HT. It is this primary axis which Colossians highlights in positive terms, creating a paradigmatic tandem of relationship and behaviour.

---

[17] Weidinger, *Haustafeln*, 74.

[18] Kramer, *Christ*, 178f. "Exhortations, both general and particular, are linked [in the Pauline corpus] with the formula 'in the Lord'. It is used to describe the character of relationships in Christ's fellowship. "In the Lord" appears in the context of ethical instruction and of particular questions, relationships and actions in the life of the church. So the church (as well as the individual Christian) in all that it does and in all that it endures is aware of being confronted by the Lord, and knows that it is accountable to him. He is therefore the Lord who is present, and by his authority every Christian activity is governed."

These observations regarding the divine-human axis can be observed most clearly in Colossians at the point of its transformation in 1:21–22. Paul assumes that divine-human relations already exist, though in a broken state of alienation. This is illustrated by the example of the Colossians themselves, who have undergone a dramatic transfer from τῆς ἐξουσίας τοῦ σκότους into the βασιλείαν τοῦ υἱοῦ τῆς ἀγάπης αὐτοῦ (1:13). Col. 1:21–22 highlights the believers' new identity in terms of the completeness of their sin and alienation, as well as the fullness of their redemption, which brings them from ὄντας ἀπηλλοτριωμένους to a place κατενώπιον αὐτοῦ. The transfer of identity comes on the heels of the Christ Hymn, creating, initially, a sharp contrast between the exalted Lord and the hearers, who, under direct address (καὶ ὑμᾶς), are brought into vertical relationship with the exalted person and deeds of Christ *at the very point of their sinful alienation*. The establishment of the new relational axis, divine-human, is effected by the death of Christ, and thereby fully dependent upon him. The scope of the transformation is fundamental, and foreshadows the ethical transformation promoted in the parenetic section of the letter:

Καὶ ὑμᾶς ποτε ὄντας
  ἀπηλλοτριωμένους
    καὶ
  ἐχθροὺς τῇ διανοίᾳ
    ἐν τοῖς ἔργοις τοῖς πονηροῖς

  νυνὶ δὲ ἀποκατήλλαξεν ἐν τῷ σώματι τῆς
  σαρκὸς αὐτοῦ διὰ τοῦ θανάτου παραστῆσαι ὑμᾶς

                    ἁγίους
              καὶ
          ἀμώμους
      καὶ
ἀνεγκλήτους κατενώπιον αὐτοῦ

The extent of the Colossians' alienation included not only distance from one another and Christ (ἀπηλλοτριωμένους), but hostile intent (ἐχθροὺς τῇ διανοίᾳ), realised in demonstrably culpable deeds (ἐν τοῖς ἔργοις τοῖς πονηροῖς). The triad of virtues, ἁγίους, ἀμώμους and ἀνεγκλήτους, contained in the second arm of the contrast, does more than perfectly displace the sinners' guilt; it establishes a new identity and relational axis, both dependent on Christ. Christ, by means of his death, has brought reconciliation on the divine-human level, establishing these redeemed individuals *before him*; this new identity, we hope to demonstrate, is ultimately that which determines relations between the believers (the intra-human axis), as well. It is important to note that the redemption portrayed within Colossians is depicted in terms of positive identification with Christ, as well as through negatively formulated contrasts, illustrated by the ποτε...νυνὶ construction of 1:21–22. The contrast between the new and old is extended into the letter,[19] highlighting the new, vertical relational axis and its theme of transfer, as well as giving the grounds for new ethical behaviour. Christ's redemptive death is placed at the fulcrum of change, where he assumes the mediating role in the new relational axis. The centrality of Christ becomes paradigmatic for relations in the letter to the Colossians; faith in him (1:4) is the orienting contingency, 1:23a: εἴ γε ἐπιμένετε τῇ πίστει τεθεμελιωμένοι καὶ ἑδραῖοι καὶ μὴ μετακινούμενοι ἀπὸ τῆς ἐλπίδος τοῦ εὐαγγελίου οὗ ἠκούσατε. Yet there is a more positive expression of the letter's ethic, which is tied uniquely to Christ. Here it is Christ who stands at the centre of the believer's new orientation as mediator and model.

Implications of the Divine-Human Axis

The absolute dominion of Christ, particularly the primacy of the divine-human axis, is extended in Colossians in terms of a number of positive, divine movements on the believers' behalf, which are immediately followed by related admonitions. These movements, notably accomplishments unique to Christ (his circumcision, death, resurrection, and future revelation), become a part of the new and unfolding context of life for the hearers, who now partake in them as their identity is increasingly defined in terms of, and therefore inextricably tied to, Christ. The benefits of Christ's salvation are com-

---

[19] Ethical behaviour is depicted in terms of its relation to Christ: περιπατῆσαι ἀξίως τοῦ κυρίου εἰς πᾶσαν ἀρεσκείαν (1:10), and contrasted with concepts and behaviours that are characterised as being κατὰ τὰ στοιχεῖα τοῦ κόσμου καὶ οὐ κατὰ Χριστόν (2:8). 3:7f., for example, repeats the direct address, καὶ ὑμεῖς, as well as employing another ποτε...νυνὶ construction. The contrasting behaviour is highlighted by old/new language, as well as by the putting off/putting on imagery in v. 8 (ἀπόθεσθε), 9 (ἀπεκδυσάμενοι), 10 and 12 (ἐνδύσασθε), indicating behaviour in terms of dynamic change. In 3:1, establishment of the vertical axis is highlighted in the contrast of the two spheres, τὰ ἄνω...τὰ ἐπὶ τῆς γῆς; hearers are to put to death (νεκρώσατε) the numerous aspects of their former life in which they walked (contrast v. 2:6), and according to which they lived (ἐζῆτε), v.3:5–7; the wicked behaviour in 3:5, 8 is contrasted with new behaviours in 3:12–17, love being the crowning virtue (σύνδεσμος τῆς τελειότητος). This phrase may have been familiar to Paul's hearers, as a philosophical expression denoting, as P.W. van der Horst, "Observations on a Pauline Expression," *NTS* 19 (1973): 181–187, argues, "the transition from...the unenlightened state to the enlightened state".

pounded in the lives of the believer, including, ultimately, the coming age. The series of Christ-centred declarations refer to their new status in *positive* terms, defining the vertical relationship, not in terms of *contrast* mentioned above, but wholly in relation to Christ. This is the pattern which Paul initiates when he reminds the hearers of his own sufferings for them, the church. As a servant of the Gospel and the church (1:23, 25), he understands his present sufferings, surprisingly, in the broader context of Christ's sufferings for *his* body, the church (ὑπὲρ τοῦ σώματος αὐτοῦ, ὅ ἐστιν ἡ ἐκκλησία, 1:24). Even unique events of salvation, such as Christ's suffering, are identified with those who now serve Christ. This personal reference illustrates the close relationship which the letter maintains between the believer's identity and the work of Christ, a theme which is critical to the understanding of the parenetic instruction within the letter.

The following declarations, found within Colossians 2:6–3:4, distinguish themselves from the letter's contrasting material in that each declaration (initiated in receiving, 2:6) is accompanied by an immediate call to a particular behaviour or attitude. They initiate a Christ-believer reality/ethical reality pattern, which is reflected, ultimately, in the instruction contained in the HT. The hearers find themselves fully identified with Christ, marked on the one hand by various *accomplished* elements of salvation, and the call to reorient their behaviour in light of this event, on the other. The interplay between the accomplished work of Christ and the earth-bound reality of life is particularly noticeable in this section: 2:6, "As you received Christ Jesus the Lord, so walk in him."; 2:8, "Make sure that no one deceives you…"; 2:16, "Let no one judge you…"; 2:20, "If you have died with Christ to the elemental principles of the world, why…"; 3:1, "Since you have been raised with Christ, seek…" ; 3:4–5, "…you will also appear with him in glory. Put to death, therefore…" Ideally, Christ's accomplished works form a seamless continuum, characterised by the believers' relationship to him; practically, however, it unfolds in two remotely analogous heavenly and earthly spheres, which are punctuated by, and ultimately united in, the appearance of Christ (3:4). These initial works of Christ distinguish themselves from the last example, found in 3:4, in two notable ways. They are, firstly, seen as achieved events in terms of Christ *and* the believer (primarily in the aorist). Secondly, they tend to introduce more general, theological admonitions, whereas the last example in 3:4 is followed by strictly ethical injunctions. It is perhaps these subtle differences which have led to the traditional bifurcation of theology and ethics in this epistle (generally being divided at 3:4). At any event, the final example will receive particular attention at the end of this section. The message of these affirmations is clear: identification with Christ, though complete in terms of salvation, is not yet fully realised in terms of behaviour and attitude. The divine-human axis is employed as a point of soteriological orientation *and* ethical-behavioural reorientation. In this manner, the vertical axis, inaugurated and sustained by soteriological events, is vitally linked to both practical and theological life issues of the Colossian recipients. The intersection, we believe, constitutes a pattern for the Christ-oriented ethic found in the letter, as seen in the examples below.

Receiving Christ. Col. 2:6, "As you received Christ the Lord, so walk in him.", represents a starting point, as well as the general rubric under which the following statements may be seen: the relationship to Christ, designated by the aorist παρελάβετε, is the foundation for the believer's earthly behaviour (ἐν αὐτῷ περιπατεῖτε). This represents the genesis of the new relationship with Christ, which is both primary and paradigmatic. It is especially noteworthy that Christ, denoted here as τὸν Χριστὸν Ἰησοῦν τὸν κύριον, assumes a position of dominion/superordination in respect to those who have received him.[20] The title of lord (κύριος) serves here as a term which not only summarises the previous material in which Christ is portrayed in cosmological dominion, but has implications for the believers' ethical behaviour, as well.[21] Verse 2:6 takes on, then, an almost paradigmatic nature, which can be seen in the following material. The indicative mood, representing the relational axis to Christ, is followed by an imperative (notably the first up to this point in the letter), which regulates the horizontal axis, establishing a pattern of relational reality/behavioural admonition. Relation to Christ as Lord, in the logic of Colossians, regulates intra-human behaviour.[22] This first command accentuates the believer's established roots in Christ, (which are grounded in the faith in which they had been instructed, 1:5–7, 23; 2:7), establishes Christ's relationship as *kurios*, and indicates the necessity that these realities be translated into the realm of behaviour. These things, Paul writes, are in accordance with their instruction, καθὼς ἐδιδάχθητε (2:7). The ensuing string of participial admonitions

---

[20] The vertical axis is marked by its reciprocal nature, the believer being called (3:12, 15) as God is actively establishing reconciliation in Christ (1:20). 2:6 acknowledges the initial human activity, which establishes, as in the human axes, a reciprocal relationship involving superordination/subordination. The various activities of Christ on the believers' behalf are consistently joined to expected ethical behaviours.

[21] The title lord has an almost regulatory function in the letter, which applies particularly to the horizontal axis. Of the fourteen references to Christ as *kurios* (1:3, 10; 2:6; 3:13, 17, 18, 20, 22, 23, 24 (2), 4:1, 7, 17), all are brought into connection with ethical behaviour or approved service within the church. This is especially so in the HT, where the *kurios* title occurs seven times in a regulatory capacity.

[22] Lincoln, "Household Code," 105, notes "The explicit language of lordship comes into play when the readers' conduct is in view".

72

(ἐρριζωμένοι, ἐποικοδομούμενοι, βεβαιούμενοι and περισσεύοντες) in v.7 encourage fidelity to Christ, the divine-human relationship representing the ultimate orientation for their Christian walk.

The Fullness of Christ. The imperative (βλέπετε) in v. 8 insists that the believer be watchful for influences which are in conflict with the above teaching, being of the world and οὐ κατὰ Χριστόν (this phrase is attached to the promoters of the false teaching in 2:19, 22 as well). In contrast to the false propositions of philosophy, the author again introduces Christ, in whom dwells all the fullness of deity in bodily form (2:9). The contrast between the fullness of Christ's wisdom and the "crafty speech" of the false teachers is familiar from 2:3–4; here the fullness of Christ, surprisingly, has been shared with the believer, ἐν αὐτῷ πεπληρομένοι. The believer, then, has no need of contending philosophies, traditions or systems. Christ is described, if there remains any doubt regarding his sufficiency, as being the head of all authority and power. The false teachers, unsurprisingly, are later depicted as being *detached* from the head, God's only provision for salvation and growth (2:19); in Christ's stead, they rely upon the observance of Law or the boastful enumeration of spiritual experiences.[23] The believer's behaviour, however, follows the elementary truths of the primary relational axis, as well as deriving its power from Christ's authority and fullness.

The Believer's Sufficiency in Christ. The sufficiency of Christ outlined in 2:9–10 (characterised as fullness) includes the following aspects of the believer's joint existence in Christ. These particular shared elements are both cultic and essential in nature, and prepare the hearer for the ensuing command in 2:16, "Let no one judge you…":

Circumcised: 2:11 proclaims that believers, having received the circumcision of Christ (περιετμήθητε…ἐν τῇ περιτομῇ τοῦ Χριστοῦ) have cultic adequacy in him; it transcends the human and fleshly practice, being ἀχειροποιήτῳ ἐν τῇ ἀπεκδύσει τοῦ σώματος τῆς

---

[23] Col. 3:11 and 16f. make clear reference to Jewish ceremonial service. The redemption in Christ is contrasted with legalistic service. The former is the substance (σῶμα τοῦ Χριστοῦ), the latter derivative, and thereby a mere shadow (σκία). For this reason, it is Christ, intersecting and redefining human relational axes, who is essential. Those who lean on the Law (2:16) or esoteric religious experience (2:18) are no longer "holding to the head." For Paul, the head of the body (1:18) is the absolute source of life and growth by God's power (3:19). Ethical categories, then, revolve around, and are substantiated by, Christ alone. For an extensive review of the various heresy theories related to Colossians, see Lähnemann, *Kolosserbrief*, 63–105.

σαρκός. In the logic of Colossians, for those in Christ, even cultic practice is influenced by the divine-human axis.

Buried in Baptism: 2:12a connects the believer, in baptism, to the burial of Christ, συνταφέντες αὐτῷ ἐν τῷ βαπτισμῷ.

Raised with Christ: 2:12b attaches the believer to the resurrection of Christ, being raised through faith in him (συνηγέρθητε). The believers have undergone not only a shift in allegiance, but of residence, as well. This radical identification with Christ places them in a new vantage point, namely at the right hand of God. The divine-human axis changes, ideally, the believer's fundamental perspective. Here the emphasis is upon the privilege of the close association with Christ, who, being raised, is vindicated of God; hence, the believer should not allow himself to be judged. The same theme of identification of the believer with the resurrection of Christ can be found in 3:1. Here the text is even more direct in its mandate to link the spiritual reality with behaviour, "If you have been raised in Christ, seek the things above, where Christ is…"

Made Alive with Christ: 2:13, συνεζωοποίησεν ὑμᾶς σὺν αὐτῷ, essentially repeats the sense of the believers being raised with Christ in 2:12b; it is an important addition to the previous verse, however, as it makes practical application of this spiritual reality in light of the false teachers, who are judging the Colossians (2:16). 2:12b closes with the reminder that God raised Christ from the dead; 2:13a picks up this language in its first phrase, καὶ ὑμᾶς νεκροὺς ὄντας ἐν τοῖς παραπτώμασιν. Being made alive with Christ displaces not only the finality of natural death, but it includes the spiritual death caused by sin. Verses 2:13–14 speak of the sufficiency of Christ's death to cover both the ceremonial (ἐν...τῇ ἀκροβυστίᾳ τῆς σαρκὸς) and ethical (τὸ καθ᾽ ἡμῶν χειρόγραφον τοῖς δόγμασιν ὃ ἦν ὑπεναντίον ἡμῖν) demands of the law, as well as disarming the rulers and authorities.

Dead: 2:20 rhetorically asks the believers, if they have *died* with Christ (εἰ ἀπεθάνετε) to the elemental teachings (τὰ στοιχεῖα τοῦ κόσμου also seen in 2:8, equally contrasted as οὐ κατὰ Χριστόν) of the world, how they can then, in full contrast, be receiving indoctrination (δογματίζεσθε) as if (concessive use of ὡς) *living* in the world? Identification with Christ in death implies a disruption of the status quo, and a new assessment of τὰ ἐντάλματα καὶ διδασκαλίας τῶν ἀνθρώπων, v. 22. Their death with Christ is again emphasised in 3:3, (ἀπεθάνετε), where their existence (ἡ ζωὴ ὑμῶν) is characterised as being κέκρυπται σὺν τῷ Χριστῷ ἐν τῷ θεῷ. As a present reality, the position of believers with God as hidden in Christ is expected to transform their perspective in this life, presumably in terms of being God or Christ-oriented. To this end, the present imperatives ζητεῖτε and φρονεῖτε are directed heavenward (τὰ ἄνω), both activities implying a circumspect lifestyle that is ultimately determined by the one with whom they have been raised, Christ. Their perspective should be Christ's. The allusion to Christ's reign in 3:1 as his being seated at God's right hand, signals the final event, yet unfulfilled in 3:4: the appearance of Christ. The emphasis, again, is that their standing in Christ determines a new posture in this world; being identified with Christ places the believer in critical opposition to the indoctrinating tendencies of false, and ultimately fleshly, teaching, v.23. This radical position, if consequently applied in context of the ethical admonitions in Colossians, could have interesting implications.

The previous verses, found in Colossians 2:6–3:3, form the groundwork of each believer's position in Christ, and establish a pattern of Christ-reality/ethical behaviour. The verb forms, expressed primarily in aorist, are cast in relational opposition to false teaching and esoteric practices troubling the Colossian fellowship. These movements illustrate the "fulfilled" sphere in terms of spiritual reality and its relationship to ethical behaviour, establishing the divine-human axis as authoritative and normative for the believer's cultic, philosophical and ethical world-view. The broad, Christ-oriented exhortations found in these sections provide a theological backdrop for the following ethical exhortations, which follow closely on the heels of the last Christ-event, the appearance of Christ in glory.

Colossians 3:4–4:6: Life in Light of the Coming Lord

The understanding and application of the believer's standing in Christ will insure that the Colossians will not be deceived (2:4), as well as having the full riches of complete understanding, to know the "mystery of God, namely Christ" (2:3). Though the first events touching upon salvation (2:6–3:3) do not constitute any systematic order, the final event stands logically at the end of the positive relationship between Christ and believer, introducing an eschatological element and motivation. It carries within it the full weight of the other movements, and as their fulfilment, it is charged with the hope of glory (1:27). Ultimately, this last movement brings with it the culmination of their salvation, as well as the resolution of the tension (things not conforming to Christ's rule) created by the parallel eternal and temporal spheres. The last propositional statement, which links the believer with Christ, is found in 3:4. Its primary motif, the revelation of Christ in glory, precedes and directly influences the tenor of the letter's final parenetic section, including the HT. It differs from the other statements regarding the believer and Christ in that it contains an element, contingent on relationship to Christ, which stands at some point in the future. Though Christ has indeed been glorified (3:1), he has not appeared in his glory, nor have those who are in him experienced this future event: ὅταν ὁ Χριστὸς φανερωθῇ, ἡ ζωὴ ὑμῶν, τότε καὶ ὑμεῖς σὺν αὐτῷ φανερωθήσεσθε ἐν δόξῃ. The subjunctive φανερωθῇ and the future passive φανερωθήσεσθε indicate to the hearers that this event, unlike the previous, indicative statements regarding their standing in Christ, stands somewhere on the horizon. The unfulfilled nature of Christ's coming brings with it a distinct element of anticipation of new divine activity, which is cast in contrast to the present, earthly behaviour characterised as τὰ μέλη τὰ ἐπὶ τῆς γῆς, and made particularly clear in the contrasts outlined in 3:5–17. The coming of Christ in glory acts as a bridge between the heavenly and earthly spheres, providing the keystone in the larger picture of salvation as depicted in Colossians. It is the last frame in a series of salvation images, all intrinsically tied to the believer's spiritual/eternal as well as ethical/temporal condition. It forms the unrealised yet defining moment of salvation, as well as the basis for the letter's largest parenetic section.

If in Christ, the believers will participate with him in all that it means to be revealed in glory. It is something for which they can prepare, as the lengthy, attendant parenetic section attests. The return of the absolute Lord elicits both hope,[24] as well as the fearful element of wrath and judgement, as seen in the following verses, 3:5–6. Judgement emerges as the regulatory force of the final parenetic section, and is, ultimately, tied to Christ. To seek in the HT a codification of divinely sanctioned natural law, or a static expression of social regulations, would effectively bypass this dynamic ele-

---

[24] The future is described in terms of heavenly hope (τὴν ἐλπίδα τὴν ἀποκειμένην ὑμῖν ἐν τοῖς οὐρανοῖς), 1:5. The rich and glorious mystery, once hidden (ἀποκεκρυμμένον), has been revealed (ἐφανερώθη), and represents Christ in them, the hope of glory (ἡ ἐλπὶς τῆς δόξης), 1:26–27. The vocabulary of the latter citation is strikingly similar to that of 3:3b–4, ἡ ζωὴ ὑμῶν κέκρυπται σὺν τῷ Χριστῷ ἐν τῷ θεῷ· ὅταν ὁ Χριστὸς φανερωθῇ, ἡ ζωὴ ὑμῶν, τότε καὶ ὑμεῖς σὺν αὐτῷ φανερωθήσεσθε ἐν δόξῃ.

ment.[25] Christ, as eschatological judge, emerges as the last criterion for ethical behaviour. Gnilka recognises the sole rule of Christ as the inherent motivation behind the HT admonitions; the person of Christ cannot be reduced to an order, and the order cannot hold pre-eminence.[26] Glorification and judgement bring resolution, where the tensions of the present earthly conditions will be drawn together in the final soteriological movement of Christ. The theme of judgement finds it fullest expression, not surprisingly, in the expanded ethical admonitions contained in the slave-master relationship of the HT, and becomes its distinctive, modifying element, as we hope to show. As an emerging eschatological reality, the coming of Christ as judge alters the otherwise fixed relationships found in the HT. The ethical tensions of the present reality will indeed find resolution; the conflation of the temporary and the eternal spheres in judgement strikes the main chord of the HT admonitions to slave and master. There is, then, a Christ-determined *continuity* between the coming kingdom (representing contrasting and absolute standards) and present behaviour; this continuity lends the following admonitions, including the HT, supreme moral significance, while simultaneously relativising the importance of the present, earthly order.

The Colossian *Haustafel*: Observations

Before we undertake our analysis of the Colossian HT in order to determine if its mandates are influenced by the person of Christ and his coming judgement, a number of general observations regarding the Colossian HT are in order. The following aspects of the HT (and the surrounding letter), including the theme of lordship, the aural nature of its commands, and the form of address it employs, all contribute to the level of mediation given Christ in their regulation.

The Theme of Lordship and the HT

In light of the theme of Christ's dominion in Colossians, it is interesting that the HT is expanded at the axis slave-master. Christ's lordship, marked seven

---

[25] Joachim Gnilka, *Der Kolosserbrief*, eds. A. Vögtle, A. Wikenhauser and R. Schnackenburg, Herders Theologischer Kommentar zum Neuen Testament, vol. 10 (Freiburg: Herder, 1980), 217. Attempts to locate the motivation of the HT in natural law (ἀνῆκεν being associated with the Stoic καθῆκον) overlook the central position of Christ in determining the HT ethic. See also Schweizer, *Brief*, 161.

[26] Ibid., 217. Since Christ is the only absolute authority, no "positive Ordnung [kann] das Endgültige sein."

times by the term κύριος in the HT alone, provides, as Gnilka observes, a point of orientation.[27] The *kurios* language provides a literary link to the broader letter's vision of Christ's dominion. It is in the HT where we find this theological aspect taking concrete, ethical form.[28] The κύριος Χρίστος assumes the central position of influence, which then creates the possibility to cast common relations in a truly Christian manner.[29] The simple, three-fold HT schema undergoes alteration, or better, additions, in order to extend the author's theological emphases and clarify the central relationship of Christ to the persons addressed, including the regulation of slave and master. It may be no coincidence that the HT is expanded at this point, the lord-servant relationship being, in essence, an expression of the Christ-believer relationship. The believer's new identity, now in subordinated relation to Christ as Lord, might well be described as servant,[30] particularly as the use of slave language becomes a leading metaphor for Christian service[31] within the letter. This could be argued *a fortiori*, since Paul, being himself an apostle, describes himself and others in Colossians as διάκονος (1:7; 1:23, 1:25; 4:7), and his fellow workers as δοῦλος (4:12) or σύνδουλος (1:7; 4:7). Though the exact level of meaning of διακονία is disputed,[32] we can assume from these

---

[27] Gnilka, *Kolosserbrief,* 226.

[28] Contra Klaus Wengst, "Versöhnung und Befreiung: Ein Aspekt des Themas 'Schuld und Vergebung' im Lichte des Kolosserbriefes," *Evangelische Theologie* 36 (1976): 14–26, who claims that the HT evades the theological concerns of the letter, not making them concrete in daily affairs.

[29] Gnilka, *Kolosserbrief,* 6. The Lord creates a new context as well as a new type of morality: "Es handelt sich nicht um billige Berufsmoral oder Ständeregeln. Im Zentrum steht der Kurios Christos, der Eheleuten, Eltern, Kindern, Herren, Sklaven die Möglichkeit anbietet, ihr fa-miliäres, berufliches Leben christlich zu deuten."

[30] Lohmeyer, *Briefe,* 159. He asserts that "der Stand des Sklaven" is "die reine Repräsenta-tion des gläubigen Daseins." Gielen, *Tradition,* 177, concurs: "Der Christ wird somit [in con-version] in der Taufe dem neuen Herrn unterstellt und wird damit δοῦλος Χριστοῦ/κυρίου. Erst dies begründet seine wirkliche Freiheit. Freiheit ist für Paulus im Sinne eines dialek-tischen Verhältnisses Freiheit in Gebundenheit, das δοῦλος-Χριστοῦ-Sein wird zum Zeichen der Freiheit und definiert geradezu das Christsein als solches." A. Standhartinger, "The Origin and Intention of the Household Code in the Letter to the Colossians," *JSNT* 79 (2000): 117–130, sees the servant language as characterising the radically egalitarian nature of the early church.

[31] M.J. Harris, *Slave of Christ: A New Testament Metaphor for Total Devotion to Christ,* ed. D.A. Carson, New Studies in Biblical Theology, vol. 8 (Leicester: Apollos, 1999), argues that the slave serves as a NT metaphor for the Christian's service to Christ. Especially helpful are his citations which illustrate the collocation of *kurios-doulos* language in the NT, 90f.

[32] Discussion regarding the meaning of διακονία ranges from menial and often vulgar work consigned to servants, to a more elevated notion of spokesman or emissary. Cf. A. Clarke, *Serve the Community of the Church: Christians as Leaders and Ministers,* ed. A.D. Clarke, First-Century Christians in the Graeco-Roman World (Grand Rapids/Cambridge: Eerdmans,

78

passages and other Pauline texts[33] that he understood himself to be a servant of Christ. The implication for the Colossian Christians should be clear enough from the example of the apostle and his fellow workers; the issue of the believer's standing in Christ, however, is not left to conjecture, but is expanded in the slave-master instruction of the HT. Here the author indicates the direct nature of the believer's service to Christ, regardless of social standing. The slaves, for instance, who hear the words of the HT, are commanded, as might be expected in their disadvantaged position, to serve *as if* serving the Lord himself (3:23). They are further commanded, however, to serve the Lord Christ (3:24), an unusual formulation.[34] This command finds its representation for the masters, as well, who are reminded that they, too, have a Lord in heaven (4:1), a unique phrase which seems to mirror the command to the slaves. These particular commands, represented in both members, intimate the universal nature of servanthood to Christ, and strengthen the general overarching rule of life in 3:17, to do all in the name of the *Lord* Jesus. The hearers of the letter to the Colossians had no reason to doubt that they, with the apostle, his colleagues, and slaves and masters, had become servants, as well. To emphasise this theological truth on the human plane is a necessary reminder of the practical reality of service to Christ; the new relationship to Christ is also the foundation for a new relationship to his body. The primary, divine-human axis, then, can be characterised in terms of Lord-Servant, making the members of Christ's body, by extension, fellow-servants. The master-slave relationship, then, reflects not only a social element within the early church, but the theological reality embodied in the terms. This schema stands in relation to the larger theology of the letter, positioned directly under the primary axis of Lord-Servant, which applies equally to all:

2000), 233–243, who argues that while the term may have a range of meanings in the broader Graeco-Roman culture, the adopted meaning in reference to such Christian leaders as Paul would indicate service, inverting "contemporary social values" of his day. Clarke interacts with the thesis of J.N. Collins, *Diakonia: Re-interpreting the Ancient Sources* (Oxford: Oxford University Press, 1990), 209f., which prefers the latter sense of spokesman. In either case, Paul understands himself to be a man under orders, and is not ashamed to be known as a σύνδουλος of Epaphras (1:7, 4:12) and Tychicus (4:7), both named in these instances as διάκονος.

[33] At other points, Paul's servanthood is directly expressed (Rom. 1:1; Gal. 1:10; Phil. 1:1), as well as that of others (1 Cor. 7:22; 2 Cor. 4:5).

[34] Lohmeyer, *Briefe*, 159, fn.2. Lohmeyer notes the unusual (and unique to the NT) collocation κυρίῳ Χριστῷ found in the Colossian HT, which he suggests guarantees a uniquely Christian emphasis. Equally noteworthy is the phrase κύριον ἐν οὐρανῷ used in 4:1. This phrase is used only here in the NT, and may be an attempt to underscore the earnestness of the matters of lordship.

Colossian *Haustafel* Relationships

Vertical Axis
Lord <<<<<<◇>>>>>Servant
Horizontal Axis
Wife<<κύριος Χρίστος>>Husband
Children<<<κύριος Χρίστος>>>Parent
Servant<<<κύριος Χρίστος>>>Lord
(expanded form)

The Aural-Communal Aspect of the HT Commands

As part of the analysis of the admonitions found in the HT, it is important to note the aural character of the letter's presentation, an aspect which is critical to the letter's method of delivering ethical mandates. One of the formal characteristics of the HT, direct address, provides the platform for a more dynamic function of the HT, the *public* announcement of correct relations in Christ. The letter, being addressed to the "holy and faithful brethren living in Colossae" (1:2), is far from a private address or personal letter, and is not intended to serve solely as a catalyst for independent, personal deliberation.[35] The context of the public reading,[36] the fellowship meeting, allows for all members to "overhear" the instruction directed to others, a critical element in understanding the moral force of the letter.[37] The form of direct address, characterised by the second person plural, is retained throughout the letter,[38] accentuating the corporate nature of the admonitions, as well as enhancing

---

[35] Paul J. Achtemeier, "Omne verbum sonat: The New Testament and the Oral Environment of Late Western Antiquity," *JBL* 109 (1990): 3–27. Achtemeier notes, 19, that early Christian documents, not originally intended for silent, solitary reading, were written for oral presentation: "NT documents…are oral to the core, both in their creation and their performance…the NT must be understood as speech."

[36] Colossians gives us an unusual glimpse into the public nature of the letter in 4:16, where Paul expects a reading παρ' ὑμῖν, presumably the normal gathering of the church. Gnilka, *Kolosserbrief*, 245, asserts that this was the case for all NT "Gemeindebriefe".

[37] Laub, *Begegnung*, 72. The public nature of the apostolic letter removes the issues of "Brüderlichkeit" between slaves and masters from the "private, individualistic sphere", making them a matter of "ecclesiastical, and thereby social and community concern."

[38] Not including participial forms, which make reference to the hearers, the tally of second person plural pronouns and finite verb forms is remarkably high, and evenly distributed throughout the letter. Pronouns, 58 occurrences: 1:1–9, 12–13, 21–24, 25, 27; 2:1, 4–5, 8, 13, 16, 18; 3:3–4, 7–8, 13, 15–16; 4:1, 6–7, 8–10, 12–14, 16, 18. Verbs, 51 occurrences: 1:4–7, 9, 23; 2:6–8, 10–12, 20; 3:1–5, 7–9, 12, 15, 17–24; 4:1–2, 5, 8, 10, 12, 15–18.

the immediacy of the content.[39] This aspect is particularly important as we consider the social implications of the HT admonitions, which feature the *highest* concentration of direct address. The original hearers, especially the superordinated members (husbands, fathers, masters; in some instances the same individual!) receive instruction which implies that the household is under new management, and subject to public scrutiny under its new, Christ-centred policies. The admonitions of the letter, then, touch the lives of *all* the listening members, drawing them, without exception, to be consciously involved in the establishment of Christ's dominion. This is particularly true of human relationships, for Christ's dominion is attached to the church as a body (1:18). Indeed, the members have not only been chosen by God (3:12), but have *already* been addressed by him in their calling into one body (3:15).[40] The gospel itself, meeting with great success (1:6–7) has been communicated to them in aural fashion (1:5–6, προηκούσατε, ἠκούσατε), as well. The original call of God, and the believers' hearing and obedience, form the foundational pattern for the ethical mandates of the letter. The aural admonitions, especially the direct address of the HT, are connected to, and follow, the larger theological context and pattern of address, hearing and response.

The pattern of direct address and moral admonition, descriptive of the ethical argumentation of Colossians, is heightened in its intensity within the HT by the *singling out* of the addressees in terms of their station in life. The effect is dramatic; at the point of the introduction of the HT, the letter ceases to be a general address to all the faithful saints (frequently addressed in some form of καὶ ὑμᾶς), being interrupted by an abrupt shift to a select group within the fellowship, αἱ γυναῖκες. That a particular group is singled out is cause for attention; the fact that responsibilities (and failings) of the reciprocal pairs are highlighted in this public fashion is nearly dramatic, as even children overhear (and we assume take careful note!) the admonitions given to their parents. The greatest surprise, however, was reserved for the slaves

---

[39] Gielen, *Tradition*, 129, fn. 69. Gielen points out the public nature of the address in the HT as contrasted with a personal letter; the character of these forms of address "lies on two different levels."

[40] καλέω, found in Ro. 4:17; 8:30; 9:7, 12, 24–26; 1Cor. 1:9; 7:15, 17–18; 20–22; 24; Gal. 1:6, 15; 5:8, 13; 1Thes. 2:12; 4:7; 5:24; 2Thes. 2:14, is almost exclusively associated with the call of God in the Pauline epistles, the exceptions being 1Cor. 10:27 and 15:9. It is in part associated with the election of Israel, yet extended to the Gentiles (Ro. 9:24). Most references have direct relation to fellowship and order within the community, including social status (1Cor. 7:22). The call is also generally attached to the gospel (2Thes. 2:14). Calling in Col. 3:15 reflects both the theological and practical emphases found in the broader Paulines, for it is a calling ἐν ἑνὶ σώματι.

and their masters, who being addressed, sensed that their culturally determined (and legally documented) boundaries were being benignly infringed upon in Christ.[41] The HT, though treating common relations, does so in a thoroughly uncommon manner: through direct address and the singling out of relational pairs. In this manner it confronts the believers at the most personal level, and with a greater intensity than that found in the broader letter. The public nature of this intense direct address only adds to the effect of forcefulness.

Addressing the Subordinate Member

Women, children and slaves, all living in subordinated relationship to the *paterfamilias*,[42] receive an unexpected manner and level of address in the HT. As subordinated members of the stereotyped pairs, they are not only addressed directly, but given order of preference. For the slave, these characteristics of the address meant more than a subtle change in relation to the head of the household; it signalled a remarkable change in his status. As innocuous as the pairing of these logically related groups might seem to the modern eye, and in spite of their common juxtaposition in antiquity,[43] the slave was not usually the *object* of address,[44] and certainly not in direct opposition to

---

[41] Werner Eck and Johannes Heinrichs, eds., *Sklaven und Freigelassene in der Gesellschaft der römischen Kaiserzeit*, Texte zur Forschung, vol. 61 (Darmstadt: Wissenschaftliche Buchgesellschaft, 1993), 3–4. The direct address of the HT recognises the slaves as persons, and the owners as responsible to another, higher law. Under the rubric "legal status of slaves", the editors have compiled a number of important sources which give us an idea of the formal relationship between slave (non-entity/property) and master (owner). Gaius, *Inst.* 1,9–11 describes two fundamental human groups, which enjoy discrete personal rights: slaves and non-slaves. Gaius, *Inst.* 1,52–53 describes the absolute power (*potestas*) which the owner has over the slave; this power is the result of unwritten law; it also includes the power over life and death, and anything which the slave might earn or produce. Ulpian, *Dig.* 50,17,32 declares that slaves do not, according to civil law, register as persons. The HT is not *overturning*, but simply *ignoring* the legal dimensions of the slave master relationship.

[42] Laub, *Begegnung*, 43. Economic treatises were not merely economic theory or anything approaching modern economic science, but rather a part of philosophy which treated the "Herrschaft des Mannes über das Ganze des Oikos, Menschen und Sachen"; the master of the house was absolute and central: "Ohne die Herrschaft des Mannes kein Oikos." The HT, in contrast, acknowledges only the lordship of Christ; the slave receives parallel and equal treatment, and thereby responsibility, before the "Lord in Heaven" (4:1).

[43] As early as Plato's *Laws* and Aristotle's *Politics* we find mention of the slave-master relationship, stations which reflected the two basic human conditions.

[44] Aristotle, *Politics*, 1.2 sets the stage for later literature on slavery and economics, discussing slaves in terms of function ("tools"), which "belong completely" to the master. Aristotle's

his master.[45] The admonition begins with the subordinated member of the section, the slave, representing a dramatic shift in perception. This is a less than subtle indication that the ethical standard is no longer cast in terms of the master only; the slave is confronted, neither as an oppressed victim, nor as a neutral economic commodity, but as a morally responsible individual. His first identity is in Christ, which effectively transcends contemporary social and economic categories, giving him individual, and morally independent status. On the basis of this new identity and social status, the slave becomes a responsible being within the social context of the HT. Whereas the literature regarding slaves was written primarily in terms of their function and profitability to their owners (in the form of unilateral advice to slave owners), the HT departs from mere pragmatic concerns and the exclusive interest of the superordinate party. Introducing a theological motivation, the HT draws both parties, by virtue of their life in Christ, into the discussion.[46] The slaves themselves, generally regarded as morally inferior and not meriting such address,[47] receive here an earnest appeal to their religious and moral responsibility.

Strengthening this view is the unusual feature of the HT, which gives priority of address to the subordinated members, women, children and slaves. The subordinated member is no longer conceived in terms of dependent relation to the superordinate member, but is given order of preference, highlighting (perhaps to overcome a stereotyped pattern?) a responsible standing before Christ, as well as in the church. This unusual order of address represents an uniquely Christian aspect of the slave-master relationship, the new and independent standing as a responsible person in Christ.[48] We may infer from

---

discussion (and those found in later economic literature), in contrast to the HT, was directed solely towards the owners.

[45] Thomas Wiedemann, *Greek and Roman Slavery* (London: Croom Helm, 1981), 61. Wiedemann observes that the "compulsion to classify all men as either free or slave" developed into a framework of thinking of these poles as good and bad; there was an "almost universal prejudice that slaves could not but be worse than their masters."

[46] Wolter, *Brief*, 208. The motivation behind the treatment of slaves in the HT, unlike the economic literature (whose primary, pragmatic interest was to insure increased efficiency), is "theologisch."

[47] Plato, *Laws*, VI, 776b–8a, declares that "There is no element in the soul of a slave that is healthy" and that a "sensible man should not trust anything into their care." Pliny the Elder, *Natural History*, 35,36: "This moral inferiority must imply that slaves are unworthy of the higher aspirations of human beings." In the same work, 33,8, he betrays disgust and wonder as he writes of how slaves have been able to "leap over" restrictions of entrance into equestrian orders, making these "full of slaves." How different their entrance and standing in Christ.

[48] Laub, *Begegnung*, 38. Though the HT is not "wesentlich verschieden" in its support of the household economy, it represents a major shift in the welfare of the slave as a responsible

the surprising nature of the address, that the hearers, especially the women, children and slaves, would note a change in their status at the human level. Even more essential, however, is the addressee's *ultimate* identity in Christ. Here the inverted order of address of the HT introduces unfamiliar, uncomfortably level ground, where both members of an unequal social relationship become relationally equal in their relation to Christ.[49] The spiritual reality, if we follow the logic of Colossians, is ultimate reality. The primary, divine-human axis sets the stage, ideally, at least, for significant modifications at the human level. It is precisely this life in Christ, establishing membership in a body, which draws disparate elements together (3:11), and creates relationships characterised by reciprocal, Christ-influenced responsibilities. The reciprocal features of the HT form transcend mere literary significance at this point: the axes are working models of a new social and ethical reality, bound to Christ, which cannot be divorced from the life in faith. The axes become illustrative vehicles, which transmit truth about the person and work of Christ; even more, they create a theological context for construing social relationships. It is for this reason that the ethical dimensions of faith and fellowship, constituting what it means to remain in Christ (in faith towards Christ, 1:4a, 2:7, and love towards others, 1:4b, 3:14) give the admonitions found in the HT an urgent dimension; the addressees' disregard of the other members (particularly those in reciprocal relationship) has implications for the well-being of the fellowship as well as for the individual. The slave-master relationship (the husband-wife, parent-children relations, as well), then, though traditional in appearance, is transformational in its anthropological and social implications.[50] The addressees are drawn from their particular (and polar) stations into a common arena, the church, which is mediated by Christ himself. The social implications of good-bad/strong-weak/entitled-powerless associated with the HT relationships undergo, by virtue of the mediation of Christ, genuine change. The HT brings the ethics

---

human being: "Die Oikonomik verspricht sich Erfolg durch geschickten und richtigen Umgang des Herrn mit dem Sklaven, die frühchristliche Verkündigung dagegen appelliert an das ethisch-religiöse Bewußtsein des Sklaven selbst und nimmt ihn damit als ethisch verantwortliche Person ernst."

[49] Wolter, *Brief*, 203. Wolter finds the "common status before the Lord" to be an unique Christian aspect of the HT; for the slave, however, this means a "double loyalty", which raises the question, to which degree the human relations find unique expression in Christ. Gielen, *Tradition*, 175, terms the slave's ontological predicament a "dialektisches Verhältnis". See also Georg Strecker, "Die neutestamentlichen Haustafeln," in *Neues Testament und Ethik: FS für R. Schnackenburg*, ed. H. Merklein (Freiburg, Basel, Wien: Herder, 1989), 371.

[50] Laub, *Begegnung*, 96. Laub insists that the HT is not attempting to lend slavery (or anti-slavery sentiments) theological justification. In spite of this, however, the HT formulates a new anthropology in Christ, which has the effect of being "subversiv ignorierend".

of the larger address in Colossians to bear on a traditional relationship, making it more than a stereotyped pair. The original slave-master relationship, which had been largely closed to outside influences, and wholly dependent upon the discretion of the master and economic considerations, has been unalterably changed in Christ. Both slave and master are being called to submit their relationship to the "Lord in heaven", the new, and ruling, arbiter of their ethical behaviour. This is especially important in understanding the force of the HT in terms of the superordinate member, the master, and his new responsibilities in Christ.

Reciprocity and Responsibility

The surprising element of the HT is its sobering and unrelenting insistence upon *mutual* human responsibility. This is a practical as well as a christianising aspect of the formal HT feature of reciprocal address. All believers are responsible first to Christ, then to the body. The first element, responsibility to Christ, takes on strong ethical contours in the previous section, 3:1–17, contrasting the old and new patterns of behaviour, categories which have been created by the transformation found in Christ. The relationship to Christ is nowhere a private matter, but invades the human sphere to the point of imitation: they should forgive, Paul writes, καθὼς καὶ ὁ κύριος ἐχαρίσατο ὑμῖν (3:13). This particular command illustrates, in compressed form, the close relationship drawn in Colossians between the work of Christ and Christian behaviour; the direct benefits of Christ are translated into reciprocal behaviours (commands) which are to be executed upon the intra-human axis. It is also interesting to note that in this particular section we find an expectant tone of reciprocity, an aspect of the letter's ethics which unfold most completely in the attendant HT.[51] The HT continues in the same vein, sharpening the focus of ethical behaviour in terms of kindred social pairs. Ethical responsibilities now fall along the individual's respective station in life, an unflinchingly *realistic* starting point for defining ethical behaviour: in terms of real-life circumstances. Husbands and wives, parents and children are commanded, in both positive and negative terms, to execute discrete duties. The third social pair, slave-master, is unique in its detailed description of the reciprocal duties and their christological motivation, where ethical responsibility is notably enhanced. The slave's responsibility towards the master, for instance, is transformed, yet fully intact. The previous relationship to the master remains prominent, and most importantly of all, very real in its call to honest, daily service (3:22–25). The slave is not extricated from the *status*

---

[51] Three reciprocal commands in 3:9, 3:13 a, b.

quo of his social world, rather this becomes the stage upon which allegiance to Christ is proven. To the degree that responsibility, in this case towards the master, is abrogated, it is to an equal degree that the slave's moral identity recedes. It should be noted that the call to responsibility is reciprocal. Ethical behaviour in Christ takes place in a relationship of bilateral responsibility; both slave and master stand before the Lord, and both receive rewards and punishments as outlined in the HT (3:24–25). The masters, as will be seen below, have enormous responsibilities towards the slaves, as well. The genuineness and completeness of the mutual responsibilities reflect the value of both members of the slave-master relationship as responsible individuals, as well as the concern that this relationship reflect behaviour *in Christ*. Ethical decisions and actions are predicated upon responsibility. Most important, however, is the backdrop which informs the intra-human axis: the ultimate responsibility towards Christ.

The HT, by virtue of its unusual form of address (direct, inverted and public), as well as its reciprocal ethic which calls members to responsible and ethical relationship before Christ, introduces uniquely Christian elements into stereotyped relational pairs. These elements indicate to believers that a new status in the Lord is being introduced. The foundation of this new status is the vertical relationship to Christ, which introduces a new, theological reality. A closer analysis of the slave-master relationship in 3:22–4:1 will illustrate the nature and extent of the change wrought by the vertical axis.

Analysis of the Expanded Instruction:
Slave and Master

The HT contained in Colossians appears at first glance to have little to do with the themes of the larger letter, and betrays no overt theological justification, save the modifier ἐν κυρίῳ, as well as other titular references in the slave-master parenesis. It is this apparent theological superficiality, along with the HT's clear structure, which led Dibelius, and others after him, to see the code as traditional material which had undergone a "leichte Verchristlichung."[52] The first impression, however, is deceiving. The Colossian HT,

---

[52] Dibelius, *Kolosser*, 46f. Dibelius notes that the author was indebted to a number of sources, OT and pagan. The HT represents a hasty attempt to draw upon the best elements of these traditions, giving them a Christian veneer, the master-slave parenesis revealing the most Christian influence. See also Weidinger, *Haustafeln*, 74f.

in particular its references to the Lord,[53] appears to be more than an altered piece of traditional material,[54] and as discussed in chapter one, displays several elements which are unique to its NT form. Yet there can be no agreement as to how the original commands were received or implemented. Even the phrase "as is fitting in the Lord", universally understood as a christianising element, has met with divergent estimations of its significance.[55] The first and second relational pairs, wives-husbands and children-parents, illustrate the difficulty in ascertaining a Christian understanding of the HT material. Though they share several formal features of the Col. HT, they are considerably less developed than the third relational pair, slave-master. Both contain reciprocal and public admonitions, giving priority of direct address to the subordinate member. The parent-children commands also contain explanatory phrases notably absent in the husband-wife relationship. The features particular to these two relational pairs raise a number of important and interesting issues,[56] but because of their extremely concise formulation, a differentiated, Christian understanding of the terms proves a difficult task. The first relationship, wives and husbands, notably the briefest formulation, represents this well:

---

[53] Lohse, *Colossians*, 156. Contra Dibelius and Weidinger, Lohse sees the HT form changed most remarkably in terms of the *kurios* language. See also Dunn, *Colossians*, 244, Laub, *Begegnung*, 92.

[54] Gielen, *Tradition*, 129. The form of the Colossian HT "steht…in der Antike singulär da." Attempts to compare the HT to literature of similar theme remain unconvincing, as with Plutarch, *Conj. Praec.* 138 B, where she points out critical differences in the form and character of address, the HT being apodictic in nature. See also Michael Wolter, *Der Brief and die Kolosser, Der Brief an Philemon*, eds. E. Gräßer and K. Kertelge, Ökumenischer Taschenbuchkommentar zum Neuen Testament, vol. 12 (Gütersloh: Gütersloher Verlagshaus Gerd Mohn, 1993), 195f. Wolter agrees with Gielen that the Col. HT is "nicht aus der antiken Ökonomik ableitbar" and that there remains a "formgeschichtliche Erklärungslücke."

[55] Gnilka, *Kolosserbrief*, 217, considers this small phrase to be the element which offers a Christian understanding and motivation. Gielen, *Tradition,*144, traces the *kurios* language through the entire HT, concluding that this expression reflects the existential reality of the servant-lord axis, giving the commands meaning which is inseparable from the christological "Begründungsstruktur" of the HT ethic; it is more than a "oberflächlich angehängte Christianisierungsformel." Weidinger, *Haustafeln*, 74, and Schweizer, *Brief*, 165, fn. 606, disagree, seeing the phrase to be a Christian legitimisation of a borrowed form. In spite of this, however, both phrases, ὡς ἀνῆκεν ἐν κυρίῳ and εὐάρεστόν ἐστιν ἐν κυρίῳ, can be said to have at *least* a regulatory function.

[56] These relationships are equally interesting in terms of the rule of Christ and his role vis-à-vis the traditional *paterfamilias*. Dunn, *Epistles*, 252, points out the "remarkably modern" psychological sensitivity shown in the child-parent relationship. See also Caird, *Letters*, 209.

3:18: Αἱ γυναῖκες, ὑποτάσσεσθε τοῖς ἀνδράσιν ὡς ἀνῆκεν ἐν κυρίῳ.
3:19: Οἱ ἄνδρες, ἀγαπᾶτε τὰς γυναῖκας καὶ μὴ πικραίνεσθε πρὸς αὐτάς.

Since ὑποτάσσειν is relatively scarce in its usage outside of the NT to describe the relationship of a wife to her husband,[57] some commentators have opted to see the phrase in an expressly Christian light.[58] Others, in contrast, have ascribed to ὑποτάσσω and ἀγαπάω no particular Christian aspect.[59] In spite of scholarly disagreement as to the ultimate meaning of these HT expressions, they remain central to its understanding. Laub cites three aspects of the Christian fellowship (all of which are, interestingly, reflected in the HT), which had no parallel in its day:

1. The concept and application of agape love;
2. The motif of the socially-levelling Christ-Lordship and the final judgment;
3. The motif of submission.[60]

The coincidence of these themes within the HT, we believe, suggests a significant theological impulse within the HT, and underscores the importance of discovering its Christian meaning. The disagreement among scholars as to the origin, meaning and significance of the HT material makes a closer analysis of the *expanded* section of the HT essential. Our discussion will, for this reason, reflect an emphasis upon the third relationship, slave-master. Though a number of theories have been put forward to explain the occasion

---

[57] Plutarch, *Conj. Praec.* 33 (ii. 142e) and Ps. Callisthenes, *Hist. Alex. Magni* i. 22.4. See also Delling's article in *TDNT*, VIII, 40.

[58] Rengstorf, "Mahnungen", 131f.; Schroeder, *Haustafeln*, 116f.; Gielen, *Tradition*, 143f. These scholars see the particular command to submit under the aspect of two modifying, and christianising influences: the complementary command towards the men to love (ἀγαπᾶτε being understood in a specifically Christian sense), and the subjection of the command to the modifying ὡς ἀνῆκεν ἐν κυρίῳ.

[59] Crouch, *Origin*, 109; Standhartinger, "Origin", 119. Crouch allows for no christianising of the commands: "...neither the instructions to the husbands nor the usage of the term ὑποτάσσειν elsewhere in the New Testament alters the nature of the exhortation to the wife. The husband's command to love is seen as the common duty of all husbands; commentators ascribing to it a specifically Christian sense are making a superficial assumption."

[60] Laub, *Begegnung*, 88. The "Dynamik" of the early church's fellowship was unique; it was concerned with realising new human relations within the context of faith in Christ. Laub pointedly suggests, 62, that this dynamic has not been witnessed in the history of the church since that time.

which might have precipitated this expansion,[61] the discussion only highlights the need for further analysis of the material. It is this relationship, by
virtue of its expanded form, which demonstrates the strongest theological
impulses, as well as a substantial relatedness to the broader text.[62] The absolute dominion of Christ can be seen most clearly in this expanded section, we
hope to demonstrate, where the unequal relations of slave and master are
subjected to the mediating presence of Christ. Perhaps the expanded material
will reveal, to a greater degree, the specifically Christian elements contained
in the HT.[63] It is our hope that this approach will inform the interpretation of
the entire HT, and prove methodologically sound under the following aspects
of consideration:

1. The slave-master relationship represents a break from the structure
   of the previous axes, signalling our attention to a particularly important concern of the Colossian HT;[64]

---

[61] Dibelius, *Kolosser*, 47f., is one of the first to posit the crisis theory related to excesses
arising from Gal. 3:28, as well as the need for a common ethic; the more common explanation,
that the expanded section is somehow connected to the incident with Onesimus, has gained
broad acceptance (see, for example, Moule, *Colossians*, 128).

[62] Gnilka, *Kolosserbrief*, 227. Gnilka sees the HT as determined by the "Makrotext", esp.
3:11, distilled in a teaching which attempts to bring Christian love of neighbour "to its most
radically possible expression."

[63] A number of commentators, including those who perceive the HT as traditional only, note
that the slave-master parenesis most closely approximates a genuine Christian ethic. It is interesting to note that Dibelius, *Kolosser*, 47, though finding the HT to be traditional in character, sees the slave-master relationship as the most "verchristlicht": "Der ganze Abschnitt ist –
im Gegensatz zu den vorhergehenden [HT relationships] – aus original-christlichen Gedanken
heraus gestaltet." See also Lohmeyer, *Briefe*, 155; Wolter, *Brief*, 208; Laub, *Begegnung*, 92f.
The opposite opinion, however, is also represented among scholars. Pokorný sees the HT as
an "Anpassung an die Welt" which, in terms of the slave master parenesis "geht da zu weit,
bis an die Grenzen dessen, was man noch christlich verantworten kann." Petr Pokorný, *Der
Brief des Paulus an die Kolosser*, eds. J. Rohde, E. Fascher and C. Wolff, Theologischer
Handkommentar zum Neuen Testament, vol. X/1 (Berlin: Evangelische Verlagsanstalt, 1987),
150. Dunn, *Epistles*, 247, downplays the uniqueness of the HT and its ethical potential as "un-
avoidably conformist rather than transformist."

[64] F. Zeilinger, *Der Erstgeborene der Schöpfung: Untersuchungen zur Formalstruktur und
Theologie des Kolosserbriefes* (Wien: Herder, 1974), 69, notes the even balance of the cou-
plets in 3:18–21; the first sentence of the slave-master relationship, however, "sprengt das
[literary] Schema", setting it apart. Gnilka, *Kolosserbrief*, 204, in agreement with most commentators, deems the expanded slave-master section as "most important", whereas Lohmeyer,
Briefe,155, goes even further, arguing that the HT was included as a traditional device *solely*
to introduce the expanded discussion regarding slaves and masters.

2. The argumentation offered in the slave-master relationship is most helpful in construing the christological reasoning behind the ethical demands of the HT;[65]

3. Finally, it is assumed that the more detailed theological and ethical arguments within the extended material of the third relationship can be helpful in interpreting the former.[66]

The HT, especially the segments dealing with the issue of slavery, has been characterised on the one hand as a cruel preservation of the *status quo*, or conversely, as a budding manifesto of the Christian gospel's message of freedom. As Franz Laub has concluded in his study, neither extreme represents the historical context or intention of the HT.[67] Another interpretative error, which affects the understanding of the slave-master relationship, has to do with the imposition of modern sociological categories such as self-determination and social injustice, which inevitably accrue in discussions regarding the ethic of the HT. These observations reflect a modern anthropological understanding of slavery and consciousness.[68] Superimposing such modern categories, however interesting and relevant, overlooks the historical aspect of slavery in the first century, and forces the admonitions of the HT into an anachronistic framework.[69] Yet the presence of slaves in a religious community raises the question as to how these community members fared in light of their common religious experience. In the following discussion we will investigate how the HT, by means of its reciprocal ethic, sought to exalt Christ in all relations; it remains to be seen whether it introduced a discernible attempt to ameliorate the slave's estate.

The early church was variegated in its makeup, and evidenced a tendency to attract members from several walks of life, including a remarkable number of slaves, as is documented by the admonitions of the biblical HT

---

[65] Wolter, *Brief*, 202, cites the expanded explanation and christological reasoning as the two features which distinguish the third section.

[66] Gielen, *Tradition*, 119, also assumes that the slave-master section exercises a "paradigmatic function", which extends to the interpretation of the other HT relationships.

[67] Laub, *Begegnung*, 9. Laub has no patience with such historically unfounded theories: "Die Dinge liefen differenzierter, als es solche Alternativlösungen mit ihrem Defizit an geschichtlicher Betrachtungsweise zunächst vermuten lassen."

[68] Wiedemann, *Slavery*, 15f., points out the profound level at which slavery was considered to be part of the natural order, though modified and confused at points by the Sophist division of natural (*physis*) and conventional (*nomos*) human institutions.

[69] Ibid., 11f. Slavery was simply a "Vorgegebenheit und Selbstverständlichkeit." The writers of the NT did not have anthropological-philosophical slave theories in mind, but rather the "every-day reality of slave existence in all of its subtle variations."

tradition and the contemporary[70] record. To a degree, this can be seen in Colossians, as well.[71] Could motifs found in the letter of Colossians such as agape love, Christ's lordship over all members and his return in glory combine to allow the slave to "obtain a free mind and receive a noble birth from the Logos"?[72] The Colossian HT, introducing new relational dynamics such as reciprocity, individual responsibility and submission to Christ, opens this very possibility. In the following sections, we will analyse the slave-master relationship by consecutive exegesis. This analysis will attempt to explicate the carefully structured and reasoned admonitions to the slaves and masters, shedding light upon the implications for both members of the relational pair, as well as uncovering the significant role of Christ in construing this relationship. It is our hope that the theological motivation behind the admonitions will become apparent.

The Slave in Christ's Service: Colossians 3:22–24

Οἱ δοῦλοι, ὑπακούετε κατὰ πάντα τοῖς κατὰ σάρκα κυρίοις, μὴ ἐν ὀφθαλμοδουλίᾳ ὡς ἀνθρωπάρεσκοι, ἀλλ᾽ ἐν ἁπλότητι καρδίας φοβούμενοι τὸν κύριον. ὃ ἐὰν ποιῆτε, ἐκ ψυχῆς ἐργάζεσθε ὡς τῷ κυρίῳ καὶ οὐκ ἀνθρώποις, εἰδότες ὅτι ἀπὸ κυρίου ἀπολήμψεσθε τὴν ἀνταπόδοσιν τῆς κληρονομίας. τῷ κυρίῳ Χριστῷ δουλεύετε.

Slaves are commanded, in unambiguous language, to obey their masters κατὰ πάντα (3:22).[73] The slave is not allowed, for example, to slacken his energies in service or maintain a well-established routine; quite the contrary! He now has an awe-inspiring *divine* supervisor, who is watching his hands as

---

[70] Origen records the words of Celsus in his apology *Contra Celsum* III, 52–54, in which Christians are accused of gathering around them uneducated persons from all walks of life, including, among others, slaves.

[71] The HT introduces us to the several relations of the household; 3:11, however, anticipates a broad spectrum in the body of Christ, including room not only for ethnic and religious diversity characterised by Jew and Greek, and social diversity in the slave and free, but in almost hyperbolic fashion, allowing for cultural outsiders in the use of βάρβαρος and Σκύθης, normally terms of disdain. Moule, *Colossians*, 121, sees the terms implying slaves of the lowest class; see O. Michel, "Σκύθης", *TDNT* 7, 447–50. Gnilka, *Kolosserbrief*, 192, suggests that these people groups reflect *actual* missionary endeavour, and hence the makeup of the church.

[72] Origen, *Contra Celsum*, III, 54.

[73] A small number of mss., including 𝔓[46], omit κατὰ πάντα; perhaps to hinder potential abuse? V. 22 retains its broad sense of full obedience from the heart, although the sense of this service is restricted considerably by the modification of the masters as being such only κατὰ σάρκα.

well as weighing his heart (3:22). In pragmatic terms, his lot in life seems identical, yet with greatly *increased* responsibility. The euphoric tones of the greater letter, particularly the images of deliverance (1:13f) and egalitarian standing through Christ (3:11), seem to stand in contrast to the slave's relationship to the master. The redeemed life in Christ *seems* remarkably like the previous life, and in some sense, even more exacting. In terms of responsibilities, this is true; the transfer into Christ's kingdom has not transformed daily work into idleness, pleasure or anything unknown to other contemporary slaves. The difference is not realised in subtracting the earthly, and often negative, elements, but by the introduction of the positive, the divine. Due to the primary axis, common slave duties become, in Christ, human *and* divine service. Hence the nature of service is given in modified language, *earthly* masters, τοῖς κατὰ σάρκα κυρίοις. Not only does this phrase naturally limit the scope of service to this life, it clearly intimates the divine sphere, which modifies the human relations in a sharp, bilateral fashion. It functions as comfort and warning. The master's authority does not stand alone, and is ultimately subject to the greater authority of Christ. Both master and slave have a common, and mediating *Gegenüber*, the Lord Christ. The slave, however, being here addressed, is placed squarely under the lordship of Christ, and is accountable for his service, which is to be done in the fear of the Lord, not as men-pleasers, and with a sincerity of heart. Φοβούμενοι τὸν κύριον is the rubric under which the service mentioned in 3:24–25 is to be performed, and relates, ultimately, to the parallel themes of reward and punishment in 3:5–6.[74] The slave's relationship to Christ is primary, indissoluble and in light of the scope of salvation and judgement, rightly awesome. It is the primary motivation of fearing Christ, likened unto the OT fear of God, as Gielen rightly points out, which forms the "integralen Bestandteil in der semantisch-pragmatischen Struktur der Kol-HT."[75] Though the service rendered is on the human level, its motivation is wholly derived from the vertical Christ-Servant axis.

---

[74] Wolter, *Brief*, 204.

[75] Gielen, *Tradition*, 172f. Gielen sees Paul's self-understanding in terms of a servant operating in the fear of the Lord. He adapts the OT tradition which combined fear and service (cf. 1 Sam. 12:14, 24; 2 Kg. 17:41; Neh. 1:11; Mal. 1:6; 3:14, 16; Ps. 2:11; 119:38), to structure his argument, giving it a "christologische Ausrichtung." The title Lord in these passages is to be understood as Christ (see also Schrage, *Ethik*, 170–171). The method of argumentation and use of "fearing the Lord" are not accidental (contra Müller, "Frauenthema," 273), but are to be understood as semantically connected to the Pauline servant language. Paul's anthropology knows only the state of servanthood; humans are slaves to sin, the law or to righteousness. See also Lohmeyer, *Briefe*, 159, who similarly connects Pauline servant language to this passage.

92

The slave is seen as belonging, first and foremost, to the Lord in Heaven. All service in the earthly sphere is to be done "as unto the Lord and not men" (3:23), the contrast between the two masters being a leading theme of the passage. The fear of the Lord effectively displaces (or significantly modifies) the fear of man, two basic approaches to service which are cast in contrastingly negative and positive terms. Here the apostle makes clever use of language, as well as OT references, to emblazon an image of fierce, inward devotion to Christ, a devotion which is manifest only *partially* in outward acts. The slave is being invited into a deeper, spiritual service and growth in Christ. Several aspects of the nature of service make this abundantly clear:

i.) 3:22a: μὴ ἐν ὀφθαλμοδουλίᾳ ὡς ἀνθρωπάρεσκοι
This word pair occurs only twice in the NT, the other occurrence being the parallel passage in Eph. 6:6. It illustrates, in particularly caustic language, how obedience to the master should *not* be carried out, and certainly not service rendered unto Christ (the admonition is framed by, and anticipates two realms of service; earthly obedience in 22a, and fearing the Lord, 22b). In the most fundamental terms, the slave is here being asked to express his *ultimate* obedience to Christ in a posture of integrity. The two realms of service, though shown in genuine contrast, do not involve the practice of duplicity, but can only be rightly integrated and practised by the very positive ἐν ἁπλότητι καρδίας. The opposite also holds true: mere ὀφθαλμοδουλία, and those attempting to please men, characterised as ἀνθρωπάρεσκοι, are contrasted with this singleness of heart, and genuine, undivided service to Christ.[76]

ii.) 3:22b: ἐν ἁπλότητι καρδίας
This phrase forms a short, yet powerful contrast to the falseness of serving under pretence, the feigned service for the sake of human eyes. The expression ἁπλότητι can be found only in letters of Pauline origin in the New Testament, twice in the HT context, Col. 3:22 and Eph. 6:5.[77] It is quite possibly of Old Testament origin,[78] re-

---

[76] Ibid., 168f. Gielen notes that Paul conceives the status of the slave of Christ to be in opposition to attempting to please men; Gal. 1:10, 1Thes. 2:4, Rom. 14:18 and 2 Cor. 5:9 also show evidence of striving to please Christ foremost in contrast to pleasing men.

[77] Other occurrences: Rom. 12:8; 2 Cor. 8:2; 9:11, 13; 11:3. See article "Einfalt" by H. Bacht, *RAC* 4, 821–840.

[78] Gielen, *Tradition*, 169, fn. 309, points out that the Hebrew word תֹּם is sometimes translated in the LXX as ἁπλότης (other Greek translations using it more frequently). She lists the

ferring to a singleness of heart, and service rendered unto God. Here we see a unique Christian emphasis which isolates Christ as the primary and ultimate source of the slave's motivation. In terms of the two masters, the potential conflict of ultimate fidelity becomes clear, as the outward, observable behaviour designated as ὀφθαλμοδουλία is contrasted with the inner realm, καρδία. It is Christ only who can see and reward inner motives; this contrast underscores the intrinsic limits of the slave-master relationship as external and incapable of securing ultimate devotion, the prerogative of God. The heart becomes the impartial courtroom of God, an unmolested environment in which the slave is encouraged to weigh out decisions in terms of ἁπλότης. Here responsibility is placed squarely upon the slave to reject a sense of victimisation attached to his outward circumstances (as real as they certainly were), and to allow new, inward motivations to determine outward behaviour. It is in this inward realm where the motivating fear of the Lord can take root and influence behaviour. Wolter notes that this model of obedience directs the slave to consider not only the present reality, but the eschatological implications of *ultimate* reward and punishment, implicit in the exercise of the fear of the Lord. The HT use of contrasts is intentional, attempting to address the awkward issue of dual loyalties, while underscoring the final authority of Christ.[79] This exercise of the heart, complicated by conflicting interests, as well as the most undesirable of human conditions, is not without its rewards (v. 24). The following verse, however, draws the slave into special relationship to Christ: service.

iii.) 3:23: ὃ ἐὰν ποιῆτε, ἐκ ψυχῆς ἐργάζεσθε ὡς τῷ κυρίῳ καὶ οὐκ ἀνθρώποις

Here the contrast between the two realms of the heavenly and earthly masters found in 3:22 is repeated[80] in more general terms, a variation in the call to obedience finding broad expression in "whatever you do". This formulation has already been encountered in the general

---

OT (LXX) references which employ this phrase in full or part: 2 Sam. 15:11; 1 Mac. 2:37, 60; 3 Mac. 3:21; 1 Chr. 29:17; Wisdom 1:1. The last two references mirror Col. 3:22 exactly.

[79] Wolter, *Brief*, 202f. The "Kontrastmahnungen", which place the Lord and human authority in opposition, are so structured as to be unmistakably clear: "Die Sklaven sollen sich bei der Erfüllung ihrer Gehorsamspflicht nicht an menschlichen Instanzen orientieren, sondern ausschließlich am erhöhten Herrn."

[80] The broader context of the passage does not allow for the master to displace Christ (ὡς τῷ κυρίῳ), but simply restates the human-divine spheres and limitations in another way.

instruction found in 3:17, (καὶ πᾶν) ὃ ἐὰν ποιῆτε, and modified there by the rather vague injunction to do all things ἐν ὀνόματι κυρίου Ἰησοῦ. The instruction to the slave, then, gives more precision to the universal requirement of 3:17, and in this manner may conceivably be understood, at least in its inward motivation, to apply to all Christian activity. This is a destabilising and uniquely Christian element which the HT introduces to the slave-master relationship. The earthly master, in a very real way, no longer administers exclusive control over the slave's tasks, but shares them with Christ. Indeed, Christ, by virtue of his cosmic authority and position as redeeming Lord eclipses the authority of the earthly master, as is reflected in the ensuing command, "Serve the Lord Christ!" (3:24). Particularly in the case of the slave, we may speak in literal terms of *Herrschaftswechsel*. Menial service, consequently, acquires the dignity of ministry and worship. The slave, as with all who undertake service unto Christ, may be regarded as a σύνδουλος of the Apostle, and a person no longer perceived in terms of human relationships *only*. Service rendered unto Christ, done in obedience, will not miss its reward (3:24). The work of the slave is ennobled, then, in two aspects: it is executed on the human level with the same honour due other servants of Christ (ministry), and it is inherently worthy as direct obedience to God (worship). Christ, as one of two masters, receives priority and ultimate obedience.

The slave's service, formerly understood in terms of the master *in the fear of the Lord*, can conceivably include other spheres, and is now to be considered as service directed unto Christ. The slave's entire existence is addressed. The emphasis is, of course, upon the inward attitude, but again transforms all menial tasks into deeds of ultimate significance, weighing the importance of the activity primarily in terms of its relationship to Christ. For this reason, ἐκ ψυχῆς takes on particular significance as a descriptor of the service rendered. Dunn reads this phrase as echoing the *Shema* of Deut. 6:4, as well as its Christian affirmation in the words of Jesus, Mk. 12:30.[81] Lohmeyer adds to this Jewish parenetic tradition as being inseparable from Paul's understanding.[82] From the OT and Christian perspective, the meaning becomes unmistakable: the slave, like others called into

---

[81] Dunn, *Epistles*, 255. He also mentions pseudo-Phocylides 50 as representative of the broader Hellenistic understanding of this phrase.

[82] Lohmeyer, *Briefe*,158, fn. 6, lists a number of OT and Jewish sources which express the basic sense of Paul's usage, Prov. 11:17; Sirach 6:26; 7:29, etc.

the life of faith in Christ, is being included among those who have a direct relationship and responsibility to the Lord. This relationship is marked in its completeness by the force of responsibility laid upon the slaves, as well as the promise of reward. The challenge to serve ἐκ ψυχῆς is a point of transition in the admonition to the slave; without it, the relationship to the Lord would be in some way mitigated and secondary. The surprising message of the HT is the equal access to Christ which the servant enjoyed. Only the prospect of reward, also linked to OT concepts, surpasses this claim.

iv.) 3:24a: εἰδότες ὅτι ἀπὸ κυρίου ἀπολήμψεσθε τὴν ἀνταπόδοσιν τῆς κληρονομίας
Following the parenetic section's theme of the returning Christ (3:4) and judgement (3:6), verse 24 makes explicit reference to this event in relation to the slaves. As the last and future movement of the believer in Christ, the revealing and glorification are yet to be realised. The future passive (ἀπολήμψεσθε) in 3:24 mirrors 3:4 (φανερωθήσεσθε) conceptually as well as morphologically, where the recompense of inheritance is seen to be an element of the appearance of Christ in glory. Verse 24 begins a three-verse segment, which can rightly be called "Gerichtsparänese",[83] balanced around, and hinged upon, v. 25. These verses draw both parties, by the use of discreetly addressed parallel clauses (3:24 and 4:1b εἰδότες ὅτι), before the judgement seat of Christ.

The sense of recompense is strong in ἀνταπόδοσιν, suggesting an understanding by the author that the slave was likely experiencing unjust treatment.[84] Lohmeyer finds this unique NT occurrence of the term to be a clear reference to the frequent Septuagint usage of the "day of judgement." This meaning also holds true for most cognate uses in the NT.[85] Though this appears to be a reference to judgement,

---

[83] Wolter, *Brief*, 208. Wolter recognises vv. 3:24–4:1 as a unit, "Gerichtsparänese", which includes by its very nature, both the slaves and owners. The reciprocal nature of judgement is related to faith in both sides, and corresponds to the "Schutzbestimmungen" found in the OT (Dt. 15:12–18, 23:16; Ex. 21:2, Lev. 25:8f., 39f.). Laub, *Begegnung*, 14f., points out that these protective measures were limited to those in faith only. See also H.L. Strack and Paul Billerbeck, *Kommentar zum Neuen Testament aus Talmud und Midrasch*, 8th ed. (München: C.H. Beck'sche Verlagsbuchhandlung, 1982), 4.2., "Das altjüdische Sklavenwesen," 698–744.

[84] Dunn, *Epistles*, 256, notes the double prefix "give back (ἀπό) in return (ἀντί)" suggests full compensation for deprivation and harsh treatment.

[85] Lohmeyer, *Briefe*, 159, fn.1. LXX, ἡμέρα ἀνταποδόσεως. ἀνταπόδομα can be found in Lk. 14:12 and Rom. 11:9. The verbal form, ἀνταποδίδωμαι, occurs more frequently, express-

it is at this point wholly positive. The κληρονομία, a theme introduced in 1:12, had, as Wolter points out, three aspects in which inheritance could be understood; these three combine here to serve as a "Vergeltung für ihre [slaves'] allein am Kurios orientierte Erfüllung der Gehorsamspflicht." The tripartite inheritance constitutes a hopeful vision of a new "Statuszuweisung" which will transform their momentary, earthly legal status.[86] Inheritance becomes here an event which would, in light of Roman law,[87] create a paradox.[88] It is perhaps this word, inheritance, which represents the zenith of the tension created by the intersection of Christ in the slave master relationship. Using OT and kingdom imagery, the author includes the slave in an ancient and divine process of promise and inheritance, effectively declaring that the slave in Christ is in some way an heir, and essentially *free*. The transformation *in Christ* of the slave status is announced as a fixed point in the unfolding sequence of salvation found in Colossians. Though it is envisioned as a future event, it is as sure as the coming of Christ. The tension created by this soteriological and eschatological transformation is very real, and poses the most acute challenge to the understanding of the HT mandates.[89]

v.) 3:24b: τῷ κυρίῳ Χριστῷ δουλεύετε

In light of the inheritance which is theirs, the slaves are again admonished, this time to serve the Lord Christ. This last command to

---

ing recompense in judgement, as well as human payment of a debt, Lk. 14:14; Rom. 11:35, 12:19; 1 Thes. 3:9; 2 Thes. 1:6; Heb. 10:3.

[86] Wolter, *Brief*, 205. He sees this use as reaching back to Jewish post-exilic, as well as early Christian eschatological thought. The reference is in terms of 1) the *Land* (Is. 60:21; Ps. 37:9, 11; Mt. 5:5, 19, 29); 2) *eternal life* (Ps. Sol. 14:10; Mk. 10:17; Mt. 19:29; Lk. 10:25); and 3) *partnership* in God's rule/kingdom (Mt. 25:34; 1 Cor. 6:9f.; 15:50; Gal. 5:21; Eph 5:5; Jn. 3:5). See also Gielen, *Tradition*, 183f; Foerster and Herrmann in *TDNT* 3, "κληρονομία, κτλ.", 758–785; Friedrich in *EDNT* 2, 298–301.

[87] The slave status did not allow the accumulation of wealth (Gaius, *Inst.* 52–53); inheritance could only fall to slaves who had been legally freed (case of inheritance from master, Ulpiani *Epit.* 1,14; Gaius, *Inst.* 2, 153–155). Even a freedman had limitations placed upon inheritances, and could encounter opposition to legal claims (Gaius, *Inst.* 3, 55–56 indicates several legal scenarios according to differing legal status; Pliny, *Ep.* 10, 104.105 gives example of the tenuous nature of freedman inheritance as seen in his successful appeal to Trajan to alter, and thereby revoke, their inheritance rights).

[88] Lohmeyer, *Briefe*, 159, sees the unrealisable promise as a "leichte Paradoxie."

[89] The slave-master relationship is drawn into a dialectical tension between inheritance, relation to Christ and present reality, questioning to what degree human relations can be relativised in light of the slave's ultimate, theological standing in Christ. See Gielen, *Tradition*, 175; Strecker, "Haustafeln", 371; Wolter, *Brief*, 203.

the slaves sharpens and conspicuously redirects the focus of slave responsibility in more exclusive terms to Christ. It is important to note here that an alternative, possibly indicative reading τῷ γαρ κυρίῳ Χριστῷ δουλεύετε is attested in several manuscripts, including the Majority Text. An indicative reading of 24b would remove the imperative force, certainly, but not the clear indication that the slaves now serve the Lord Christ. The following points, however, lend support to an imperative reading of this verse segment. Firstly, the reading omitting γάρ is found in the most ancient and reliable texts. Its presence elsewhere may be explained as an editorial addition, γάρ being inserted, perhaps, to help the sentence halves flow more smoothly together. The more abrupt and forceful reading would in this case be preferable. In addition, an indicative reading would break with the general imperative tone of the HT (the long string of present imperatives found in the broader letter are also well-represented in the HT: ὑποτάσσεσθε, ἀγαπᾶτε, πικραίνεσθε, ὑπακούετε [2x, v. 20, 22], ἐρεθίζετε, ἐργάζεσθε, δουλεύετε, παρέχεσθε). 24b, appearing directly before the pivotal announcement of impartial judgement in v.25, may also reflect an intentional, grammatically parallel construction to that of the masters found in 4:1 (both verses containing εἰδότες ὅτι, coupled with a statement regarding their relation to Christ, which is understood to justify the respective commands δουλεύετε v.24b, or παρέχεσθε), which would also indicate an imperative understanding. In any event, the verse illustrates the radical implications of the establishment of the divine-human axis for the slave. From obedience to the master only in the fear of the Lord (3:22), and the rather broad command to do all things with a whole heart as unto the Lord (3:23), verse 24 takes the next logical step: the slave has direct responsibility to serve Christ. The three levels of responsibility function as a staircase, which elevates the slave's service from broad, human categories to specific, divine allegiance, and we might assume, the option for participation in Christian ministry in some form. It is probably not insignificant that the title Lord Christ is singular in its NT usage at this point, and unlikely to be an accidental occurrence.[90] Its employment here may be to underscore, at this particularly important moment in the HT, the absolute nature of the Christ's mediation, both titles being used

---

[90] Kramer, *Christ*, 214, points out that Lord and Christ were titles in their own right, the joining here singular in the NT. The frequent use of titles, and the wide variety present in the NT, argues against a coincidental usage.

98

for emphasis[91] and clarity.[92] The displacement of the *earthly* master as the primary and ultimate authority represents the unique Christian emphasis found in this section of the HT, as well as a genuine basis for social change. The slave, master and church would not have missed the significance of this command. The slave is ultimately Christ's.

Justice before Christ: The Transition

Colossians 3:25: ὁ γὰρ ἀδικῶν κομίσεται ὃ ἠδίκησεν, καὶ οὐκ ἔστιν προσωπολημψία.

Every verse of the slave-master section is weighed and logically ordered; verse 25, however, is perhaps the most significant, for it represents the surprising turn in the *Gerichtsparänese*. While the words "Serve the Lord Christ!" were still looming with the sense of responsibility and new allegiance, verse 25 cuts through the slave-master section like a two-edged sword. The slaves, still being addressed, are now hearing the balance of the negative aspects of the coming of Christ and his judgement. The sense of receiving a positive recompense (ἀπολήμψεσθε τὴν ἀνταπόδοσιν τῆς κληρονομίας) cannot exclude the opposite contingency of negative judgement at Christ's appearing (κομίσεται ὃ ἠδίκησεν).[93] The verse, however, cuts in the other direction, as well, leading, like a swinging door, into the address to the masters. The illicit behaviours intimated in verse 24 by ἀδικῶν and ἠδίκησεν find their positive counterpart, furthermore, in the master's expected behaviour, τὸ δίκαιον καὶ τὴν ἰσότητα, in 4:1, making it unlikely, as some have thought,[94] that verse 25 was directed only towards the slave. Verse 25 becomes the hinge, the interpretative key, to both sections of the slave-master relationship, and deserves particular attention. It is here that the centrality of Christ and his role as absolute authority can be most clearly seen.

---

[91] Gnilka, *Kolosserbrief*, 233, sees this unique collocation as an emphasis to insure that the hearers know "who the Lord is, and whom they have to serve."

[92] Martin Hengel, *Studies*, 2, points out that the title *Christos* would have had little meaning for the Greek, who, having little or no knowledge of the titular sense of Jewish messiah, would have confused it with either a proper name, or the normal sense of anointing.

[93] κομίζω also carries the general sense of judgement found in reward, punishment and realised promises (Mt. 25:27; 2 Cor. 5:10; Eph. 6:8; Heb. 10:36, 11:19, 11:39; 1 Pet. 1:9, 5:4).

[94] Lohse, *Colossians*, 161. Interesting to note that the parallel passage in Eph. 6:8 includes εἴτε δοῦλος εἴτε ἐλεύθερος.

Regardless of social standing, evil behaviour will be recompensed by the impartial judge, Christ. The use of προσωπολημψία, possibly a Christian formulation, guarantees that this sense of egalitarian justice is not missed.[95] This term is almost always used in connection with God's action on behalf of those who are denied rights. As Gnilka points out, v. 25 makes use of "sober, almost legal language" to communicate the last judgement; it constitutes an "equalising force" which cannot be bribed, and creates, for this reason, confidence among the slaves.[96] The Lord Christ, the seat of present authority, as well as the initiator of the coming judgement, shows himself here to be aligned only with righteousness. The event of the judgement is inextricably joined to the person of Christ and his character, and is wholly initiated by him. Both slave and master, already in vertical relationship with the Lord, hear how he will remain between them as witness and final arbiter of their relationship. The HT is, at the unlikely point of judgement, most reflective of its christocentric nature.[97] It is at this point that Christ, and the divine ethic, are most central and determinative. Here the agent of rescue extends salvation by decisively terminating inequity and distributing reward and punishment. In the consequent logic of judgement, the Christ who was denied a central role in earthly dealings, must now assume a more enhanced role in judgement. Injustice and righteousness, however unevenly known in the present, will be exposed and rewarded in perfect measure at his coming.

The forceful and law-like character of the HT commands becomes one of its defining features,[98] and has opened the question of whether verse 25 reflects a formulaic expression of *jus talionis*. Pokorný concludes that it is in-

---

[95] Other NT occurrences in Rom. 2:11; Eph. 6:9; Jas. 2:1 (verbal usage, Jas. 2:9); see also *Testament of Job* 43:13 and Polycarp, *Philippians* 6:1. All are in reference to the impartial judgement of God regarding human behaviour. Gnilka, *Kolosserbrief*, 223, points out that this term is probably a Pauline creation (contra Lohmeyer), playing on the LXX phrase πρόσωπον λαμβάνειν (Lev. 19:15; 2 Kg. 3:14; Mal. 1:8f., 2:9, etc.); more likely Lohmeyer, *Kolosser*, 159, fn. 4, and Dunn, *Epistles*, 258, suggesting a Christian creation, playing off the numerous OT occurrences, in particular, the citation from Sirach 35:12–13, which contains not only the term πρόσωπον λαμβάνειν, but the sense, as well. See Lohse's article in *TDNT* 6, 779–80.

[96] Gnilka, *Kolosserbrief*, 223. He sees v. 25 as a "Satz heiligen Rechts", in which all human behaviour is placed in opposition to the judgement of God and Christ "in der Form der Talio."

[97] Wolter, *Brief*, 205. It is Christ himself who decides "letztinstanzlich über Heil und Unheil."

[98] Gielen, *Tradition*, 200f. (with Schroeder, Gnilka, Pokorný, Ernst, Hartman, Hahn, Käsemann), concludes that the HT differs from other similar literature in its use of apodictic law sentences.

deed a *Talionsformel,* a "Satz heiligen Rechts,"[99] which couples all ethical behaviour with its corresponding reward or punishment, including the possibility of condemnation. It represents the reverse side of the promise found in v. 24, adding the balance of negative rewards, as well as extending the general sense of judgement initiated in 3:6.[100] As Hahn points out, the language which touches upon the future work of Christ, particularly the judgement, is characterised by "ausgesprochene forensische Termini" found notably in the form "eines heiligen Rechtssatzes."[101] The *Talionsformel* becomes, in NT usage, inextricably connected to judgement.[102] So we find the same pattern of Christ's return in judgement predicating the ethical mandates of the Colossian HT, in particular, the very form of verse 25.

The forensic language of v. 25 assumes the vigilance of God in ethical matters, and is characterised by the reality of future judgement, whether positive or negative. This creates an ethical tension, which Käsemann describes as "oddly dialectic" in its effect.[103] Käsemann's observation sheds light on the present and future force of verse 25. The hearer, presumably a believer in full relationship to Christ, is called to consider judgement in the hope that he

---

[99] This term is first used by Ernst Käsemann in his article "Sätze heiligen Rechtes im Neuen Testament," *NTS* 1 (1954–55): 248–260, in which he describes NT formulations (such as Mk. 8:38; 1 Cor. 3:17; Rom. 10:11, 13; Gal. 3:12; Rev. 22:18f.) which imitate and extend certain OT prophetic expressions, offering the young church a form in which to cloak its own prophetic "Sätze heiligen Rechtes." These terse formulations impart a sense of prophetic proclamation, heralding God's decisive and retributive activity in the final judgement. Paul, in using such phrases, is assuming a prophetic role, and announcing that God's judgement is, even apart from the apostle's presence, among them: "Die Proklamation des Gesetzes, nach welchem Gott an seinem Tage handeln wird, bedeutet für sie [the church], daß sie sich dereinst nicht entschuldigen können. Sie sind fortan mit ihrer Schuld behaftet. Die Verkündigung des Gerichtes ist darum mehr als eine Drohung. In ihr vollzieht sich bereits ein Gerichtetwerden." Klaus Berger, in his article "Zu den sogenannten Sätzen Heiligen Rechts," *NTS* 17 (1970–71): 10–40, places the genesis of these formulations not in the prophetic traditions, but in wisdom literature. He contests the eschatological emphasis bound to the understanding of law, preferring a more limited scope, which affects the hearer "innerhalb seines Lebens und ist individuell" (See also Wolter, *Brief,* 206). We agree here with Pokorný, *Kolosser,* 155, fn. 40, and Gnilka, *Kolosserbrief,* 223, that his argument is not convincing, since the wisdom literature, though showing some outward similarities (cf. Prov. 22:8), differs in function from the NT occurrences, which do not impart wisdom for daily life, but rather confront the hearer with the question of life and death in terms of the eschatological judgement.

[100] Pokorný, *Brief,* 155.

[101] Hahn, *Hohheitstitel,* 34.

[102] Ibid., 34, fn. 1, "Entscheidend für das Talionsmotiv im NT ist der Bezug auf das eschatologische Gericht; hierdurch ist es allein von der Sache her zum heiligen Recht geworden, ganz gleich, wie es mit den dabei angewandten Stilformen stehen mag."

[103] E. Käsemann, "Sätze Heiligen Rechtes im Neuen Testament," *NTS* 1 (1954–55): 248–260.

might, above all, escape judgement. Life in Christ's body, though over-whelmingly benevolent, includes, for all those in Christ, the *present* initiation of judgement. The HT admonitions to slave and master convey this unique Christian emphasis with a sense of immediacy. Though the coming of Christ remains a future event, in a very real way, it contains force for the present. The establishment of the primary axis, Lord-Servant, carries with it a certain degree of contingency, and does not afford the hearers the indulgence of ig-noring the earthly relations of the HT. The formulation of the verse leaves the hearer without doubt that it includes all behaviour, all parties and in-volves the very root of Christian existence, present and future.[104] The fact that the letter has been read before the church implies a certain level of social pressure to conform to its admonitions, as well as the possibility of disci-pline; the real force, however, lies in the call to be aligned with Christ, now *and* in his appearing. Not to do so is separation from the head, Christ him-self. The HT reflects both the immediate danger of a human level of inequity brought on by deeds of unrighteousness, as well as the ultimate danger of condemnation. On the one hand, the believer's salvation waits in hope (διὰ τὴν ἐλπίδα τὴν ἀποκειμένην ὑμῖν ἐν τοῖς οὐρανοῖς 1:5), yet it is equally contingent on remaining in faith (εἴ γε ἐπιμένετε τῇ πίστει τεθεμελι-ωμένοι καὶ ἑδραῖοι καὶ μὴ μετακινούμενοι ἀπὸ τῆς ἐλπίδος τοῦ εὐαγγελίου οὗ ἠκούσατε, 1:23). It is this very contingency which gives the slave-master section of the HT its unusual force, and separates the HT ethic from other, similar literary forms.[105] The ethic transcends pragmatic catego-ries of utility or social stability, and attaches its mandates to the person and judgement of Christ. Here, if nowhere else, slave and master have found a level field.

Earthly Masters and the Lord in Heaven

Colossians 4:1: Οἱ κύριοι, τὸ δίκαιον καὶ τὴν ἰσότητα τοῖς δούλοις παρέχεσθε, εἰδότες ὅτι καὶ ὑμεῖς ἔχετε κύριον ἐν οὐρανῷ.

Verse 4:1 continues the theme of present and future judgement, with express mention of the slave masters. The verse is connected here logically and the-

---

[104] Gnilka, *Kolosserbrief*, 223, points out that the broad scope of this verse (ὁ γὰρ ἀδικῶν) encompasses the entirety of the Christian life, and is decisive in determining salvation or damnation.

[105] Wolter, *Brief*, 208. Wolter notes, correctly, that in the economic literature "die differen-zierte Behandlung der Sklaven pragmatisch begründet wird und zur Steigerung der Arbeit-sleistung eingesetzt werden soll."

102

matically to the previous verses, as one might expect, but also contains linguistic parallels which insure that the slave owners understand their common standing, with the slaves, before an impartial judge. They are addressed directly, and in parallel[106] with the slaves (3:22, Οἱ δοῦλοι; 4:1, Οἱ κύροι), a remarkably bold feature in terms of the social standing of the masters. The masters are also admonished in similar manner to the slaves (3:24a) in 4:1b, their instruction prefaced with the identical words εἰδότες ὅτι. These small parallels form a significant bridge between the respective instruction, placing their conscious ethical behaviour in the context of the broader perspective of Christ, and particular, his judgement.[107] Christ, conspicuously titled κύριος, gives a compass to the instruction presented to the slaves and masters, and thus provides a mediating influence. Most notable is the contrast between the earthly masters (3:22a) and the master in heaven (4:1b). The juxtaposition of these two instances of dominion frame the passage, underscoring the tension between the two realities, as well as serving as a reminder to the masters that their authority is, ultimately, relative. They stand, in concert with the theology of the letter,[108] in notable contrast. The heavenly master cannot represent the status quo, but introduces the standards of the kingdom. The earthly masters, in contrast (κατὰ σάρκα), are limited by the very term; the heavenly master emerges as the only ultimate authority. This small but ingeniously formulated parallel highlights the message to the masters: the Lord Christ is arbiter of all relations, which should be marked by justice[109] and equity (τὸ δίκαιον καὶ τὴν ἰσότητα).[110] The formulation takes into account both rela-

---

[106] The parallels, hinging upon verse 25, are simultaneously contrasting more than their status; the slaves are encouraged, whereas the masters receive a clear admonition.

[107] Wolter, Brief, 208. Wolter points out that this parallel shows Paul applying the same measure to the slave owners, and extending his argument, which is notably "gerichtsparänetisch."

[108] As noted above, Colossians highlights the dual realities of the earthly and heavenly spheres; cf. Col. 1:5, 13, 16, 20; 2:5, 8, 17, 20–23; 3:2, 5, 9–10; 4:1.

[109] See Quell and Schenk's article, δίκη, κτλ., in TDNT, 2, 174–225. Here the authors point out that the rather sparse NT usage is linked to the righteousness of God and judgement based on his character, both aspects of OT (LXX) thought. The law of God is assumed as the standard, and ethical behaviour is regulated in the context of relationships to God and others.

[110] Here Wolter, Brief, 206 and Gnilka, Kolosserbrief, 224f., point out that τὴν ἰσότητα refers to equity, not equality. See also Stählin's article in TDNT 3, 343–355. Standhartinger, "Origin", 128f., disagrees, seeing in ἰσότης an "interpretative key" which underlies the radical egalitarianism found in Col. She notes that this term, absent in Eph., "in fact means equality between groups of varying status in ancient society." Citing its use in Aristides, Regarding Rome, 26.39, where Roman law is praised for granting equality (ἰσότης) to divergent societal groupings, and Philo, Omn. Prob. Lib. 79, where the Essene refusal to hold slaves reflected a view that this practice was illicit, unnatural, and destroyed equality (ἰσότης), Standhartinger opens the possibility for such a translation. The term, as Balch, "Moralists",

tional axes, its language intimating the interplay between judgement and ethical behaviour. The masters, as the slaves, are called to parallel, responsible action. The "Lord in Heaven" awaits them with a common standard. The slave-master section closes on a firm note of equity: the judgement.

Conclusion

In this chapter we have attempted to demonstrate the ethic of Colossians as dependent upon the establishment of two relational axes, expressed in terms of faith towards Christ and love towards the saints. The former, divine-human axis, is the vertical relationship, established by the soteriological work of Christ. This axis, initiated by the transfer of the believer into a new kingdom, implies a fundamentally new allegiance to Christ as absolute Lord, and the change in status which this implies. In keeping with the manner of its initiation, the axis is characterised by an identification with Christ at the points of his earthly life and passion, as well as his future coming. The ethical admonitions of the letter are closely tied to, and emanate from, these soteriological movements. For this reason, the nature of the lordship found in Colossians, and assumed in the HT ethic, are appropriately located in the redemptive activity and person of Christ. Hence the Colossian HT ethic, if consistent with the letter's theology, cannot be fully understood in terms of natural law or power only; Christ's central position in the letter as lord, as well as his unique position as saviour, should make for an ethic which is based upon *relationship*. The benevolent transfer into Christ's kingdom implies, moreover, a relationship of master (king) and servant (subject), to which all believers subscribe, and which we found, interestingly, reduplicated in the slave-master relationship. This, we believe, becomes the *primary and irreducible* relationship of every believer, creating a new and egalitarian standing for all believers before Christ (3:11).

The second relational axis, intra-human, is, ideally, determined and re-ordered by the first; members within Christ's body are addressed in surprisingly egalitarian terms, their identity now being understood in relation to Christ and his body, the church. The believers' solidarity in sin and relationship to Christ as servants radically modify the *prima facie* implications of the HT commands. A subtle indication of this new status can be detected in its

---

ANRW, II 26.1, 406, points out, was not used among the neopythagorean moralists in reference to slaves, suggesting a unique usage here. ἰσότης, may have, then, in its original context, intimated some sort of equality; it does not, however, carry the entire weight of the author's arument. It is, rather, the larger context of Christ's coming judgement which establishes equality before the divergent social groups, slave and master.

mode of address, call to reciprocity and the centrality of Christ as the lord of new relations. It is in the expanded HT section, slave-master, however, where the instruction is most clearly expressed in terms of Christ, his central position as *kurios* working remarkable changes in a previously inequitable relationship. Following the pattern of the general letter, it is the approaching reality of Christ's appearing and the final judgement (directly antecedent to the HT parenesis) which informs the extended mandates. The centrality of the person of Christ as lord, as well as the theme of impartial judgement, play a decisive role in the formulation of the slave-master instruction. The point of union of this present life and the next is not only an event, but the person of Christ, who figures in verses 3:22–4:1 no less than four times as *kurios*. The Lord of salvation, who has rescued each believer (1:13), is declared in surest terms to be judge, as well. Christ's rule is normative in its moral authority from both aspects.[111] Salvation, being associated with Christ from beginning to end, finds it consummation in judgement. The rule of Christ, and in particular, the event of judgement, create a distinct Christian element of the HT tradition.[112] Regardless of the present reality known to the slaves and their masters, the language reflects unashamed confidence in the present mediation and the future judicature of Christ. The slave-master relationship, then, serves as an example of how stratified relationships within the church undergo fundamental re-ordering according to both the achieved and unrealised works of Christ.

The early form of the Christian HT found in the letter to the Colossians illustrates the author's concern with bringing the person of Christ to bear upon the church's daily life, in particular the common duties of the household. In spite of the letter's egalitarian tone and emphasis upon the mediation of Christ, the HT makes no pretence of abolishing slavery or subordinated relationships, *per se*. The HT cannot be construed as the formal beginnings of a "Freiheitsbewegung".[113] Its purpose of illustrating the role of Christ among the various human conditions, though profound, is limited in its

---

[111] Gielen, *Tradition*, 143, points to the absolute use as well as the "normierende Authorität" of the *kurios*-title in this section. See also Werner, *Christ*, 172f. He lists a number of features of Paul's use and understanding of *kurios* as absolute and relevant for present ethical behaviour, giving the ethical instruction "a note of urgency and of obligation." The aspect of judgement also plays a significant role in present behaviour: "The idea of being confronted by, or belonging to, the *Lord* does indeed provide a kind of back-cloth, but the actual content of ethical propositions is drawn from elsewhere, e.g. from the slave-master metaphor…"

[112] Laub, *Begegnung*, 88. Besides the element of agape love found in the HT tradition, Laub cites the unique "Motiv der 'gleichmachenden' Christusherrschaft und des Gerichts."

[113] Ibid., 8. Laub warns against this overly simplified reading, as well as dismissing the *opinio communis* that the apostolic teachings regarding love and equality inevitably led to the slavery's abolition.

scope, and must be understood in terms of the *totality* of the message of Colossians. The HT axes cannot, in the breadth of only a few lines, properly reflect the sheer complexity and personal dynamics which are found in the faith relationship to Christ, which is to be lived out within his body, the church. The HT ethic is, then, best understood, in terms of the theology of the entire epistle. Its skeletal form and concrete admonitions, though containing important theological impulses, remain dependent upon a broader theological compass to understand its ethical trajectory. The HT, when removed either from the interpretative paradigm found in the person of Christ, or the broader context of the letter, resists any *interpretatio christiana*. That being said, the role of Christ constitutes a profoundly theological and uniquely Christian element within the HT. The Colossian HT possesses, then, a theological point of orientation in which all stations of life are indivisibly united *in Christ*. As an expression of the letter's distinctive Christ-reality/believer-behaviour pattern, the form can be helpful in understanding how the early church understood genuine piety, ethical behaviour, and perhaps even social change. The importance of the Colossian HT's theological motivation should not be overlooked; if the theological impulses can be found and traced in the early forms, it may be possible to find a common denominator (as well as shifts in reasoning) among the later forms. Such theological impulses can help build a bridge towards understanding and interpreting the HT for today.

Chapter Three
The Relationship of Colossians
and Ephesians

Introduction

An investigation of the Ephesian HT cannot be engaged without careful attention being paid to its place within the development of the HT form.[1] A general consensus has emerged within NT scholarship, which views the Ephesian HT as dependent upon the older, Colossian *Vorlage*. This is also the opinion of our study. In spite of the general consensus, objections have been raised against this assumption, and will be treated in the first section of this chapter. It is our hope that this investigation will not only support our thesis, but will render useful solutions towards resolving the complex nature of the letters' relationship. After having established the likelihood of Colossian HT priority, our inquiry will consider the numerous innovations which the author of Ephesians has employed in his version of the HT. It is our hope that an analysis of the letters' respective HT forms will uncover a pattern of thoughtful adaptation of the Colossian original by the hand of the Ephesian redactor.

The remarkable amount of common material found in Colossians and Ephesians, as well as the identical order of appearance in the respective epistles, suggests some form of literary relationship between them.[2] This has given rise to a number of contrasting yet interrelated theories[3] touching upon the provenance, authorship and relative priority of the letters. As early as the 19th century, the priority of Colossians (and the literary dependence of Ephe-

---

[1] Though a number of studies make mention of the Col.-Eph. relationship, this particular aspect has been, as T. Moritz, *A Profound Mystery: The Use of the Old Testament in Ephesians*, eds. A.J. Malherbe and D.P. Mössner, Supplements to Novum Testamentum, vol. 85 (Leiden: E.J. Brill, 1996), 219, points out, "somewhat neglected."

[2] Mitton, *Epistle*, 12, finds the similarities "exceedingly close and curiously intricate." Figuring conservatively, he has found 25% of Ephesians to be taken from Colossians; this common material makes up 34% of the Colossian text.

[3] Ernst Percy, *Die Probleme der Kolosser- und Epheserbriefe* (Lund: C.W.K. Gleerup, 1946), and A.Van Roon, *The Authenticity of Ephesians*, ed. W.C. van Unnik, Supplements to Novum Testamentum, vol. 39 (Leiden: Brill, 1974). Both longer studies, they analyse the interrelated elements of authorship and priority, which Merklein, *Das Kirchliche Amt*, 35, characterises as "indissolubly bound together." For a good overview of more recent scholarship, see J.B. Polhill, "The Relationship between Ephesians and Colossians, " *Review and Expositor* 70 (1973): 439–50.

108

sians) had become an assumption among the majority of critical scholars,[4] as in our day.[5] In light of the general consensus among scholars, Best's recent criticism of this state of affairs is not exaggerated.[6] The majority opinion has placed Ephesians in dependent relationship to Colossians, and at the end of a (deutero) Pauline literary trajectory.[7] Determining whether the letters stand in some form of dependence is important to our study, particularly as we analyse the largest body of coincidental material, the HT. The following examination of recent objections to the majority view is not intended to dismiss the complexity of the Col.-Eph. redaction, but to offer possible solutions which highlight the author's redactional intentions, as well as suggesting the most probable scenario of dependence. C.L. Mitton's discussion represents the fullest modern expression of Col.-Eph. scheme of dependence, and comprises the following elements:

1. The priority of Col. is an almost universally accepted conclusion; previous attempts to argue Ephesian priority rely on a "very debatable hypothesis";[8]
2. The development in theology between the letters is best explained in terms of Eph. redaction;[9]
3. Ephesians evidences "improvements" over Colossians;[10]

---

[4] H.J. Holtzmann, *Kritik der Epheser- und Kolosserbriefe auf Grund einer Analyse ihres Verwandschaftsverhältnisses* (Leipzig: Wilhelm Engelmann, 1872), 32. Holtzmann notes that the dependence of Ephesians has been merely assumed; his study, in contrast, intends to take critical questions "aus der Sphäre des Behaupteten in diejenige des Bewiesenen."

[5] A sampling of scholars who defend Colossian priority: Dibelius, *Kolosser*, 57; Gnilka, *Epheserbrief*, 13; Schnackenburg, *Brief*, 27; Mußner, *Brief*, 18; Lincoln, *Ephesians*, l; Merklein, "Rezeption", 195 and "Paulinische Theologie", 27, where he notes that this position has become the *opinio communis* among exegetical scholars.

[6] A dissenting voice in similar vein to Holtzmann is Ernest Best, "Who Used Whom? The Relationship of Ephesians and Colossians," *NTS* 43 (1997): 72–96. He notes that Colossian priority has wrongly come to be an "accepted tenet" and "proven fact" among modern scholars.

[7] C.L. Mitton, *The Epistle to the Ephesians* (Oxford: Clarendon Press, 1951). Mitton's treatment of this position in *Epistle* has become a standard; A.T. Lincoln, *Ephesians*, ed. Ralph P. Martin, Word Biblical Commentary, vol. 42 (Dallas: Word Books, 1990), xxxv–lxxiii, represents a more recent expression of the position.

[8] Mitton, *Epistle*, 70. He notes that 11 of 12 dissenting scholars base their opinion on the assumption that Ephesians is the lost letter mentioned in Col. 4:16, τὴν ἐκ Λαοδικίας.

[9] Ibid., 71. Developments in the meaning of "church" or "the second coming of Christ" show later development in the thought of the author/redactor.

[10] Ibid., 71. The HT is expanded to address the first two relational pairs more fully; Col. 3:25 gives example of redaction: elements such as the severity of the instruction to the slaves

4. Ephesians generalises the particular concerns of Colossians;
5. Ephesians "conflates" passages from Colossians.

Mitton, primarily concerned with the question of authorship of Eph., rests his case for Col. priority with this observation: "Each of these five arguments could be enlarged, but fuller treatment seems unnecessary, since there is no champion who still cares to advocate the priority of Ephesians."[11] Mitton's observation describes scholarly opinion up to our day. There are, however, dissenting contemporary voices, which we will survey below.

The Current Discussion of Dependence

Merklein, a strong proponent of Ephesian dependence upon Colossians, admits that the majority position is not without some difficulties.[12] The complexity of the two letters' interrelatedness has given rise to alternative theories regarding the process of confluence and redaction. H.J. Holtzmann's detailed critical study of the relationship between the letters was the first modern attempt to challenge the consensus by highlighting several parallel passages, demonstrating, in many instances, that Colossians could possibly be seen as being dependent upon Ephesians. He postulated a complex Col.-Eph.-Col. redaction, which could explain the phenomenon he saw as "wechselseitige Abhängigkeit."[13] More recently, Best[14] and Muddiman[15] have reasserted Holtzmann's concern to consider alternate scenarios of the letters' relationship. Best develops this argument most fully, suggesting that the letters' common elements are the result of traditional materials available to a Pauline school. Discrete authors, working from a "Pauline pool", would have

---

is lessened, while the masters receive more specific instruction regarding impartiality. This represents editing of Col. 3:25 into Eph. 6:8–9. A case for the originality of the Eph. passages would be, then, an "extremely hard task."

[11] Ibid., 72.

[12] H. Merklein, "Eph 4,1–5,20 als Rezeption von Kol 3,1–17 (zugleich ein Beitrag zur Problematik des Epheserbriefes)," in *Kontinuität und Einheit* (FS F. Mußner), eds. P.-G. Müller and W. Stenger (Freiburg: Herder, 1981), 194–210. He characterises the relation of dependence as "äußerst komplex".

[13] Holtzmann, *Kritik*, 83. "Das doppelte schriftstellerische Verhältnis beider Briefe" is a result of the original and authentically Pauline Colossians undergoing a revision (interpolation) under the influence of the later, deutero-Pauline Ephesians. The passages treated by Holtzmann were: Eph. 1:4; 1:6–7; 3:3,5,9; 3:17–18; 4:16; 4:22–24 and 5:19.

[14] Best, "Relationship of Ephesians and Colossians," *NTS* 43 (1997): 72–96.

[15] J. Muddiman, *The Epistle to the Ephesians*, ed. M.D. Hooker, Black's New Testament Commentaries (London: Continuum, 2001).

had contact within this school, and perhaps at some points, collaboration.[16] This fluid contact, Best reasons, obscures the redactional relationship between the letters. As to the ultimate resolution of the nature of dependence, Best remains agnostic, however, allowing only a "slight probability" of Eph. priority.[17] Muddiman, though equally unconvinced of Holzmann's overall theory,[18] makes a case for a singular occurrence of a second, Eph.-Col. redaction, as well as presenting a problematic parallel, both of which will be treated below. A limited number of scholars, making use of brief arguments employed to illustrate Colossian priority, reach more positive conclusions concerning the literary relationship.[19] The matter of priority, we believe, merits consideration at this point, as it carries significant ramifications for the understanding of the Ephesian HT. The large amount of common parenetic material between the letters, particularly the HT, afford us opportunity for comparison at the redactional level. If the Eph. HT represents a reception and modification of the Col. original, the redaction implies some theological/ethical intention on the author's part; if a literary relationship cannot be established, then the particular features of the respective HT may be treated in nothing more than a comparative manner.

John Muddiman

Muddiman's analysis of the Col.-Eph. relationship, though brief, deserves attention at this point. He correctly observes that many of the verbal similarities between the letters are limited to "just a few words in otherwise differ-

---

[16] Best, "Relationship", 91. Best is cautious with his proofs, however; he insists that the authors drew from memory (no *Vorlage*), hymns, traditional materials and "normal epistolary formulae", showing randomness in their selection. Such traditional material, he rightly observes, cannot be used to argue priority. He admits, however, that "…most of the arguments [for Ephesian priority] can be turned the other way around."

[17] Ibid., 79. See also Van Roon, *Authenticity*, 430, fn. 2. Van Roon also argues for a Pauline school and the use of traditional materials, yet admits only a "feeble" argument for Ephesian priority. The Pauline school, however, worked primarily from a singular "blueprint" source.

[18] Muddiman, *Epistle*, 209.

[19] Most notably John Coutts, "The Relationship of Ephesians and Colossians," *NTS* 4 (1957–58): 201–207. He argues that the general nature of the epistle suggests an earlier use as a homily, from which Colossians was drawn; several words and phrases are given as examples of conflation from Ephesians; here he makes reverse use of Mitton's arguments. That Ephesians contains more material from earlier Pauline letters has been suggested by the majority of scholars to be a sign of compilation, and thus a later date; W. Munro, "Evidences," 434–47, however, cites earlier Pauline material to suggest a closer affinity with the letter, and thus Ephesian priority.

ently constructed sentences."[20] In spite of this, he concedes exact parallels between Col. 4:7–8 and Eph. 6:21–22, as well as the two parenetic "clusters," Col. 2:19/Eph. 4:15b–16 and Col. 3:16f./Eph. 5:18b–20. His listing is not intended to be exhaustive, yet the remarkable absence of the HT as a significant and extensive parallel illustrates the brevity of his analysis, which overlooks the centrality of the parenetic material (the HT representing not only the longest amount of parallel material, but displaying both preservation *and* significant extension) in the Eph. author's ethic. In spite of this critical omission, Muddiman offers two examples which support a possible later interpolation of Eph. material into Col., or, alternately, illustrate the ambiguous relationship of the cited parallels. The first example which he notes as a parallel which has been ignored in critical scholarship, "both because it occurs very late in Colossians and also because it is very problematic" [to the advocates of Col.-Eph. sequence of dependence].[21] The new parallel is Col. 3:12 and sections of Eph. 1:4, 6. The coincidental elements of the texts read as follows:

Col. 3:12: Ἐνδύσασθε οὖν, ὡς ἐκλεκτοὶ τοῦ θεοῦ ἅγιοι καὶ ἠγαπημένοι...and Eph. 1:4, 6, which contain similar ideas, if not vocabulary:

Eph. 1:4: καθὼς ἐξελέξατο ἡμᾶς ἐν αὐτῷ πρὸ καταβολῆς κόσμου εἶναι ἡμᾶς ἁγίους καὶ ἀμώμους κατενώπιον αὐτοῦ ἐν ἀγάπῃ, as well as this segment of Eph.:

Eph. 1:6: εἰς ἔπαινον δόξης τῆς χάριτος αὐτοῦ ἧς ἐχαρίτωσεν ἡμᾶς ἐν τῷ ἠγαπημένῳ.

Muddiman draws our attention to the common ideas within these two parallels, particularly the attributes given to the saints in Colossians: being *elect of God, holy* and *beloved*. He notes that similar modifiers are found in the Eph. passages, yet the final attribute, "beloved" refers to believers in Col. (ἠγαπημένοι) and to Christ in Eph. (τῷ ἠγαπημενῳ). This Eph. expression as a reference to Christ is unique to the NT, and deserves closer attention in an attempt to postulate its relation to Colossians. It must be noted, firstly, that the first parallel is only approximate, ἐκλεκτοὶ τοῦ θεοῦ and ἐξελέξατο

---

[20] Muddiman, *Epistle*, 8.

[21] Ibid., 9. Mitton, *Ephesians*, 281, had already noted the similarities, yet considered the parallel improbable.

112

conveying a similar idea of being chosen. Only ἅγιος remains consistent in terms of verbal agreement and referent. That this proposed parallel is problematic, Muddiman would agree. Having proposed this difficult parallel, he asks, "Is there any method in this alleged dependency? Is it psychologically credible?"[22] Considering the loose verbal agreement between the verses, the considerably divergent placement of the parallels within the respective letters, as well as the conflicting references to "beloved", it may be that Muddiman's observations reveal not a mismatched and confusing parallel, but no parallel at all. The challenge to this contention, of course, is to suggest a more tenable argument for explaining both alleged parallels independently.

It seems, first of all, that Col. 3:12, though certainly reflecting the theology of its own broader context,[23] has no direct redactional relationship to Eph. 1:4, 6. The phrase ὡς ἐκλεκτοὶ τοῦ θεοῦ ἅγιοι καὶ ἠγαπημένοι represents a unique and independent formulation[24] within the Col. parenetic section (Col. 3:5–17) which was not directly adapted by the author of Ephesians in this otherwise similar parallel passage (Eph. 4:17–5:20). The broader message of the Col. passage (putting on and putting off imagery), however, can be located within the corresponding parenetic section of the Ephesian letter.[25]

The formulations found in Eph. 1:4, 6 can be shown to be more than a contrived borrowing from the parenetic section of Colossians, reflecting a logical parallel found within the corresponding theological section in Col. The phrases found in Eph. 1:4, 6, we hope to show, are dependent upon the earlier Col. form, drawing from the Col. formulations as they appear, closely grouped in 1:13, 14, and subsequently in 1:22 (verses 15–18, the Christ Hymn, being omitted as such in the Eph. redaction). These three verses account for the Ephesian expression, demonstrating a close verbal connection, as well as an explanation for the Ephesian association of "beloved", not with believers, but with Christ. If we allow that the Ephesian verbal formulation

---

[22] Ibid., 9.

[23] Cf. Col. 3:10, ἐνδυσάμενοι; 1:2, 4, 12, 22 and 26 for examples of the usage of ἅγιος referring exclusively to believers; usage of ἀγάππη in 1:4, 8, 13; 2:2; 3:14; ἀγαπητός in 1:7; 4:7, 9, 14; whereas the verb ἀγαπάω finds expression only in the parenetic section in 3:12 and the HT in 3:19.

[24] The adjectives ἅγιοι καὶ ἠγαπημένοι can be found throughout the letter (cf. fn. 23). ἐκλεκτός, however, is found only here in Col. and is absent in Eph.; similar citations referring to believers can be found in Rom. 8:33, τίς ἐγκαλέσει κατὰ ἐκλεκτῶν θεοῦ; and 16:13, ἀσπάσασθε᾽ Ροῦφον τὸν ἐκλεκτὸν ἐν κυρίῳ and may indicate a stock phrase in Pauline usage.

[25] ἐνδύσασθε found in Col. 3:12 finds its counterpart in the same parenetic section of Ephesians, 4:24: ἐνδύσασθαι.

ἐξελέξατο to stand alone (it is unique to both letters),[26] we will need to illustrate how, if at all, the author of Ephesians came to his formulations in Eph. 1:4, 6, particularly the "holy" state of believers as well as the surprising relation of "the beloved" to Christ.

Eph. 1:4 ἁγίους as designation for believers. Parallels to this particular adjective can be found at several points in the letter to the Colossians, and taken in isolation, the comparisons would be misleading. Ἁγίους, however, finds itself embedded in a larger parallel, which is located in the theological section of Col., previously noted by Mitton:[27]

Colossians 1:22: νυνὶ δὲ ἀποκατήλλαξεν ἐν τῷ σώματι τῆς σαρκὸς αὐτοῦ διὰ τοῦ θανάτου παραστῆσαι ὑμᾶς **ἁγίους καὶ ἀμώμους** καὶ ἀνεγκλήτους **κατενώπιον αὐτοῦ**.

Ephesians 1:4: καθὼς ἐξελέξατο ἡμᾶς ἐν αὐτῷ πρὸ καταβολῆς κόσμου εἶναι **ἡμᾶς ἁγίους καὶ ἀμώμους κατενώπιον αὐτοῦ** ἐν ἀγάπῃ.

The theological significance of Col. 1:21–22, the shift of the believers' alienation to reconciliation with God, has not been overlooked by the author of Ephesians. The content is remarkably similar, though abbreviated (most notably the omission of the negative aspect, a characteristic of the Eph. author's redaction). It appears that Col. 1:22 offers a closer parallel, and a better explanation for the characteristic of holiness attributed to believers in Eph. 1:4.

Eph. 1:6: ἐν τῷ ἠγαπημένῳ. Muddiman's observation that this adjectival noun refers to Christ, and not believers, is correct. It can be said that nearly every reference to love in Col., whether in verbal, adjectival or noun form, pertains directly to believers, or their behaviour. Love is seen as being actively expressed on the human level, or acknowledged as a passive state, in which the believer is characterised as "beloved", the recipient of love from both God and other believers. To link these human references directly to Christ would represent a shift in the original intention of the Col. author. For this reason, Muddiman's connection of Col. 3:12 (or any number of other

---

[26] It could be argued that ἐξελέξατο expresses the sense of election in Col. 1:12,13: εὐχαριστοῦντες **τῷ πατρὶ τῷ ἱκανώσαντι** ὑμᾶς εἰς τὴν **μερίδα τοῦ κλήρου** τῶν ἁγίων ἐν τῷ φωτί: **ὃς ἐρρύσατο** ἡμᾶς ἐκ τῆς ἐξουσίας τοῦ σκότους καὶ **μετέστησεν** εἰς τὴν βασιλείαν τοῦ υἱοῦ τῆς ἀγάπης αὐτου.

[27] Mitton, *Ephesians*, 281.

instances where believers are meant) with Eph. 1:6 is mistaken. There is, however a singular exception in the Col. author's employment of love as a regulating/descriptive element of human relations. This can be found in Col. 1:13: ὃς ἐρρύσατο ἡμᾶς ἐκ τῆς ἐξουσίας τοῦ σκότους καὶ μετέστησεν εἰς τὴν βασιλείαν τοῦ υἱοῦ τῆς ἀγάπης αὐτοῦ. Here we find clear reference to the comprehensive work of salvation, which includes transfer into the kingdom of the Son, who is, in this unique formulation, described as "beloved". It is possible that the author of Eph. has taken both elements of this pivotal verse, and reformulated them in the corresponding theological section of Eph. 1:5–6.[28] This transfer in Col. 1:13 loses its negative element ἐκ τῆς ἐξουσίας τοῦ σκότους (typical of the author of Eph.), yet the aspect of being placed into (εἰς) the kingdom of the Son μετέστησεν εἰς τὴν βασιλείαν τοῦ υἱοῦ τῆς ἀγάπης αὐτοῦ is transformed by the author of Eph. By accentuating the purposes of God,[29] the author of Eph. depicts the transfer in terms of its result, a relationship characterised as being destined unto (εἰς) sonship. The notion of sonship is unique here, and has likely been influenced by the Col. formulation βασιλείαν τοῦ υἱοῦ, Eph. 1:5: προορίσας ἡμᾶς εἰς υἱοθεσίαν διὰ Ἰησοῦ Χριστοῦ εἰς αὐτόν, κατὰ τὴν εὐδοκίαν τοῦ θελήματος αὐτοῦ. The elements of transfer into, and belonging to, the Son's kingdom are retained and reformulated in positive, static terms in Eph. 1:5. The following verse, 1:6, though primarily a new formulation, gives expression to the unique phrase in Col. 1:13, τοῦ υἱοῦ τῆς ἀγάπης αὐτου, Eph. 1:6: εἰς ἔπαινον δόξης τῆς χάριτος αὐτοῦ ἧς ἐχαρίτωσεν ἡμᾶς ἐν τῷ ἠγαπημένῳ. This, it should be noted, is the only occurrence in Eph. where Christ/God is the recipient of love, making the coincidental appearance of this phenomenon in both letters highly unlikely. The Eph. formulation represents a change from the Col. original; however this corresponds to the tendency of the author's style.[30]

In conclusion, the formulations found in Eph. 1:4, 6 can be explained in terms of dependence upon the Col. original, taken and transformed from the

---

[28] Placing Col. 1:13 and Eph. 1:5–6 in parallel relationship. Eph. 1:7, it might be added, forms a close parallel to Col. 1:14, suggesting that the immediately preceding material may have been drawn in sequence, as we have argued.

[29] θέλημα occurs seven times in Ephesians, over against three in Col.; only 2:3 refers to human will. The word features prominently in this section (1:5, 9, 11), and represents a significant expansion and development of its usage in Col. 1:9 from being an object to be grasped to its representation in Eph. as a determining force in the execution of the believer's salvation.

[30] Both the authors of Col. and Eph. tend to employ ἐν+ dative to qualify a state of being or behaviour; Eph. extends this usage considerably, particularly in direct reference to God or Christ (34 instances against 19 in Col.).

corresponding theological sections. Muddiman's proposed parallel with Col. 3:12, an attempt to display the arbitrary nature of the Col.-Eph. redactional relationship, should be dismissed in terms of its unconvincing features as a parallel, making way for more tenable solutions.

Muddiman's next evidence against a Col.-Eph. redaction lies in his analysis of the parallel found in Col. 2:19 and Eph. 4:15b–16, notably the only parallel which he admits as conclusive.[31] Several features of the Col. parallel, including style, grammar and vocabulary, suggest a later interpolation of the Eph. material into the Col. text. The parallel texts are as follows:

Col. 2:19: καὶ οὐ κρατῶν τὴν κεφαλήν, ἐξ οὗ πᾶν τὸ σῶμα διὰ τῶν ἁφῶν καὶ συνδέσμων ἐπιχορηγούμενον καὶ συμβιβαζόμενον αὔξει τὴν αὔξησιν τοῦ θεοῦ.

Eph. 4:15–16: ἀληθεύοντες δὲ ἐν ἀγάπῃ αὐξήσωμεν εἰς αὐτὸν τὰ πάντα, ὅς ἐστιν ἡ κεφαλή, Χριστός, ἐξ οὗ πᾶν τὸ σῶμα συναρμολογούμενον καὶ συμβιβαζόμενον διὰ πάσης ἁφῆς τῆς ἐπιχορηγίας κατ᾽ ἐνέργειαν ἐν μέτρῳ ἑνὸς ἑκάστου μέρους τὴν αὔξησιν τοῦ σώματος ποιεῖται εἰς οἰκοδομὴν ἑαυτοῦ ἐν ἀγάπῃ.

Muddiman notes, firstly, the lack of gender agreement in the Colossian formulation, τὴν κεφαλήν, ἐξ οὗ, due to the lack of a masculine referent. He correctly observes that the Ephesian formulation, in contrast, shows agreement with its antecedent, Christ, ὅς ἐστιν ἡ κεφαλή, Χριστός, ἐξ οὗ, making clear grammatical sense. The author of Col., he reasons, has clumsily adapted the familiar Eph. passage, his subsequent interpolation omitting the clear masculine referent found in the original. Grammatical dissonance is thereby created in his positioning of κεφαλή in close relationship to the masculine pronoun. Several observations are necessary here. The masculine referent in Col. is given in the context of the passage, and would have been understood by the hearers as intimating Christ. In his larger discourse, the author of Col. has represented Christ as the universal head, encompassing both the church (1:18, αὐτός ἐστιν ἡ κεφαλὴ τοῦ σώματος τῆς ἐκκλησίας), as well as the powers and authorities (2:10, ὅς ἐστιν ἡ κεφαλὴ πάσης ἀρχῆς καὶ ἐξουσίας). This unique appellation is particularly important in the author's attempt to display Christ as pre-eminent (1:18). It is especially true of the immediate context of 2:19, where the author exposes elements of the false teaching which had gained a hearing in Col. Against such

[31] Muddiman, *Epistle*, 209.

116

shadowy claims Christ is depicted as substance, 2:17: ἅ ἐστιν σκιὰ τῶν μελλόντων, τὸ δὲ σῶμα τοῦ Χριστοῦ. The author of Col., still arguing for Christ's pre-eminence as the source of growth in the body in 2:19, would rely on the previous context (in which Christ figures as the ultimate authority) for his masculine antecedent. Having established a contrast between the claims and troubling practices of the Col. innovators and Christ, it is clear, then, that those who are boasting in their esoteric experiences, μηδεὶς ὑμᾶς καταβραβευέτω θέλων ἐν ταπεινοφροσύνῃ καὶ θρησκείᾳ τῶν ἀγγέλων, ἃ ἑόρακεν ἐμβατεύων, εἰκῇ φυσιούμενος ὑπὸ τοῦ νοὸς τῆς σαρκὸς αὐτοῦ (v.18), are not holding to the head, namely Christ. 2:19 shows little sign, then, of being an interpolation, as the elements of the verse continue the thought of v. 18, promote the pre-eminence of Christ, and signal continuity with the explicit use of κεφαλή, the contextual marker for Christ.

Muddiman, discussing the content of the parallel, notes that the "context of Colossians fails to explain the emphasis on the church's growth", whereas this is a central theme in Ephesians. The verse is "at home" in Ephesians, but represents an "intrusion" in the Col. context.[32] His observation in respect to Eph. is correct, where the church is indeed depicted as being built up through the ministries and spiritual gifts, moving towards maturity (contrasting εἰς ἄνδρα τέλιον and νήπιοι), a mutual "growing" (αὐξήσωμεν) into Christ the head (Eph. 4:11–15). This might be expected, as the author of Ephesians develops his theology and ethics in more explicit terms of the church.[33] Growth, however, relating to the believer and the life of faith, can be shown to represent a comparably important theme in Colossians. A listing of mutual occurrences, at several points actually expanded in Col., shows this clearly:

(i.) αὐξάνω
The verb "to grow" figures prominently in both letters, and is related in Eph. 2:21 and 4:15 to the corporate church and individuals respectively; the use in Colossians, *three* occurrences, 1:6, 1:10 and 2:19 (as well as the noun form here) relates to the faith of the individual in terms of God. Though slightly different in emphasis, the concept of growth is present in Colossians.

---

[32] Ibid., 208. Both letters reveal an interest in growth imagery, perhaps related to early teaching derived from the remarkably similar vocabulary of the sower parable found in the synoptics (ῥίξα, καρπός, αὐξάνω, καρποφορέω, μυστήριον) in Mk. 4, Mt. 13 and Luke 8.

[33] The listing of offices and gifts employed in the church (2:19–20, 4:11), its unique placement as the mediator of God's plan (3:9–10), as well as the larger number of references to the church (primarily in the expanded HT), point to this development.

(*ii.*) ῥιζόω

Both letters have a single occurrence of the admonition to be "rooted" (ἐρριζωμένοι), a part of the growth imagery of the letters found in Eph. 3:17 and Col. 2:7. The Eph. reference relates to the more general concept of love (modified by the phrase ἐν ἀγάπῃ); the Col. citation is connected to Christ, in whom the believer is to be rooted and built up, ἐρριζωμένοι καὶ ἐποικοδομούμενοι ἐν αὐτῷ.

(*iii.*) ἐποικοδομέω

"Being built up" is also equally represented in the letters in Eph. 2:20 and Col. 2:7. The Ephesian reference, however, refers to the placement of believers into the household of God, built upon the foundation of the apostles and prophets, whereas the Col. reference is again related directly to Christ and faith.

(*iv.*) συμβιβάζω

To be "knit" or "joined together" is found once in Eph. at 4:16; it refers to the body of Christ as it is being joined in love. Col. shows *two* occurrences, 2:2 and 2:19. 2:2 refers to the hearts of individual believers being knit together, whereas 2:19, though similar to Eph., associates the joining of the body directly with God's activity. Beyond these *common* verbal forms which express growth in both letters, Col. employs two verbs which extend its growth metaphor: βεβαιόω, "to establish, make firm" is linked to faith in v. 2:7, accentuating the idea of being established in the faith: ἐρριζωμένοι καὶ ἐποικοδομούμενοι ἐν αὐτῷ καὶ βεβαιούμενοι τῇ πίστει. Even more significantly, καρποφορέω, "to bear fruit", finds expression at two points (in notable conjunction with αὐξάνω), Col. 1:6, 10, both references speaking of the believers' life in faith as it bears good works in the Gospel. Though the Col. references to growth apply primarily to the life of the members as they live out the Gospel in faith, and differ in this to their Eph. counterparts, they represent a significant emphasis of the author, so that the growth vocabulary found in Col. 2:19 cannot be construed as an "intrusion" into the text.

In spite of Muddiman's acute observations, it is more likely that the longer (and smoother) reading of the Ephesian parallel represents an expansion (the *nature* of the growth within the body is explicated) and clarification (making express reference to Christ, which is a particular feature of the Eph. redaction) upon the earlier Col. form.[34] It is also more general in its formulation, representing an adaptation of the particular (and deleted) concerns of the Col. author. It is difficult to imagine how this longer, more generally formulated reading, which clarifies and expands the material in Col., would have been adapted in such a defective manner at this point in the Col. letter.

Ernest Best

E. Best has also given recent treatment to the question of Col.-Eph. dependence. His more thorough analysis, which includes reference to the HT material, draws the reader's attention to the traditional nature of a number of passages which reveal remarkable similarities in their phraseology.[35] The parallel passages, he reasons, share a common traditional source, and cannot be employed as an indication of dependence in either direction. This observation is correct insofar as we are able to discern a common formulation, or suggest the original *Sitz im Leben* of the passages at hand.[36] Best's extensive list offers a number of genuine possibilities for understanding a third, traditional and *independent* reservoir of traditions, which might explain a number

---

[34] Muddiman, *Epistle*, 209, notes that the Col. formulation αὔξει τὴν αὔξησιν τοῦ θεοῦ does not fit the passage, being "abrupt" and "elliptical". He observes that the meaning is not clear, stating, "God after all does not grow!" The unusual formulation, perhaps needing explication, is no proof of dependence, however (cf. just two of the unique, yet notably undefined NT formulations in Eph.: 4:18, ζωῆς τοῦ θεου; and particularly 3:19, which is equally elliptical and in need of clarification: ἵνα πληρωθῆτε εἰς πᾶν τὸ πλήρωμα τοῦ θεου); if, as he observes, the Eph. letter explicates this formulation, it might be argued that the author of Eph. has intentionally expanded and clarified this concept by means of his ecclesiological emphasis.

[35] The parallel passages are treated in the following order, with Best's proposed designation immediately after: Eph. 1:10/Col. 1:16, 20; hymn; Eph. 5:3,5/Col. 3:5; vice list; Eph. 1:1–2/Col. 1:1–2; epistolary formula; Eph. 1:17/Col. 1:3; liturgy; *HT material designated as traditional*; Eph. 5:19–20/Co. 3:16–17; common patterns of worship; Eph. 5:6/Col. 3:6; universal NT concept; Eph. 5:15–16/Col. 4:6; common phrase; Eph. 4:22–24/Col. 3:8–12; catechetical instruction; Eph. 4:15b–16/Col. 2:19; common image within Pauline school; Eph. 4:2/Col. 3:12–13; pre-existing list; Eph. 1:4/Col. 1:22; phrase of Pauline school; Eph. 1:7/Col. 1:14, 22; church tradition; Eph. 1:8b, 9a/Col. 3:16; 1:27; OT; Eph. 1:17–17/Col. 1:4, 9, 3, 10; Pauline phrase; Eph. 1:15/Col. 1:4; Pauline phrase; Eph. 1:18/Col. 1:27; Pauline phrase; Eph. 1:20/Col. 2:12; 3:1; common NT theme; Eph. 1:22/Col. 1:17–19, 24; hymn; Eph. 2:1/Col. 2:13a; traditional couplet; Eph. 2:16/Col. 1:20–22; traditional hymn.

[36] Mitton, *Epistle*, 58, concedes this point for clearly identifiable formulae; Best follows Greeven's observation, Dibelius, *Kolosser*, 113, that "Col und Eph nicht unmittelbar voneinander, sondern beide von einer Tradition bestimmt sind."

of common passages proposed by Mitton in his extensive treatment of the Col.-Eph. relationship. A limited number of parallels could, then, be dismissed in this manner as coincidental, traditional usage. It is the sheer number and disparate nature of these potentially traditional passages, however, which diminishes the force of Best's argument. The unusually high number and diversity of the parallels suggest a dependent relationship between the letters. If every instance of an independent source suggested by Best were allowed as an explanation of the relationship between the letters, including the coincidental ordering of the traditional material along theological and parenetic lines, the parallels would be a remarkable coincidence, indeed. Best is aware that the letters reflect an alignment of their theological and parenetic sections. In spite of this, he dismisses Merklein's observation that the placement of the HT within the respective letters cannot be attributed to traditional borrowing, but reveals a reception of both content and order.[37] Although Best notes both similarities and unique features within the parenetic section, these fail to lessen the significance of Merklein's contention. The appeal to traditional material alone cannot account for the sheer amount or orderly coincidence of material found between the letters.

Best does not rely on a sole appeal to traditional material, however, to argue his point. He briefly examines the relationship between several of the common texts he lists, citing the arguments from both Mitton and Holtzmann, and pronouncing them inconclusive. The inconclusive nature of their relative dependence is taken as an indication of a third, independent source. The HT material of the two letters forms no exception. Best postulates a traditional, Christianised version of the HT, which served as a foundation for the known HT forms as found in Col. and Eph. The authors of our HT knew this form, and borrowed particular stock phrases, albeit from memory. He does not attempt to account for the remarkable (and from memory alone improbable) agreement in argumentation, structure and verbal coincidence. As a test case, Best analyses the passages regarding the third relational pair, slaves and masters, to illustrate the arbitrary relationship evidenced by unique aspects of the HT forms. This relational pair, expanded in its Col. form, offers a larger amount of coincidental material, and as we shall see, a number of important differences. It should be noted at this point that Best represents the only treatment of the HT material which questions the Col.-Eph. redactional sequence. Again, Best suggests that the variations are due to

---

[37] Merklein, "Rezeption", 195. He assumes Eph. dependence, yet shows convincingly how the material preceding the HT reveals a reception of Col., including the ordering of the parenetic section.

an independent source, which has been appropriated according to the interests of the respective authors. A closer examination of his evidences may prove helpful in ascertaining the pattern of dependence (if at all), or whether the HT stand in a "purely random" relationship.[38]

Any comparison of the two HT forms will show that the Eph. HT has expanded the material considerably in the first two relational pairs, creating a broader Christian argument for the desired behaviour. The third pair, slave-master, demonstrates the *least* amount of additional material, but shows innovation nonetheless. Best takes note of this particular aspect, first of all, ascribing to the Eph. HT a "greater Christian context".[39] This is seen in the addition of the motivation to the slaves in 6:5, Οἱ δοῦλοι, ὑπακούετε τοῖς κατὰ σάρκα κυρίοις μετὰ φόβου καὶ τρόμου ἐν ἁπλότητι τῆς καρδίας ὑμῶν ὡς τῷ Χριστῷ, particularly the phrase ὡς τῷ Χριστῷ. This singular citation of the Eph. author's christianising of the HT ethic (we hope to cite more below) is inconclusive for determining dependence, however, for as Best indicates, the Col. HT can be shown to extend the Christian context of the Eph. HT, as well. The instance is found in Col. 3:22, Οἱ δοῦλοι, ὑπακούετε κατὰ πάντα τοῖς κατὰ σάρκα κυρίοις, μὴ ἐν ὀφθαλμοδουλίᾳ ὡς ἀνθρωπάρεσκοι, ἀλλ᾽ ἐν ἁπλότητι καρδίας φοβούμενοι τὸν κύριον, where he suggests that the author "relates the slave's fear to the Lord and not the owner."[40] This observation deserves special attention. First of all, Best is correct in locating the Col. HT motivation as divine, and *directly* related to the slaves, all their duties of obedience being executed while "fearing the Lord". This element of Col., so Best, though not fully lost in Eph., is located solely upon the human level of motivation, being directed in 6:5 towards the masters, as indicated in the phrase "with fear and trembling". The phrase μετὰ φόβου καὶ τρόμου, however, is not a random alteration drawn from an independent source,[41] but rather replaces the intention of the present participle φοβούμενοι found in Col. (which here likewise modifies the imperative ὑπακούετε) with a stereotyped word pair. Not only does this use of word pairs (stereotyped, synonymous and simple) fit the style of the author of Eph.,[42] it introduces a thoroughly divine aspect to the Eph. motivation as

---

[38] Best, "Relationship", 81.

[39] Ibid., 80.

[40] Ibid., 80.

[41] Though this phrase can be found in 1 Cor. 2:3, 2 Cor. 7:15 and Phil. 2:12 (occurrences which may have influenced the author), the impulse for choosing the expression lies in within the original Col. text.

[42] Dibelius, *Kolosser*, 84, points out a characteristic of the Eph. author's style as the "Häufung synonymer Ausdrücke." These are typically found in noun/verbal pairs and triplets,

found in the OT. The familiarity of the OT phrase, as well as its referring exclusively to fear towards God, makes it highly unlikely that this usage by the author of Eph. would indicate a mere human level of motivation. The element of fear and trembling (similarly φοβούμενοι in Col.) modifies the slaves' obedience, and is ultimately limited by, and subject to, the final modifying phrase ὡς τῷ Χριστῷ. The realm of obedience is indeed human; the motivation, however, is towards Christ. To this it might be added that the author of Eph. has already indicated in Eph. 5:21 that the motivation of fear is to be understood as regulating *all* relations in terms of Christ. The Eph. HT, though evidencing clear differences in vocabulary, cannot be shown to promote a less christianised ethic than its Col. counterpart. The notable differences, furthermore, do not indicate an independent source, but show a tendency to retain the fullness and logic of the Col. argument, albeit in the distinctive style of the Eph. author.

In similar manner, Best maintains that certain significant phrases found in the Col. HT are lost, noting the absence of the important and unique phrase in Col. 3:24, τῷ κυρίῳ Χριστῷ δουλεύετε. At first glance, this appears to be true. Upon closer inspection of the Eph. HT, however, we dis-

---

adjectivally joined synonyms, or among the many (95 within 115 verses!) genitive constructions. The HT shows several examples of word pairs: 5:27a, σπίλον ἢ ῥυτίδα; 5:27b, ἁγία καὶ ἄμωμος; 5:29b, ἐκτρέφει καὶ θάλπει; 6:4b, παιδείᾳ καὶ νουθεσίᾳ; 6:5, φόβου καὶ τρόμου. The broader letter reveals this as an element of the author's style: 1:4, ἅγίος καὶ ἀμώμους; 1:5, τὴν εὐδικίαν τοῦ θελήματος; 1:8b, ἐν πάσῃ σοφίᾳ καὶ φρονήσει; 1:11a, προορισθέντες κατὰ πρόθεσιν; 1:11b, κατὰ τὴν βουλήν τοῦ θελήματος; 1:6, 12, 14, ἔπαινον (τῆς) δόξης; 1:14, ἀρραβὼν τῆς κληρονομίας...ἀπολύτπωσιν τῆς περιποιήσεως; 1:19 (6:10), τοῦ κράτους τῆς ἰσχύος; 1:23 (3:19), πλήρωμα...πληρουμένου; 2:2, αἰῶνα τοῦ κόσμου; 2:2b, ἄρχοντα τῆς ἐξουσίας; 2:3, τά θελήματα τῆς σαρκὸς καὶ τῶν διανοιῶν; ἐν ταῖς ἐπιθυμίαις τῆς σαρκός; 2:14, μεσότοιχον τοῦ φραγμοῦ; 2:15, νόμον τῶν ἐντολῶν ἐν δόγμασιν; 2:19, ξένοι καὶ πάροικοι; 2:20 (3:5), ἀπολτόλων καὶ προφητῶν; 3:6, συγκληρονόμα καὶ σύσσωμα καὶ συμμέτοχα; 3:7, δωρεὰν τῆς χάριτος; 3:7 (3:20), ἐνέργειαν τῆς δυνάμεως; 3:9, τοῦ μυστηρίου τοῦ ἀποκεκρυμμένου; 3:10, ταῖς ἀρχαῖς καὶ ταῖς ἐξουσίναις; 3:12, παρρησίαν καὶ προσαγωγήν; 3:15 (1:10), ἐν οὐρανοῖς καὶ ἐπὶ γῆς; 3:17, ἐρριζωμένοι καὶ τεθεμελιωμένοι; 3:20, ὑπὲρ πάντα ποιῆσαι ὑπερεκπερισσοῦ; αἰτούμεθα ἢ νοοῦμεν; 3:21, εἰς πάσας τὰς γενεὰς τοῦ αἰῶνος τῶν αἰώνων; 4:1(4:4), κλήσεως ἧς ἐκλήθητε; 4:2, ταπεινοφροσύνης καὶ πραΰτητος; 4:14, κλυδωνιζόμενοι καὶ περιφερόμενοι; κυβείᾳ...πανουργίᾳ...μεθοδείαν; 4:16, συναρμολογούμενον καὶ συμβιβαζόμενον; τὴν αὔξησιν...οἰκοδομήν; 4:23, πνεύματι τοῦ νοός; 4:24, ἐν δικαιοσύνῃ καὶ ὁσιότητι; 4:31, πικρία καὶ θυμὸς καὶ ὀργὴ; 5:2, προσφορὰν καὶ θυσίαν; 5:3, πορνεία δὲ καὶ ἀκαθαρσία; 5:4, μωρολογία ἢ εὐτραπελία; 5:9, ἀγαθωσύνη καὶ δικαιοσύνη; 5:19, ψαλμοῖς καὶ ὕμνοις καὶ ᾠδαῖς πνευματικαῖς; ᾄδοντες καὶ ψάλλοντες; 6:12, αἷμα καὶ σάρκα; τὰς ἀρχάς...τὰς ἐξουσίας; 6:18, προσευχῆς καὶ δεήσεως; 6:21, ἀδελφὸς καὶ...διάκονος.

cover that the elements of this phrase are actually preserved and enhanced by the author of Ephesians. Eph. 6:6 incorporates both elements of the Colossian command to the slaves by denoting them as servants of Christ, making use of the title: ὡς δοῦλοι Χριστοῦ ποιοῦντες τὸ θέλημα τοῦ θεοῦ. The idea is further developed in 6:7, where the nature of the slaves' obedience (the Col. command) is expressed in terms of service: μετ' εὐνοίας δουλεύοντες ὡς τῷ κυρίῳ καὶ οὐκ ἀνθρώποις. The author of Ephesians has replaced the singular verb form of Col. (δουλεύετε) with noun and participle forms of the verbal command, as well as representing both titles, Christ and Lord. This, joined with the Eph. author's emphasis upon the will of God, combines the impulses of both authors. Here we see expansion, rather than a deletion of the Col. HT message.

Best further observes that many of the phrases shared between the two HT forms have been moved about, such variations intimating a third source from which the authors randomly borrowed. His first example is the most significant, for it implies much more than a slight shift in location within a closed argument, indeed a change in the implications of the argument itself. προσωπολημψία, he notes, has been moved from its original position in Col. 3:25 to the final sentence of the Eph. HT, 6:9. This in itself would not be particularly remarkable, except that it appears that this piece of instruction, originally directed towards the slaves (Col. 3:25) has now been applied to the masters in Eph. 6:9. His observation, however, does not allow for the transitional and bilateral regulatory function of Col. 3:25, which we discussed at length above. The verse regulates *both* sections of the slave-master relationship as found in Col.; the author of Eph. has simply applied the principle of impartial judgement to the masters in this case. This complies with the tendency of the author of Eph. to further mediate the slave-master relation in terms of Christ, creating a more pronounced Christian ethic.[43] Other examples which Best enumerates refer to movement of particular phrases within a closed thought. These examples show nothing more than the author's crea-

---

[43] Best, "Relationship", 81, admits that the Eph. HT "sets slaves and masters more firmly on the same plane before God than does Colossians." This can be further seen in the deletion of the Col. slave's duties κατὰ πάντα, as well as in the startling expansion in the instruction to the slaves, which frames the warning found in 6:8 in more specific, inclusive terms: τοῦτο κομίσεται παρὰ κυρίου εἴτε δοῦλος εἴτε ἐλεύθερος. Finally, the instruction to the masters begins with a reciprocal command in 6:9a, which extends the previous material to them: τὰ αὐτὰ ποιεῖτε πρὸς αὐτούς. The author of Eph. transforms the Col. HT by mediating its commands, introducing reciprocal responsibilities, and making the ethic of just recompense (Col. 3:25) explicitly bilateral.

tive hand in crafting his argument, and cannot be employed to suggest an independent source.[44]

Best also notes incidences where words are employed in a differing manner in each HT. Although this might be expected as a result of the editorial process, Best again sees these variations as an indication of an independent source. κομίσεται, he points out, refers to punishment in Col. 3:25, but to reward in Eph. 6:8. Here both examples given by Best may be joined, as their emphases (Eph. good-reward; Col. injustice-punishment) correspond. Logically, the context would allow for either emphasis, yet he is correct in noting this significant difference. Later in his article, he cites the same pair of verses as evidencing another significant change: the Col. passage forbids wrongdoing (ὁ ἀδικῶν), whereas the Eph. author stresses doing good (ἕκαστος ἐάν τι ποιήσῃ ἀγαθόν). These examples, we would suggest, are not the result of an independent literary source, but of conscious editorial activity. The author of Eph. tends to express his ethic in positive terms.[45] Another example of change which Best cites is κληρονομία, found in the Col. HT in 3:24, but finding no expression in the Eph. HT whatsoever. This appears unusual, since it is used elsewhere by the author of Eph. in 1:14, 18 and 5:5. The absence of κληρονομία in the Eph. HT, however, cannot rule out a direct relationship between the letters. The singular and significant occurrence of this word in Col. within the expanded and christianised slave-master relationship of the HT may have influenced the author of Eph. to incorporate the term into both the theological and parenetic sections at the three points mentioned; the command to the slaves in Colossians is, further, reflected in Eph. 6:8, εἰδότες ὅτι ἕκαστος ἐάν τι ποιήσῃ ἀγαθόν, τοῦτο κομίσεται παρὰ κυρίου εἴτε δοῦλος εἴτε ἐλεύθερος, being expanded in explicit terms of who shall receive the recompense (slave and free), yet compressed in terms of this particular expression (reward being implied by τοῦτο, whose antecedent in 6:8a is ἀγαθόν). It is noteworthy that the author of Eph. emphasises

---

[44] The following changes, noted by Best, imply only editorial freedom: the reversal of ἐν ἁπλότητι καρδίας and ὀφθαλμοδουλία; the reference to fear moves its relative position.

[45] This can be seen, of course, in these two instances in Col. 3:25 and Eph. 6:8. Further examples are found in the deletion of the negative command to the husbands in Col. 3:19b, which is substituted with the positive admonitions of loving as Christ in Eph. 5:25–26; children are given positive instruction in Eph. in the form of a scriptural promise, which extends the motivation far beyond that found in Col.; fathers in both Col. and Eph. are instructed not to provoke their children; the Col. motivation is negative, ἵνα μὴ ἀθυμῶσιν; the Eph. motivation substitutes a further, positive admonition: ἀλλὰ ἐκτρέφετε αὐτὰ ἐν παιδείᾳ καὶ νουθεσίᾳ κυρίου; in keeping with the shift mentioned above, the instruction to the slaves in Eph. adds positive elements to the otherwise negative formulations found in both texts, θέλημα τοῦ θεοῦ/μετ᾽ εὐνοίας/ἀγαθόν.

both positive intention (μετ᾽ εὐνοίας δουλεύοντες, 6:7a) and behaviour (ποιήσῃ ἀγαθόν/ποιοῦντες τὸ θέλημα τοῦ θεοῦ) of the slave in this section. It is this *positive* behaviour which is linked to the received recompense (τοῦτο). The omission of κληρονομία indicates the editorial activity of the author of Eph., who has expanded the influence of the original slave instruction of Col. 3:24 to both parties, while retaining the sense of reward through his emphasis on correct behaviour and corresponding recompense.

Other differences in the HT form noted by Best include the Eph. author's phrase ποιοῦντες τὸ θέλημα... in 6:6, which he notes "is simpler than the corresponding phrase in Col. 3:23." This phrase is actually an addition to the HT material,[46] and cannot be construed as a simplification of Col. 3:23, whose elements are adopted into the Eph. HT.[47]

Though Best has noted a number of unique characteristics of the HT forms in Col. and Eph., his examples fail to indicate how a third, independent source might lie behind these various additions, slight changes in order, and omissions. From such a variety of alterations it becomes practically impossible to construe an earlier christianised form of the HT from which both Col. and Eph. might have been drawn. Without a clear indication of how this might have occurred, and from what original constructions, Best's theory remains rather speculative. The agnostic nature of his thesis, though effectively defusing the dependence question, proposes no *necessary* conclusions, nor does it adequately account for the remarkable similarities of the HT material in terms of order, verbal agreement or development. For this reason, arguments tendered for the priority of Colossians (regardless of the authorship issue) appear to us to provide the least complicated scenario of redaction, while offering cogent explanations for similarities and variations found in both letters. Mitton's thorough analysis of the literary relationship, though not in all points incontrovertible, remains convincing in terms of sheer evidence (particularly his observations regarding conflation and tenability). More important for our study is to determine how, and at which points, Ephesians and Colossians coincide or diverge in their theological and pare-

---

[46] τὸ θέλημα θεοῦ and its derivatives are found seven times in Eph., an expansion over the three instances found in Col. 1:1, 9 and 4:12. In Col. all instances refer to the will of God in an abstract, statal, determinative sense; Eph. carries this meaning in 1:1, 5, 9, 11, but is more direct in applying the known will of God to ethical behaviour in 2:3 (corrupt human desire), 5:17 (knowing the will of God in combination with wise behaviour) and 6:6 (*doing* the will of God).

[47] Only the command ἐργάζεσθε has been replaced by the participle δουλεύοντες, perhaps as a displacement of this verb form in 3:23 in favour of the unique command to serve Christ (τῷ κυρίῳ Χριστῷ δουλεύετε) in Col. 3:24.

netic concerns, and, of course, to trace, at a later point, the unique theological impulses found in Ephesians.[48] Regarding the individual characteristics of the two letters (and their parenesis) there is remarkable agreement among commentators: there is no slavish imitation in either style or theology between them.[49] We hope that a close examination of this relationship will reveal the "particular goals" of the writer of Ephesians, while noting any "shift in perspective" which might influence its theology or parenesis.[50] Here we would agree with Merklein that Eph. represents not a copy, but a "Rezeption" of the Colossian material, encompassing "Interpretation, Innovation und Transformation", particularly in its parenesis.[51] Gese sums up well:

> Viel wesentlicher als die Entscheidung dieser Alternative [priority-dependence] ist jedoch die Beobachtung, daß mit der Rezeption des Kolosserbriefes im Epheserbrief zugleich eine theologische Weiterentwicklung einhergeht. Es zeigt sich nämlich, daß die aus dem Kolosserbrief übernommenen Wendungen nicht einfach nur wiederholt, sondern zugleich charakteristisch umgeformt werden.[52]

HT Comparison

The HT, representing the longest parallel between the letters, also incorporates the most extensive level of change, illustrating Gese's observation.[53]

---

[48] Dibelius, *Kolosser*, 84, suggests analysis which combines attention to common *termini* and *schema*, yet takes particular note of the differences, as well.

[49] Van Roon, *Authenticity*, 432, concludes that although the letters have a common source, "each has its own character." Schnackenburg, *Brief*, 28, insists that Eph. must not be seen only in the "wake" of Col., and Lincoln, *Ephesians*, lv, characterises the literary dependence as "free and creative."

[50] J. Gnilka, *Der Epheserbrief*, eds. A. Vögtle, R. Schnackenburg and A. Wikenhauser, Herders Theologischer Kommentar zum Neuen Testament, vol. 10 (Freiburg: Herder, 1971), 13. He warns that statistical analysis alone can lead to false conclusions re. the message of Ephesians; though Col. was used as a *Vorlage*, the author has "eigene Ziele." Schnackenburg, *Brief*, 28, cites several unique concerns of Eph., which he aptly terms *Blickverschiebung*.

[51] Merklein, "Rezeption", 196, points out that the process of "Rezeption", which involves significant transformation, can be seen especially clearly in the HT.

[52] M. Gese, *Das Vermächtnis des Apostels: Die Rezeption der paulinischen Theologie im Epheserbrief*, eds. O. Hofius and M. Hengel, *WUNT*, vol. 99 (Tübingen: Mohr Siebeck, 1997), 40f. and 109. Following Schnackenburg, he speaks of a "Perspektivenwechsel"and an "einheitliches Umformungsprinzip." Cf. also Lona, *Eschatologie*, 39.

[53] More than any phrase, conflation or formula (even the lengthy parallel greeting, Col. 4:7–9/Eph. 6:21–22), the HT contains the most common material and follows the same schema, while introducing the lengthiest expansions/changes.

The following comparison[54] offers an overview of passages, both unique and common, in Col. and Eph.:

Ref. Col.	Colossians	Parallel Material	Ephesians	Ref. Eph.
1:1,2		Prologue		1:1,2
			Eulogy	1:3–14
1:3–14		Thanksgiving / Intercession		1:15–23
1:15–20	Christ Hymn			
			Reminder of Salvation	2:1–10
1:21–23		Alienation to Reconciliation	(Jews and Gentiles)	2:11–22
1:24–2:3		Suffering Apostle, Ministry of Mystery		3:1–13
2:4–3:4	Warnings			
			Intercession, Prayer and Doxology	3:14–21
2:19		Head and Body Language	(Exhortation to Unity, 4:15,16)	4:1–16
3:5–17		Exhortation Regarding Old/New, Conduct, Worship	(Light/Darkness, 5:8–14)	4:17–5:20
3:18–4:1		*Haustafel*	(Christ and Church 5:22–32)	5:21–6:9
			Spiritual Warfare	6:10–17
4:2–4		Exhortation to Pray		6:18–20
4:5,6	Conduct w/ Outsiders			
4:7–9		Regarding Tychicus		6:21–22
4:10–17	Greetings			
4:18	Autograph	Benediction	(Peace and Love)	6:23–24

[54] A similar chart was originally developed by J. Schmidt, *Der Epheserbrief des Apostels Paulus: Seine Adresse, Sprache und literarischen Beziehungen* (Freiburg: Herder, 1928), 412. See also J. Ernst, *Die Briefe an die Philipper, an Philemon, and die Kolosser, an die Epheser* (Regensburg: Pustet, 1974), 254–255; Lincoln, *Ephesians*, xlix; and O'Brien, *Ephesians*, 9–10.

It is clear from the above outline that Col. and Eph. share a skeletal frame-work, their common material having coincidental sequence within their re-spective letters. The differences between the letters are remarkably few, and are conspicuous in their careful placement, which preserves the common or-der. In nearly every instance, the material designated as unique to the Ephe-sian redaction can be shown to reveal a significant influence from Colossian vocabulary.[55] The shared material, in contrast, represents the foundation of the letters' structure. The close and numerous links between the letters in terms of order, themes and vocabulary make the suggestion that the letters' common material arises from shared traditional sources unlikely. The com-mon structure shared by the letters can be observed especially well in the immediate context of the HT, where its reciprocal admonitions are couched between a larger parenetic section (Col. 3:5–17 and Eph. 4:1–5:20) and a common exhortation to prayer (Col. 4:2–4 and Eph. 6:18–20). Ephesians, however, expands the parenetic section considerably, with additional mate-rial being introduced before the HT (especially in 4:1–16 with its emphasis upon the church and unity, and 5:8–14, light/darkness contrast), as well as after (6:10–17 spiritual warfare). The parallel and common sections of pare-nesis can be characterised as being influenced by the vocabulary of Colos-sians, but certainly not bound to its formulations; apart from the uniquely

---

[55] The unique sections of Ephesians are not discrete formulations, uninformed by the Colos-sian text. These sections reveal an affinity with a number of Col. texts, including several cita-tions from texts which appear above as unique to the Col. letter: Eph. 1:3–14 contains phrases from Col. 1:9, 13, 16, 20, 22 and 3:16; Eph. 2:1–10 echoes Col. 1:10; 2:13 and 3:7; Eph. 3:14–21 incorporates terminology from Col. 1:16, 20, 23, 27; 2:7, 9; Eph. 4:1–16 shows bor-rowings from Col. 1:10; 3:12, 14; the HT expansion in Eph. 5:22–32 reveals elements taken from Col. 1:18, 22, 28; finally, Eph. 6:10–17 incorporates one element of the Christ hymn, Col. 1:16. It should be noted that in these sections, several Col. texts appear more than once (Col. 1:9 [2x], 10 [2x], 16 [3x], 20 [2x], 22[2x]), suggesting the *expanded* use of the Col. text by the Eph. redactor. Elements of the Christ hymn (Col. 1:15–20), remarkably, appear five times throughout Ephesians in 1:7, 10; 3:15; 5:23; 6:12. All of these instances are found in segments of Ephesians which do not correspond to the Col. text. If the Col. author had re-dacted these sections (most of the material is fully omitted), it is unlikely such disparate and highly edited segments would produce a passage of such beauty and cohesion as the Christ hymn. More probable is the Eph. borrowing of this central passage to inform thanksgiving, prayer, the HT and the passage on spiritual warfare. Col. 1:22 provides another example of a central theological passage which finds expression in the Ephesian expansions of the Eulogy (Eph. 1:4) and the HT (Eph. 5:27). It appears likely that the Eph. author has taken this central theme and applied it to two of his expansions, including metaphorical use in 5:27; to suggest a Col. redaction which deletes the surrounding material of Ephesians, yet manages to extricate this passage, limit its meaning and press it into the concise and balanced formulation found in Col. 1:21–22, would be strained.

heavy level of coincidence found between the corresponding HT forms, borrowed phrases within the longer parenetic section of Eph./Col. have no more than one or two words[56] in common, usually in random arrangement. The important exceptions to this fairly loose borrowing from Col. (given in full text below) can be seen in the verses originally preceding and following the Col. HT, Col. 3:16–17/Eph. 5:18–20 and Col. 4:2–4/Eph. 6:19–20, respectively. In both instances, these verses reflect a higher degree of coincidence in word order and vocabulary, as well as preserving the meaning of the Col. text. This suggests that the original position of the HT within the parenetic section (as found in Colossians) was still present in the memory of the writer, being meticulously retained in spite of its transmission to a new literary context. Even if a *Vorlage* is allowed, the importance of the parenesis to the writer of Ephesians cannot be overlooked; his editorial activity both preserves *and* extends the influence of the original parenesis found in Col., indicating the importance of the received material to the author, as well as his intention in writing, to maintain and extend the Col. ethic.[57] Because of the author's concern for the maintenance and extension of ethical instruction, the parenetic elements of Ephesians reveal a tendency to retain the highest level of similarity to Colossians on the one hand, while freely introducing a surprising amount of new material on the other. The HT material represents the clearest example of this pattern of preservation and innovation, where the form and vocabulary of Col. are preserved with only minor changes, for example, in the reciprocal relations of slave-master and parent-child. Innovation, however, is detected in the expansion of the HT: it grows to twice the size of its Col. counterpart, the husband-wife relationship expanding from

---

[56] The only exception being Col. 3:6 and Eph. 4:6, sharing the phrase ἔρχεται ἡ ὀργὴ τοῦ θεοῦ. It should also be noted that Eph. 4:16 borrows from the theology and near-identical wording of Col. 2:19, creating another longer incidence of confluence; the vocabulary, however, can also be found in Ephesians' theological section in 1:22. The parenesis of Ephesians, though following the outline of Col. and its parenesis, makes limited use of the "doctrinal" section of Col. 1:1–3:4. A number of these uses, however, can be traced to the Ephesian text, as well. Clear examples are: Eph. 4:1, Col. 1:10; Eph. 4:14, Col. 2:22; Eph. 4:16, Col. 2:19 (but also Eph. 1:22); Eph. 4:17, Col. 2:4; Eph. 5:27–28, Col. 1:22; Eph. 6:12, Col. 1:16 (but also Eph. 1:10 and 1:21).

[57] Luz, "Überlegungen zum Epheserbrief und seiner Paränese," in *Neues Testament und Ethik, FS für R. Schnackenburg*, ed. H. Merklein (Freiburg: Herder, 1989), 376f., notes that the parenetic section of Ephesians is larger than the theological section, a relation of 6:5. This is unique, and in contrast to Col. and the Paulines, it represents a remarkable development: "Umfangmäßig hat sich das Schwergewicht im Epheserbrief auf die Paränese verlagert." This represents the "particular intention of the author", for whom parenesis "das eigentlich Wichtige war."

two to twelve (!) verses. In spite of the high level of coincidence and expansion, the Eph. HT has been largely regarded, with Col., as a reception of traditional material. For this reason, the Eph. parenetic material, especially the HT, has received little attention in the discussion of the letter's theological development.

As mentioned above, scholarly opinion regarding the dependence of Ephesians upon Colossians is nearly unanimous. Beyond the question of priority, representatives of this majority position have posited several tenable solutions for the occasion and authorship of the letter, as well. The natural result of maintaining Col.-Eph. dependence is to see Ephesians in *transformed relationship* to Colossians, where particular accent is given to the common structure,[58] as well as highlighting numerous changes in common theological termini such as σῶμα, κεφαλή, μυστήριον and ἐκκλησία. This method has been very helpful in discerning genuine differences between the letters, locating several discernible connections drawn from earlier Paulines, and suggesting particular emphases unique to Ephesians.[59] The order of dependence Col.-Eph. carries with it an assumed flow of development in theological concepts, yet these are usually treated in a somewhat broad, independent manner.[60] Here scholarly emphasis has been placed upon the process and theological concerns of redaction, de-emphasising, in effect, the integrity of Ephesians as a coherent and intentional theological whole. The parenesis, likewise, has been seen primarily in terms of its relationship to, and development from, the original theological impulses found in Colossians, making it little more than a transmission of familiar convention.[61] Though this ap-

---

[58] Structural similarities are clear. The division doctrine-parenesis (in Eph. 1:1–3:21; 4:1–6:20) is followed. Shared elements, including the HT, occur in almost identical sequence, forming a skeletal framework from which individual elements then deviate. The Eph. HT conforms to this pattern, treating the horizontal relationships in corresponding order to Col. Interesting to note is the inclusion of nearly identical material before and after the HT, which "brackets" it within the concerns of a worshipful lifestyle and thanksgiving (Col. 3:16/Eph. 5:19–20), the Apostle's call to prayer (Col. 4:2–4/Eph. 6:18–20) and final greetings, suggesting a perceived cohesion between these parenetic elements and the HT.

[59] Luz, "Überlegungen", 378, is rightly critical of approaches which attempt to categorise the message of Ephesians solely under a particular theological rubric derived from this vocabulary. The letter, he argues, shows balance between theology and ethical behaviour.

[60] The changes in theology and language are traced in broad terms, and the letter is seen, primarily, as leaning heavily on tradition and the earlier Paulines. Cf. Mitton, *Epistle*, 82f.; Gnilka, *Epheserbrief*, 26; Lincoln, *Ephesians*, lvi.

[61] Dibelius, *Kolosser*, 87. He suggests that the author of Eph. "mehr tradiert als produziert"; Mußner, *Epheser*, 133, considers the content of the parenesis familiar and "inhaltlich koventionell." Fischer, *Tendenz*, 147, concurs, designating a majority of the parenetic material as disparate, dualistic and theologically dislocated traditional forms, which were employed in the

proach can serve as a valuable method of analysis, it unwittingly bypasses the important intermediate stage and function of the theological concepts *as they are found in the text of Ephesians*.[62] The derivative nature of Ephesians, it seems, has been overstated.

Though the parenesis of the letter has received a more precise transmission than the purely theological sections in terms of its close relationship to Colossians,[63] it has received little attention in its own right.[64] This is particularly surprising, as the parenetic section not only makes up the *largest* body of coincidental material, but evidences the strongest verbal agreement between the letters. It is our contention that a close examination of the Eph. HT, the lengthiest common parenetic feature between the letters, will reveal both common and unique elements in relationship to Colossians, as well as demonstrating, ultimately, a thoroughgoing affinity to the theology of the Ephesian redactor. Far from being a dutiful adaptation of familiar traditional material, the large amount, close adaptation and prominent place of parenesis in Eph. speaks for the author's intention to maintain, yet transform, the Col. ethic.

Exegesis: The Immediate HT Context

The Ephesian HT is noteworthy in that it is joined[65] to the previous parenetic section by means of verbal dependence upon a present participle,

---

absence of a distinctive and developed ethic [Alltagsethik]. Interestingly, Fischer notes that the most recognisable form, the HT, possesses a "substantially different" structure, which allows significant and differentiated ethical development along its intra-human axes.

[62] Mitton, *Epistle*, 12f. Here Mitton's excellent parallel readings of Eph./Col., 279–315, show this tendency, where, for example, Eph. 5:23–24 is linked to a parallel in Col. 1:18. The Ephesian parallel is actually 1:22–23; the text found in the Eph. HT is properly connected to the Ephesian reference.

[63] Ulrich Luz, "Überlegungen", 377, notes that the theological portions of Col. 1–3 are loosely adapted ("nur gelegentlich und eher assoziierend benutzt") into the text of Eph., if at all. Yet the parenetic material found in Col. 3:5–4:6 is nearly taken in its entirety. "Das Interesse des Verfassers liegt also bei der Paränese des Kolosserbriefs."

[64] Ibid., 377f., "Die Paränese wird nur selten als Proprium des Briefes ernst genommen." Luz notes the mistaken tendency to see the parenesis in terms of some overarching theological scheme, and the lack of attention to the entire epistle; if the message of Eph. is to be understood, parenetic passages must receive equal consideration, balancing the author's concern with theology and lifestyle [*Wandel*]. He suggests locating points of assimilation between the theology and parenesis.

[65] There is much discussion regarding the division of the passage, consigning v. 21 either to the previous section, or to the HT (UBS Greek text places break after v.21, the NA after v.

ὑποτασσόμενοι, which is found in verse 21. The participles flow in tight succession in verses 19–21: λαλοῦντες, ᾄδοντες, ψάλλοντες, εὐχαριστοῦν-τες and ὑποτασσόμενοι. The final participle in 5:21 provides the verbal expression[66] for verse 22, αἱ γυναῖκες τοῖς ἰδίοις ἀνδράσιν, drawing the HT material into a more immediate relationship with the preceding material.[67] Here it seems that the author has made intentional use of ὑποτασσόμενοι, not only to introduce the theme of submission which initiates, and to some degree characterises, the HT material,[68] but to create a smoother transition than we see in Col., as well. The grammatical and thematic link created by v. 21 reveals, we believe, the author's creative attempt to integrate the HT material into its broader parenetic field.[69]

Verse 21, when considered apart from its grammatical and transitional function, introduces an undeniably unique aspect of the Eph. parenetic material in its emphases upon mutual submission and its motivation, the fear of Christ.[70] In analysing this verse, we hope to highlight the unique aspects of the author's formulation, which in turn will have implications regarding his *intentions* in joining the parenetic material and the HT.

---

20). Both positions have merit, yet assigning a firm position overlooks the intentionally transitional nature of the verse. E. Best, *Ephesians*, New Testament Guides (Sheffield: JSOT Press, 1993), 515f., gives this editorial question an excellent treatment.

[66] Though a considerable number of texts insert ὑποτασσέσθωσαν or ὑποτάσσεσθε after either γυναῖκες or ἀνδράσιν in verse 22, this would be a departure from the author's succinct style, and is most likely a scribal insertion intended to insure clarity. See Metzger, *A Textual Commentary on the Greek New Testament*, 608f., or Best, *Ephesians*, 531, for helpful discussions in favour of the simpler reading.

[67] N. Baumert, *Frau und Mann bei Paulus* (Würzburg: Echter Verlag, 1993), 193, correctly identifies this verse as a *Bindeglied*, joining the two sections under the more general admonitions of the preceding section. The Greek text shows *variae lectiones* in the reversed order of vv. 20–21, however. Though supported by 𝔓⁴⁶, D, F and G, the reversed order makes little sense, and leaves verse 22 without a predicate. The traditional reading is well attested by ℵ, A, B, D², Ψ and the Majority Text. Gielen, *Tradition*, 206, fn. 6, postulates a scribal error due to familiarity with the Col. text.

[68] E. Kamlah, "Ὑποτάσσεσθαι in den NT Haustafeln," in *Verborum Veritas: FS Stählin*, eds. O. Böcher and K. Haacker (Wuppertal: R. Brockhaus, 1970), 238, cites the uniqueness of this HT emphasis: "…im Gebot der Unterordnung ein Spezifikum der urchristlichen Haustafel liege; denn in keiner anderen ähnlichen Ermahnung, wie sie sich in Texten der stoisch beeinflüßten Popularphilosophie und des hellenistischen Judentums finden, ist es auch nur belegt, von einer derart dominierenden Rolle ganz zu schweigen."

[69] Contra Tanzer, "Traditions," 341, who follows Munro's arguments closely, seeing the previous material as "clumsily attached to the household code."

[70] Mutual submission is unique to the Eph. HT; the fear of Christ is found only here in the NT.

132

Scholarly debate regarding the relationship of this verse to the HT has revolved around the "unresolved tension between authority and mutuality"[71] which its unique formulation engenders. At the root of the discussion lies the judgement as to whether this injunction found in 5:21 (Ὑποτασσόμενοι ἀλλήλοις ἐν φόβῳ Χριστοῦ, calling for mutual submission) is in fundamental conflict with the following HT admonitions (clearly unilateral commands, including submission and obedience), or in some way can be understood to explicate, expand or perhaps mediate the fundamental injunctions to the three relational pairs. In either case, the tension needs to be considered from several possible perspectives. If a conflict has indeed been created, then we might allow for unintentional discrepancy in logic on the part of the author (with no discernible intention), or conversely, suggest a scenario in which he might have intended to create such a tension. Finally, it may be that the author sensed the tension created by this formulation, yet chose, nonetheless, to retain it as an integral part of his larger theological redaction.

In the first instance, the author may have *unwittingly* created an antithetical conflation of material present in Col. Reciprocal injunctions containing ἀλλήλους and ἀλλήλων stood in relatively close proximity to the Col. HT (3:9, μὴ ψεύδεσθε εἰς ἀλλήλους; the reciprocal formulations and sense of 3:13, ἀνεχόμενοι ἀλλήλων καὶ χαριζόμενοι ἑαυτοῖς ἐάν τις πρός τινα ἔχῃ μομφήν· καθὼς καὶ ὁ κύριος ἐχαρίσατο ὑμῖν, οὕτως καὶ ὑμεῖς; not to mention the obvious influence of ἑαυτούς in 3:16, ἐν πάσῃ σοφίᾳ διδάσκοντες καὶ νουθετοῦντες ἑαυτούς). These might have led the author to create another reciprocal construction (complementing the ἑαυτοῖς in Eph. 5:19?), by employing ὑποτασσόμενοι, not indiscriminately, but as it came to mind as the first verbal expression of the Col. HT.[72] The two influences were consciously drawn upon by the author, without an awareness of the tensions created. This scenario seems unlikely, however. The construction makes a clever connection between preceding verbal forms and the HT theme of submission, which seems to preclude undeliberated or unintentional formulation. It is more likely that the author is indeed extending the reciprocal ethic found in both letters, making similar and conscious use of the reciprocal constructions found in Col., as well as extending similar constructions employed in the parenesis of Ephesians. This deliberate construction looks back to the preceding material, whereas ὑποτασσόμενοι and the phrase ἐν φόβῳ Χριστοῦ (overlooked in this connection) *anticipate* the HT.

---

[71] Best, *Ephesians*, 517, engages the discussion thoughtfully, and rightly points out this fundamental tension.

[72] So Best, *Ephesians*, 517.

Whereas ὑποτασσόμενοι introduces a familiar HT theme initiating the Col. HT, 5: 21b lends further support to the deliberate nature of the formulation. The motivational phrase found here, ἐν φόβῳ Χριστοῦ,[73] is an unique collocation in NT usage, meriting special attention. The unusual phrase suggests that the author was not unconscious of his formulation, but was actually introducing something important and new, to be developed, or at least represented, in the following parenetic material: the motivation of fear, which finds a new Christian aspect in the person of Christ.[74] This observation is borne out on both counts in the attendant HT material. The author develops the concept of fear within the HT in 5:33, ἡ δὲ γυνὴ ἵνα φοβῆται τὸν ἄνδρα[75] and 6:5, μετὰ φόβου καὶ τρόμου, as well as making nearly exclusive use of Χρίστος (a notable departure from Col.) as the title for the Lord in 5:25, 29; 6:5, 6.[76] The novelty of the phrase, as well as its considerable representation in the HT, suggest that the author constructed the verse in a most meticulous and innovative manner to imply a close connection between the general parenesis and that of the HT. If we allow, then, the construction to be deliberate in nature, might it be held that it represents an intentional conflict? This position has been posited by Sampley, who understands 5:21 as "the author's critique of the basic stance of the *Haustafel* form wherein one group is ordered to be submissive to another group vested with authority over it."[77] This position seems to be unlikely in light of the expansions within the HT,

---

[73] The last word of this formulation, Χριστοῦ, has competing textual variants: F, G read Ἰησοῦ Χριστοῦ; D reverses this; K and bo-mss read κυρίου; 6. 81. 614. 630. 1881. *pm* Cl and Ambst-mss read θεοῦ. An overwhelming majority of the texts, including substantial witnesses, support the adopted reading. Its unusual (and therefore difficult) formulation also speaks for its originality. The first two variants can be explained as attempts to achieve clarity and completeness of the more familiar title of Christ; the second two variants reflect common NT usage (Lk. 18:2, 4; 23:40; Ac. 9:31; 10:2, 22, 35; 13:16, 26; Rom. 3:18; 2 Cor. 5:11; 7:1; Col. 3:22, 1 Pet. 2:17; Rev. 11:18; 14:7; 19:5), as well as OT influences already noted in Col. (See Gielen, *Tradition*, 170f., Best, *Ephesians*, 518).

[74] The traditional OT formulation φόβος κυρίου is prominent in wisdom literature and the Psalms as a fundamental aspect of wise and ethical behaviour, upon which the author, in the tradition of Col., draws (see Balz and Wanke's article, "φοβέω κτλ." in *TDNT*, 9, 189–219). The author of Eph., by the substitution of Χρίστος for κύριος, intentionally introduces a specifically Christian aspect to the HT ethic.

[75] Most commentators agree that 5:33 comprises an inclusio; Best's observation, *Ephesians*, 516, that this should actually occur at 6:9, is correct; the two occurrences, however, are more than accidental, as he suggests.

[76] The only exception is the word-play created by the opposition of κύριοι and κύριος, which the author necessarily retains in 6:9.

[77] J.P. Sampley, *"And the Two Shall Become One Flesh": A Study of Traditions in Eph. 5:21–33* (Cambridge: CUP, 1971), 117.

134

which appear to develop the HT ethic, rather than diminish its authoritative nature.[78] If the intention of the author had been to discredit the HT, then we must agree with Best: "...he would have made this clearer."[79]

If 5:21 is not construed as being in conflict with the HT material, it remains to be shown in what manner its singular injunction of mutual submission in the fear of the Lord represents a new development, and how this relates to the HT admonitions. It may be that the apparent lack of clarity between the general admonition found in 5:21 and the particular HT injunctions can be explained in terms of the author's editorial activity and intentions. The discrepancy may simply be the result of the author's redactional attempts to preserve and conflate the most important, uniquely Christian elements of the Col. HT form (including the full expression of reciprocity, the theme of submission and the motivation given to the slaves in the prominent slave-master relationship, ἐν ἁπλότητι καρδίας φοβούμενοι τὸν κύριον), in an attempt to construe the most christianised ethic possible.

It appears that v. 21 introduces the theme of submission in a broader, and perhaps more nuanced form,[80] yet traditional relationships, it must be said, remain intact, their subordinate/superordinate characteristics firmly in place.[81] The familiar discussion over the interpretation of this verse in terms of either mutual submission or support of the HT mandates may not adequately encompass the original concerns of the author, who has, we believe, intentionally taken the Eph. HT in a new direction. A possible point of understanding this innovation presents itself in its point of departure: the expanded slave-master section of the Col. HT. As we discussed above, the Col. HT ethic builds upon the general understanding within the letter that believ-

---

[78] One would not expect the HT to expand to twice the size of the Col. HT, nor to include elements which appear to add stronger or even absolute nature to the admonitions to the subordinated members: cf. 5:22, where the women are called to submit, not as is fitting in the Lord (Col. 3:18), but ὡς τῷ κυρίῳ (v.22) and ἐν παντί. To this is added the imagery of male headship after the model of Christ. Children are admonished to obey *and* to honour parents, with OT support (Dt. 5:16, v. 6:3). Slaves are to obey with φόβου καὶ τρόμου, 6:5.

[79] Best, *Ephesians*, 516.

[80] Franz Mußner, *Der Brief an die Epheser*, eds. E. Gräßer and K. Kertelge, Ökumenischer Taschenbuchkommentar zum Neuen Testament, vol. 10 (Würzburg: Echter Verlag, 1982), 154, notes the specifically Christian aspect of the familiar term as encountered in the HT: "Die neuen Kontexte, in die im Neuen Testament die Haustafeln gestellt sind, wie besonders im Epheserbrief, verschieben auch die Semantik übernommener Lexeme wie 'unterwerfen'."

[81] Peter T. O'Brien, *The Letter to the Ephesians*, ed. D.A. Carson, The Pillar New Testament Commentary (Grand Rapids: Eerdmans, 1999), 402, notes that the attempts to construe v.21 in an egalitarian manner do not correspond to normal usage of ὑποτάσσομαι, nor to the reality of the HT. See also Gielen, *Tradition*, 223.

ers stand in a redeemed relationship to Christ, which is analogous to the master-servant relationship found in the HT. Paul and his hearers, for this reason, share a certain level of solidarity with the slaves addressed in the HT. The admonitions and christological motivation enjoined to the slaves are particularly significant for the general reader, if not paradigmatic for the Christian life. The centrality of the slave-master parenesis in determining the HT ethic would not have escaped the attention of the writer of Ephesians, who would have closely scrutinised the theological motivation contained within the notable expansions found in the slave-master relationship. It is important, then, to note that Col. 3:22b introduces the *singular* motivation for the slave's activities as the fear of the Lord, φοβούμενοι τὸν κύριον.[82] It would not be surprising, then, if the author of Ephesians were to incorporate faithfully this central theme into his own HT, giving it an appropriately prominent and similar position of regulating the motivation for *all* the HT admonitions. The unique formulation ἐν φόβῳ Χριστοῦ departs slightly from the Colossian formulation in its notable use of Χρίστος as an alternative title for κύριος.[83] This may reflect a borrowing from the unusual christological title found in the Col. slave parenesis in 3:24, κύριος Χριστός, the expanded admonitions of Col. again exercising a strong influence upon the Eph. author's choice of words. Verse 21 would, then, not only reflect the earlier christological motivation incorporated in Col., but also represent a conflation of the Col. HT's vocabulary with its special use of the title of Christ.[84] It appears that the author of Ephesians has not only inserted v. 21 with the intention of creating a smooth transition, but also to establish, from the beginning, the central motivating element of the HT, which builds upon the uniquely Christian elements of the Col. HT.[85]

---

[82] This can be construed as the general rubric under which behaviour is regulated, as well as the appropriate response to the rewards (punishments being omitted in the Eph. redaction) promised. In this regard, the fear of the Lord regulates the masters' behaviour, as well.

[83] The title *kurios*, used eight times in reference to Christ in the Col. HT, is reduced to five occurrences (omitting the doubtful insertion of *kurios* in 29b) in Eph., these following the usage of Col. in the slave-master relation in 6:7 [Col.3:23], 6:8 [Col. 3:24], 6:9 [Col. 4:1], as well as reflecting the vocabulary of the instruction to the wives in 5:22 [Col. 3:18]. The fifth occurrence, 6:4, qualifies the nature of the instruction (ἐν παιδείᾳ καὶ νουθεσίᾳ κυρίου). The author tends to employ the title of Christ (used only once in Col. HT) in the Eph. HT: 5:21, 23, 24, 25, 29, 32; 6:5, 6.

[84] Verses 3:22b (motivation, φοβούμενοι τὸν κύριον) and 3:24b (title, τῷ κυρίῳ Χριστῷ) represent both central and unique elements of the Col. HT, which might have influenced the author's formulation of this motivational rubric.

[85] Here Gielen, *Tradition*, 233, sees the call to mutual submission as paradigmatic, replacing the *kurios-doulos* relationship of Col.: "Der Aufruf zur gegenseitigen Unterordnung ist also

136

The position of v. 21 and its theological motivation represent a significant organisational shift in the HT form.[86] Here the author expands the regulating force of the fear of the Lord (implicit in Col., yet formally limited to
the slave-master relation), by explicit inclusion of *all* relations within the HT
under its rubric.[87] The fear of the Lord, then, becomes the overarching theological touchstone for regulating HT relations, as well as a clear indicator
that the mediating authority of the Lord over all relations (now by the title
Christ) is a chief concern of the Eph. editor. The author of Ephesians, then,
not only introduces a significant change in the HT *form* and a homogenising
of its *motivation* to all its relations, but gives us this important signal for the
interpretation of the following relations, as well. The combination of conscious alterations, borrowed vocabulary and stylistic craft evidenced in v.21
should not be underestimated when weighing its significance to the understanding of the following HT material. Here we would agree with Gese's
thesis that in Ephesians, style is intricate and conscious, and follows intention:

> Da der Verfasser hier [Eph. 5:19f. and 6:18–20] jedoch bewußt umformuliert, muß
> diese Verschmelzung von ihm gewollt sein. Sie kann also nicht in stilistischer Un-
> beholfenheit ihren Grund haben, sondern muß inhaltlich bedingt sein. Offensichtlich
> möchte der Verfasser die innere Verbindung der Rahmenaussage (Gottesbeziehung)
> mit der Aussage der gerahmten Stücke (Leben in menschlichen Beziehungen) stil-
> istisch unterstreichen. Das heißt aber, daß der Verfasser mit *grammatischen* Struk-
> turen *theologische* Zusammenhänge markieren möchte.[88]

In summary, Ephesians 5:21 illustrates the author's intention to join the
broader parenetic section into close relation with the HT form. This he does
by carefully combining vocabulary and grammatical forms from both sections. His reliance upon the formulations found within the slave-master section of the Col. HT indicates a concern to preserve and simultaneously expand the uniquely Christian motivation of the Col. HT to all relations in the
Eph. HT. This illustrates the tendency of the author of Eph. to maintain much

---

nichts anderes als die auf die zwischenmenschlichen Relationen übertragene Forderung, dem
Herrn zu dienen."

[86] Contra Schweizer, *Brief*, 246, who characterises the Eph. HT as having "die gleiche Rei-
henfolge, die gleiche Intention."

[87] Gielen, *Tradition*, 218f., notes that the "überraschende Schlußperspektive" found in the
slave-master relation of Col. HT loses its original function, and becomes the assumed beginning point in Eph. In this manner, the surprising and unique christological perspective is extended to all relations.

[88] Gese, *Vermächtnis*, 99.

of the Col. parenesis in form and content, while making considerable expansions. Verse 21 becomes, by virtue of its general character, the new motivational rubric under which the Eph. HT might be understood: relationships construed in the fear of Christ.

The Ephesian HT: Transformation

In contrast to the innovation of 5:21, it is notable that the Ephesian HT makes no alteration in the ordering of the reciprocal relations within the Col. HT. The original content of the Col. HT is largely preserved as well, reflecting the highest coincidence in vocabulary and word order between the letters. An appeal to common traditions, though possible at points of the letters' formation, cannot adequately explain this high level of coincidence. The Ephesian author's intentions are reflected at some points by subtle additions, or even larger expansions of the Col. material. These expansions, though present in all three relational pairs, are unequally distributed, as we shall see. It is this new material, we believe, which will not only illustrate the unique formal aspects and ethical argumentation of the Eph. HT, but reveal the intention of the author of Ephesians, as well. The following discussion will attempt to uncover the particular elements within the parenesis of the Ephesian HT which the author has employed to effect a transformation; it is hoped that our analysis of the several differences between the Col. and Eph. HT will first of all illustrate the unique characteristics of the Ephesian adaptation. This, in turn, will lay the groundwork for a later discussion of the theological tendencies and intentions of the author.[89]

The following chart may be helpful to the reader in gaining a visual impression of the similar structure of the Col. and Eph. HT forms, while highlighting the clear editorial expansions of the Eph. redactor:

Key: underlined words represent similar, related formulations; words in **bold type** represent more exact correspondence in vocabulary. The comparison does not take into account exact or similar formulations elsewhere in the letters.

Ephesians 5:19–6:9	Colossians 3:16–4:1
λαλοῦντες ἑαυτοῖς [ἐν] ψαλμοῖς καὶ ὕμνοις καὶ ᾠδαῖς πνευματικαῖς, ᾄδοντες καὶ ψάλλοντες τῇ καρδίᾳ	ὁ λόγος τοῦ Χριστοῦ ἐνοικείτω ἐν ὑμῖν πλουσίως, ἐν πάσῃ σοφίᾳ διδάσκοντες

[89] Gielen, *Tradition*, 226, agrees that the differences found between the HT traditions best illustrate the "actual intention" of the author.

138

ὑμῶν τῷ κυρίῳ, εὐχαριστοῦντες πάντοτε ὑπὲρ πάντων ἐν ὀνόματι τοῦ κυρίου ἡμῶν Ἰησοῦ Χριστοῦ τῷ θεῷ καὶ πατρί.	καὶ νουθετοῦντες ἑαυτούς, ψαλμοῖς ὕμνοις ᾠδαῖς πνευματικαῖς ἐν [τῇ] χάριτι ᾄδοντες ἐν ταῖς καρδίαις ὑμῶν τῷ θεῷ· καὶ πᾶν ὅ τι ἐὰν ποιῆτε ἐν λόγῳ ἢ ἐν ἔργῳ, πάντα ἐν ὀνόματι κυρίου Ἰησοῦ, εὐχαριστοῦντες τῷ θεῷ πατρὶ δι᾽ αὐτοῦ.
Ὑποτασσόμενοι ἀλλήλοις ἐν φόβῳ Χριστοῦ, αἱ γυναῖκες τοῖς ἰδίοις ἀνδράσιν ὡς τῷ κυρίῳ, ὅτι ἀνήρ ἐστιν κεφαλὴ τῆς γυναικὸς ὡς καὶ ὁ Χριστὸς κεφαλὴ τῆς ἐκκλησίας, αὐτὸς σωτὴρ τοῦ σώματος· ἀλλὰ ὡς ἡ ἐκκλησία ὑποτάσσεται τῷ Χριστῷ, οὕτως καὶ αἱ γυναῖκες τοῖς ἀνδράσιν ἐν παντί.	Αἱ γυναῖκες, ὑποτάσσεσθε τοῖς ἀνδράσιν ὡς ἀνῆκεν ἐν κυρίῳ.
Οἱ ἄνδρες, ἀγαπᾶτε τὰς γυναῖκας, καθὼς καὶ ὁ Χριστὸς ἠγάπησεν τὴν ἐκκλησίαν καὶ ἑαυτὸν παρέδωκεν ὑπὲρ αὐτῆς, ἵνα αὐτὴν ἁγιάσῃ καθαρίσας τῷ λουτρῷ τοῦ ὕδατος ἐν ῥήματι, ἵνα παραστήσῃ αὐτὸς ἑαυτῷ ἔνδοξον τὴν ἐκκλησίαν, μὴ ἔχουσαν σπίλον ἢ ῥυτίδα ἤ τι τῶν τοιούτων, ἀλλ᾽ ἵνα ᾖ ἁγία καὶ ἄμωμος. οὕτως ὀφείλουσιν [καὶ] οἱ ἄνδρες ἀγαπᾶν τὰς ἑαυτῶν γυναῖκας ὡς τὰ ἑαυτῶν σώματα. ὁ ἀγαπῶν τὴν ἑαυτοῦ γυναῖκα ἑαυτὸν ἀγαπᾷ. οὐδεὶς γάρ ποτε τὴν ἑαυτοῦ σάρκα ἐμίσησεν ἀλλὰ ἐκτρέφει καὶ θάλπει αὐτήν, καθὼς καὶ ὁ Χριστὸς τὴν ἐκκλησίαν, ὅτι μέλη ἐσμὲν τοῦ σώματος αὐτοῦ. ἀντὶ τούτου καταλείψει ἄνθρωπος [τὸν] πατέρα καὶ [τὴν] μητέρα καὶ προσκολληθήσεται πρὸς τὴν γυναῖκα αὐτοῦ, καὶ ἔσονται οἱ δύο εἰς σάρκα μίαν. τὸ μυστήριον τοῦτο μέγα ἐστίν· ἐγὼ δὲ λέγω εἰς Χριστὸν καὶ εἰς τὴν ἐκκλησίαν. πλὴν καὶ ὑμεῖς οἱ καθ᾽ ἕνα, ἕκαστος τὴν ἑαυτοῦ γυναῖκα οὕτως ἀγαπάτω ὡς ἑαυτόν, ἡ δὲ γυνὴ ἵνα φοβῆται τὸν ἄνδρα.	Οἱ ἄνδρες, ἀγαπᾶτε τὰς γυναῖκας καὶ μὴ πικραίνεσθε πρὸς αὐτάς.
Τὰ τέκνα, ὑπακούετε τοῖς γονεῦσιν	Τὰ τέκνα, ὑπακούετε τοῖς

ὑμῶν [ἐν κυρίῳ]: τοῦτο γάρ ἐστιν δίκαιον. τίμα τὸν πατέρα σου καὶ τὴν μητέρα, ἥτις ἐστὶν ἐντολὴ πρώτη ἐν ἐπαγγελίᾳ, ἵνα εὖ σοι γένηται καὶ ἔσῃ μακροχρόνιος ἐπὶ τῆς γῆς.	γονεῦσιν κατὰ πάντα, τοῦτο γὰρ εὐάρεστόν ἐστιν ἐν κυρίῳ.
Καὶ οἱ **πατέρες**, **μὴ** παροργίζετε **τὰ τέκνα ὑμῶν** ἀλλὰ ἐκτρέφετε αὐτὰ ἐν παιδείᾳ καὶ νουθεσίᾳ κυρίου.	Οἱ **πατέρες**, **μὴ** ἐρεθίζετε **τὰ τέκνα ὑμῶν**, ἵνα μὴ ἀθυμῶσιν.
Οἱ **δοῦλοι**, **ὑπακούετε τοῖς κατὰ σάρκα κυρίοις** <u>μετὰ φόβου</u> καὶ τρόμου ἐν **ἁπλότητι** τῆς **καρδίας** ὑμῶν <u>ὡς τῷ Χριστῷ</u>, μὴ κατ᾿ <u>ὀφθαλμοδουλίαν</u> ὡς **ἀνθρωπάρεσκοι** ἀλλ᾿ <u>ὡς δοῦλοι Χριστοῦ</u> ποιοῦντες τὸ θέλημα τοῦ θεοῦ **ἐκ ψυχῆς**, μετ᾿ εὐνοίας δουλεύοντες **ὡς τῷ κυρίῳ καὶ οὐκ ἀνθρώποις**, **εἰδότες** ὅτι ἕκαστος ἐάν τι ποιήσῃ ἀγαθόν, τοῦτο **κομίσεται** <u>παρὰ</u> **κυρίου** εἴτε δοῦλος εἴτε ἐλεύθερος.	Οἱ **δοῦλοι**, **ὑπακούετε** κατὰ πάντα **τοῖς κατὰ σάρκα κυρίοις**, μὴ <u>ἐν ὀφθαλμοδουλίᾳ</u> ὡς **ἀνθρωπάρεσκοι**, ἀλλ᾿ ἐν **ἁπλότητι καρδίας** <u>φοβούμενοι</u> τὸν κύριον. ὃ ἐὰν ποιῆτε, **ἐκ ψυχῆς** <u>ἐργάζεσθε</u> **ὡς τῷ κυρίῳ καὶ οὐκ ἀνθρώποις**, **εἰδότες** ὅτι <u>ἀπὸ</u> **κυρίου** ἀπολήμψεσθε τὴν ἀνταπόδοσιν τῆς κληρονομίας. <u>τῷ κυρίῳ Χριστῷ δουλεύετε:</u> ὁ γὰρ ἀδικῶν **κομίσεται** ὃ ἠδίκησεν, καὶ οὐκ ἔστιν προσω-πολημψία.
Καὶ οἱ **κύριοι**, τὰ αὐτὰ ποιεῖτε πρὸς αὐτούς, ἀνιέντες τὴν ἀπειλήν, **εἰδότες** ὅτι καὶ <u>αὐτῶν καὶ ὑμῶν ὁ</u> **κύριός** <u>ἐστιν</u> ἐν οὐρανοῖς καὶ **προσωπολημψία** οὐκ ἔστιν παρ᾿ αὐτῷ.	Οἱ **κύριοι**, τὸ δίκαιον καὶ τὴν ἰσότητα τοῖς δούλοις παρέχεσθε, **εἰδότες** ὅτι καὶ <u>ὑμεῖς ἔχετε</u> **κύριον** ἐν οὐρανῷ.

The Eph. HT, particularly in the first two relational pairs, illustrates the thoroughly expanded nature of the redaction. At the macro level (we will discuss in more detail individual changes below), it becomes clear that the direction of redaction was either towards expansion (Col.-Eph) or reduction (Eph.-Col.). As discussed above, the Ephesian expansion in 5:21 appears to be a clever attempt to integrate the HT into the surrounding material, as well as emphasising elements of the expanded slave-master axis. The editorial deletion of Eph. 5:21 in Col., it might be argued, represents an attempt to place the HT form in starker relief to the surrounding material. A clearer, more abrupt division and "leaner" admonitions might serve to emphasise the HT as a didactic form, as well as highlighting its reciprocal character. This would explain, perhaps, the further deletions found within the first two relational pairs. The third relational pair, however, which retains the expansions of

140

Eph., causes problems for the theory of Eph.-Col. dependence. The Eph.-Col. redactor has reformulated the Eph. admonitions with very little change and much the same length. For this feature of the redaction, there seems to be no explanation. It can only be supposed that the features of the Ephesian slave-master relationship corresponded with the emphases of the Col. redactor, and were retained. This supposition, however, would better explain the expansion as part of the Col. original; it seems unlikely that the author of Col. would craft his theological argument in such a reactive manner. A corresponding question arises when considering the deleted material: why would the Col. redactor suppress elements in the Eph. HT (such as OT references or the christological analogy), which are otherwise features of the Colossian redaction?[90] A redaction which features selective adoption or deletion of the Eph. material, must have some sort of theological or organisational principle which explains these features. Proponents of Eph.-Col. redaction have yet to suggest a scenario of redaction which might account for the uneven adoption of the HT material. Col.-Eph. redaction, in contrast, suggests a tendency towards expansion throughout the letter, with a corresponding tendency of retaining the central and most christianised elements of the Col. original. The Col. *Vorlage* has been largely retained.[91] The expansions upon the Col. original are characterised by extensive OT citation, a more explicit emphasis upon Christ's love, substitution through word pairs and positive formulations, as well as other original additions. These features, most of which build upon elements present in Col., suggest a process, employing creative methods of clarification and intentional expansions wrought by a redactor. The result is a broader, if not more general epistle, which has incorporated and expanded upon the *essence* of Col., while losing only its *occasional* elements. An Eph.-Col. redactional model cannot, we maintain, demonstrate

---

[90] OT references in Colossians are fewer, but nonetheless present: Col. 1:16b–17 appears to associate the vocabulary linked to wisdom (Prov. 8:23–27) with Christ; Col. 2:3 locates wisdom (Prov. 2:3) and hidden riches (Is. 45:3) in Christ; Col. 2:22b, the "human commands and teachings" echoes Is. 29:13; Col. 3:1 refers to Christ's being seated at God's right hand (Ps. 110:1); Col. 4:1 reflects the commands found in Lev. 25:43, 53 as well as the observation of Eccl. 5:8. The christological analogy, (including the emphasis upon love) found in the Eph. HT is clearly reflected in similar language in Colossians. Love: Col. 1:4, 8, 13; 2:2, 12, 14; 3:19; Christ: head over all powers, 2:10; head of the body the church, 1:18; his body, which is the church, 1:24.

[91] The Christ hymn is represented within the Eph. redaction, see fn. 55 above. The occasional elements in 2:4–3:4 and 4:5–6 are, as might be expected, not fully represented in the Eph., redaction, though some of the phrases can be found integrated within Eph.: Col. 2:4 in 3:17; Col. 2:7 in 2:20, 3:17; Col. 2:9 in 3:19; Col. 2:11 in 2:11; Col. 2:13 in 2:2, 5; Col. 2:14 in 2:15; Col. 2:19 in 2:21, 3:16; Col. 3:7 in 2:2; and Col. 4:5 in 5:16.

such a clear pattern of adoption and innovation. The following analysis will attempt to demonstrate how the individual admonitions of the Ephesian HT can be seen as arising from the Col. original, representing reception and extension of the original Col. HT ethic.

The First Relational Pair: Husband and Wife

In contrast to the Col. HT, Eph. undergoes its most remarkable expansion in the *first* relational pair, husband-wife. It is here that the author increases his words nearly twenty-fold to convey to the hearers the implications and theological foundation of the commands regarding submission and love. In similar manner to the slave-master relationship of the Col. HT, it might be expected that this relational pair has been chosen by the author for special development along the thematic lines of the larger letter. At the very least, it is within this first section that the author shows a free hand in developing his own ethical concerns.[92]

Eph. 5:22: αἱ γυναῖκες τοῖς ἰδίοις ἀνδράσιν ὡς τῷ κυρίῳ.
Col. 3:18: Αἱ γυναῖκες, ὑποτάσσεσθε τοῖς ἀνδράσιν ὡς ἀνῆκεν ἐν κυρίῳ.

Besides the omission of a finite verb form[93] as found in Col., the author of Eph. has changed this first command considerably in terms of the motivation and force. On the one hand, the author appears to clarify and insure by the use of τοῖς ἰδίοις submission within the husband-wife relation only.[94] In spite of this limiting modification, however, the command undergoes a significant intensification in terms of the wives' former posture of submission found in Col. 3:18b, ὡς ἀνῆκεν ἐν κυρίῳ. The author retains the original

---

[92] Gielen, *Tradition*, 233, notes that the author reaches "his greatest degree of independent thought" within the first reciprocal pair; for this reason, verses 22–33 deserve "primäre Aufmerksamkeit" in determining the pragmatic intentions of the author.

[93] Some texts do supply a verb form after ἀνδράσιν or γυναῖκες, see fn. 66.

[94] That the listening wives are meant here, and not women in general, can be argued by the use of the nominative case with the article to form the vocative (see F. Blass and A. Debrunner, *A Greek Grammar of the New Testament and Other Early Christian Literature*, trans. R.W. Funk (Cambridge: CUP, 1961), 147, [3]. This, in combination with the adjective ἴδιος (which had, by the time of the writing of the NT, the function of a reflexive or possessive pronoun), limited the scope of the command to the marital relationship. See W. Bauer, *A Greek-English Lexicon of the New Testament and Other Early Christian Literature*, trans. W.F. Arndt and F.W. Gingrich, 2nd, Rev. F.W. Gingrich and F. Danker, eds. (Chicago: University of Chicago, 1979), 369.

ὡς phrase, an indication of his reliance on the Col. original. The new explicatory phrase in Eph., however, replaces the ambiguous Col. formulation, indicating a more direct level of identification of the wives' behaviour with their relation to Christ. The sense of propriety, or even duty towards a recognised norm (ἀνῆκεν), is superseded by another, more intimate motivational force: relationship to Christ. The relationally unconnected and indirect appeal to an accepted norm is displaced by Christ himself. Propriety is, then, measured in terms of Christ and his relationship to believers. This significant change most probably reflects the author's tendency, noted above, to lean more heavily on the expanded section of the Col. HT, in particular the motivation found given to the slaves in 3:23: ὃ ἐὰν ποιῆτε, ἐκ ψυχῆς ἐργάζεσθε ὡς τῷ κυρίῳ. The motivation which implied direct service for the slaves is now implemented in Eph. to generalise the intense and unmitigated nature of Christ's lordship in *all* HT relations.

> Eph. 5:23: ὅτι ἀνήρ ἐστιν κεφαλὴ τῆς γυναικὸς ὡς καὶ ὁ Χριστὸς κεφαλὴ τῆς ἐκκλησίας, αὐτὸς σωτὴρ τοῦ σώματος.

Though the HT form has been characterised as typically having three elements of *Anrede*, *Weisung* and *Begründung*, the last element, the explanatory/motivational phrase is noticeably defective in the first relational pair of Col., the husbands and wives.[95] Here the author of Eph. makes a considerable addition to the material, expanding the parenetic aspect of the pericope by adding extensive theological support to his mandates. The expansion, remarkably, retains the mediating influence of Christ within the relational pair, yet casts the common elements of human relationships (formerly [Col. HT] under the absolute authority of Christ) into a new relational pattern. The distinctive relational pattern, at least for the husband and wife, is now characterised as Christ-Church.[96] This use of analogy is unique to the Eph. HT redaction, and a significant development over the Col. HT. The depiction of Christ as head[97] is derived from the Col. text, and certainly forms the basis for this expansion: Col. 1:18a, as head of the church, καὶ αὐτός ἐστιν ἡ κεφαλὴ

---

[95] Gielen, *Tradition*, 4f. She correctly notes the exceptions in the address to the men in Col. 3:19, as well as to the fathers in Eph. 6:4. Neither receives a formal *Begründung* for the required behaviour. The instruction to the wives in Col. 3:18 indicates, similarly, only that the behaviour is fitting.

[96] Gielen, *Tradition*, 232, notes a paradigm shift from the "alle umfassenden Herrschaft Christi" to the "Relation Christus-Kirche".

[97] Though Christ is also depicted as saviour of the body here, and represents another aspect of his exemplary function, this image is more fully developed in 5:25–26.

τοῦ σώματος τῆς ἐκκλησίας; 2:10b, as head over all other authority, ὅς ἐστιν ἡ κεφαλὴ πάσης ἀρχῆς καὶ ἐξουσίας, and 2:19, as being the source, ...καὶ οὐ κρατῶν τὴν κεφαλήν, ἐξ οὗ πᾶν τὸ σῶμα διὰ τῶν ἁφῶν καὶ συνδέσμων ἐπιχορηγούμενον καὶ συμβιβαζόμενον αὔξει τὴν αὔξησιν τοῦ θεοῦ. The author of Eph. is indebted here to the language of Col., which advances the concept of Christ's lordship over, and sustaining power in, all relations. This understanding of Christ's pre-eminence is the author of Ephesians point of departure, which is reflected throughout the letter. That Christ is head of the church is known to the hearers by means of the declarations in Eph. 1:22 and 4:15; the surprising development of the Eph. HT is the direct manner in which the author introduces his analogy, and thereby the mediating influence of Christ. More than its Col. counterpart, the Eph. HT develops a distinctively theological argumentation for the first relational pair, intentionally couched in terms of the letter's distinctive κεφαλή vocabulary.

Eph. 5:24: ἀλλὰ ὡς ἡ ἐκκλησία ὑποτάσσεται τῷ Χριστῷ, οὕτως καὶ αἱ γυναῖκες τοῖς ἀνδράσιν ἐν παντί.

The author resumes his argument[98] and expands the force of his analogy in explicit terms; the verb ὑποτάσσω is introduced to denote an aspect of the relationship between Christ and the church as normative for the husband-wife relation. Though reversing the structure of v. 23 (where he first commands, then gives christological support in the form of analogy), the author underscores the emphasis upon the analogical nature of the relationships Christ-Church/husband-wife already introduced by the parallel structures in 5:23a and b. The author of Eph. repeats the command to the wives (see discussion of 5:28 below for similar technique regarding the husbands). Verse 24, however, by reiterating (and we can assume reinforcing) the command to submit in more explicit terms, introduces a *limiting* aspect to the larger analogy, as well. It is only the aspect of submission which is expressly developed and allowed as being an analogous, and therefore identifiable, relational pos-

---

[98] Lincoln, *Ephesians*, 372, points out that ἀλλά functions here as an adversative, "providing a contrast with the immediately preceding words in 23c." This seems correct, as the last phrase regarding Christ as σωτήρ does not find correspondence with any human activity, as is indicated by emphatic αὐτός (see Schnackenburg, *Brief*, 252, fn. 627). Here the author is likely expressing his consciousness of the limits of the analogy, particularly as it incorporates soteriological elements. Gielen, *Tradition*, 227, notes, "Die Apposition bleibt nun auf der Seite der zwischenmenschlichen Relation zwischen Mann und Frau ohne Entsprechung, so daß hier von einem gewissen semantischen Überhang gesprochen werden darf."

ture (ruling out other potential aspects known to the Christ-Church relationship such as the soteriological) between husband and wife.

While limiting the analogy to the aspect of submission, the author intensifies the formulation regarding the wives' submission through the insertion
of ἐν παντί. Here it appears that the author has again generalised an element
of the Col. HT found in verses 3:20 and 3:22, where children and slaves are
instructed to obey (ὑπακούετε) κατὰ πάντα. The extension of the absolute
lordship motif into the entire HT schema, which would be evidenced by a
tendency to generalise the absolute character of the commands, may lie at the
root of this expansion. This generalisation and application of κατὰ πάντα to
the first relational pair may also be due to the nature of the analogy which the
author has chosen: the absolute nature of the Christ-church relationship
dominates the analogy and its admonitions. Κατὰ πάντα may at this point be
more determined by the Christ-church relation, revealing an inherent unevenness within the analogy. Apart from this possible influence, and the express use of ὑποτάσσω, verse 24 represents unique developments of the Eph.
author.

Eph. 5:25: Οἱ ἄνδρες, ἀγαπᾶτε τὰς γυναῖκας, καθὼς καὶ ὁ
Χριστὸς ἠγάπησεν τὴν ἐκκλησίαν καὶ ἑαυτὸν παρέδωκεν ὑπὲρ
αὐτῆς.
Col. 3:19: Οἱ ἄνδρες, ἀγαπᾶτε τὰς γυναῖκας καὶ μὴ πικραίνεσθε
πρὸς αὐτάς.

The instruction to the husbands represents the largest expansion of the Eph.
HT to any single member of the household. Here the author shows a free
hand in developing an extended theological argument for regulating relations
between husband and wife. The similarities to the Col. HT are minimal, and
are limited to the opening words, Οἱ ἄνδρες, ἀγαπᾶτε τὰς γυναῖκας. The
author retains the positive element of Col. 3:19, the command to love their
wives (corresponding to the Eph. redactor's tendency to present his ethic in
positive terms), yet, he omits Col. 3:19b, μὴ πικραίνεσθε πρὸς αὐτάς, the
injunction not to be harsh.[99] The author has apparently decided to draw his
argument along positive lines only, perhaps due to the unfolding collocation
between the husband's behaviour and Christ. The reference to the negative
behaviour of harshness (certainly a human reality), does not fit the analogy of

---

[99] The Col. HT is otherwise preserved in a remarkably complete form, with most changes
occurring along the lines of intensification of the original. The other instance of omission is
6:4b.

Christ-church, and would inevitably work against his aim of construing a Christ-oriented ethic based upon this comparison. The additions found in 25b underscore the author's intention to present a *positive* model, derived from the work of Christ. The act of self-giving displaces the selfish human activity of harshness; the author has consciously changed the focus of the mandate to the husbands from the human (with its manifold frailties) to the divine sphere. 5:25 in this way qualifies the startling expansion of 5:24, ἐν παντι, to include only those behaviours that would be in keeping with the character of Christ. The singular theme regarding the husbands' behaviour has been limited, by this small omission, to love.

Eph. 5:26, 27: ἵνα αὐτὴν ἁγιάσῃ καθαρίσας τῷ λουτρῷ τοῦ ὕδατος ἐν ῥήματι, 5.27 ἵνα παραστήσῃ αὐτὸς ἑαυτῷ ἔνδοξον τὴν ἐκκλησίαν, μὴ ἔχουσαν σπίλον ἢ ῥυτίδα ἤ τι τῶν τοιούτων, ἀλλ᾽ ἵνα ᾖ ἁγία καὶ ἄμωμος.

Verses 26–27 introduce three short ἵνα clauses that are dedicated to explicating the positive results of Christ's giving of himself for the church; this is the beginning of a departure from the Col. HT in both style of argumentation and content, though clearly leaning upon the formulation in Col. 1:22: νυνὶ δὲ ἀποκατήλλαξεν ἐν τῷ σώματι τῆς σαρκὸς αὐτοῦ διὰ τοῦ θανάτου παραστῆσαι ὑμᾶς ἁγίους καὶ ἀμώμους καὶ ἀνεγκλήτους κατενώπιον αὐτοῦ. The general effects of Christ's death are here applied to the motivational aspect of the husband-wife relation. The clauses introduce a parallel concern of the author to not only impart ethical instruction to the relational pair (in this case the husbands), but to introduce and highlight *Christ*, the antecedent of the clauses, as the new ethical standard. Here the emphasis is upon Christ's sacrifice, his activity as saviour[100] determining the tenor of the ethic. The material relating to Christ in this section, being true of the entire church, can be generalised to the other relational pairs, as well. The statements regarding Christ in the Eph. HT, then, are not only unique to the HT form, but represent a broadening of the ethic in terms of universal application in the church. Whereas the person of Christ can be seen as a mediating influence upon relations in the Col. HT, the Eph. HT characterises the ethical ideal in his person and soteriological activity. In this manner, the author en-

---

[100] The instruction to the women includes this important appellation of Christ in 5:23b (αὐτὸς σωτὴρ τοῦ σώματος), a corresponding feature of his headship over the body. The motivation is an appeal not only to his sheer authority, but, additionally, to the character of his sacrifice.

hances the immediacy and universal scope (and thereby the importance) of the Christ-centred ethic.

Eph. 5:28, 29: οὕτως ὀφείλουσιν [καὶ] οἱ ἄνδρες ἀγαπᾶν τὰς ἑαυτῶν γυναῖκας ὡς τὰ ἑαυτῶν σώματα. ὁ ἀγαπῶν τὴν ἑαυτοῦ γυναῖκα ἑαυτὸν ἀγαπᾷ. 5.29 οὐδεὶς γάρ ποτε τὴν ἑαυτοῦ σάρκα ἐμίσησεν ἀλλὰ ἐκτρέφει καὶ θάλπει αὐτήν, καθὼς καὶ ὁ Χριστὸς τὴν ἐκκλησίαν.

In contrast to the terse instruction found in the Col. HT, the author of Eph. illustrates the admonition to love by extending the use of familiar somatic language.[101] Occurrences in the broader letter are linked exclusively to Christ and the church, including the HT reference in 5:23b. Here the husbands, in like manner to the wives, receive repeated instruction to love their wives (5:25), the author again reversing the order of argumentation in 5:25 from command to example of Christ. The example of Christ, particularly his redemption of the church,[102] now leads the analogy. The somatic language found in these sections of Eph. reflects a positive understanding of σῶμα, which is consistently carried over into the HT usage. This wholly positive understanding, linked by analogy to Christ and the church, creates a context in which the term σῶμα, undeniably understood in its human expression, is ennobled. Σάρξ, though used throughout the letter in both a neutral and negative sense, is also understood in positive terms, perhaps anticipating the OT use in v. 31. Again it is the primary concern of the author to indicate the exemplary nature of Christ in construing human relationships; the behaviour required of the husbands (5:28–29) is framed within, and illustrated by, the summary activity of Christ in 5:26–27 and 5:29b. This material finds neither correspondence within the Col. HT, nor in its broader context.

Eph. 5:30: ὅτι μέλη ἐσμὲν τοῦ σώματος αὐτοῦ.

Although this ὅτι construction resembles the form of the *Begründungssatz* from the earlier Col. HT form, the expansion does not reflect a borrowing

---

[101] Cf. Eph. 1:23; 2:16; 4:4, 16. These examples refer to Christ and his relationship to the church, or to the church itself. Though similar somatic language can be found in the broader text of Col. (1:18, 22, 24; 2:11, 17, 19, 23; 3:15), it is not extended to the HT, nor does it share the uniformity of meaning and wholly positive tenor of Eph.

[102] The author borrows heavily at this point from the theological motifs of Col. 1:22, 28: παραστῆσαι ὑμᾶς ἁγίους καὶ ἀμώμους καὶ ἀνεγκλήτους κατενώπιον αὐτοῦ; ἵνα παραστήσωμεν πάντα ἄνθρωπον τέλειον ἐν Χριστῷ.

from Col.[103] The somatic language is extended, momentarily, to expressly include the entire church, without a corresponding reference to the relational pair. This brief, generally inclusive statement is characteristic of the universal, christological ethic of Eph. The uneven flow of the analogy seen here is equally characteristic, and poses the difficulty in interpreting the expanded section.[104] The ethic which the author of Ephesians is promoting in the husband-wife relationship is, by virtue of its Christ-church analogy, universal to the believer, and to some degree, transferable to all relations in the church. This corresponds to the innovative approach of the author to generalise his ethic in terms of submission in the fear of the Lord in v. 21. Such general statements regarding the church's relation to Christ characterise the expanded section of the Eph. HT, and represent a unique development over against its Col. counterpart.

Eph. 5:31: ἀντὶ τούτου καταλείψει ἄνθρωπος [τὸν] πατέρα καὶ [τὴν] μητέρα καὶ προσκολληθήσεται πρὸς τὴν γυναῖκα αὐτοῦ, καὶ ἔσονται οἱ δύο εἰς σάρκα μίαν.

The quotation of Gen. 2:24 represents one of the distinctive hallmarks of the Eph. HT, the use of OT scriptures in supporting the HT ethic (also seen in 6:2). The citation strikes a more conservative note, as it is invoked to lend recognised authority to the human aspect of the author's analogy. The believers are encouraged to "understand the will of the Lord" in 5:17, and here the author provides clear evidence of God's intention in marriage. The marriage ethic is based, in contrast to Colossians, not in a sense of propriety in the Lord, but in the ontological reality created by the marriage union as described in scripture. That this human reality is in some way paralleled by the paradigmatic relation Christ-church, lends further weight to the significance of the author's admonitions. The Eph. HT, by appealing to scripture, highlights the mandatory nature of the instruction, while affirming the God-ordained nature of marriage.

Eph. 5:32: τὸ μυστήριον τοῦτο μέγα ἐστίν· ἐγὼ δὲ λέγω εἰς Χριστὸν καὶ εἰς τὴν ἐκκλησίαν.

---

[103] Besides the uneven range of meaning of σῶμα in Col., μέλος is also used only negatively in Col. 3:5. The usage here corresponds more closely to the integrated use in Eph. 4:25, perhaps akin to usage in Rom. 12:4–5 and 1 Cor. 12.

[104] The textual variant which includes a clarifying reference to Gen. 2:23 at the end of this verse is probably an attempt to introduce the ensuing OT quote (Gen.2:24), as well as maintaining the Christ-church/relational pair balance of the analogy.

The author's use of analogy to express the essence of his HT ethic, is, as mentioned above, a new stylistic development over against the Col. HT. It brings with it, as with all analogies, the difficulty of drawing lines of demarcation between the elements, Christ-church and husband-wife. The former element, Christ-church, is his innovation, and a departure from the singular regulatory function (though equally Christ-oriented) of the Col. HT. The concern for regulating intra-human relations under the lordship of Christ, the apparent intention of the Col. HT, is significantly augmented by a second, theological, concern of the author of Eph. The Eph. HT regulates human behaviour, while simultaneously introducing dogmatic elements which are equally concerned with illustrating the Christ-church relationship. There are clearly elements, then, as the author indicates in v.32, which are to be understood as pertaining to Christ and the church *only*. This represents a new use of the HT form by the author of Eph.: as a vehicle of theological instruction. The two concerns, which might be characterised as intra-human/ethical and Christ-church/theological, may be helpful in determining the limits of the analogy being drawn by the author. Verse 32 indicates the author's awareness of the two functions for which the HT is being employed, as well as the analogy's necessary limits.

Eph. 5:33: πλὴν καὶ ὑμεῖς οἱ καθ᾿ ἕνα, ἕκαστος τὴν ἑαυτοῦ γυναῖκα οὕτως ἀγαπάτω ὡς ἑαυτόν, ἡ δὲ γυνὴ ἵνα φοβῆται τὸν ἄνδρα.

This summary statement, reversing the original order of address, returns to the author's intra-human concerns, reiterating the command to love (husbands), as well as introducing a new command to the wives to respect (fear) their husbands. It is particularly notable that the author reformulates the address to both members in the singular; this feature, which intensifies the effect of the admonition, has no correspondence in any of the New Testament HT forms.[105] The admonition to love is formulated to reflect the OT command of love of neighbour, Lev. 19:18, the author making further use of authoritative texts to support his ethic. The verb φοβέομαι, found in the expanded instruction to the slaves in the Col. HT (3:22), is incorporated here to express the wife's posture towards her husband. Φόβος undergoes expanded use in the Eph. HT, providing the general motivation for mutual submission in 5:21, as well as the slave's attitude in rendering service. This general ad-

---

[105] O'Brien, *Ephesians*, 436, notes how the singular form of this summary injunction focuses upon the individual's responsibility to heed the apostle's instruction.

aptation of the fear-motif, as well as its representation in the Eph. HT, lend a sense of cohesion unknown to the Col. HT.

The Second Relational Pair: Parents and Children

The second intra-human relation, parent-children, though undergoing less alteration than the husband-wife relation, reveals several significant innovations which are unique to the Eph. HT.

Eph. 6:1: Τὰ τέκνα, ὑπακούετε τοῖς γονεῦσιν ὑμῶν [ἐν κυρίῳ]: τοῦτο γάρ ἐστιν δίκαιον.
Col. 3:20: Τὰ τέκνα, ὑπακούετε τοῖς γονεῦσιν κατὰ πάντα, τοῦτο γὰρ εὐάρεστόν ἐστιν ἐν κυρίῳ.

The first injunction to obey, though thoroughly recognisable, departs at several points from the Col. original, betraying independence of thought and the particular intentions of the author.[106] The modifying phrase κατὰ πάντα, found in the Col. text, has been left out, perhaps to avoid potential confusion or abuse (similarly in 6:5); the admonition to the children, at any rate, is extended in its particulars in 6:2, providing example and motivation for the less specific κατὰ πάντα. This small omission, notably replaced by the familiar ἐν κυρίῳ of Col., modifies the instruction with specifically Christian content.[107] The motivation has been changed, as well, the required obedience being characterised as "right" or "righteous" (δίκαιον) rather than "pleasing" (εὐάρεστόν) in the Lord. This slight motivational shift from pleasing the Lord to the rightness of the behaviour anticipates the attendant motivational appeal in v. 2, which is based in the OT Law.[108] Here the author has possibly been influenced again by the appearance of this word δίκαιον in the ex-

---

[106] Schnackenburg, *Brief*, 266, rightly argues that these departures are more than literary independence on the part of the Eph. author (so Schlier, 280f.), and should be seen as "seinen besonderen Gestaltungswillen."

[107] κατὰ πάντα appears to have been intentionally replaced by ἐν κυρίῳ, as Schnackenburg, *Brief*, 267, suggests, cleverly incorporating the specifically Christian element found in the general motivational phrase of Col. 3:20. ἐν κυρίῳ, a disputed reading, has support from a large number of reliable manuscripts, see Metzger, *Commentary*, 609, Best, *Ephesians*, 564, for a thorough discussion.

[108] Moritz, *Mystery*, 171f., contends that the author, familiar with OT collocations between right behaviours and the Law, combines the "concepts of what is right and what is demanded by the Law."

panded instruction to the slaves, Οἱ κύριοι, τὸ δίκαιον καὶ τὴν ἰσότητα τοῖς δούλοις παρέχεσθε, in Col. 4:1a.[109]

Eph. 6:2,3: τίμα τὸν πατέρα σου καὶ τὴν μητέρα, ἥτις ἐστὶν ἐντολὴ πρώτη ἐν ἐπαγγελίᾳ, ἵνα εὖ σοι γένηται καὶ ἔσῃ μακροχρόνιος ἐπὶ τῆς γῆς.

The author again makes explicit use of OT scripture, this instance from the Decalogue.[110] He underscores the importance of the promise, drawing the reader's attention to the command's motivation; this feature is characteristic of the Eph. redaction. The original command to obey is explicated in terms of a second command, which is certainly the intention of the author. The OT citation, however, lends the admonition indisputable authority, as well. The author of Eph., in contrast to the same passage in Col., promotes the HT ethic by means of clarifying expansions which appeal to scriptural authority.

Eph. 6:4: Καὶ οἱ πατέρες, μὴ παροργίζετε τὰ τέκνα ὑμῶν ἀλλὰ ἐκτρέφετε αὐτὰ ἐν παιδείᾳ καὶ νουθεσίᾳ κυρίου.
Col. 3:21: Οἱ πατέρες, μὴ ἐρεθίζετε τὰ τέκνα ὑμῶν, ἵνα μὴ ἀθυμῶσιν.

In 6:4a, the author adheres closely to the formulation of Col., but displaces the verb ἐρεθίζετε of Col. 3:21 with παροργίζετε. Whereas ἐρεθίζω may have a positive or negative sense in "to stir up" (2 Cor. 9:2, the only other NT occurrence, is clearly positive), the verb παροργίζω conveys the negative sense of to "stir to anger, provoke ".[111] The negative sense is underscored in the Eph. 4:26, where the author employs the noun form, anger (παροργισμός), to depict an undesirable ethical condition. Best explains the two forms by appealing to a third, independent source.[112] The meanings of these

---

[109] Contra Best, "Relationship", 81, who suggests that this change is arbitrary.

[110] The LXX rendering of Ex. 20:12 (Dt. 5:16 adds historical perspective in ὃν τρόπον ἐνετείλατό σοι κύριος ὁ θεός σου) is nearly exact, although the initial phrase ἐπὶ τῆς γῆς serves to abbreviate "the good land which the Lord God will give you", minimising the original (primarily Jewish) OT context. This omission also serves to generalise the scope of meaning of the promise. Similarly in Rom. 7:7, where the particulars of Ex. 20:17 are abbreviated with the opening words, οὐκ ἐπιθυμήσεις.

[111] The only other occurrence of this verb can be found in Rom. 10:9, which is a quote from Dt. 32:21, where Israel has provoked the Lord to anger (παρώργισάν με) by idolatry; the Lord reciprocates by provoking the nation to anger (παροργιῶ αὐτούς).

[112] Best, Ephesians, 568.

two verbs, however, are not synonymous; this, joined with the significant alterations within the second phrase of the verse, make a third source unlikely. Col. 3:21 undergoes significant alteration in both its command *and* motivational aspects, a shift from negative-negative to a clearer and more balanced negative-positive formulation. It appears that the author of Eph. has selected παροργίζω, which, by its singularly negative connotation, clarifies and strengthens the meaning of the Col. *Vorlage*. The clearly negative behaviour of provoking to anger also provides a fitting contrast to the author's restructuring of the motivational phrase in terms of *positive* behaviour, as well. This represents a stylistic and didactic improvement over the vague Col. formulation. The author replaces the original ἵνα clause, with its negative contingency of discouragement, with an alternative and positive admonition. Though the Col. motivational phrase is omitted, the instruction is extended. The author makes use of a familiar OT expression, which refers to God's discipline of Israel, thus capitalising upon the appropriateness of the instruction in achieving right behaviour.[113] The inclusion of νουθεσία emphasises the aspect of instruction, adding balance, as well as being characteristic of the author's use of synonymous doublets, as mentioned above. The genitive κυρίου underscores the author's intention that all admonition be understood as being vitally connected to the will of God (5:17).[114]

The Third Relational Pair: Masters and Slaves

As found in the second relational pair, the author of Eph. adheres closely to the formulation and content of the Col. *Vorlage*, yet departing at points to develop his own particular emphases.

---

[113] See Bertram's article "παιδεύω κτλ.", in *TDNT*, 5, 596–625; the OT has no particular concept or terminus for education in the modern sense; however, the expression is generally used in reference to God's activity of correction and instruction of the people as they strayed from obedience to the covenant. The LXX, then, makes use of παιδεία, but the word pair παιδεία καὶ νουθεσία does not occur. Bertram notes (fn. 103) an instance in Josephus, *Ant.* 8,217, where the LXX παιδεύειν is replaced with νουθετεῖν, perhaps because παιδεία "was alien to the literary usage of Hellenism in this sense." Either this or the tendency to employ synonymyous word pairs, may explain the Eph. author's use of similar expressions. Schnackenburg, *Brief*, 268, notes that this expression (bedeutsamer Ausdruck) would have been recognised from OT tradition.

[114] Gnilka, *Epheserbrief*, 299, sees this genitive usage as qualifying/limiting, not subjective, offering a point of reference, namely Christ. See also Schlier, *Brief*, 283.

Eph. 6:5: Οἱ δοῦλοι, ὑπακούετε τοῖς κατὰ σάρκα κυρίοις μετὰ φόβου καὶ τρόμου ἐν ἁπλότητι τῆς καρδίας ὑμῶν ὡς τῷ Χριστῷ.

Col. 3:22: Οἱ δοῦλοι, ὑπακούετε κατὰ πάντα τοῖς κατὰ σάρκα Κυρίοις, μὴ ἐν ὀφθαλμοδουλίᾳ ὡς ἀνθρωπάρεσκοι, ἀλλ᾽ ἐν ἁπλότητι καρδίας φοβούμενοι τὸν κύριον.

The author again deletes the phrase κατὰ πάντα (cf. 5:22), perhaps to avoid abuse, but apparently not to diminish the level of service, as the rest of the admonitions make clear. φοβούμενοι τὸν κύριον is not adopted for use, but finds a substitute phrase μετὰ φόβου καὶ τρόμου, which makes use of a stereotyped word pair, as well as introducing a known OT phrase, both noted aspects of the author's style.[115] Though the order of appearance is changed, "with singleness of heart" continues to modify the obedience, yet is strengthened by the phrase ὡς τῷ Χριστῷ. The title of Christ, perhaps reflecting the singular HT usage in Col. 3:24, complements the instances of the title of *kurios*, and certainly reflects an element of the Eph. author's style.[116]

Eph. 6:6: μὴ κατ᾽ ὀφθαλμοδουλίαν ὡς ἀνθρωπάρεσκοι ἀλλ᾽ ὡς δοῦλοι Χριστοῦ ποιοῦντες τὸ θέλημα τοῦ θεοῦ ἐκ ψυχῆς.
Col. 3:22: ...μὴ ἐν ὀφθαλμοδουλίᾳ ὡς ἀνθρωπάρεσκοι...
Col. 3:23a: ὃ ἐὰν ποιῆτε, ἐκ ψυχῆς ἐργάζεσθε...
Col. 3:24b: τῷ κυρίῳ Χριστῷ δουλεύετε.

The author adopts in 6a nearly the exact wording of Col. 3:22. The injunction of Col. 3:24b "to serve the Lord Christ" is assumed as an ontological fact in Eph. 6:6b, ὡς δοῦλοι Χριστοῦ, evidence of the influence of the Col. passage on the author's thinking. Service is ennobled here, as the author employs the honourable title δοῦλος Χριστοῦ to the slaves.[117] 6:6b evidences even more change, particularly a shift in perspective. Whereas Col. 3:23 admonished slaves to work ἐκ ψυχῆς, Eph. connects this attitude with attaining the will

---

[115] Cf. Gen. 9:2; Ex. 15:16; Dt. 2:25; Ps. 2:11; Is. 19:16; OT usage refers exclusively to God. Also familiar through usage in the Paulines: 1 Cor. 2:3; 2 Cor. 7:15; Phil. 2:12.

[116] The title *Christos* finds expression 47 times in Eph. (compare to 25 instances in Col.), so that the eight occurrences in the HT cannot be explained only in terms of the single usage in Col. 3:24. It appears to be the favoured appellation of the Eph. author.

[117] Phil. 1:1; Rom. 1:1; Gal. 1:10.

of God (5:17). Right behaviour for the author of Eph. is, as mentioned above, more emphatically connected to the person and will of God.[118]

> Eph. 6:7: μετ᾽ εὐνοίας δουλεύοντες ὡς τῷ κυρίῳ καὶ οὐκ ἀν-
> θρώποις.
> Col. 3:23b: ...ὡς τῷ κυρίῳ καὶ οὐκ ἀνθρώποις.

Only 6:7a introduces change (6:7b representing a direct quote of Col. 3:22b), where the author, in typical fashion, extends the instruction of the HT in positive terms. The author is apparently attempting to underscore the appropriateness[119] of the service, as well as reiterating the direct responsibility implied in service to Christ.

> Eph. 6:8: εἰδότες ὅτι ἕκαστος ἐάν τι ποιήσῃ ἀγαθόν, τοῦτο
> κομίσεται παρὰ κυρίου εἴτε δοῦλος εἴτε ἐλεύθερος.
> Col. 3:24a: εἰδότες ὅτι ἀπὸ κυρίου ἀπολήμψεσθε τὴν
> ἀνταπόδοσιν τῆς κληρονομίας.
> Col. 3:25: ὁ γὰρ ἀδικῶν κομίσεται ὃ ἠδίκησεν, καὶ οὐκ ἔστιν
> προσωπολημψία.

The author of Eph. conflates elements of Col. 3:24 and 25 to reformulate the reciprocal ethic of divine compensation. He leaves out, however, the reference to the reward of inheritance (3:24b), as well as the reference to the wrongdoer (3:25a); the negative formulation is replaced, typically of the author of Eph., with the more positive ἕκαστος ἐάν τι ποιήσῃ ἀγαθόν. Inheritance is implied, however, by the focus upon positive behaviour. Complementing this positive addition is the author's inclusion of both slave and freedman, εἴτε δοῦλος εἴτε ἐλεύθερος. The formulation may have its roots in Col. 3:11, where both groups, δοῦλος, ἐλεύθερος are mentioned in terms of their equal standing before Christ. Whereas Col. 3:24, 25 did not directly implicate the behaviour of the masters, the author of Ephesians has removed the ambiguity in the clear inclusion of both slave and free (cf. 1 Cor. 12:13). The formulation may reflect, then, the author of Eph. understanding of the

---

[118] Schnackenburg, *Brief*, 270, suggests that this usage may be an intentional echo of Dt. 6:5, ἐξ ὅλης τῆς ψυχῆς.

[119] εὔνοια found only here in NT; usage was common in antiquity, however, particularly as a virtue among slaves. See Gnilka, *Epheserbrief*, 301, fn. 4.

154

Col. ethic of equal standing before Christ, as well as his desire to enhance the force of the HT reciprocal ethic.[120]

Eph. 6:9: Καὶ οἱ κύριοι, τὰ αὐτὰ ποιεῖτε πρὸς αὐτούς, ἀνιέντες τὴν ἀπειλήν, εἰδότες ὅτι καὶ αὐτῶν καὶ ὑμῶν ὁ κύριός ἐστιν ἐν οὐρανοῖς καὶ προσωπολημψία οὐκ ἔστιν παρ' αὐτῷ.
Col. 4:1: Οἱ κύριοι, τὸ δίκαιον καὶ τὴν ἰσότητα τοῖς δούλοις παρέχεσθε, εἰδότες ὅτι καὶ ὑμεῖς ἔχετε κύριον ἐν οὐρανῷ.

Eph. 6:8b has already made clear that the Lord will recompense both slave and free for doing good. The author of Eph. extends this thought, commanding the masters to do these things, τὰ αὐτά, notably in the plural. It may be that he was influenced by the dual responsibilities contained in the original Col. construction τὸ δίκαιον καὶ τὴν ἰσότητα; at any rate, the author of Eph. expects the masters, as with the slaves, to be engaged in various deeds related to the good (τὸ ἀγαθόν). This further enhances the author's intention to show the slave-master relationship as unambiguously as possible: both parties are expected to behave in light of Christ, and find equality before him.[121] Threatening is singled out as a negative behaviour, perhaps to give concrete expression to the deleted reference to wrong behaviour in Col. 3:25. 6:9b reformulates Col. 4:1b, making the reference to the "Lord in heaven" apply equally to both slave (αὐτῶν) and master (ὑμῶν).

Conclusion

Our brief exegetical examination of the Eph. HT has shown that the author, demonstrating a conservative tendency, has preserved the order, as well as a substantial portion of the content, of the Col. HT and its immediate context. The large amount of common material, as well as the coincidence of its ordering, indicate an intricate literary relationship between the two forms. Particular elements which have been retained in the Ephesian HT include the order, number and recipients of the Colossian address, including its reciprocal and direct nature. The primary verbal admonitions, though slightly modi-

---

[120] He signals reciprocity here and at two further points in the slave-master relation: 6:9 demands of the masters *like* behaviour, τὰ αὐτὰ ποιεῖτε πρὸς αὐτούς; 6:9 also adjusts the Col. formulation (which presents a hierarchy of heavenly master-earthly master-slave), placing both master and slave in parallel relation to the Lord: ὅτι καὶ αὐτῶν καὶ ὑμῶν ὁ κύριός ἐστιν ἐν οὐρανοῖς.
[121] Gnilka, *Epheserbrief*, 271, notes the call for corresponding behaviour, which is evidence of the "Gleichstellung vor Christus."

fied, also reflect close correspondence.[122] The christological motivation, though significantly expanded in the Eph. HT, constitutes the primary theological impulse of both forms, the Eph. HT adapting the highly christianised motivation of the Col. slave-master relationship as its starting point. It appears, then, that the author is not only familiar with the Col. HT form, but has attempted to preserve, by means of imitation and clever adaptation, its basic form and motivation. The Ephesian redaction is, then, certainly conservative.

In spite of the redaction's conservative nature, the author of Ephesians demonstrates a creative tendency in his adaptation of the Col. material. Our analysis has shown, we hope, that the Eph. HT form has *grown* from the formulations found within the Col. HT, while borrowing from central theological formulations found in the broader letter of Colossians. For this reason, the Ephesian HT must be analysed along the lines of its expansions. It is precisely these expanded elements which make the Col.-Eph. direction of redaction more plausible. The author of Eph. introduces stylistic elements which work together to produce a thoroughly *revised* form of the HT, marking him as an independent and creative thinker. A number of stylistic features contained within the Eph. HT represent innovation in respect to its Col. counterpart. These significant stylistic developments reveal not only the intention of the author to modify the HT form and ethic, but belong to his general writing style and particular vocabulary as expressed across the entire epistle. That several of these stylistic elements and vocabulary can be found in the larger letter does not detract from their significance in modifying the HT form; on the contrary, their presence outside the HT shows conscious application of the author's concerns in both the theological and parenetic sections of the letter. It is therefore difficult to imagine that these features, which clarify and extend the HT admonitions, would be intentionally removed by a later Colossian redactor. The innovations take several forms. The author, citing mutual submission in the fear of Christ, sets a distinct and intentional measure for regulating the mandates along intra-human and reciprocal, yet Christ-directed lines. The motivational sections of all three relationships are expanded, these being expressed in distinctly positive terms and with more specific instruction. Negative elements of behaviour are substituted with positive examples, which are more in keeping with the direct analogy being drawn to the behaviour of Christ, as well as reflecting the au-

---

[122] All lead-in admonitions are identical, with the exception of Eph. 5:21, where the imperative ὑποτάσσεσθε of Col. 3:18 is expressed by the use of the present participle ὑποτασσόμενοι.

thor's style. The use of word pairs, an element of the author's style within the larger letter, finds expression in HT, as well. The author introduces OT passages[123] to the motivational clauses, providing illustration, while enhancing their authoritative and distinctively Christian character. Christ, certainly the mediating influence of the Col. HT as saviour and coming judge, takes a more direct role in the Eph. HT ethic as *exemplar*. This is accomplished by means of the author's use of the Christ-Church analogy, as well as the employment of somatic and head language to further illustrate the regulatory nature of the life, death and rule of Christ in the church. The extended use of analogy transforms the ethical aspects of the HT, making it a vehicle of theological instruction, as well. These significant modifications to the HT form indicate creativity and a sense of freedom on the part of the author of Eph. to modify the tenor of the Col. HT; the competing proposal of an Eph.-Col. redaction simply lacks the elements of adaptation and theological intention which these innovations demonstrate. Though it can certainly be shown that the Ephesian HT might have been heavily edited by a proposed Col. redactor, there is no positive pattern which might be construed as an attempt to craft the Col. HT to the author's particular theological or ethical goals. On the contrary, the omissions appear arbitrary; OT citations, numerous clarifications, distinctively Christian modifications and the christological analogy are suppressed, yet similar material in the slave-master relation, as well as the general letter, is retained. Though it must be conceded that such a drastic and inconsequent redaction is possible, its probability is limited, we believe, when contrasted with the logical and demonstrable innovations of the Ephesian editor. Having made these observations, it remains to be seen if the modifications and expansions found in the Eph. HT can be understood as an expression of the style and general theological message of Eph. This will be our undertaking in the following chapter.

---

[123] Moritz, *Mystery*, 220, sees the many OT references within Eph. as a deliberate attempt on the part of the author of Eph. to enrich the Col. *Vorlage*, a vital editorial aspect in understanding the letter, with which we would agree. The employment of OT references represents a development in the formation of the HT ethic.

Chapter Four
The Ephesian *Haustafel*
in Theological
Context

Introduction

Up to this point in our discussion, we have limited ourselves to an analysis of the Eph. HT in terms of its continuity with, and divergence from, its Col. *Vorlage*. This approach, we hope, has served to highlight the uniqueness of the Eph. HT, and suggested the need to treat its admonitions as expressions of the ethical vision of the Eph. author. Our analysis has shown signs of intentional preservation of the Col. HT material and form, while evidencing substantial and creative change. The scope of this manner of analysis, however, remains too limited to ascertain the theological intentions of the author of Eph., or to indicate any paradigm for understanding the Eph. HT admonitions. This, we believe, can be found in the careful examination of the larger letter, particularly innovations and subtle changes in terms of vocabulary, theological themes and unifying emphasis. In this chapter we will consider shifts in the author's theological perspective, with attention given to these elements as encountered in the Ephesian HT. These elements, if shown to be present in both the letter and the HT, may yield clues to understanding the intention of the author in his unique HT formulations.

Determining the dominant theological theme(s) contained within the theological and parenetic sections of Ephesians is not necessarily a matter of recognition (a glance over any Eph. bibliography shows that the letter can be, and certainly has been, treated from several perspectives), but of determining, if possible, whether the several important emphases and editorial features constitute a unified thematic concern of the author. Can the various themes and editorial choices be understood as representing a coherent perspective from which the author is promoting his ethic? Do unique developments within Ephesians, including significant shifts from the perspective of Col., contribute to such a unified understanding? It is our contention that Ephesians not only contains such a coherent perspective, but that this perspective has influenced the formulations and emphases of the HT, as well. This perspective, we hope to argue, emerges from the author's conviction that the church represents the expression of God's unfolding will and saving work in Christ, and embodies the necessary context for construing ethical relationships. The prominence of the church in the author's thinking gives rise to a number of significant shifts in perspective (from the Col. material), while serving as the basis for creative innovation. This can be seen, we hope to demonstrate, in the letter's unique theological emphases and vocabulary. No *single* element of the author's vocabulary, style or perspective, however, can be employed to argue our point convincingly; the letter's complexity will not allow it. The following material will, then, attempt to trace several of the strands of thought within Eph. which constitute the fundamental emphasis upon the Christ and the church.

The Ephesian Redaction

The author of Eph., though preserving much of the Col. material, introduces several fundamental changes in theological and relational perspective. These shifts in perspective correspond to the new importance with which Christ and the church are regarded in defining relational categories and regulating ethical behaviour, and go far towards systematising the author's ethic in terms of the *horizontal* axis. By drawing the reader's attention to the particular illustrative texts within the body of the letter, we hope to establish an intentional pattern of emphasis upon the horizontal axis; ultimately, our discussion will attempt to ascertain whether this tendency can be clearly identified within the HT mandates. The modifications discussed below represent, then, significant changes in the primary Colossian relational axes, in both their inter-human and divine-human expressions.

The most fundamental shift in perspective between the two letters involves their common theological/ethical division of the universe into opposing spheres of influence. This division, construed in Colossians along earthly-heavenly and present-future lines in Col. 3:1–4, serves as a backdrop for regulating the divine and human relational axes in that epistle, as discussed above. It is at this point of opposing ethical axes that the author of Ephesians has made a remarkable change. At several points within the letter, he has displaced the original Col. antithesis, "heavenly-earthly" with the more horizontal and ethically demonstrable "heathen-Christian" bifurcation. Merklein, noting a change in the Eph. author's ethical reasoning, characterises the shift in perspective as a "Verschiebung der Antithetik".[1] This shift,

---

[1] Merklein, "Rezeption", 210. His treatment includes Eph. 4:1–5:20, as well as comparisons of Eph. 2:11–22 and Eph. 3 with the theological section of Col. The change in perspective can be seen in the transitional sections of Col. 3:1–4 and Eph. 4:17–24, where both passages formulate the reasoning (*Begründung*) behind the coming parenetic sections. It is the transitional position of these texts, he reasons, which gives weight to the perspective in terms of the ensuing parenesis. The Col. passage contrasts earthly and heavenly, present and coming realities;

contends Merklein, indicates the pragmatic concern of the author to avoid the potential drift of the Asian churches into heathen practice.[2] Though this pragmatic concern likely played a significant role in the new formulation of the antithesis, it is a shift which redefines the realm of human experience in earthly, horizontal terms, and indicates a new theological perspective which places an emphasis upon the church and her practice. The Eph. author has received the antithetical model of Col., yet refocuses the sphere of ethical behaviour, placing it upon an earthly, horizontal axis. The Col. antithesis, reflecting the vast differentiation between earth and heaven, has been transformed to reflect the conflict between the world and the church and its teachings. The numerous references to the former life/worldly practice[3] illustrate the author's immanent concern regarding the influence of worldly thinking and behaviour, as well as recognising the church's struggle with evil. It also serves to illustrate the antithetical poles of heathen practice and church life. This new emphasis does not completely eliminate reference to the former heavenly perspective,[4] yet the theology and ethics of the letter are cast primarily along earthly, horizontal lines. It is particularly important for our investigation to assess the new and various elements of the author's ethical vision, in an attempt to determine if this perspective is found, ultimately, in the mandates of the Ephesian HT. The following examples illustrate the Eph. author's new perspective.

In his theological argument in Eph. 2:11–22, the author depicts the readers in terms of ethnicity, distance from God, and alienation from the promises of Israel, into which they have gained entrance through Christ. Reflecting the language found in Col. 1:21 (ἀπηλλοτριμένους- ἀπηλλοτριμωνένοι, ἐχθρούς-ἐχθραν, ἀποκατήλλαξεν- ἀποκαταλλάξῃ), the Eph. employment of the terms estrangement, enmity and reconciliation are not primarily related to God, but to the faith community (as represented by citizenship in Israel); the

---

Eph. notably leaves this element out, contrasting heathen thought and practice with the new life in Christ, Eph. 4:20.

[2] Ibid., 210. Though Merklein does not make this distinction, it should be noted here that the antithesis is ethical in nature (Eph. 4:17–19 implicates heathen practice, yet the letter is clear that such *previous* behaviours include the entire church, 2:3: ἐν οἷς καὶ ἡμεῖς πάντες ἀνεστράφημέν ποτε...ὡς καὶ οἱ λοιποί) and is not only ethnic; the letter is remarkably positive in regards to the status of the heathen as an ethnic-societal entity within the church (cf. Eph. 2:11–14, 18–19; 3:6, 8).

[3] Gentile outsiders become members of God's household, clearly the church, 2:11–22; the mystery of the gospel makes Gentiles heirs with Israel in the one body, 3:6; former Gentile life contrasted with church teaching, 4:17–25; formerly darkness, but now light, 5:8–14.

[4] Though much of the theology and ethics are concerned with the present, earthly condition, it would be incorrect to suggest that the author of Eph. limits his theological world view or ethical argument to the earthly sphere. Cf. 1:10, 20b–21; 2:6; 3:10, 15; 4:8–10; 6:9, 12.

emphasis here being upon sociological and cultic transformation, highlighted in this section by contrasting images such as near-far, alien-citizen and hostility-peace. The benefits of new standing in Christ are distilled in the formation of a new sociological unity, the *church*. The church, notably, as Israel, represents a level of earthly tradition, being built upon the prophets and apostles (2:20; 3:5). The addressees of Ephesians have exchanged, from the author's theological perspective (and in contrast to Col.), both identity and tradition along a horizontal, heathen-Christian axis. This ontological transfer carries with it an ethical dimension, which the author develops in the parenetic section of the letter. Not surprisingly, the admonitions reflect the antithesis between the two poles, as seen in the instruction of Eph. 4:1–5:20. Buried within the numerous commands and warnings, we find reference to the distinct heathen-Christian spheres. In Eph. 4:17 the hearers are admonished in light of their former life: μηκέτι ὑμᾶς περιπατεῖν, καθὼς καὶ τὰ ἔθνη περιπατεῖ ἐν ματαιότητι τοῦ νοὸς αὐτῶν. This negative behaviour is expanded upon in the following verse, describing the hearers as darkened in their understanding and alienated from the life of God (interestingly, the author again employs the language of Col. 1:21, ἀππηλλοτριμωνένοι). The antidote to this dire situation is found in 4:20–21, where the corruption of the heathen mind and practice is countered by the teaching of truth as heard in the church: ῾Υμεῖς δὲ οὐχ οὕτως ἐμάθετε τὸν Χριστόν, εἴ γε αὐτὸν ἠκούσατε καὶ ἐν αὐτῷ ἐδιδάχθητε, καθώς ἐστιν ἀλήθεια ἐν τῷ ᾿Ιησοῦ. The author appeals, then, to traditions known to his readers, and associated with the church. The church, its teachings and leaders provide the antithesis to the world, its thought-systems and lifestyle. Even super-human, evil forces are countered in the present, earthly realm with the weapons given by God to the saints; the author gives particular attention to the cognitive fields related to truth, faith, the gospel, salvation and the word of God, as well as the practice of prayer (Eph. 6:10–18). The Christian is instructed to engage the present struggle in the world with the weapons available to the church as a whole; the absence of any eschatological reference to heavenly/future resolution of this situation is remarkable. Though the author's recasting of the antithesis may appear insignificant in terms of behaviour, the departure from the "earthly-heavenly" perspective (and motivation) represents a major shift in the author's ethical and theological reasoning. The church, now representing the positive locus for ethical and theological orientation, assumes a character of authority unknown in Colossians. The author of Ephesians has, without removing Christ from his ultimate role in divine-human relations, elevated the church's role in the believer's life of faith. This significant addition represents a modifying element in the Eph. author's theological and ethical framework, one which subtly promotes a shift in the Col. relational axes. The horizontal axis of Ephesians now offers a parallel ethical model (the church) which augments the solitary vertical, heavenly model previously regulating the ethical vision of Colossians. Both Christ *and* the church represent points of reference for the believer's behaviour in respect to the world. This does not mean, however, that Christ is diminished in his ethical authority as the representative of the heavenly realm. The vertical, divine-human axis, though augmented, is left fully intact.[5] Not surprisingly, however, it also undergoes significant change.

The modification of the divine-human axis in Ephesians cannot be overlooked at this point. If the author of Ephesians has construed the *ethical* universe along horizontal lines (formerly an element of the Col. vertical axis), it might be expected that the Ephesian vertical axis would demonstrate further adjustments in perspective, as well. This does indeed take place, as the author of Eph. modifies particular *elements* of the Col. perspective. The changes, which we have designated as a systematisation of the horizontal axis, do not do away with the vertical axis; yet the author of Eph. feels free to appropriate the language from the Col. vertical axis for his own ecclesiastical and ethical concerns. This tendency can be seen in the following examples:

The genesis of the divine-human axis found in Colossians, initiated by the saving act of Christ (Col. 1:20, 22), is retained, and even expanded, in the Eph. reception, though with different language.[6] The verb designating reconciliation (ἀποκαταλλάσσω, unique to Col. and Eph. in the NT) plays a central role in the formation of the divine-human axis in Col., describing the reconstitution of divine-human relations through Christ. In Eph., however, this verb is employed to illustrate the *inter-human* benefits of Christ's death, the reconciliation of Jew and Gentile (Eph. 2:16). This significant change illustrates the author's concern with the horizontal axis, particularly as it touches upon all relationships within the church.[7] Divine-human reconciliation, though certainly assumed in Eph., includes with it an inter-human element, as well. The author of Eph. shows a distinct tendency to interpret the divine aspects of salvation upon the inter-human level. The direct sote-

---

[5] Ephesians retains the clear faith-love distinction which highlights the two axes in both letters, Col. 1:4 and Eph. 1:15.

[6] The emphasis is clear in the language of election and the will of God (1:4, 5, 9, 11, 13), as well as the author's emphasis upon previous heathen lifestyle of sin, hopelessness and alienation (2:1–22).

[7] The peace and health of the church is certainly a central concern of the letter; the unusual emphasis given here to reconciliation between Jew and Gentile may be due to significant Jewish presence in Western Asia Minor. See Moritz, *Mystery*, 220.

riological relationship which is established by means of the vertical axis in Col. is diffused in Eph., creating a more *generalised* and *indirect* aspect of the divine-human relation, which has its accent in the earthly realm. This becomes particularly clear in the HT admonitions to husband and wife, as we shall investigate below.

Another indicator of this tendency is the displacement in Eph. of the relational model *doulos-kurios*, which characterised the divine-human axis of Colossians. Not only is the slave-master relationship balanced (and superseded) by the instruction to the other relational pairs in the HT, all references to δοῦλος outside of the HT are omitted.[8] The *doulos-kurios* relationship cannot be construed as representing the relational character of the divine-human axis as found in Eph. As Gielen has pointed out, the author of Eph. has changed the direct and more individual relational paradigm of Colossians to a more *general* relationship characterised by the church:

> Der Unterschied besteht allein im Austausch des aus den bisher untersuchten Mahnungen vertrauten Paradigmas κύριος-ἄνθρωποι/δοῦλοι, das man als christlich-anthropologisches Paradigma bezeichnen kann, gegen das Paradigma Χριστός-ἐκκλησία, das demgegenüber als christologisch-ekklesiologisches Paradigma zu bezeichnen ist. Mit diesem Austausch geht einher, daß die Gebundenheit des einzelnen Getauften an Christus, die im christologisch-anthropologischen Paradigma direkt gegeben ist (δοῦλοι κυρίου), im christologisch-ekklesiologischen Paradigma nur indirekt über die Zugehörigkeit der Getauften zur Ekklesia (vgl. 5,30: ὅτι μέλη ἐσμὲν τοῦ σώματος αὐτου) zu erheben ist.[9]

The author of Eph. further modifies the divine-human aspect by limiting or eliminating an important element which regulated the Col. vertical axis. The theme of the coming of Christ (Col. 3:4), which represented an uniquely divine aspect of the vertical relational axis, as well as serving to regulate the HT mandates, has undergone significant change in the Eph. author's redaction. In spite of the fact that the author has taken much of the Col. slave-master relationship to form the Eph. HT, particularly the regulating fear of the Lord, this fear is associated exclusively with judgement (cf. Eph. 5:6, 6:8). The mediating influence of the parousia is missing from the ethical argument. One would expect to find some (even veiled) reference to Christ's return, at the very least as a partial motivation for the extensive parenetic material. This is, surprisingly, not the case in Eph.[10] On the contrary, the

---

[8] Col. includes references to δοῦλος and σύνδουλος in 1:7; 3:11; 4:7, 12; these refer both to believers, as well as the Apostle and his co-workers.

[9] Gielen, *Tradition*, 235f.

[10] Mitton, *Epistle*, 70, traces a trajectory within the early Paulines, Col. and Eph., noting an ebbing prominence of the parousia.

church appears to enjoy a continuity which extends for generations, Eph. 3:21: αὐτῷ ἡ δόξα ἐν τῇ ἐκκλησίᾳ καὶ ἐν Χριστῷ Ἰησοῦ εἰς πάσας τὰς γενεὰς τοῦ αἰῶνος τῶν αἰώνων, ἀμήν. Whereas judgement plays a central role in the motivation of the general parenesis of Col. (3:4f), as well as the HT (Col. 3:25–4:1), it finds only modified representation in the Eph. HT.[11] The fear of the Lord, though retained as a motivational and regulatory aspect of the Eph. HT, is not connected with the coming of Christ. This omission seems to be more than a matter of style, particularly for an author who is otherwise strongly influenced by earlier Pauline material.[12] The author has modified both of these aspects of Christ's role in the divine-human axis, effectively de-emphasising their importance in regulating ethical behaviour. This, along with the shift away from the individual *doulos-kurios* model in favour of the more general Christ-church model, illustrates the ultimate orientation of the Eph. author. The vertical ethic of Colossians has given way to a more horizontal, communal understanding of ethical behaviour within the context of the church. The role of Christ, though certainly Lord of the body, is diminished by the omission of his coming.

The church, conversely, shares, to a larger degree, Christ's regulating authority. This is illustrated by the Eph. author's free use of πλήρωμα. In Col., this term is used in two manners. It refers, first of all, to Christ, in whom the fullness, even divine fullness, dwells (described in the Christ hymn, Col. 1:19: ἐν αὐτῷ εὐδόκησεν πᾶν τὸ πλήρωμα κατοικῆσαι; in contrast to false teachings, 2:9: ἐν αὐτῷ κατοικεῖ πᾶν τὸ πλήρωμα τῆς θεότητος σωματικῶς. Both of these references, it should be noted, occur in segments of Col. which have not been fully included in the Ephesian redaction). The word is used to illustrate the relationship between Christ and the Father, and represents the primary emphasis of the Col. author. The second usage, found in a single reference in Col. 2:10, refers to believers, who by virtue of their relation to Christ, also experience fullness in him: ἐστὲ ἐν αὐτῷ πεπληρωμένοι. The Col. author introduces an *ecclesiastical* dimension of participation in the fullness of Christ, though this reference is directed in the second person plural to the church members; it does not indicate the generalised entity of the church as encountered in Ephesians. In spite of this difference, the author of Eph., certainly not unaware of the primary use of the term in Colossians in relation to Christ, has developed the horizontal, eccle-

---

[11] Much of the Col. formulation is retained, but the negative of Col., ὁ γὰρ ἀδικῶν κομίσεται ὃ ἠδίκησεν (and its corresponding negative consequences), are notably omitted.

[12] These themes figure strongly in earlier Pauline material from which the author of Eph. has drawn, particularly Rom., Gal. and 1 Cor. See Gese's excellent overview of parallels, *Vermächtnis*, 76f.

164

siastical aspect found in Col. 2:10 to the exclusion of the divine aspect found in Col. 1:19 and 2:9. The shift is once again away from a predominantly Christ-orientation to a horizontal, church orientation.

The first instance, found in Eph. 1:10, simply indicates the common sense of the word in the genitive phrase τοῦ πληρώματος τῶν καιρῶν, and is otherwise unremarkable. The following three occurrences, however, reveal a surprising development on the part of the author's thinking: the fullness of Christ, characterised by the author of Col. as a designation of his deity, lordship and relation to the Father, is extended *exclusively* to the church and her members, as seen in Eph. 1:22–23: καὶ πάντα ὑπέταξεν ὑπὸ τοὺς πόδας αὐτοῦ καὶ αὐτὸν ἔδωκεν κεφαλὴν ὑπὲρ πάντα τῇ ἐκκλησίᾳ, ἥτις ἐστὶν τὸ σῶμα αὐτοῦ, τὸ πλήρωμα τοῦ τὰ πάντα ἐν πᾶσιν πληρουμένου. The formulation is unusual, but the meaning is clear: it is the church in which Christ's fullness resides.[13] It may be possible that the author has, at this point, through the force of the analogy, *unintentionally* transferred this quality to the church. The following examples, however, reinforce our observation that the church is being vested with new authority, and therefore make this suggestion unlikely. In Eph. 3:19, fullness language is applied directly to the hearers, γνῶναί τε τὴν ὑπερβάλλουσαν τῆς γνώσεως ἀγάπην τοῦ Χριστοῦ, ἵνα πληρωθῆτε εἰς πᾶν τὸ πλήρωμα τοῦ θεοῦ. The formulation, expressed in the second person plural, demonstrates the closest links to the *sense* of Colossian formulation in 2:10, yet it employs the very language of Col. 1:19 and 2:9, which had formerly belonged to Christ, πᾶν τὸ πλήρωμα τῆς θεότητος σωματικῶς. Apart from redirecting the fullness language from Christ to the members of the church, 3:19 reflects the particular emphasis of the Ephesian author in accentuating Christ's love towards the church, the new vertical axis of the Eph. redaction. In similar vein, the fullness of Christ finds direct application to the church members in 4:13: μέχρι καταντήσωμεν οἱ πάντες εἰς τὴν ἑνότητα τῆς πίστεως καὶ τῆς ἐπιγνώσεως τοῦ υἱοῦ τοῦ θεοῦ, εἰς ἄνδρα τέλειον, εἰς μέτρον ἡλικίας τοῦ πληρώματος τοῦ Χριστοῦ. The hopes of the Eph. author that the church be built up reflect the language and sense of Col. 1:22, 28, where the verb παρίστημι[14] introduces the threefold effects of salvation wrought by Christ (1:22), as well as the results of the threefold ministry of preaching, admonition and teaching, 1:28, ἵνα παραστήσωμεν πάντα ἄνθρωπον τέλειον ἐν Χριστῷ. The perfected man in Eph., however, is characterised as *possessing* the fullness of

---

[13] Mitton, *Epistle*, 96, admits that this formulation is "indeed most unexpected", yet he concludes: "The important point to notice, however, is that it is not Christ whose significance is explained by πλήρωμα, but the Church."

[14] παρίστημι appears only in Eph. 5:27, where the HT expresses the activity of Christ.

Christ. The fullness of Christ, which the author of Col. employed to describe the superlatives of the Christ hymn and to provide contrast to the empty teachings troubling the church, is now accessible to the church and her members.[15] The church, for the author of Eph., shares in the power and authority of Christ. It is not surprising, then, in light of the theological shifts which the author of Eph. has introduced, that the church plays a more prominent role in the theology and ethics of the letter.

These examples illustrate the remarkable shift which the author of Eph. has introduced in systematising the horizontal axis. The Col. emphasis upon divine reconciliation characterised by the *kurios-doulos* relationship has been redirected to the horizontal transformation realised in heathen-Christian conversion, the church becoming the terminus of salvation. Correspondingly, as the importance of Christ's coming in judgement fades, it is the church which adopts regulative authority for human relationships. Christ's regulatory role, then, is tied closely to the church and her ministries. The close relationship of Christ to the church is that which ultimately characterises the ethical force of the Eph. author's admonitions; in the following sections, we hope to highlight aspects of this relationship, in an attempt to illustrate its importance in construing, ultimately, the theological basis for the HT mandates. Emerging in the place of the *kurios-doulos* pattern, the Christ-church model becomes the *new* relational basis for the vertical axis.

Theological Features of the Ephesian Redaction

If the author of Ephesians has indeed introduced a shift in perspective which emphasises and systematises the horizontal axis in terms of its regulation of his ethic, it might be expected that other, prominent theological elements of his redaction would reflect related ecclesiastical concerns. This appears to be the case, as the author construes the Christian life as participation in the community of the church. This participation takes on traditional character in the expansion of the regulatory use of the OT; it also features an emphasis upon the exercise of love as modelled in Christ. Both elements figure importantly in construing an ethic which ensures unity through an appeal to authority and the believers' common experience in Christ.

---

[15] H. Merklein, *Christus und die Kirche: Die theologische Grundstruktur des Epheserbriefs nach 2,11–18*, eds. R. Kilian, H. Haag and W. Pesch, Stuttgarter Bibelstudien, vol. 66 (Stuttgart: KBW Verlag, 1973), 87, notes the author's tendency to interpret formerly cosmic terminology in an ecclesiological sense.

Universal Ecclesiastical Perspective

In concert with the significant shifts of emphasis in the relational axes mentioned above, the author leaves the reader with no doubt that he is *expressly* concerned with the church. He uses the term ἐκκλησία no less than nine times in the letter, as compared with four instances in Colossians.[16] The majority of these occurrences are found in the parenetic section of the letter; in particular, there are six instances in the HT, which suggests that his interest is closely tied to the connection between theology and ethics. In Col., the term reflects two meanings. Within the theological section of the letter, it signifies the church universal, the body, whose head is Christ (1:18, 24). These two references from the theological section of Col. appear to be the foundation of the Ephesian redactor's understanding of the church. Later in the Colossian epistle, however, Paul uses the term twice to designate a particular church, first in a home, 4:15, Ἀσπάσασθε τοὺς ἐν Λαοδικείᾳ ἀδελφοὺς καὶ Νύμφαν καὶ τὴν κατ᾽ οἶκον αὐτῆς ἐκκλησίαν, then the more general location of Laodicea, 4:16: καὶ ὅταν ἀναγνωσθῇ παρ᾽ ὑμῖν ἡ ἐπιστολή, ποιήσατε ἵνα καὶ ἐν τῇ Λαοδικέων ἐκκλησίᾳ ἀναγνωσθῇ. This second, particular meaning for ἐκκλησία does not find expression in Ephesians.[17] The expanded use of ἐκκλησία in Eph. does not introduce innovation or an extension of the meanings found in Col. It reveals, rather, a surprising continuity of meaning: the church is projected exclusively in universal and theological terms. This, it seems, suggests that the author not only has a highly developed and focused ecclesiology, but that he is also concerned with communicating to his readers a certain level of instruction regarding the nature of the universal church. The unique and formulaic references to Christ as the head of the church, his body,[18] found in Col. 1:18a, 24b, appear to be the Eph. redactor's primary impulse in accentuating the universal church and its relation to Christ :

---

[16] Col. 1:18, 24; 4:15, 16. Eph. 1:22–23; 3:10, 21; 5:23, 24, 25, 27, 29, 32.

[17] Mitton, *Epistle*, 69, points out that Eph. represents the end of a transitional trajectory: earlier Paulines refer exclusively to local churches, Col. to both universal and local churches, Eph. only to the latter.

[18] Though teaching regarding the somatic nature of the church can be found outside of Col.-Eph., it is not as developed, nor does it collocate the terms body, head (being Christ) and church to form a full-bodied metaphor relating to Christ. This is unique to Col.-Eph. Σῶμα describes the whole of the many parts in Rom. 12:4–5; 1 Cor. 10:17; 12:12–27; only 1 Cor. 12:28 makes an indirect, though clear, connection between 12:12–27 and the word ἐκκλησία. Κεφαλή figures only once in relation to Christ, in the limited sense of 1 Cor. 11:3, παντὸς ἀνδρὸς ἡ κεφαλὴ ὁ Χριστός ἐστιν.

- Col. 1:18a: αὐτός ἐστιν ἡ κεφαλὴ τοῦ σώματος τῆς ἐκκλησίας.
- Col. 1:24b: τοῦ σώματος αὐτοῦ, ὅ ἐστιν ἡ ἐκκλησία.

These verses lay the foundation for the Eph. author's ecclesiological perspective. The theological section of the letter, particularly Eph. 1:22–23, is strongly influenced by these Colossian formulations, as well as the Christ hymn, where Christ is named head over *all* things, not only the church. The head language found there is employed in Eph. to embrace the full authority of Christ. Similarly, the church's authority expands within the universal sweep of Christ's authority. Eph. 3:1–10 declares that the hidden mystery of the gospel is now being revealed to the Gentiles as well as the rulers and authorities in the heavens; the latter, notably, appertain God's wisdom *through the church*, v. 10: ἵνα γνωρισθῇ νῦν ταῖς ἀρχαῖς καὶ ταῖς ἐξουσίαις ἐν τοῖς ἐπουρανίοις διὰ τῆς ἐκκλησίας ἡ πολυποίκιλος σοφία τοῦ θεοῦ. It is in the church where the glory of God is revealed; the doxology of Eph. 3:21 surprises the reader with a close association of God's glory in Christ *and* the church, αὐτῷ ἡ δόξα ἐν τῇ ἐκκλησίᾳ καὶ ἐν Χριστῷ Ἰησοῦ.[19]

It is in the HT, however, where the somatic metaphor found in Col. 1:18, 24 is most clearly employed, the collocation of the head-body/Christ-church language being fully retained in 5:23,[20] ὁ Χριστὸς κεφαλὴ τῆς ἐκκλησίας, αὐτὸς σωτὴρ τοῦ σώματος ὁ Χριστὸς κεφαλὴ τῆς ἐκκλησίας, αὐτὸς σωτὴρ τοῦ σώματος. The church is highlighted within the HT in its universal form, with particular attention to her relation to Christ. The universal and relational aspects can be seen in several instances. The church submits to Christ, 5:24: ὡς ἡ ἐκκλησία ὑποτάσσεται τῷ Χριστῷ. The church is the recipient of Christ's love in 5:25, ὁ Χριστὸς ἠγάπησεν τὴν ἐκκλησίαν καὶ ἑαυτὸν παρέδωκεν ὑπὲρ αὐτῆς. Verses 5:26, 27 express the benefits of Christ's love to the church, as well as Christ's intention to initiate ongoing relations. Especially important is the inclusion of presentation language in 5:27, which the author has apparently borrowed from Col. 1:22,[21] παραστῆσαι ὑμᾶς ἁγίους καὶ ἀμώμους καὶ ἀνεγκλήτους κατενώπιον αὐτου. It is Christ, then, who ultimately cares for the church, 5:29b, ἐκτρέφει καὶ θάλπει αὐτήν, καθὼς καὶ ὁ Χριστὸς τὴν ἐκκλησίαν. The relationship

---

[19] Lincoln, *Ephesians*, 227, notes that this unique formulation reflects the dominant interests of the writer.

[20] Eph. 5:23 reflects, quite possibly, 1 Cor. 11:3, παντὸς ἀνδρὸς ἡ κεφαλη ὁ Χριστός ἐστιν, κεφαλὴ δὲ γυναικὸς ὁ ἀνήρ κεφαλη`δε`τοῦ Χριστοῦ ὁ θεός. The Eph. formulation generalises the principle, placing Christ as head over the *church*.

[21] The concept has possibly been influenced by 2 Cor. 4:4 and 11:2; the verbal correspondence to Col. 1:22 is striking.

between Christ and the church, to some degree analogous to the union of man and wife, is characterised as a great mystery, 5:32: τὸ μυστήριον τοῦτο μέγα ἐστίν· ἐγὼ δὲ λέγω εἰς Χριστὸν καὶ εἰς τὴν ἐκκλησίαν. The author of Ephesians preserves the unique metaphorical language employed in Col., yet extends the relational implications of the metaphor Christ-church, head-body.

The term σῶμα, so important in the Eph. author's expression of the Christ-church metaphor, deserves attention at this point. Employed with diverse meaning in Colossians,[22] σῶμα undergoes homogenisation in Ephesians as a synonym for the church.[23] This development appears to be more than arbitrary, as the respective occurrences remain identical in number,[24] yet their placement and meaning within Ephesians has undergone significant change. In Colossians, seven instances are to be found concentrated in the theological section of the letter, whereas in Ephesians, the majority of the references are contained in the parenetic section. This shift suggests a particular interest on the part of the author of Eph. to construe his ethic in terms of a somatic understanding of the church, the church playing a central role in defining and regulating moral behaviour.[25] More significant, however, is the aspect of homogenisation of the term σῶμα. The author of Eph. has limited its meaning within the epistle. He has, first of all, eliminated the sense of human nature/physicality. There are, for instance, two references in Colossians which refer to the physical body (not Christ's), both appearing in the theological section, Col. 2:11 (τοῦ σώματος τῆς σαρκός) and 2:23 (ἀφειδίᾳ σώματος). These particular references are omitted in the Eph. redaction. We find only one exception within the letter, Eph. 5:28, the sole plural form referring to the physical bodies of the husbands, yet clearly indicating, by analogy, the church as well. The force of the Christ-church analogy, as well as the consistent use of σῶμα throughout the letter as a reference to the church, make it unlikely that the author would employ another word at this

---

[22] Half of the references pertain to the church: 1:18, 24; 2:19, 3:15; two refer to Christ: 1:22, 2:17; two to the human body: 2:11, 23.

[23] All instances refer to the church, with the exception of 5:28, which indicates the human body.

[24] Both letters contain eight occurrences: Col. 1:18, 22, 24; 2:11, 17, 19, 23; 3:15. Eph. 1:23; 2:16; 4:4, 12, 16; 5:23, 28, 30.

[25] Somatic references in the parenetic section are applied to ethical behaviour: 4:4, ἓν σῶμα is applied to the nature of the calling in unity which regulates all behaviour; 4:12 refers to the building up of the church in order to achieve unity and Christ-likeness; 4:16 speaks of the growth of the body through truth and love; 5:23 cites the head-body relationship of Christ as exemplary for the husband-wife relation; 5:30 reminds the congregation of the role of love in their union in the body of Christ.

point. Notably, where the author departs from the sense of this analogy, he is careful to avoid the confusion of using the same word.[26] The author's primary concern remains in attempting to delineate the nature and extent of the love of Christ for his body, the church.

The author of Col., when not referring to the church or the general, physical human body and its nature, twice makes reference to Christ in terms of σῶμα. Both instances fall in the theological section of the letter, Col. 1:22 and 2:17. Verse 2:17 pits the Colossian schismatics and their practices against the present and coming reality[27] of Christ: ἅ ἐστιν σκιὰ τῶν μελλόντων, τὸ δὲ σῶμα τοῦ Χριστοῦ. This verse, reflecting one occasion of the Colossian letter, might not be expected to find its way into the Eph. redaction. The second instance, however, 1:22, represents a central element of the Col. theological argument, which finds loose though complete representation in several verses in the Ephesian redaction: Col. 1:22: νυνὶ δὲ ἀποκατήλλαξεν ἐν τῷ σώματι τῆς σαρκὸς αὐτοῦ διὰ τοῦ θανάτου παραστῆσαι ὑμᾶς ἁγίους καὶ ἀμώμους καὶ ἀνεγκλήτους κατενώπιον αὐτοῦ. The author of Eph. has retained the elements of reconciliation, new standing and sacrifice. The recipients of reconciliation in Eph., as noted above, experience this at both the inter-human and divine levels, indicating a shift of emphasis from the Col. *Vorlage*:

Eph. 1:4b: εἶναι ἡμᾶς ἁγίους καὶ ἀμώμους κατενώπιον αὐτοῦ (divine axis);
Eph. 2:14b: ὁ ποιήσας τὰ ἀμφότερα ἓν καὶ τὸ μεσότοιχον τοῦ φραγμοῦ λύσας, τὴν ἔχθραν ἐν τῇ σαρκὶ αὐτοῦ (inter-human axis);
Eph. 2:16a: καὶ ἀποκαταλλάξῃ τοὺς ἀμφοτέρους ἐν ἑνὶ σώματι τῷ θεῷ διὰ τοῦ σταυροῦ (inter-human axis).

The phrase ἐν τῷ σώματι τῆς σαρκὸς αὐτοῦ, in which Col. joins σῶμα and σάρξ to designate the physical body of Christ[28], loses the somatic reference in Eph., rendering a simpler construction, ἐν τῇ σαρκὶ αὐτοῦ. It is remarkable that the author of Eph., fond of collocating synonyms, dispenses with both occurrences of the distinctive Col. phrase. The omission reflects an important aspect of the Eph. author's use of somatic language. Σῶμα is reserved for use in reference to the church, whether direct or as an element of the Christ-

---

[26] When speaking of hating the body in 5:29 (not a behaviour attributed to Christ), the author is careful to insure distance from the analogy by the use of σάρξ.

[27] See Dunn's treatment of the schism and the contrasting formulation of 2:17 in *Epistles*, 171f.

[28] This identical phrase can also be found in Col. 2:11, in reference to the human body.

170

church analogy; σάρξ, in contrast, is employed for references to the physical body as well as negative behaviour.[29] In the redaction of Eph., the church has been given a prominent position, which is illustrated by a consistent and designated use of vocabulary such as σῶμα. This development reflects the tendency of the author of Eph. to homogenise diversified concepts in order to represent a more unified picture of the universal church.

Besides making significant shifts in the theology of the letter, as well as employing key terms to signify the universal church, the author of Eph. introduces a number of clear indices of the priority of his ecclesiological emphasis. Both letters are clear and consistent in presenting Christ as the head of the church.[30] Ephesians, however, promotes a certain level of authority within the church, which complements Christ's headship, notably expressed in the formulations of Eph. 4:11, 2:20 and 3:5. It is none less than Christ himself who has instigated the intermediary church offices for the building up of the body, 4:11–12.[31] The offices of apostle and prophet are invested with significant authority. In a surprising formulation, Eph. 2:20 places them alongside Christ, the corner stone: ἐποικοδομηθέντες ἐπὶ τῷ θεμελίῳ τῶν ἀποστόλων καὶ προφητῶν, ὄντος ἀκρογωνιαίου αὐτοῦ Χριστοῦ Ἰησοῦ. This is certainly a bold statement for an author who is familiar with earlier Pauline material,[32] and a stark indicator of the importance of these church functions. Equally important is the emphasis these offices receive in respect to the mystery of Christ. Both letters give prominent place to the concept of mystery as a term which describes the unfolding of God's plan of salvation.[33] In Col. 1:26, this mystery has been revealed to the saints, τὸ μυστήριον τὸ ἀποκεκρυμμένον ἀπὸ τῶν αἰώνων καὶ ἀπὸ τῶν γενεῶν-νῦν δὲ

[29] Eph. 2:3: designates sinful behaviour; 2:11a: reference to heathen descent; 2:11b: fleshly circumcision; 2:14: refers to the earthly body of Christ; 5:29: the husband's body; 5:31: physical union; 6:5: reference to earthly lords.

[30] Col. 1:18, (19); 2:19; Eph. 1:22; 4:15; 5:23b.

[31] The Ephesian formulation resembles 1 Cor. 12:28, though the Cor. list of church functions is larger: "...ἀποστόλους...προφήτας...εὐαγγελιστάς...ποιμένας...διδασκάλους." The author of Ephesians appears to be familiar with this passage, and promotes a more developed sense of church office.

[32] Gese, *Vermächtnis*, 76f, lists several connections between 1 Cor. and Eph.; the author of Eph., however, freely alters the meaning of 1 Cor. 3:11: θεμέλιον γὰρ ἄλλον οὐδεὶς δύναται θεῖναι παρὰ τὸν κείμενον, ὅς ἐστιν᾽ Ἰησοῦς Χριστός.

[33] Col. 1:26, 27; 2:2; 4:3 all refer to the revelation of the Gospel in the church and the nations; Eph. 1:9; 3:3, 4, 9; 5:32; 6:9 also speak of the mystery of God's plan revealed in Christ. Only verse 5:32 may represent a slight departure from this basic meaning. See C.C. Caragounis, *The Ephesian Mysterion: Meaning and Content*, eds. L. Hartman, H. Riesenfeld and B. Gerhardsson, Coniectanea Biblica, New Testament Series, vol. 8 (Lund: CWK Gleerup, 1977), 59.

ἐφανερώθη τοῖς ἁγίοις αὐτοῦ, and reflects the general character of the revelation of this mystery to the saints and the nations. In Eph., however, the mystery is now made known to an individual (the author),[34] as well as the apostles and prophets, Eph. 3:5: ὃ ἑτέραις γενεαῖς οὐκ ἐγνωρίσθη τοῖς υἱοῖς τῶν ἀνθρώπων ὡς νῦν ἀπεκαλύφθη τοῖς ἁγίοις ἀποστόλοις αὐτοῦ καὶ προφήταις ἐν πνεύματι. This development indicates a more clearly defined sense of church office,[35] and places the authority of the transmission of the mystery in the hands of humans. Indeed, the author is given the privilege of declaring God's hidden purposes, 3:8–9, ἐμοὶ τῷ ἐλαχιστοτέρῳ πάντων ἁγίων ἐδόθη ἡ χάρις αὕτη, τοῖς ἔθνεσιν εὐαγγελίσασθαι τὸ ἀνεξιχνίαστον πλοῦτος τοῦ Χριστοῦ καὶ φωτίσαι [πάντας] τίς ἡ οἰκονομία τοῦ μυστηρίου τοῦ ἀποκεκρυμμένου ἀπὸ τῶν αἰώνων ἐν τῷ θεῷ τῷ τὰ πάντα κτίσαντι, and it is through the church that God's wisdom is revealed, 3:10: ἵνα γνωρισθῇ νῦν ταῖς ἀρχαῖς καὶ ταῖς ἐξουσίαις ἐν τοῖς ἐπουρανίοις διὰ τῆς ἐκκλησίας ἡ πολυποίκιλος σοφία τοῦ θεοῦ.

The vertical axis, so prominent in Col., is significantly modified in Eph. by the horizontal influence of the church. The Eph. author's shift in perspective has wrought a number of changes in the ethical model found in Colossians. Vocabulary primarily employed in reference to Christ in Col. now indicates the present functioning of the church and her offices. The Christ-church relationship represents a model which places particular emphasis upon the church as a universal entity; in spite of this universal understanding, the author retains and even develops a sense of the intimacy of the Christ-church bond. The church and its relation to Christ become an integral part of the author's ethic, representing in the HT the positive pole of human experience, as well as being the collective term for all who stand in relation to Christ. The author of Eph. augments this significant shift in the relational models with two further elements which distinguish the Ephesian redaction: the use of the Old Testament and the emphasis upon an ethic of love, modelled upon Christ.

The OT and the Ephesian Redaction

A prominent development emerging between the two letters is the extensive use of OT references in Ephesians to illustrate and substantiate both theological and ethical concerns. The application of the OT is remarkably thor-

---

[34] Eph. 3:3.
[35] τοῖς ἁγίοις becomes an adjective; Dibelius, *Kolosser*, 56, sees this as a "kirchliche Weiterbildung von Kol. i. 26." Merklein, *Amt*, 33, notes an "Einengung" of the meaning of Col., where the original sense becomes "streng ekklesiologisch".

ough, and includes the HT form. In Col., as we have noted, the references to the OT scriptures are not direct, possessing a more veiled character.[36] Two of the three *direct* OT quotations found in Eph. are located, notably, in the HT, the third quotation also located in the parenetic section in 4:8. Both theological and practical concerns are addressed by means of these quotations.[37] Direct citation indicates not only a familiarity with the OT text, it also assumes a level of familiarity with the OT text on the part of some of the hearers.[38] Most of all it reveals a willingness on the part of the author of Eph. to apply OT concepts to the theology and practice of the church. By introducing scriptural texts, the author raises a theological and moral standard for church members, and sets a unifying hermeneutical principle. This particular standard, it should be noted, is lacking in the reasoning within the correspondence to the Colossians. The author is apparently redressing the lack of clear scriptural support in the Col. argumentation, while simultaneously setting a pattern for the church. The word of God is taken to be part of the believer's "equipment" for daily life.[39]

The use of the OT scriptures may also have their basis in the author's desire to promote peace and unity along the prominent line of ethnic demarcation within the church, Jew and Gentile, as seen above. This corresponds

---

[36] Col. 2:16 mentions OT regulations, but as a negative example; 3:6 could be construed as a Jewish formulation, but the concept of judgement was known in the ancient world, see Dunn, *Epistles*, 216f.; the HT mandates to the slaves/master, as noted above, contain OT concepts (fear of the Lord, inheritance and *jus talionis*), though without any clear OT indication.

[37] Direct quotations, a unique development, are limited to the parenetic section, 4:8 (Ps. 68:18); 5:31 (Gen. 2:24); 6:2, 3 (Ex. 20:12). Eph. 4:8, though located in the parenetic section, provides a profound theological support for the apportioning of faith. The rest of the letter, however, is informed by an intimate knowledge and conscious editorial appropriation of the OT text. Examples have been catalogued by Moritz. He notes in *Mystery*, 19, that "it has also become clear that Ephesians shows an awareness of the OT *Vorlage* which goes beyond the level of *Wirkungsgeschichte* and which extends to the level of the OT text itself." See also A.T. Lincoln, "The Use of the OT in Ephesians", *JSNT* 14, 1982, 16–57, and D.C. Smith, *Jewish and Greek Traditions in Ephesians 2:11–22*, Yale University Dept. of Religion thesis, 1971.

[38] Moritz, *Mystery*, 216f., rejects theories which propose an exclusively Gentile community; he suggests that the author is attempting to speak to a congregation with a "more Jewish component." Though Jews may have been counted among the members of the fellowship and its leadership, the letter implies a primarily Gentile audience, Eph. 2:11, Διὸ μνημονεύετε ὅτι ποτὲ ὑμεῖς τὰ ἔθνη ἐν σαρκί, οἱ λεγόμενοι ἀκροβυστία ὑπὸ τῆς λεγομένης περιτομῆς ἐν σαρκὶ χειροποιήτου, and 4:17b, μηκέτι ὑμᾶς περιπατεῖν, καθὼς καὶ τὰ ἔθνη περιπατεῖ ἐν ματαιότητι τοῦ νοὸς αὐτῶν.

[39] Eph. 6:17 describes the word of God (ῥῆμα) as a sword; this may refer to the prophetic word (Is. 49:2), but certainly the message of the Gospel. The NT features this image in Heb. 4:12; Rev. 1:16; 2:12; 19:15, 21.

with the author's development of the new horizontal axis along heathen-Christian lines. The transformational event of salvation is along horizontal lines, being the sphere and vehicle by which Gentiles are included in the blessings of the church, and thereby the inheritance of Israel. Unity is achieved by the far-near approach of the heathen to the church, the locus of salvation. This is formulaically expressed in the general call for unity in Eph. 4:3–6, the author reminding the hearers to preserve the unity they have in the church by the recognition of their common ground: one body, one spirit, one hope, one Lord, one faith, one baptism, one God and Father. The promises of OT scripture constitute another element of their *common* inheritance. The author tends to indicate the blessings of faith as the result of promise, a characteristic notably absent in Colossians. The sense of promise courses through the letter serving as a cipher for anticipated blessings in several forms. Examples of this tendency can be seen in Eph. 1:13, 2:12, 3:6 and 6:2:

1. Eph. 1:13: ἐσφραγίσθητε τῷ πνεύματι τῆς ἐπαγγελίας τῷ ἁγίῳ. It is interesting to note that the promised Spirit is also guarantor of "our inheritance", v. 14: ὅ ἐστιν ἀρραβὼν τῆς κληρονομίας ἡμῶν. The Gentiles are clearly being included, perhaps in keeping with the promise of Joel 2:28a (3:1a LXX): Καὶ ἔσται μετὰ ταῦτα καὶ ἐκχεῶ ἀπὸ τοῦ πνεύματός μου πᾶσαν σάρκα.

2. Eph. 2:12: ὅτι ἦτε τῷ καιρῷ ἐκείνῳ χωρὶς Χριστοῦ, ἀπηλλοτριωμένοι τῆς πολιτείας τοῦ Ἰσραὴλ καὶ ξένοι τῶν διαθηκῶν τῆς ἐπαγγελίας, ἐλπίδα μὴ ἔχοντες καὶ ἄθεοι ἐν τῷ κόσμῳ. The separation (ἀπηλλοτριωμένοι) of the Gentiles hearkens back to Col. 1:21, which characterised the recipients as being separated from God; the Eph. author makes a connection between salvation and the promises of Israel. Formerly the exclusive possession of those holding the "citizenship of Israel", the promises[40] of scripture are now open to those who have been drawn near, Eph. 2:11–17. Though clearly falling on the side of Jewish sensibilities and level of familiarity, the OT scriptures and traditions offer an authoritative point of departure in determining the church's ethic, which can now be seen as transcultural, in that they are now available to *all* in Christ. The au-

---

[40] The author retains the Pauline emphasis upon OT priority of promise to the law, and associates the word with the reception of the Gospel. Cf. Rom. 4:13, 14, 16, 20; 9:4, 8, 9; 15:8; 2 Cor. 1:20, 7:1; Gal. 3:14, 16, 17, 18, 21, 22, 29; 4:23, 28.

thor not only employs direct OT quotation, but also embeds OT concepts within his phraseology and argumentation.[41] The reference to being drawn near, itself an OT concept, underscores the new horizontal relationships created in the church through Christ.[42] It seems certain that the readers of Ephesians would not have missed their newly found inclusion in the traditions and promises of Israel. The scriptures represent a *part* of the inheritance of those who were formerly distant. In particular, we find stark contrasts drawn between the Jewish and Gentile destinies, joined only in Christ:

Gentile Characteristics	Believer Characteristics
Gentiles/uncircumcised (2:11)	Circumcised (2:11)
Without Christ/excluded/outside	
Foreigners/without hope/without God (2:12)	Citizenship of Israel, Covenants of Promise
Enmity (2:14, 16)	Peace (2:14, 15)
Far (2:13, 17)	Near (2:13, 17)

3. Eph. 3:6: εἶναι τὰ ἔθνη συγκληρονόμα καὶ σύσσωμα καὶ συμμέτοχα τῆς ἐπαγγελίας ἐν Χριστῷ Ἰησοῦ διὰ τοῦ εὐαγγελίου. The creative use of συν- prefixes underscores the author's intent of including the Gentiles in the blessings of Israel, now in Christ. The mystery of the Gospel, according to the author of Eph., is essentially summed up in 3:6 as the sharing of the benefits of the new relation in Christ, and as such, the shared inheritance becomes a factor for church unity.[43] Such a standard and common inheritance would be necessary to build the unity envisioned by the author, who builds his ethic upon the assumption of unity and mutuality, 4:25, Διὸ ἀποθέμενοι τὸ ψεῦδος λαλεῖτε ἀλήθειαν ἕκαστος μετὰ τοῦ πλησίον αὐτοῦ, ὅτι

---

[41] See fn. 37.

[42] The author adapts the restoration language of Is. 57:19; those far and near, who repent, receive comfort, healing and forgiveness from the God of Israel. The author interprets Is. 57 in terms of Gentile conversion, now brought near in Christ. See Moritz, *Mystery*, 37.

[43] Cf. also Eph. 2:19, συμπολῖται τῶν ἁγίων καὶ οἰκεῖοι τοῦ θεοῦ and 2:22, συνοικοδομεῖσθε εἰς κατοικητήριον τοῦ θεοῦ. The common standing as one new man constitutes the formation of the church, and correspondingly, the building of the church contributes to unity, 4:12–13.

ἐσμὲν ἀλλήλων μέλη.[44] The extended use of the OT promises and instruction not only assumes free access on the part of the hearers, but actively encourages the formerly heathen component of the church to incorporate its teachings. The church, built upon Christ, the apostles and prophets, has become the "holy temple" (2:21). Indeed, the author of Eph. departs from the traditional Pauline categories with no mention of the typical terms designating Jew and Gentile[45] (with its elements of Jewish priority or the necessity of the rejection of Israel) to the degree that the distinction in Ephesians is essentially lost.[46] The author is unmistakably including the heathen within the scope of Israel's OT promises, and this takes place in the central theological and ethical community: the church.

4. Eph. 6:2, 3: τίμα τὸν πατέρα σου καὶ τὴν μητέρα, ἥτις ἐστὶν ἐντολὴ πρώτη ἐν ἐπαγγελίᾳ, ἵνα εὖ σοι γένηται καὶ ἔσῃ μακροχρόνιος ἐπὶ τῆς γῆς. This final example, taken from the HT, illustrates the principle of blessing being brought into connection with adherence to an OT command. Gentiles hearing this would be left without doubt that the OT scriptures are now their own.

The expanded use of OT scriptures in Eph. is, then, likely motivated by several concerns. Colossians, we have noted, provides very little scripture as evidence for its ethical reasoning, a lack which the author of Eph. addresses. The author's bifurcation of the universe along the horizontal lines of heathen-Christian poles sets the stage for an ethic that is defined by common, measurable standards. The need for unity posed by such a fundamental division would also need to be addressed. The author of Eph. does this by defining the *former* heathen in terms of a faith community, the church, closely associated with the covenant people of Israel and her covenant promises. The scriptures define the faith community, and regulate its behaviour; the author's concern for the unity and well-being of the church nearly mandates such a standard.

---

[44] Interestingly, even the admonitions of Eph. 4:25–30 are solidly based in OT commands. See Moritz, *Mystery*, 88–95.

[45] No use is made of either term, so prevalent in the Paulines. The contrast formerly drawn (cf. Rom. 1:14, 16; 2:9, 10; 3:9; 10:12; 1 Cor. 1:22, 24; 10:32; 12:13; Gal. 3:28; Col. 3:11) is minimised in Eph. in the interest of church unity.

[46] Gese, *Vermächtnis*, 103, notes that Ephesians "hebt...die Abgrenzung der Heiden gegenüber den Juden völlig auf...eine Voranstellung Israels ist darin nicht mehr erkennbar."

If the author is concerned with unity among the believers in the church, his conception of how this union should be realised is through a dual emphasis: the cultivation of love among its members, as well as increasing holiness, which involves, for the author of Eph., a graduated departure from the former life of impurity. These emphases reflect the vocabulary of the Colossian *Vorlage*,[47] and correspond to the relational axes of Col., which are retained in the Ephesian redaction, 1:15: Διὰ τοῦτο κἀγὼ ἀκούσας τὴν καθ᾽ ὑμᾶς πίστιν ἐν τῷ κυρίῳ Ἰησοῦ καὶ τὴν ἀγάπην τὴν εἰς πάντας τοὺς ἁγίους. The author of Eph., however, explores the implications of this verse in his redaction. The development can be traced in the expansion of love as the ethic's central force, and Christ as its prime representative.

Christ and the Mediation of Love

The concept of love plays a central role in the theology and parenesis of the letter of Eph. It represents, first of all, a significant expansion of the theme of love over against its Col. counterpart, in both the theological and parenetic sections of the letter. References to love within Col. are limited to seven instances, whereas the Ephesian redaction incorporates twenty.[48] Of the seven original references in Col., only three can be shown to be directly related to the Eph. formulations, making the Eph. expansion a more striking and original phenomenon.[49] The Eph. redaction reveals a shift and expansion of the love vocabulary to the parenetic section, as well.[50] This is not to say, however, that the Col. emphasis upon love is insignificant, or has remained unnoticed by the Eph. redactor. On the contrary, Colossians sets the stage for the strong emphasis in Eph. The formulation of Col. 3:12–14 is important in understanding the Eph. author's ethic. This Col. passage introduces love as a guiding ethical principle. The Col. author sums up his several admonitions with an appeal to the example of Christ, καθὼς καὶ ὁ κύριος ἐχαρίσατο

---

[47] Both concepts are represented in Col. References to love in Col. are seven, ἀγαπάω, 3:12, 19; and ἀγάπη, 1:4, 8, 13; 2:2; 3:14, nearly evenly divided between the theological and parenetic sections. Holiness, limited to six adjectival and pronominal forms of ἅγιος, refers to the state of believers (not in reference to some behaviour), and is found primarily in the theological section.

[48] Both ἀγαπάω and ἀγάπη undergo expanded usage in Eph. 1:6; 2:4; 5:2, 25 (2X), 28 (3X), 33; 6:24 and 1:4, 15, 2:4, 3:17, 19; 4:15, 16; 5:2; 6:23, respectively.

[49] The three related formulations are Col. 1:4 and Eph. 1:15; Col. 2:2 and Eph. 4:16; Col. 3:19 and Eph. 5:25.

[50] Col. locates four references in the theological section, only three in the parenetic section; Ephesians, in contrast, places seven references in the theological section, with the balance of thirteen references located in the parenetic section.

ὑμῖν, οὕτως καὶ ὑμεῖς, and a final admonition to (put on) love *above all*: ἐπὶ πᾶσιν δὲ τούτοις τὴν ἀγάπην, ὅ ἐστιν σύνδεσμος τῆς τελειότητος. The author of Ephesians not only preserves this passage to a large degree in his redaction,[51] but notes the importance of both love and the example of Christ as regulating principles for the compressed admonitions found in this section of Col. Interestingly, the "putting on" language of this passage also figures significantly in the Eph. author's ethic.[52] It is not, then, just the expanded number of references to love which attract attention to this feature of Ephesians, but also the direction in which the love vocabulary is being used. It is here that we see several unique features of the Eph. author's appropriation of the Col. material, which reveal particular aspects of the Eph. understanding of love.

The Ephesian redaction shows a remarkable emphasis upon love as the *regulating* force in both the theological and ethical aspects of the letter. The author indicates, from the onset, the centrality of love to the salvation event (so critical in Col.) by modifying the important formulation of Col. 1:22b: παραστῆσαι ὑμᾶς ἁγίους καὶ ἀμώμους καὶ ἀνεγκλήτους κατενώπιον αὐτοῦ. He makes love a defining marker of the Ephesians' salvation, as well as describing Christ's work on behalf of the Church. The centrality of love in the Christian life becomes unmistakable; the Col. *Vorlage* is edited to include the aspect of love in Eph. 1:4: εἶναι ἡμᾶς ἁγίους καὶ ἀμώμους κατενώπιον αὐτοῦ ἐν ἀγάπῃ. Here, the central event of salvation is modified in terms of love. This is the first of a string of ἐν-ἀγάπῃ prepositional phrases,[53] which modify both theological concepts, as well as ethical behaviour within Ephesians. Several of these phrases, as in the example above, are attached to the original Colossian formulation, making the author's emphasis and intention easily recognisable. Eph. 3:17b, for example, ἐν ἀγάπῃ ἐρριζωμένοι καὶ τεθεμελιωμένοι is taken from the formulation found in Col. 2:7, the only other occurrence of ῥιζάω in the New Testament. Both verses make reference to Christ and faith, yet the Eph. re-

---

[51] Eph. 4:2–4 preserves several elements, most notably ταπεινοφροσύνης καὶ πραΰτητος, μετὰ μακροθυμίας, ἀνεχόμενοι ἀλλήλων, which is appended with the author's generalising phrase, ἐν ἀγάπῃ.

[52] The language of Col. 3:12–14 is partially retained in the Eph. redaction in 4:1–4. The emphases, however, are expanded, notably the "putting on" metaphor (ἐνδύω, found only in these letters, figures three times in Eph. 4:24; 6:11, 14) which finds its ultimate expression in love, Col. 3:14: ἐπὶ πᾶσιν δὲ τούτοις τὴν ἀγάπην. The Eph. editor did not overlook this central emphasis.

[53] ἐν+ dative is a favourite stylistic device of the author. Of the six phrases found in Eph. (1:4; 3:17; 4:2, 15, 16; 5:2), there is only one correspondence between the letters in Eph. 4:16 and Col. 2:2, the only instance of the phrase in Col.

178

daction modifies this foundational element in terms of love. Another instance is found in Eph. 4:2b: ἀνεχόμενοι ἀλλήλων ἐν ἀγάπῃ. Aside from the reference to love, the Eph. redaction reflects the formulation of Col. 3:12, 13 almost exactly. Both references are found in parallel segments, where ecclesiological and ethical concerns (reciprocal admonitions) dominate the passages. Our next example can be found in Eph. 4:15: ἀληθεύοντες δὲ ἐν ἀγάπῃ αὐξήσωμεν εἰς αὐτὸν τὰ πάντα, ὅς ἐστιν ἡ κεφαλή, Χριστός. Here love can be understood as modifying either speaking the truth or growth; the relationship, however, is not absolutely clear.[54] The growth metaphor, an important image in Col., is retained by the author of Eph.[55] At the very least, the explicit admonition to the truth touches upon the process of growth, and the regulatory effect of love can be seen as operating in Eph. 4:16: ἐξ οὗ πᾶν τὸ σῶμα συναρμολογούμενον καὶ συμβιβαζόμενον διὰ πάσης ἁφῆς τῆς ἐπιχορηγίας κατ᾽ ἐνέργειαν ἐν μέτρῳ ἑνὸς ἑκάστου μέρους τὴν αὔξησιν τοῦ σώματος ποιεῖται εἰς οἰκοδομὴν ἑαυτοῦ ἐν ἀγάπῃ.[56] Here we find the language of growth and the building up of the body unmistakably linked with the aspect of love, which describes the nature and resultant character of the process. The author of Eph. shows dependence upon the formulation in Col. 2:2 (which is notably the only occurrence of the ἐν ἀγάπῃ within the letter), as well as the formulation of Col. 2:19. It appears that he has conflated the contents of both, wedding συμβιβασθέντες ἐν ἀγάπῃ of 2:2 with 2:19b: ἐξ οὗ πᾶν τὸ σῶμα διὰ τῶν ἁφῶν καὶ συνδέσμων ἐπιχορηγούμενον καὶ συμβιβαζόμενον αὔξει τὴν αὔξησιν τοῦ θεοῦ. This is the only example of the use of love which does not represent an expansion on the part of the Eph. author.

The final example is the general admonition of Eph. 5:2: περιπατεῖτε ἐν ἀγάπῃ. The author of Col. employs περιπατέω four times, denoting both good (1:10; 2:6; 4:5) and undesirable (3:7) behaviour. It is a significant expression in terms of its role in denoting proper behaviour. This pattern can be seen in the author of Eph. as well, though significantly expanded; both positive (2:10; 4:1; 5:2, 8, [15 both behaviours contrasted]) and negative behaviours (2:2; 4:17; [5:15 both]) are denoted. Though several of the Eph. formulations involving περιπατέω can be traced to the Col. *Vorlage*, Eph. 5:2

[54] Lincoln, *Ephesians*, 260, convincingly argues against joining ἐν ἀγάπῃ and αὐξήσωμεν for contextual reasons, yet admits a conceptual link between speaking the truth and growth.

[55] Col. 1:6, 10; 2:19 (2X); Eph. 2:21; 4:15, 16. The noun αὔξησις is found only within the Col.-Eph. redaction in the NT in vv. 2:19 and 4:16, respectively.

[56] Best, *Ephesians*, 406, rightly notes that this command "makes explicit the idea of growth which was already implicit in passages like 2:20–2 and present in the καταντήσωμεν of v. 13 with its implication of movement towards maturity. See also Lindemann, *Epheserbrief*, 81.

stands unique in its usage of ἐν ἀγάπῃ. Only Ephesians modifies this important verb in explicit terms of love.

The expansion of love as a regulating principle within the Eph. theology and ethical mandates is significant in terms of its broad representation throughout the letter, and placement in central themes of relationship to Christ and Christian behaviour. The HT, as we shall see, is not an exception. It is important to note that love characterises both the vertical and horizontal relational axes in these examples. This becomes especially significant as we encounter Christ as the exemplar of love in the HT admonitions, as well as the clear horizontal admonition to love; both heavenly and earthly expressions of love are joined in the author's use of marriage as metaphor. The emphasis upon love, however, has its origins in the person of Christ.

Christ as the Exemplar of Love

The ethical force of love, in spite of its prominence as a regulatory element of the Ephesian ethic, also includes a personal element, which contributes to the fullness of the author's ethical vision. This element is embodied in the person of Christ. Within Colossians, references to love can be connected to Christ in only one instance in 1:13, where the believers have been transferred into the kingdom, apparently Christ's, designated as the βασιλείαν τοῦ υἱοῦ τῆς ἀγάπης αὐτου βασιλείαν τοῦ υἱοῦ τῆς ἀγάπης αὐτου. This sole reference[57] stands in stark contrast to the role which Christ plays in forming the ethical mandates within Ephesians, particularly the manner in which the listeners are to understand and apply the ethic of love. The Col. reference to Christ in 1:13, 14 is retained by the author of Eph. in 1:6, 7, though with significant changes: εἰς ἔπαινον δόξης τῆς χάριτος αὐτοῦ ἧς ἐχαρίτωσεν ἡμᾶς ἐν τῷ ἠγαπημένῳ. Ἐν ᾧ ἔχομεν τὴν ἀπολύτρωσιν διὰ τοῦ αἵματος αὐτοῦ, τὴν ἄφεσιν τῶν παραπτωμάτων, κατὰ τὸ πλοῦτος τῆς χάριτος αὐτοῦ. These verses contain nearly all the information of its Col. counterpart, though the reference to the kingdom is omitted.[58] Most important, however, is the unique formulation with which the author of Eph. denotes Christ in 1:6. He is characterised as the beloved, ὁ ἠγαπημένος. This appellation, here constituting a unique christological title,[59] is otherwise reserved for believers

---

[57] Possibly formulated from familiarity with Gospel accounts, Mk. 1:11; 9:7; 12:6 and parallels.

[58] An unusually long set of coincidental words, Ἐν ᾧ ἔχομεν τὴν ἀπολύτρωσιν...τὴν ἄφεσιν.

[59] Schnackenburg, *Brief*, speaks of a "titulären Klang"; Gnilka, *Epheserbrief*, 74, refers to this as a "im NT einmaligen Christusprädikat." See also Caragounis, *Mysterion*, 90.

in both OT and NT usage,[60] and represents a transference of this community designation to Christ.[61] The author, in using this designation, has built a bridge between the believer and Christ, who both now receive, in unmistakably strong language,[62] the love of God. Christ becomes, then, in this respect, a template for receiving the love of God. He stands not only as *mediator* of the salvation which they have received, but is, as the beloved of God, the penultimate model of its ethical mandates as one who equally stands in relationship to God. Christ's role then, is expanded along horizontal lines in the Eph. redaction. For the author of Ephesians, as with Colossians, Christ mediates, by virtue of his saving lordship, all horizontal relationships. This mediation, however, is primarily characterised in Eph. by love. The vertical axis of Colossians remains intact, but is augmented in Ephesians by this unique aspect of Christ's relationship to God. The horizontal axis receives, in this manner, prominence within the Ephesian redaction. The horizontal ethical model is presented by the author of Eph. in terms of parallel relationships which find analogy in their dependence upon the common element of love. The author, in developing his ethic (particularly in the HT), encourages his hearers to draw their motivation from the example of Christ, and indeed, to understand their lives in analogical terms to him:

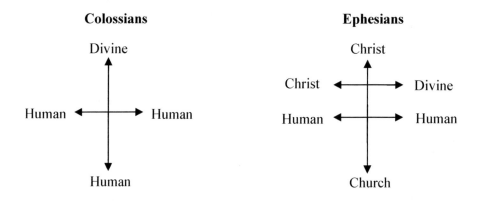

---

[60] Note the use of ὁ ἠγαπημένος in the Paulines: 1 Thes. 1:4; 2 Thes. 2:13; Rom. 9:25; Col. 3:12.

[61] Lincoln, *Ephesians*, 26f., notes the OT usage of beloved as denoting God's people by special designation of a "pet name" (Deut. 32:15; 33:5, 26; Isa. 44:2), as well as adjectival usage (Deut. 33:12; Isa. 5:1, 7; Jer. 11:15; 12:7); these are carried over into the Paulines, the author of Eph. applying this to Christ.

[62] Gnilka, *Epheserbrief*, 74f., points out that ἀγαπητός, familiar to the hearers via the Gospel tradition as a referent of Christ, had lost its "verbale Kraft"; the author attempts, by means of familiar OT language (references to ὁ ἠγαπημένος denoting both Israel and individuals

We find, then, a tendency of the Eph. author to join characteristics of God (and Christ) and expected Christian behaviour in parallel, which is an unique aspect of the Eph. redactor's ethical vision in general, and a distinctive feature of the HT mandates in particular. The divine-human axis is pressed into service by the author of Eph. to regulate horizontal, inter-human behaviour. Correct behaviour, for instance, is characterised, as might be expected, in contrast to the world (4:17–19) in 4:20–5:21. This negative behaviour, however, is not initially countered by means of forbidden activities or laudable deeds,[63] but is prefaced with the knowledge of Christ. The following admonitions hinge on the hearers' previous knowledge of Christ, who is the paradigm of behaviour as well as the embodiment of truth, 4:20–21: ὑμεῖς δὲ οὐχ οὕτως ἐμάθετε τὸν Χριστόν, εἴ γε αὐτὸν ἠκούσατε καὶ ἐν αὐτῷ ἐδιδάχθητε, καθώς ἐστιν ἀλήθεια ἐν τῷ Ἰησοῦ. The knowledge of Christ, not moral rigour, is the antidote of evil behaviour, and provides the model of correct behaviour. The acquisition of Christian maturity is closely associated with Christ in 4:13, where the church's multifaceted call to service, unity and knowledge of Christ is depicted in terms of maturity (εἰς ἄνδρα τέλειον), which is notably equated with the fullness of Christ (εἰς μέτρον ἡλικίας τοῦ πληρώματος τοῦ Χριστοῦ). The mature church should, above all, resemble Christ. A significant aspect of knowing and reflecting Christ is betrayed by the author in 3:17–19, where his prayer is that the believers will know Christ in their hearts through faith, and grow in love (v.17). This relational basis is critical for understanding the love of Christ, which appears to be the apex of the believer's knowledge of God, v. 19: γνῶναί τε τὴν ὑπερβάλλουσαν τῆς γνώσεως ἀγάπην τοῦ Χριστοῦ, ἵνα πληρωθῆτε εἰς πᾶν τὸ πλήρωμα τοῦ θεοῦ. The realisation of this prayer is expressed most clearly in the broad admonitions of Eph. 5:1–2. Here we find a unique call to imitate,[64] not only the sacrificial love of Christ, but God himself; in particular, the desired behaviour is love, modelled upon Christ. The ethic is based in loving, vertical relationship (τέκνα ἀγαπητά), while presenting Christ as exemplar, Eph. 5:1–2: γίνεσθε οὖν μιμηταὶ τοῦ θεοῦ ὡς τέκνα ἀγαπητὰ καὶ περιπατεῖτε ἐν ἀγάπῃ, καθὼς καὶ ὁ Χριστὸς ἠγάπησεν ἡμᾶς καὶ παρέδωκεν ἑαυτὸν ὑπὲρ ἡμῶν προσφορὰν καὶ θυσίαν τῷ θεῷ εἰς ὀσμὴν εὐωδίας.

[Dan. 3:5; 2 Chr. 20:7; Sir. 45:1; 46:13]), to connect the relationship of Christ and God's people.

[63] 4:22 opens an extended series of positive and negative admonitions which flow into the HT.

[64] Paul calls believers to imitate him in 1 Cor. 4:6 and 11:1; 1 Thes. 1:6 expects believers to imitate the apostle(s) and the Lord, whereas 2:14 calls for imitation of other churches' behaviour.

The Eph. ethic of love, then, is nothing other than the imitation of God as revealed in Christ. The centrality of Christ represents the emphasis upon love, and vice-versa. The two become inextricable components of the Eph. author's ethical vision, where both divine and human spheres are illustrative of the Christian life. This particular aspect of the author's ethic plays a prominent role in the formulation of the HT mandates to husband and wives, where reciprocal responsibilities are framed in terms of divine *and* human action. This feature corresponds to the observations we have made in our analysis of the Eph. author's systematising of the horizontal axis; elements of the divine-human axis in Col. have been adapted to the human sphere, in particular, the church. It is the church which not only shares *attributes* formerly associated with Christ, but also the role of Christ in regulating ethical behaviour along the horizontal axis.

Summary

The author of Eph. has introduced in his redaction of Col. a new emphasis upon the horizontal axis. In doing this, he has displaced several elements of the Colossian relational model, while presenting his own theological perspective. The Colossian bifurcation of the universe into heavenly-earthly realms undergoes a decidedly horizontal shift in the Eph. author's introduction of the heathen-Christian axis. In this new model, the church becomes the locus for theological and ethical orientation for the believer; this new aspect of authority, previously unknown in Col., is shared with Christ. It is Christ who stands in direct relation to the *church* as his body, the former *doulos-kurios* relationship of Colossians being replaced by this broader, more inclusive model. These shifts in perspective represent the Eph. redactor's understanding of the church as the central relational reality in which ethical relationships are initiated and regulated. The OT plays a significant role in defining the church in terms of promise and contrast to the world, as well as providing clear ethical direction for the Christian community. Finally, it is Christ himself who stands in relationship to both God and the church, representing and defining correct relations in their horizontal and vertical aspects. The love which characterises these relationships becomes the rubric under which the author construes his ethic.

The Theology of the Ephesian HT Admonitions

Having determined a significant shift in the Eph. author's theological understanding of the universe, as well as new emphases regarding the roles of

Christ and the church in determining his ethic, it might be expected that certain elements of these theological impulses would be detectable in some form within the HT. Following the observations derived from our treatment of the Colossian HT, such recognisable aspects of the letter's distinguishing traits should present themselves in particular relief in the expanded sections of the household code. The author of Eph. has expanded the first relational axis, husband-wife, most significantly, and, as we hope to demonstrate, it is here that his particular theological emphases and innovations find their most significant expression. The parent-child and slave-master relationships undergo less innovation, the latter reflecting the original, expanded Col. formulation to the greatest degree. For this reason, the first relational pair will inevitably receive the most attention in our analysis, and will be treated following shorter comments regarding the parent-child and slave-master relationships.

The Parent-Child Relationship

As noted in the stylistic analysis of the parent-child relationship in the previous chapter, the author of Ephesians has retained the basic structure of the admonitions to both parent and child. Yet through slight omissions, subtle substitutions and the addition of OT concepts, the author has shown a tendency to bring the understanding of the HT admonitions within the broader context of OT regulations and concepts. This appears to adhere to the broader letter's use of OT scripture in an appeal to authority which might regulate ethical behaviour within the church. The following examples, we hope, will illustrate this pattern within the child-parent relationship.

The insertion of δίκαιον as a substitution for Colossian's εὐάρεστον appears to be a deliberate, redactional alteration of the Col. *Vorlage*, in an attempt to locate this term in parallel with behaviour which is expected in the Law.[65] Such a minor change would not in itself warrant particular attention, particularly if the author is simply making an editorial or stylistic choice; it may be that he has been influenced by the similar formulation in the Col. slave-master relation (Col. 4:1), which we have observed to be a common feature of his redaction. The preservation of the Col. formulation at this point (and its uniquely Christian emphasis and OT overtones) would not *necessar-*

---

[65] Contra Best, *Ephesians*, 565, who suggests independent formulations here. The relative rarity of the word in the NT, as well as its coincidence in both HT make this unlikely. The author of Eph. employs εὐάρεστον in 5:10 to indicate correct behaviour which is pleasing to the Lord. The use of δίκαιον reflects in this context the original Col. HT usage of behaviour according to the law, suggesting intentionality. Gielen, *Tradition*, 294, sees the change as adding a "rechtliche Nuance" which anticipates the Decalogue quotation.

ily suggest any tendency on the author's part to be promoting an ethic which involves the OT,[66] or reflect an awareness of this subtle emphasis within the Col. instruction. Furthermore, if such a conscious alteration were allowed, it would not necessarily represent the ethic of the larger letter. Here the broader text of Eph. affords us clues to the author's use and understanding of δίκαιον.

In contrast to Colossians, which employs δίκαιος only in verse 4:1, the author of Eph. has expanded the use of this concept within the parenetic section to regulate behaviour.[67] Importantly, these instances are found at junctures where the author is summing up the type of behaviour which is expected of the hearers. The centrality and frequency of the examples within the parenesis suggest a conscious intent of the author to regulate behaviour along the familiar OT notion of righteousness. The three instances found within the parenetic section (Eph. 4:24; 5:9 and 6:14) follow a pattern of *negative behaviour-admonition-negative behaviour*, in which the charge to live according to righteousness is contrasted with, or given as an antidote to, negative behaviours and influences. The noun δικαιοσύνη figures prominently in each of the following examples:

1. Eph. 4:24: καὶ ἐνδύσασθαι τὸν καινὸν ἄνθρωπον τὸν κατὰ θεὸν κτισθέντα ἐν δικαιοσύνῃ καὶ ὁσιότητι τῆς ἀληθείας. Following a description of the blindness and excess of the heathen, the author advises the hearers to "put off the old man", and in our verse, to put on the new. Holiness and righteousness are modified by truth, which, in this example, stands in contrast to lies and blindness found in the surrounding material. The description of the "new man" is given in passive terms of God's creation, but appeals, nonetheless, to the behaviour of the believer.[68] The combination of holiness and righteousness can be

---

[66] δίκαιον is related, in OT texts, to the fulfilling of the Decalogue and righteous behaviour, which is fundamentally relational in obedience to God and right actions towards others. See G. Quell and G. Schenk's article, δίκη, κτλ., in *TDNT*, 2, 174–225; also Moritz, *Mystery*, 172.

[67] The parenetic usage differs significantly from Pauline forensic/static usage (esp. Rom. and Gal.). The emphasis here is clearly upon lawful and right behaviour.

[68] Lincoln, *Ephesians*, 288, points out the close connection between God's activity and the new man; the parenetic context, he notes, indicates the author's desire that the believers appropriate these virtues, as well.

construed as attributes of God,[69] but may be applied to human character as well.[70] In any event, the believer is expected to live according to a measure of holiness and righteousness, which, in OT fashion, is related both to God's character and to human behaviour. The following examples give further illustration of both uses of δικαιοσύνη in which the author makes a clear connection to human or divine righteousness.

2. Eph. 5:9: ὁ γὰρ καρπὸς τοῦ φωτὸς ἐν πάσῃ ἀγαθωσύνῃ καὶ δικαιοσύνῃ καὶ ἀληθείᾳ. The author again enumerates the scandalous behaviour of the surrounding culture ("sons of disobedience"), this time characterising the former life in terms of darkness (σκότος), against which the believers are light in the Lord and children of light (5:8). In this example it is the believer who is expected to bear fruit, including that of righteousness.

3. The final example comes from the author's depiction of the world in terms of diabolical powers, which threaten to overcome the believer (6:10–12). The antidote consists of several defensive and offensive weapons which make up the panoply of the believer; one of which is the breastplate of righteousness, Eph. 6:14b: ἐνδυσάμενοι τὸν θώρακα τῆς δικαιοσύνης. Although the believer is admonished to put on this breastplate, Best is correct in asserting that this righteousness is to be linked with the earlier phenomenon in 4:24, where it is God who must initially give righteousness.[71] The human activity of righteousness, however construed in this instance, is ultimately linked with the concept of God's righteousness. Again, the concept can be traced to the OT concept of God, in this case as warrior, in whom the qualities which the author expects, can be found.[72]

---

[69] Note Ps. 144:17 (LXX); Deut. 9:5; 32:4; Rev. 16:5 show these paired virtues to be attributes of God. This would be consistent with the *imitatio* ethic of 5:1, and correspond to the author's promotion of Christ as exemplar.

[70] Best, *Ephesians*, 437, giving copious literary examples, notes that the word pair commonly formed a "comprehensive phrase for virtuous living" known to the hearers of the day. The use of this common word pair lends the passage a new, Christian emphasis and "ethical slant" which the same metaphor in Col. lacks. As applied to human virtue in scripture, see Wis. 9:3; Lk. 1:75; 1Thes. 2:10; Tit. 1:8.

[71] Best, *Ephesians*, 598.

[72] The Lord is depicted in terms of the belt/breastplate of righteousness, Isa. 11: 4, 5; 59:17 and Wis. 5:18. Schnackenburg, *Brief*, 283, notes that the entire analogy is characterised by

These examples show that the author of Eph. is promoting an ethical vision which includes the OT concept of righteousness, both divine and human. This concept applies to God's character, as well as to behaviour that is in keeping with his character and the Law. Though this subtle relationship may not have been understood by his hearers, the author of Eph. becomes explicit in his desire to promote behaviour, where applicable, in keeping with God's character and law. In the child-parent relationship of the HT, he illustrates the meaning of obedience and τὸ δίκαιον by direct appeal to the Decalogue. This is an expansion in terms of style and argumentation, of course, but it adds the element of *Begründung* which was missing in the Col. version.[73] The OT scriptures are used here, as elsewhere in the letter, not only to illustrate, but to establish an ethical benchmark, as well.[74] The author ties this scriptural reference to his formal *Begründung*, highlighting its importance[75] and drawing the hearers' attention to the *positive* nature of the promise attached to the command: ἥτις ἐστὶν ἐντολὴ πρώτη ἐν ἐπαγγελίᾳ. The concern of the author to establish a viable Christian mode of discipline is unmistakable, as he admonishes the fathers to instruct in the παιδείᾳ καὶ νουθεσίᾳ κυρίου.[76] This instruction, it appears, following the prescriptive nature of the author's instruction, takes its first impulses from the traditions of OT law.

The Master-Slave Relationship

Though the slave-master relationship undergoes significant changes in its formulation, with slight omissions and additions, it remains remarkably similar to the Col. original, retaining nearly all of its distinctive features. This is to be expected, as the Col. HT was significantly expanded at this point, containing a high degree of uniquely Christian thought, as well as OT concepts.[77] In keeping with the author's emphasis upon the OT, the phrase μετὰ

---

plays upon, and reminiscences of, OT passages. The passage hopes to display that the believer is equipped with nothing less than the weapons of God.

[73] The τοῦτο γὰρ εὐάρεστον phrase of Col. is not actually *Begründung*.

[74] Moritz, *Mystery*, 177, concludes that the OT usage illustrates "the author's essential agreement in matters of ethics with the God revealed in the Jewish Scriptures."

[75] The Eph. author's contention, ἥτις ἐστὶν ἐντολὴ πρώτη ἐν ἐπαγγελίᾳ, probably does not consider the reference in Ex. 20:4–6 as a promise. It is interesting to note that other NT occurrences (Mt. 15:4; 19:19; Mk. 7:10; 10:19 and Lk. 18:20) do not include this element. Perhaps the author includes the promise to underscore the command's importance.

[76] The word pair may suggest discipline executed in deed and word, but it is more likely that this is a synonymous pair, typical of the author's style, see Mußner, *Brief*, 163.

[77] Concepts such as the fear of the Lord, serving the Lord in singleness of heart (Deut. 6:5) and the *jus talionis*; in spite of the commonality, Eph. reflects the OT in a more direct manner.

φόβου καὶ τρόμου expands its explicit usage in this portion of the Eph. HT. The author has moved Christ even more to the centre of the ethic by his explicit mention of his title in 6:5 ὡς τῷ Χριστῷ and 6:6, ὡς δοῦλοι Χριστοῦ. These are small indications of the author's tendencies discussed above, and contribute to an ethic which is regulated by Christ and OT motifs. More significant at this juncture is the emphasis within the slave's instruction upon executing God's will, τὸ θέλημα τοῦ θεοῦ ἐκ ψυχῆς. Here the author connects the behaviour of the slave with an important expansion of the Eph. redaction,[78] the emphasis upon the appreciation and understanding of the will of God as determinative for salvation and ethics. The author of Col. had associated God's will with known activities in this present age: 1:1, the calling of the Apostle; 1:9–11 the knowledge of the will to determine wisdom, knowledge of God and fruitful behaviour; and 4:12, a prayer that the Colossians might know the will of the Lord. This same emphasis can be found in Eph. 1:1, 5:17 and 6:6, where the will of God is a present reality, and the basis for ethical admonition. For the author of Eph., however, the will of God has acquired a new aspect which links it to events which transpire outside human history, and involve mystery, as well as election. This added realm of God's activity expresses the notion of God's will as timeless and transhistorical, and decisive in securing the Ephesians' salvation. It is God's will, ultimately, which establishes the divine-human axis. The importance of this element cannot be overstated in this context. The event of salvation, so central to the Col. letter, is augmented by the element of God's will, so that God's will becomes, for the writer of Ephesians, much more than a category for ethical behaviour; it represents an achievable, demonstrable goal. It becomes the genesis of the hearers' relationship to God, an inextricable element from which all else depends and originates:

1. Eph. 1:5: προορίσας ἡμᾶς εἰς υἱοθεσίαν διὰ Ἰησοῦ Χριστοῦ εἰς αὐτόν, κατὰ τὴν εὐδοκίαν τοῦ θελήματος αὐτου.

2. Eph. 1:9: γνωρίσας ἡμῖν τὸ μυστήριον τοῦ θελήματος αὐτοῦ, κατὰ τὴν εὐδοκίαν αὐτοῦ ἣν προέθετο ἐν αὐτῷ.

Moritz, *Mystery*, 153, notes the closer affinity of Eph. 6:9 (Col. 4:1) to the original text of Lev. 25:43.
[78] Seven instances in Eph. 1:1, 5, 9 11; 2:3; 5:17; 6:6. Col. 1:1, 5; 4:12. Of these, only 1:1 is a clear parallel.

3. Eph. 1:11: ἐν ᾧ καὶ ἐκληρώθημεν προορισθέντες κατὰ πρόθεσιν τοῦ τὰ πάντα ἐνεργοῦντος κατὰ τὴν βουλὴν τοῦ θελήματος αὐτοῦ.

That the author of Eph. would include reference to God's will in the HT admonition to the slaves is more than coincidence, and reflects the centrality of this concept for the writer. Though the slave-master relationship reflects a high level of Christian motivation, it receives a further regulating element in the appeal to the will of God. For the author of Eph., the will of God establishes the relational axes in Christ (divine and inter-human), and regulates relationships within the church.

The Husband-Wife Relationship

Although the parent-child and slave-master relations show affinities with the style and theological emphases of the larger letter, it is the expanded relationship between the husband and wife which most closely reflects the unique theological impulses and intentions of the author. Here both the style and theological innovation of the Eph. author converge to produce a highly theological piece of ethical instruction. In the following paragraphs, we hope to illustrate how the Eph. HT instruction to the husbands and wives incorporates the letter's broader tendencies within its highly compressed form. As with the theological emphases of the letter, the points of coincidence are several.

First of all, the author of Ephesians has adopted the Col. author's penchant for expressing theological truth regarding the church by means of comparative illustration. Here we note an expanded and more consistent use of the head-body metaphor,[79] as well as the influence and importance of growth language to describe the church and its relation to Christ.[80] The author extends the parenetic section in 6:10–17 with the unique panoply illustration, further underscoring his desire to impart theological truth by means of comparison between the hearers' common experience and greater, spiri-

---

[79] Note christological-ecclesiological usage in Col.: 1:18, 24; 2:10, 17, 19; as well as Ephesians, 1:22, 23; 2:16; 4:4, 12, 15, 16; 5:23, 30. Col. also incorporates common usage, 1:22; 2:11, 23, whereas somatic and head-language in Eph. consistently refers to the church, with the single exception in the HT instructions to the husband, 5:23a, 28, a reference, however, clearly used in tandem with the Christ-church metaphor.

[80] Col. 1:6, 10; 2:7, 19. As noted earlier, the author retains and even extends the concept of growth in his argument. Eph. 2:21; 3:17; 4:15–16; these incidents of growth are joined by the Eph. author to the concept of building, and indicate the corporate sense of the analogy, see 2:21; 4:12, 16, 29 for references to the οἰκοδομή; 2:22, συνοικοδομεῖσθε.

tual realities. This tendency is most clearly seen in the HT instruction to the wives and husbands, where the author takes the somatic and head analogies in a new direction,[81] tying the letter's theology to its ethical mandates in an unprecedented parallel.[82] Here we find the author's primary theological concerns, located in the person of Christ and the entity of his church (representing the divine-human axis), joined in parallel with aspects of the intra-human axis. This parallel not only represents a sophisticated method of drawing out similarities and subtle nuances in both relationships, but is equally a reflection of the Ephesian author's development of the Colossian original.[83] The discrete relational axes of the Col. *Vorlage* are retained, yet with the added aspect of being drawn in parallel for the sake of analogy. As discussed above, the common experience of being loved of God has placed the believers in parallel, analogous relation to Christ. The addition of the relational axis, God-Christ, has allowed the author to build a bridge between divine and human experience, allowing, at least to some degree, a certain level of analogy based upon the love of God. The new and parallel theological reality gives rise to parallel ethical constructions; in our case, an analogy based on the model and thinking *Urbild-Abbild*.[84] In the Eph. HT, the analogy is drawn most clearly into focus through the mandates given to man and woman. It is interesting to note that love determines, at least primarily, the motivation of the husband-wife ethic.[85] The Ephesian HT instruction to husbands and wives represents a *continuation* of the author's expanded emphasis upon love, as well as incorporating the author's explicit call to imitation of Christ in love, 5:1–2: γίνεσθε οὖν μιμηταὶ τοῦ θεοῦ ὡς τέκνα ἀγαπητὰ καὶ περιπατεῖτε ἐν ἀγάπῃ, καθὼς καὶ ὁ Χριστὸς ἠγάπησεν ἡμᾶς καὶ παρέδωκεν ἑαυτὸν ὑπὲρ ἡμῶν προσφορὰν καὶ θυσίαν τῷ θεῷ εἰς ὀσμὴν εὐωδίας. The formulation, which isolates the divine as sole object for imita-

---

[81] The author's formulation in Eph. 5:23 is likely to have been influenced by the 1 Cor. 11:3; this passage lacks, however, the clear and intentional parallelism between Christ-church/husband-wife.

[82] Mußner, *Brief*, 159, expresses amazement that the author would attempt such a risky parallel.

[83] The Col. author provides the seeds for the more extensive use of Christ as exemplar in Ephesians in Col. 3:13b, καθὼς καὶ ὁ κύριος ἐχαρίσατο ὑμῖν, οὕτως καὶ ὑμεῖς. The Eph. author, however, accentuates the element of love, deriving his model from both divine-human as well as divine-divine relations.

[84] See Gielen, *Tradition*, 242, fn. 120.

[85] The wife is not, of course, specifically required to love the husband, though this might be assumed; the majority of the material, however, directed towards the husband, is regulated by love. The parallels of God-Christ, Christ-church and husband-wife represent superordinate-subordinate relations characterised by love (superordinate) and submission (subordinate).

tion, is unique[86] to the author of Eph., and represents his Christ-oriented approach to construing the daily Christian ethic. This command is reflected, and takes on concrete form in the HT admonition to the husbands, in Eph. 5:25 and 29, where even Christ's soteriological activity serves as example to the husbands: Οἱ ἄνδρες, ἀγαπᾶτε τὰς γυναῖκας, καθὼς καὶ ὁ Χριστὸς ἠγάπησεν τὴν ἐκκλησίαν καὶ ἑαυτὸν παρέδωκεν ὑπὲρ αὐτῆς and οὐδεὶς γάρ ποτε τὴν ἑαυτοῦ σάρκα ἐμίσησεν ἀλλὰ ἐκτρέφει καὶ θάλπει αὐτήν, καθὼς καὶ ὁ Χριστὸς τὴν ἐκκλησίαν. The original command of Col. 3:19 is formulated in positive terms only (μὴ πικραίνεσθε πρὸς αὐτάς being dropped), in keeping with the author's positive style, and as might be expected in order to avoid confusion in the analogy. The surprising element is the manner in which the author draws the activity of Christ into *direct* analogy to the husbands' expected behaviour. The analogy is so direct, in fact, that most commentators of the Eph. HT mediate the injunctions in some manner. This observation is not limited to the husbands, but is extended to the wives, as well. The author's instruction to the wives is strengthened in its force,[87] and notably expanded in the parallel drawn between Christ and the church.

The instruction to the husbands and wives follows, as noted above, the author's tendency to employ analogy, incorporate the motif of love, and locate Christ as the motivational centre of the parenetic motivation. In this respect, the HT is a clear extension of the general thought of the larger letter. This provides the author with a backdrop upon which he places the particular images of his ethical vision. Not surprisingly, much of the vocabulary which makes up the extended HT admonitions can be shown to reflect the concerns and stylistic character of the letter, as well.

Though the author has elevated Christ to a central, analogical position in determining the HT ethic, as well as dealing with concrete issues of particular inter-human relations, his concern for the church remains evident, and presents a second, unique element of the author's instruction to husbands and wives. It is the church, as we have noted, which comprises the earthly pole of the author's vertical axis, a critical shift in emphasis over the individual groupings found in Colossians. The church is so important, in fact, that the instruction of 5:22–33 includes six explicit references in terms of her relation

---

[86] μιμητής, consistently joined with γίνομαι and the descriptive genitive, is normally related to humans or human activity in the NT: 1 Cor. 4:16; 11:1, of Paul (μου); 1Thes. 2:14, of the churches (τῶν ἐκκλησιῶν), Heb. 6:12 of other believers (τῶν κληρονομούνψῶν); 1 Thes. 1:6 combines both human and divine aspects (ἡμῶν...καὶ τοῦ κυρίου). The verb μιμέομαι and its accusative object reveal the same tendency of imitating primarily human behaviour: 2 Thes. 3:7, 9 (ἡμᾶς); Heb. 13:7 (τὴν πίστιν); 3 Jn. 11 (τὸ ἀγαθόν).

[87] The ὡς τῷ κυρίῳ of Col. 3:23 is adopted here.

to Christ.[88] The author never loses sight of the ecclesiastical aspect of his instruction, as if this concern were almost competing with instruction concerning household relations. Twice, for example, he interrupts his instruction to the husbands to make observations as to the nature of the church. Both examples break with the standard HT form, and deserve closer attention. The first instance, which changes the address to the first person plural, echoes the sentiments of 4:25. Adopting a confessional tone, the author affirms an ecclesiastical truth related to his teaching to the husbands, 5:30: ὅτι μέλη ἐσμὲν τοῦ σώματος αὐτοῦ. This departure from the typical direct address of the HT form reflects the author's intention to instruct the entire congregation in the ecclesiastical implications of the mandates, and is singular in the NT.[89] The second instance, similarly, attempts to direct the present aspect of his ethical and theological argument towards the church, 5:32: τὸ μυστήριον τοῦτο μέγα ἐστίν· ἐγὼ δὲ λέγω εἰς Χριστὸν καὶ εἰς τὴν ἐκκλησίαν. The normal HT form is again modified to include first-person discourse, a feature which is unique to the Ephesians HT. The commentary upon the OT citation of Gen. 2:24 reveals the author's intention of shared, if not primary, emphasis upon instruction concerning the church.[90]

This emphasis can be further observed in the extension of the head-body metaphor, which features so prominently in both Col. and Eph. The author of Eph. draws upon this familiar[91] metaphor to illustrate, in creative and nuanced fashion, the implications of Christ's lordship to the most intimate of relations, man and wife, and connect the HT mandates to the theological tenor of the larger letter. The head-body metaphor, employed in Col. only *outside* the HT, renders double service in Ephesians. It depicts, in stylistically parallel terms, the degree of coincidence the author has allowed be-

[88] The six references in the HT represent the expansion of the term over against Col.; the meaning in the HT is consistent with the universal church depicted in the broader letter.

[89] We have noted in our study that the HT form is characterised by direct address in the second person plural.

[90] Here Lindemann, *Epheserbrief*, 105, is correct to point out that the author employs emphatic language (ἐγὼ δὲ λέγω) and the modifier great (μέγα) to underscore the importance of the ecclesiastical aspect; the use of δὲ, often construed as a signal that there were competing interpretations, is probably used to lend weight to the following interpretation (for similar usage cf. Rom. 3:22; 1 Cor. 10:11; Phil. 2:8). This would be most in keeping with the central role of the church in the broader letter, as well as in the HT.

[91] Certainly familiar from the Col. *Vorlage* and borrowing from the Paulines (1 Cor. 11:3; see Gese, *Vermächtis*, 76–7 for listing); the head-body concept was also known in the broader cultural context of the time. For an overview of possible parallels, see K.M. Fischer, *Tendenz und Absicht des Epheserbriefes*, eds. E. Käsemann and E. Würthwein, Forschung zur Religion und Literatur des Alten und Neuen Testaments, vol. 111 (Göttingen: Vandenhoeck & Ruprecht, 1973), 72–78.

tween the primary axes, and becomes an illustration of both relationships. In this manner, the shared use of the somatic metaphor serves to illustrate the author's theological innovation of placing the primary axes in parallel, analogical relation. The clever technique is much more than stylistic finesse, however. The Eph. author manifests a genuine, *dual* interest in the relational pairs conjoined by the metaphor. The two relations, Christ-church and husband-wife, receive equal treatment within the somatic metaphor, yet there remain elements within the HT instruction which are obviously intended to remain unique to either Christ-church or husband-wife. The juxtaposition of the two axes within the framework of the HT underscores the author's genuine intention to impart instruction regarding marriage *and* the church. It is the latter element which distinguishes the redactional expansion and perspective of the Eph. author.

This observation of dual emphasis might be surmised from the concerns of the larger letter, but it is illustrated in the following examples from the Eph. HT, where the behaviours of the husbands and Christ *cannot* be held in parallel. As noted above, it is in the HT where the author has departed (Eph. 5:28) from an otherwise positive and homogenous usage of the term σῶμα to denote the church; the husbands' bodies can only fit the Christ-church analogy tangentially. The analogy between the Christ-church and husband-wife relationships displays, then, limitations. At these points, which make up a significant amount of the instruction, the focus appears to be on Christ's historical accomplishments on behalf of the church:

Eph. 5:23a: Parallel: The husband is head over the wife as Christ to the church;
Eph. 5:23b: Disanalogy/Exclusive to Christ: αὐτὸς σωτὴρ τοῦ σώματος.[92]

This verse introduces the church to the passage, which becomes its dominant feature.[93] The phrase σωτὴρ τοῦ σώματος is unique to the NT, and anticipates the discourse regarding Christ in 5:25. The soteriological language makes this aspect of the comparison humanly untenable.[94]

---

[92] Some MSS attempt to make this point even more clearly with the addition of καὶ (αὐτός) ἐστίν.

[93] So Best, *Ephesians*, 535.

[94] Gnilka, *Brief*, 277, rightly states that "der Vergleich ein ungleichmäßiger ist." Dibelius, *Kolosser*, 93, sees the phrase as not belonging to the analogy (*Nebengedanke*), and allows no parallel in human marriage.

Eph. 5:25–27, the first instruction to the husbands to love their wives, is illustrated in terms of Christ and the church. The husband's behaviour is not described, but Christ's; in particular, his love for the church and his soteriological activity, which produce results attributable to none other than Christ. In both length and subject, Christ and the church dominate this segment:

Eph. 5:25a: Parallel: Husbands to love wives as Christ the church;
Eph. 5:25b–27: Disanalogy/Exclusive to Christ: ἑαυτὸν παρέδωκεν ὑπὲρ αὐτῆς, ἵνα αὐτὴν ἁγιάσῃ καθαρίσας τῷ λουτρῷ τοῦ ὕδατος ἐν ῥήματι, ἵνα παραστήσῃ αὐτὸς ἑαυτῷ ἔνδοξον τὴν ἐκκλησίαν, μὴ ἔχουσαν σπίλον ἢ ῥυτίδα ἤ τι τῶν τοιούτων, ἀλλ' ἵνα ᾖ ἁγία καὶ ἄμωμος. ἑαυτὸν παρέδωκεν ὑπὲρ αὐτῆς, ἵνα αὐτὴν ἁγιάσῃ καθαρίσας τῷ λουτρῷ τοῦ ὕδατος ἐν ῥήματι, ἵνα παραστήσῃ αὐτὸς ἑαυτῷ ἔνδοξον τὴν ἐκκλησίαν, μὴ ἔχουσαν σπίλον ἢ ῥυτίδα ἤ τι τῶν τοιούτων, ἀλλ' ἵνα ᾖ ἁγία καὶ ἄμωμος.

The vocabulary of these verses is strikingly representative of the larger letter, passages which are, notably, linked exclusively to Christ. Christ giving himself, for instance, (ἑαυτὸν παρέδωκεν) refers to his love and sacrifice as illustrated in the pivotal verse in Eph. 5:2, ὁ Χριστὸς ἠγάπησεν ἡμᾶς καὶ παρέδωκεν ἑαυτὸν ὑπὲρ ἡμῶν. The result of his sacrifice is that the church might be holy and blameless, the very result of the author's introductory remarks concerning Christ and the church in Eph. 1:4: καθὼς ἐξελέξατο ἡμᾶς ἐν αὐτῷ πρὸ καταβολῆς κόσμου εἶναι ἡμᾶς ἁγίους καὶ ἀμώμους κατενώπιον αὐτοῦ ἐν ἀγάπῃ. The language of this important passage is reflected in the HT formulation of 5:27b. Both instances from the broader letter, reflected in this Eph. 5:25–27, remind the reader, in quite clear tones, of soteriological activity unique to Christ.

Can the same be said of the rather enigmatic clauses of Eph. 5:27, ἵνα παραστήσῃ αὐτὸς ἑαυτῷ ἔνδοξον τὴν ἐκκλησίαν, μὴ ἔχουσαν σπίλον ἢ ῥυτίδα ἤ τι τῶν τοιούτων? Though there is no strict agreement as to the exact meaning of these phrases, the following options illustrate how commentators generally assign these clauses to soteriological activity/ecclesiastical reality on the behalf of believers. The first option is that 5:26a, ἵνα αὐτὴν ἁγιάσῃ καθαρίσας τῷ λουτρῷ τοῦ ὕδατος ἐν ῥήματι, apparently refers to the believer's baptism, or perhaps a baptismal formula (though the exact meaning of ῥῆμα in this connection is disputed).[95] The subject here is still understood to be Christ; the activities of purifying by *the* water and *the* word indicate familiarity, perhaps with a ritual; human agency seems unlikely in this context.

The formulation can likewise be explained in terms of several possible *hieros gamos* traditions.[96] This would include the OT marriage of Yahweh and Israel, as well as the later Gnostic conceptions of divine union contained in the Sophia myth, or perhaps the divine marriages of mystery religions.[97] If this is indeed the tradition which influenced the author's vocabulary, then we may assume that the author understands *Christ* to be the divine agent of the spiritual union with the church.

Others take 5:26a to be a reference to Jewish and pagan bridal bath traditions. Gnilka suggests that the "Hochzeitsritus des Brautbades" is represented in the phraseology of Eph. 5:27.[98] This ritual, performed before the marriage ceremony, is undertaken, he suggests, in OT literature by God himself (Ezek. 16:19f),[99] and has been adopted into Christian thought. If the bridal bath tradition has shaped the formulation of Eph., it is most probable that Eph. 5:27 anticipates *divine* activity and relates to Christ and the church.[100] A scenario where a human bridegroom is encouraged to wash his bride-to-be (whatever the intended result) seems, at best, peculiar. Furthermore, the resultant qualities of the church's cleansing, ἵνα ᾖ ἁγία καὶ ἄμωμος, hearken back to the unique work of Christ found in Eph. 1:4 (Col. 1:22), where believers are chosen to be ἁγίους καὶ ἀμώμους before God.

Finally, the formulation can be understood primarily in terms of its presentation language. This view allows for the traditional influences mentioned

---

[95] Generally construed to be either the Gospel or a baptismal formula. See Dibelius, *Kolosser*, 93f., for an insightful discussion of the meaning of ῥῆμα. He points out that grammatical arguments cannot locate the precise meaning of the word; the brevity of the expression assumes familiarity on the part of the hearers. Also Best, *Ephesians*, 543f.

[96] See Sampley, *One Flesh*, 15–76, for a thorough discussion of the various *hieros gamos* interpretations.

[97] Lincoln, *Ephesians*, 362–3, records some of the shortcomings of the Gnostic and pagan sources.

[98] Gnilka, *Epheserbrief*, 280. He cites several sources which attest to the ritual in Jewish and pagan contexts.

[99] Muddiman, *Ephesians*, 265, correctly notes that this citation can only be cautiously applied, as it refers to the washing of a new-born.

[100] The church is named as the recipient of the cleansing in v. 27; the effects of the cleansing, μὴ ἔχουσαν σπίλον ἢ ῥυτίδα (!) ἤ τι τῶν τοιούτων, ἀλλ᾽ ἵνα ᾖ ἁγία καὶ ἄμωμος cannot be understood merely in terms of a ritual bath.

above,[101] yet sees them employed to illustrate a more ultimate reality, the presentation of the church before Christ. It also corresponds to the reasoning of the text, which makes presentation the result of the cleansing, ἵνα παραστήσῃ αὐτὸς ἑαυτῷ ἔνδοξον τὴν ἐκκλησίαν, as well as reflecting the theology of Eph. 1:4 (Col. 1:22), which places the church holy and blameless κατενώπιον αὐτοῦ ἐν ἀγάπῃ. It is also possible, given the author's tendency to draw from Pauline material, that this is an adaptation of the presentation theme of 2 Cor. 11:2. In our text, Christ is depicted in the apostle's role; the universal church sublimates the local church context of 2 Corinthians. At any event, it appears clear that Christ alone is construed as presenter in these verses, making an interpretation involving human correspondence improbable.[102]

The genesis of the formulation of Eph. 5:25–27 may have a simpler, redactional explanation. Sampley, in his discussion of the several possible meanings of παρίστημι, notes that the verb may be understood in a sacrificial manner.[103] This possibility seems likely when we consider the strong influence of Col. 1:22 upon the formulation of this passage, particularly 1:22b: παραστῆσαι ὑμᾶς ἁγίους καὶ ἀμώμους καὶ ἀνεγκλήτους κατενώπιον αὐτοῦ, which contains both elements of presentation related to Christ, as well as the corresponding sacrificial language. In this verse it is the church which attains sacrificial purity through the Christ's death, ἀποκατήλλαξεν ἐν τῷ σώματι τῆς σαρκὸς αὐτοῦ διὰ τοῦ θανάτου.[104] The sacrificial purity[105] which the church has attained in Col. 1:22 and Eph. 1:4 may help explain the language applied to the church/bride in Eph. 5:27b: μὴ ἔχουσαν

---

[101] Schnackenburg, *Brief*, 257, suggests that the complex images found in Eph. 5:27 must be understood in terms of Christ and the church, which unify the author's borrowing of "verschiedene Gedanken."

[102] The emphatic use of αὐτός makes this clear. See Sampley, *One Flesh*, 134.

[103] Sampley, *One Flesh*, 135f., notes an indebtedness to Jewish sacrificial language within the larger passage.

[104] This type of presentation involving the body as sacrifice is a Pauline concept, Rom. 12:1b: παραστῆσαι τὰ σώματα ὑμῶν θυσίαν ζῶσαν ἁγίαν εὐάρεστον τῷ θεῷ.

[105] Gnilka, *Brief*, 283, sees the passage influenced by OT "Opfersprache" pertaining to the perfection of the offering. The reference to the absence of wrinkles (ῥυτίδα is unique to Bible) probably corresponds to the OT requirement that the offering be less than one year old (Lev. 6–9). The adjective ἄμωμος is common in OT (LXX) usage to describe purity, particularly that of sacrificial animals (Num. 19:2; 28:3, 9, 11; 29: 17, 26), but also of humans (Dt. 32:5; Job 11:15; Song 4:7 [Heb. 9:14]). Μὴ ἔχουσαν σπίλον seems to correspond to ἄμωμος in meaning both in sacrificial (1 Pet. 1:19) and ethical (1 Tim. 6:14; 2 Pet. 3:13; 3:14; Jude 12) terms. Though σπίλος is not attested in the LXX, it is apparently associated with purity, see 2 Pet. 2:13, σπίλοι καὶ μῶμοι; 3:14, ἄσπιλοι καὶ ἀμώμητοι.

σπίλον ἢ ῥυτίδα ἤ τι τῶν τοιούτων.[106] If the author of Ephesians has indeed been influenced by the formulation of Col. 1:22, this would add another reason for understanding Eph. 5:25–27 in solely christological terms.

In summary, the images presented in Eph. 5:25–27 appear to refer solely to the sacrifice of Christ, and the benefits wrought on behalf of the church. The association of the agency or work of Christ in these verses with the human axis cannot be sustained on grammatical grounds, and are equally unlikely in terms of the theological emphasis of sacrifice and redemption. The author of Ephesians displays, in this manner, his concern to use the HT form as a vehicle to illustrate both horizontal *and* vertical axes; though the use of analogy brings the axes into confluence at several points, the vertical, Christ-church relation remains a distinct feature of his redaction.

Lastly, the author of Ephesians (as noted above) makes use of the OT scriptures to a greater degree than that which is found in Colossians, and especially so in his edition of the HT. This usage betrays a familiarity with, and affinity towards, Jewish traditions. The OT commands and inferences add a traditional element to the Ephesian redaction, as well as functioning in a regulatory manner. In the expanded husband-wife instruction, we note direct OT citation, as well as the presence of *embedded* OT tradition. This can be seen, for example, in the OT sacrificial imagery found in Eph. 5:25–27, as discussed above. The author not only reminds the reader of the sacrifice of Christ (Eph. 1:4), but extends the image by adapting the presentation language of Col. 1:22 on the one hand, and adding further sacrificial language on the other.

Eph. 5:33 represents another possible example. It calls the husbands to love their wives, ἕκαστος τὴν ἑαυτοῦ γυναῖκα οὕτως ἀγαπάτω ὡς ἑαυτόν, connecting the letter's theme of love to the broader instruction found in Lev. 19:18 (LXX), ἀγαπήσεις τὸν πλησίον σου ὡς σεαυτόν.[107] This reference is, of course, embedded in the text, and may not have been understood by the original hearers as originating from the OT. Yet it illustrates the author's intention to bring OT principles to bear upon the themes of the letter, as well as its practical concerns.

The following example found in Eph. 5:31, however, is unmistakable: ἀντὶ τούτου καταλείψει ἄνθρωπος [τὸν] πατέρα καὶ [τὴν] μητέρα καὶ

---

[106] Muddiman, *Ephesians*, 267, correctly differentiates this description of the church from any analogy to human beauty, noting the sacrificial nature of the language.

[107] First recognised by Samply, *One Flesh*, 30–34, who indicates the influence of this concept upon the larger husband-wife section; the inexactness of the citation (γυναῖκα for πλησίον) is accounted for in numerous examples taken from Jewish literature, where the concepts are held in parallel, or even substituted as in Song 1:9, 15; 2:2, 10, 13; 4:1, 7; 5:2; 6:4.

προσκολληθήσεται πρὸς τὴν γυναῖκα αὐτοῦ, καὶ ἔσονται οἱ δύο εἰς σάρκα μίαν.[108] Gen. 2:24 functions as authoritative support for the author's command to the husbands to love, yet καὶ ἔσονται οἱ δύο εἰς σάρκα μίαν, in keeping with the dual nature of the somatic analogy, illustrates the author's broader concern for unity in the body, as well.[109] Unity occurs within the church across a broad range, incorporating both the human and divine-human spheres. The citation of Gen. 2:24 serves both the horizontal and vertical axes.

The author's motivation for including the Genesis quotation seems to follow his tendency to substantiate his theological and ethical views with OT scripture. This is arguably the case in terms of the husband-wife relation. As Moritz has convincingly shown,[110] extracanonical use of Gen. 2:24 was primarily limited to discussions regarding the legality of divorce, constituting a "grave misuse" of the concept of marriage in contemporary thought. It may be that the author is augmenting the Colossian original with a clear mandate of creation to counter this negative contemporary perception, and establish an ethical standard for the church. This pattern is true of the Gospel accounts; it may be that the author of Ephesians has adopted Christ's emphasis upon the precedence of creation over Law.[111] Even closer at hand, however, is an example from the Paulines. We have noted that the author of Eph. has been influenced at several points by the theological formulations of 1 Corinthians; the vocabulary and reasoning of 1 Cor. 6:12–20 may have influenced the author's formulation here, where we find an unusual coincidence of somatic language, christological reasoning, the close juxtaposition of the horizontal and vertical axes, and, of course, the citation of Gen. 2:24.[112] The context of this passage is the *abuse* of the Corinthian believers' sexuality, which

---

[108] καὶ προσκολληθήσεται πρὸς τὴν γυναῖκα αὐτοῦ is omitted in a number of texts, and probably represents a textual emendation, perhaps in light of docetic tendencies, cf. Gnilka, *Epheser*, 286.

[109] Eph. 2:12–18; 4:3–5 speak of unity, notably in somatic terms.

[110] Moritz, *Mystery*, 121–130, compiles a number of Jewish discussions on marriage, which indicate that Gen. 2:24 was either not being interpreted in terms of the marriage bond, or left out altogether. Nearly all discussion involved the legal aspects of divorce. This is collaborated in the accounts of Mk. 10 and Mt. 19, where it is Jesus who introduces the creation aspect of union contained in Gen. 2:24.

[111] Mk. 10 and Mt. 19 contrast the Law (Dt. 24:1f.) and creation as found in Gen. 1:27 and 2:24. Note the words of introduction in Mk. 10:6a: ἀπὸ δὲ ἀρχῆς κτίσεως or Mt. 19:4a: ὁ κτίσας ἀπ᾽ ἀρχῆς, and 19:8b, ἀπ᾽ ἀρχῆς δὲ οὐ γέγονεμ οὕτως. The creation of God supersedes the Law in Eph., as well, 2:15: τὸν νόμον τῶν ἐντολῶν ἐν δόγμασιν καταργήσας, ἵνα τοὺς δύο κτίσῃ ἐν αὐτῷ εἰς ἕνα καινὸν ἄνθρωπον ποιῶν εἰρήνην.

[112] The reciprocal form of the HT follows that found in 1 Cor. 7:3–5a.

is found in a much larger parenetic section beginning in 1 Cor. 5. If Moritz' theory is correct, perhaps the author of Ephesians has adopted elements of the Corinthian sexual ethic in order to confront inappropriate or deficient sexual/ethical attitudes with a positive, Christ-centered and somatic under-standing of marriage. The expansion to the Colossian original appears to in-clude several elements from 1 Cor. 6, as seen in the following examples.

In 1 Corinthians we find the fullest expression of the somatic understand-ing of the church in the NT.[113] 1 Cor. 6:15–20 is particularly interesting in connection with the Eph. HT, because it also brings somatic language to bear upon sexual ethics. Paul's argument in this passage is drawn to a climax as he poses the question in 6:15, οὐκ οἴδατε ὅτι τὰ σώματα μέλη Χριστοῦ ἐστιν; This somatic connection to Christ is placed in opposition to the unde-sirable joining with a harlot, v. 15b. In a similar manner, the author of Ephe-sians employs the somatic union with Christ to regulate proper behaviour in the HT.[114] Loving behaviour is contrasted with hating one's own flesh (not properly loving the wife), Eph. 5:28–29; 5:30 offers similar christologi-cal/ontological reasoning for the author's desired behaviour: ὅτι μέλη ἐσμὲν τοῦ σώματος αὐτοῦ. Though the elements of the metaphor (μέλος, σῶμα) are reversed, the collocation of the terms in relation to Christ is unique to these two passages, and suggests that the author of Eph. has adopted the Co-rinthian somatic metaphor and christological reasoning here.

The authoritative and regulatory use of Genesis 2:24 is also a remarkable characteristic of both passages. In 1 Cor., the author hopes to correct a par-ticular sinful pattern (joining with harlots) by pointing out the ontological realities of sexual union. In Ephesians, the author augments his description of the marriage bond with similar results. The notion of "one flesh" illustrates, in both passages, the intimacy of human sexual union in the first instance. The secondary and correlative meaning, however, is also present in both pas-sages, revealing a similar technique of presenting the human and divine axes in parallel. In 1 Cor., the believer is strictly admonished to avoid intimacy with a harlot, not due to the repercussions within the marriage bond, but be-cause of union with Christ. The two realities are held in contrast in 6:13b, τὸ δὲ σῶμα οὐ τῇ πορνείᾳ ἀλλὰ τῷ κυρίῳ, καὶ ὁ κύριος τῷ σώματι, 6:15b, ἄρας οὖν τὰ μέλη τοῦ Χριστοῦ ποιήσω πόρνης μέλη; μὴ γένοιτο. In-

---

[113] Rom. makes extensive use of somatic language, though in a negative or neutral sense; 12:4–8 employs somatic language (both μέλος and σῶμα) in terms of the church. The use in 1 Cor. is more extensive and consistent in meaning (1 Cor. 6:13, 15, 16, 18, 19, 20; 10:17; 12:12, 13, 14, 15, 16, 17, 18, 19, 20, 22, 23, 24, 25, 26, 27). Interestingly, apart from Rom. and 1 Cor., it is only in Eph. where these terms are joined to speak of the church.

[114] It is interesting that both passages speak of the undesirable behaviour as mistreatment of the body.

deed, the physical union with the harlot is placed in parallel with the spiritual union with Christ: ὁ κολλώμενος τῇ πόρνῃ ἓν σῶμά ἐστιν of 6:16 gives the identical pattern for 6:17: ὁ δὲ κολλώμενος τῷ κυρίῳ ἓν πνεῦμά ἐστιν. The Corinthian parallel highlights both similarities and stark contrasts between the two axes. The author of Eph. also places the human and divine axes in parallel relation; the contrasts do not receive primary attention, however, as the author is presenting positive ethical behaviour.

As the concept of unity, both physical and spiritual, is highlighted in 1 Cor. 6 and the Eph. HT, the author of Eph. employs a familiar term in an attempt to quantify the nature of union on both the inter-human and divine-human axes: *mysterion*. Much discussion has been generated concerning the meaning of the reference to μυστήριον found in 5:32.[115] The several references within the letter (1:9; 3:3, 4, 9; 6:19) would suggest that the author is *extending* the meaning found there[116] to the HT; this interpretation would serve our thesis well! The HT usage, however, though certainly related to the mystery of God revealed in Christ, becomes more particular in explicating at least one element of the mysterion: the union of Christ and the church.[117] Though representing a departure from the meaning of the word as used elsewhere in the epistle, it would correspond with the author's ecclesiastical emphasis in the broader letter, and the husband-wife relation in particular. The possible influence of 1 Cor. 6 may be instructive at this point. Given the several similarities between Eph. 5 and 1 Cor. 6, it may be that the author of Eph. has not only adopted much of the vocabulary and parallel structure of 1 Cor. 6: 13–20, but its understanding of union with Christ, as well. 1 Cor. 6:17, as mentioned above, makes explicit reference to a spiritual union which parallels physical union: ὁ δὲ κολλώμενος τῷ κυρίῳ ἓν πνεῦμά ἐστιν. Both passages, notably, represent commentary upon the *mia sarx* element found in Gen. 2:24. It is clear that the author's use of Gen. 2:24 could be legitimately understood in terms of physical union, this being construed as the "great mystery" of verse 32a. The author of Ephesians is apparently aware of the possibility of understanding his commentary in physical terms, hence the spiritual and ecclesiastical clarification with the predication ἐγὼ δὲ λέγω.[118]

---

[115] Lincoln's discussion, *Ephesians*, 380–82, cites the several positions; his conclusion that the usage is highlighting an aspect of the mysterion, namely the union of Christ and the church, seems correct.

[116] The mystery is characterised as the heretofore veiled plan of God in Christ, made known in the Gospel.

[117] Caragounis, *Mysterion*, 30, sees this usage in terms of Christ and the church.

[118] Best, *Ephesians*, 555, notes that there is no clear indication as to what the author opposes; the physical-spiritual aspects of the parallel, however, offer a solution. See also Moritz, *Mystery*, 118f.

If the author of Eph. were familiar with the Cor. passage, it is more likely that he is making reference to the more extraordinary element of the two meanings, the spiritual union of Christ and the believer. The usage of μυστήριον in the HT connects the mandates to the broader letter's usage as a cipher for the activity of God revealed in Christ; in the HT, however, the mystery takes more particular form in the union of Christ and the church. The author connects the HT in this manner to the broader theology of the letter, while emphasising the centrality of the church as locus of the mystery.

Christ not only provides both passages with positive relational parallels, but constitutes the motivation for the sexual ethic. In both incidences, the passage is initially regulated by the citation of OT scripture, which is then applied allegorically to Christ. In Eph. we note the author's expansion of the instruction to the wives, Christ being named as "saviour of the body", 5:2; this soteriological theme courses through the entire husband-wife section of the HT, and is the basis for the husbands' treatment of their wives. The vertical axis Christ-body determines the horizontal behaviour. Similarly, the motivation of 1 Cor. 6:15–20 rests upon the relationship established by the work of Christ, 6:19–20a: ἢ οὐκ οἴδατε ὅτι τὸ σῶμα ὑμῶν ναὸς τοῦ εΟν ὑμῖν ἁγίου πνεύματός ἐστιν οὗ ἔχετε ἀπὸ θεοῦ, καὶ οὐκ ἐστὲ ἑαυτῶν; ἠγοράσθητε γὰρ τιμῆς· δοξάσατε δὴ τὸν θεὸν ἐν τῷ σώματι ὑμῶν. Christ, by virtue of his redemption of the body, establishes his relational authority in the church, an authority which is characterised by union.

Conclusion

We have argued in this chapter that the author of Ephesians, though adhering to a great degree to much of the Colossian letter's thought and form, has introduced several changes in theological perspective. The fundamental change of perspective from the Colossian original is what we have characterised as the systemisation of the horizontal axis; this entails the Eph. author's tendency to incorporate the central aspects and implications of salvation in Christ in horizontal, inter-human terms. In particular, we have noted a present-oriented emphasis upon the church (its unity, its authority, and its direct relation to Christ) which has superseded the Col. emphasis upon the parousia. In concord with the adoption of a horizontal and present-oriented perspective, the vertical relational *kurios-doulos* model has been displaced by a more communal model, Christ-church. The original Col. sense of transformation, which ran along antithetical present-future/heavenly-earthly lines, is understood by the author of Eph. to fall along horizontal lines, a human spectrum demarcated by its heathen-Christian extremes. The believer is understood, then, as having undergone passage into the Church, which stands, as a body, in direct relation to Christ. It is the church and its teachings, ultimately, which comprise the Christian sphere of existence, and the author's primary concern. This ecclesiastical concern is distilled in his emphasis upon the church, its offices, and its regulation; the introduction of traditional material found in the OT suggests an attempt to codify correct behaviour. It is the Christ-church relationship, however, which provides the author with his most profound theological insights and ethical model for behaviour. Christ is characterised as the mediator and exemplar of God's love; his relation to the church, though clearly representing the divine-human axis, serves as model and motivation of the parenetic discourse and its inter-human demands.

The theology and ethical motivation of the broader letter finds expression in the HT mandates, as well. We have found an expansion of explicit OT regulation in its regulation, as well as specific instances where the Eph. author has introduced modifications to suit his interests and literary style. It is his concern for the church, however, which determines the most striking emphases and stylistic choices. In the expanded husband-wife instruction, it is the church's relationship to Christ which regulates, and often dominates, the passage. The divine-human axis serves, as in the rest of the letter, as the model of love and correct behaviour between believers. The implications of Christ's role as head of the Church are explored in the particulars of the marital duties, resulting in an analogy which is drawn in tension between the realities of the axes Christ-church and husband-wife. In keeping with the author's primary emphasis, the analogy is often weighted towards an ecclesiastical, soteriological understanding, including the unity and purity of the church. The HT functions, then, as parenetic instruction to husband and wife, which draws upon the profound mysteries of the Christ-church relationship; in similar manner, it can also be characterised as theological instruction, in which the author presses the human analogy with dramatic effect. The result of the Ephesian author's redaction is a HT which is, to a greater degree than its Colossian counterpart, a vehicle of the author's theological motifs.

Having examined the theology of Col. and Eph. both comparatively and in relation to their broader letter contexts, we hope that the reader has gained an appreciation for the unique nature of each letter's theology and ethical vision, particularly as this is codified in the expanded sections of their respective HT. We move now to a much broader comparison of the HT with ancient and contemporary Hellenistic sources, in an attempt to locate significant elements of similitude and contrast. It is our hope that this comparison will highlight elements of the HT which might be characterised as common tradition, as well as those uniquely Christian.

Chapter Five
A Comparison of Household Regulations

Introduction

As early as the fifth century BC (and certainly earlier!), philosophers were musing over, and often energetically disputing, the very nature of household authority relationships and their regulation. Though distant from the New Testament HT in terms of time, and couched in much broader discussions of ontology, ethics and statecraft, their concerns and categories prove to be similar to those of the NT household codes. Regulations of household relations continued to develop up to the time of the New Testament HT, and both periods have received scholarly treatment in light of the HT. The attention given to such material, both antecedent and contemporary to the HT, has been dominated, however, by the questions of *Form-* and *Traditions-geschichte* in an attempt to establish a "genetic link" in the HT's evolutionary development. Without denying the importance of these studies to the question of HT origins, it seems that a *comparison* of the most full-bodied and relevant sources might serve to highlight the similarities, and perhaps reveal unique characteristics of the HT form and message. The task of isolating significant elements within particular Hellenistic authors may help to counteract the tendency of treating individual sources as undifferentiated constructs or representatives of a larger, political or religious phenomenon; often, a particular author may evidence remarkable independence of thought.[1] The comparative analysis of several sources and periods, it is hoped, will illustrate the remarkable variety of assumptions and concerns among the Hellenistic thinkers, as well as the considerable level of discontinuity between their conclusions. The ancient thinkers cannot, we hope to show, be properly organised according to a monolithic scheme, nor do they

---

[1] Klaus Thraede, for instance, suggests that Philo represents the *status quo* of Jewish thought, in which all the HT relationships suffer discrimination; any mediating influences upon the HT would not have come from this corner, but rather from (non-Jewish) Greek sources, "Ärger mit der Freiheit. Die Bedeutung von Frauen in Theorie und Praxis der alten Kirche," in *"Freunde in Christus werden... " Die Beziehung von Mann und Frau als Frage an Theologie und Kirche*, ed. Gerta Scharffenoth (Berlin: Gelnhausen, 1977), 89. Elsewhere ["Hintergrund", 367] he brands Philo with "unverblümtes Herrschaftsdenken." This is a remarkable conclusion, for although Philo is conservative in his treatment of the husband-wife and parent-child relationships, he is peerless in his liberality towards slaves, and his concept of freedom surpasses even that of the Stoics.

demonstrate a particular progression of ideas or seamless continuity. The HT, for this reason, cannot be rightly regarded as a distillation of any particular thinker or school.[2] The numerous differences raise, rather, questions in terms of the sources' relationship to the HT. Do, for instance, the ancient forms employ similar regulatory means, or share assumptions regarding the human constitution? Are particular elements such as sacrificial love (Eph. 5:25) uniquely Christian? A comparison of coincidence and contrast between ancient and contemporary treatments of HT relations may be helpful towards attaining a better understanding of the HT message.

To provide a basis for our analysis, we have selected six authors for comparison with the HT; three ancient authors, and three which are contemporary to the New Testament HT. Plato, Aristotle and Ps.-Aristotle represent the former group. Their treatments are especially suitable for comparison with the HT due to their completeness and focus upon the household relations; most ancient references to the household relation are, in contrast, fragmentary, or simply repeat the earliest sources.[3] Although primarily interested in the political ramifications of HT regulation, Plato, Aristotle and Ps.-Aristotle incorporate a philosophical element which makes a comparison with the HT especially interesting. Later treatments of the household evidence other characteristics. In the centuries which passed before the writing of the New Testament HT, political and philosophical reflection continued to

---

[2] Elisabeth Schüssler Fiorenza, in *A Critical Feminist Ekklesia-logy of Liberation* (London: SCM Press, 1993), 213f., generalises the thought of Plato and Aristotle in terms of "patriarchal dominion." This stream of thought, she suggests, has found its way into the NT canon via the HT; the connection to Aristotle is depicted as direct and undiluted, the church having adopted the "Aristotelian pattern of patriarchal submission." Overlooking significant and divergent influences such as Hellenistic Judaism and Stoic thought, she sees the HT as an adoption of "Roman imperialist-patriarchal structures." In "Colossians," in *Searching the Scriptures: A Feminist Commentary*, ed. E. Schüssler Fiorenza (New York: Crossroad Publishing, 1994), 313–324., M.R. D'Angelo concurs that "The Household Code is a pattern of exhortation derived from a tradition of philosophical politics already articulated by Aristotle"; likewise, in the same volume, "Ephesians", 331, S. Tanzer believes that the HT succeeds in "christianising the patriarchal Aristotelian ethics." Though ancient authors, including Aristotle, evidence similarities to the HT form, such statements are too undifferentiated to be helpful; they overlook significant differences in ontological assumptions, ultimate concerns and, most tellingly, the concrete advice given in the respective sources.

[3] Discussion of the household is often limited to the mention of one of the relations (i.e., fathers) within broader lists of societal groupings, which, in some cases, include their related duties. Philosophers such as Areius Didymus and Xenophon provide examples of adapted schemas (both borrowing from Aristotle). Hierocles, though writing in the second century AD, is a notable exception, and will receive mention below.

influence questions related to household government, yet to a notably lesser degree. Although the impression of earlier thinkers is evident in the categories of the later writings, a number of changes and new emphases can be traced, as well. Three first century writers, Philo, Plutarch and Musonius Rufus, preserve for us detailed discussions of the household which are contemporary to the New Testament HT mandates, and which illustrate the subtle shift away from strictly political concerns and ontological arguments. These authors will be analysed in the section immediately following our treatment of the most ancient sources.

Ancient Treatments: Plato

Plato's observations regarding the household are intended to be axiomatic in determining the larger structure of the ideal state, the primary concern of his discussion. Writing in the fifth century BC, his thoughts reflect the current debate of the principles and nature of state government. The household, he argues, cannot be formally separated from the discussion of state, for both, ultimately, are organised under the same principle of rule. The nature of rule, as understood by Plato, can be found in *Laws*, iii. 689e–690c. Here, in a lively dialogue between Clinias, Megillus and the wise Athenian stranger, it is agreed that the state is to be ruled, first of all, in wisdom; the Athenian stranger then proposes two classes of citizens, announcing that society must be divided into rulers and subjects:

῎Αρχοντας δὲ δὴ καὶ ἀρχομένους ἀναγκαῖον ἐν ταῖς πόλεσιν εἶναί του. (*Laws*, iii. 690a)

Following this observation, the philosophers agree that it is necessary to discover the rights and claims of these two groups, both at the broad level of the state, as well as those within the household:

Very well then: what and how many are the agreed rights or claims (ἀξιώματα) in the matter of ruling or being ruled, alike in States, large or small, and in households (ἔν τε πόλεσι...ἔν τε οἰκίαις)? (*Laws*, iii. 690a)

The ruler/ruled dichotomy becomes the ontological basis for ensuing discussions of stratified relationships and their regulation, including, among others, the HT relations parents/children and masters/slaves.[4] Though the dichotomy expresses the pragmatic, organisational reality of the political and domestic order, it also reflects a corollary and *essential* aspect of the natural order, which Plato terms as κατὰ φύσιν. Those who rule in strength, he reasons, do so according to nature; "the natural rule of law...over willing subjects", by extension, is not against nature (παρὰ φύσιν), but according to it (κατὰ φύσιν, *Laws*, iii. 690b–c). The establishment and regulation of authority relationships is based, then, not on potential abilities, but ultimately in the rule of natural law among the various relations.[5] He lists several natural rights or claims to rule, which spring from nature:

> The right of father and mother to rule (ἄρχειν)...is
> a claim universally just (ἀξίωμα ὀρθὸν πανταχοῦ);
> The right of the noble to rule over the ignoble...;
> The right of older people to rule and of younger to be ruled;
> Slaves ought to be ruled, and masters ought to rule;
> The stronger should rule and the weaker be ruled;[6]
> The man without understanding should follow, and the wise man lead and rule.[7]
> (*Laws*, iii.690 a–b)

All relations falling in these categories are to be regulated, ideally, by the State. The unfolding dialogue within Plato's *Laws* reflects the attempt to distil, both from natural law and its traditional expression in the "written and unwritten laws", general rules for establishing order in personal, and above all, authority relationships. The context of Plato's discussion is ultimately the State; for this reason, there is relatively little material touching upon the household itself. The parent-child and husband-wife relationships are par-

---

[4] Plato also recognises husband and wife in his discussion in *Republic*, viii. 14. Tyranny, he reasons, arises out of the abuse of liberty, where citizens no longer tolerate any type of servitude, and throw off the laws, both "written and unwritten." Plato illustrates this development, where "this anarchical temper...must penetrate into private homes." As a result, parents fear their children, while children feel neither awe nor fear; slaves become as free as their owners, and women enjoy equality with men.

[5] It would be incorrect to assert that native ability does not figure in Plato's thoughts; on the contrary, there is a tension here: see *Republic*, v.454–456a (discussion re. women), or *Republic*, v. 469b–c (the taking of Greek slaves). In the end, however, he appeals to natural law in regulating matters of equality and authority.

[6] This particular category includes the husband-wife relationship, cf. *Republic*, v. 456a.

[7] A final form of rule is named, which underlies the natural ruler/ruled dichotomy: heaven decides, by cast of lot, who will rule, or "take his place among the ruled."

ticularly limited; it is the least private of the household relations, the slave-master relationship, which receives the most attention.

Plato and Household Regulation

Wives. The formal appeal to natural law, though not present in the regulation of the HT mandates, provides the primary rationale for construing household relations within Plato. This can be seen to a limited degree in Plato's discussion of both the husband-wife and parent-child relationships. He insists, as noted above, that in determining relations, both public and private, the stronger should rule over the weaker (*Laws*, iii. 690b); this premise would ensure that the rule of the man over the woman, or parent over child, is virtually guaranteed.[8] Though this text does not explicitly mention the husband-wife relationship, the woman is considered elsewhere in Plato to be weaker according to nature (κατὰ φύσιν, *Republic*, v. 455d–e) and inferior in goodness to men (*Laws*, vi. 781b). Indeed, Plato assumes the negative answer to the rhetorical query, "Do you know, then, of anything practised by mankind in which the masculine sex does not surpass the female on these points [physical and intellectual abilities]?"[9] Thus Plato's ontological assumptions regarding human nature and the natural rule of law appear to envision a subordinated role for the women in either state or domestic affairs, all rights of rule being consigned to men. The natural ability to rule provides Plato with a foundation for stratified, subordinated relationships, particularly the husband-wife relationship.

Children. Plato, as with many Hellenistic authors, devotes relatively little space to the parent-child relationship. Consistent with all stratified relationships treated in *Laws*, his primary concern is not the child's relationship to

---

[8] Warnings regarding freedom within the HT relationships are given in *Rep*. viii. 14; in particular, that women might become men's equals. This is ruled out in *Rep*. viii. 563b, where Plato speaks clearly against the "liberty and equality of the sexes." Bosanquet, *A Companion to Plato's Republic*, 2nd ed. (London: Rivington, Parcival & Co., 1895), 335, points out the malicious tone of this passage, which juxtaposes women and inferior animals.

[9] *Republic*, v. 455c–d. This stands in curious contrast to his apparent egalitarian tones in *Republic*, v. 451e, 454e, where he envisages women of the guardian class enjoying both the education and employments of men. The discussion concludes, however, v. 455e, that although natural abilities may be found distributed among both sexes, the male evidences greater ability. See Julia Anna's article, "Plato's Republic and Feminism," in *Plato*, ed. Gail Fine (Oxford: Oxford University Press, 2000), 747–761, for a detailed feminist analysis of Plato's position.

208

the parents, but to the ideal state. Behaviour, as with the husband-wife relationship, is regulated by natural law. Plato's insistence upon the right of the
parent to rule over the children as one of the primary ruler-ruled relationships
(*Laws*, iii. 690a) assumes the natural order of subordination in this relational
pair; indeed, a society where the roles of parent and children are reversed
reflects excess of liberty and the undermining of social order through the disregard of written and unwritten laws, οὐδὲ τῶν νόμων φροντίζουσι γε-
γραμμένων ἢ ἀγράφων (*Republic*, viii. 562–3). This suggests a general approval of the traditional view of household relations, and secures a subordinated parent-child relationship. Plato's intention in the *Republic*, however, is
to appeal for a state-sponsored training of children, where the traditional role
of the parents is displaced by state-appointed guardians and communal rearing. The context of the Col.-Eph. HT is, then, discarded.[10] Children are classified, at least in the period of their training, among slaves and herd animals,
in need of a tutor as the others are in need of masters and herdsmen. Until
reason has taken hold of a child, it remains a "treacherous, sly and insolent
creature" (*Laws*, vii. 808d). Again we see an appeal to the natural order of
things to validate the behaviour towards the subordinated member. The training of children (παιδείαν) involves activities such as sport and musical instruction, but also includes instruction in the "middle path"; this middle path,
interestingly, is contained in the repository of ancient knowledge known as
the "unwritten laws" (ἄγραφα νόμιμα) or "ancient customs" (πατρίοι
νόμοι).[11] Though his treatment is brief, and in the context of state-sponsored
education, we may assume that the traditions which the children are to learn
would not deviate significantly from the contemporary ethical norm.

The Master-Slave Relationship, Laws, vi. 776D–777E. The institution of
slavery generated much interest among ancient writers, and Plato proves no
exception. The slave-master relationship is included among those he characterises in terms of rule which corresponds to nature (κατὰ φύσιν, *Laws*, iii.
690a–b). Beyond being subordinated according to the laws of nature,[12] the
slave is to be categorised among the impersonal possessions of the master's
estate; indeed, the subject of slavery emerges from the discussion of posses-

---

[10] Children, he says, should be removed from their homes, and subjected to the agreed training of the state, *Republic*, vii. 541a; in *Republic*, ix. 590e, he announces the control (rule) of
the state over children (ἡ τῶν παίδων ἀρχή), in order that the laws might be formed in
them.
[11] *Laws*, vii. 793a–b.
[12] The slave is characterised as a "witless creature" in need of a herdsman, *Laws*, vii. 808d.

sions in *Laws* vi. 776b. In spite of this apparently static and utilitarian view of the slave, it is clear from Plato's discussion that slave ownership presents the lawmaker with both theoretical and pragmatic difficulties, rooted in the slave's nature.[13] The practice of slave-holding can be particularly disruptive when encountered in the Greek context.[14] Ultimately, the instability of the slave's nature presents a danger to the efficiency of the master's commercial interests; appropriate regulatory measures, therefore, must be taken.[15] The reader would expect the discussion in *Laws*, vi. 776–7 to resemble other ancient writers' concern for harsh control over the slave and the slave's responsibilities.[16] Plato presents, however, a surprising shift at this point from the sheer pragmatics of economic theory to the *just regulation* of the master-slave relationship. The solution given by Plato is equally unexpected within a broader discussion of financial management: after comparing the options, Plato concludes that, for the sake of the slaves, and even more so the masters' economic interests, the slaves should be treated in a proper and just manner, *Laws*, vi. 777d:

> ...to try...to accord them proper treatment (τρέφειν δ' αὐτοὺς ὀρθῶς), and not only for their sakes, but still more for ourselves. Proper treatment of servants consists in using no violence towards them, and in hurting them even less, if possible, than our own equals.

Though the context and motivation are primarily economic, Plato's concern for just treatment of the slaves must be seen as more than generous pragmatism. We find in his treatment of the slave-master relationship a fuller explication of what he described as the "agreed rights or claims in the matter of

---

[13] In *Laws*, iii. 776–777, the dialogue admits that a slave can possess a noble soul, and be of great benefit to his master; yet there is also the opinion that the "soul of a slave has no soundness in it, and that a sensible man should never trust that class at all." In either case, a slave is "no easy chattel", not always willing to accept the "necessary distinction between slave and free-born in actual experience", resulting in rebellion.

[14] *Republic*, v. 469b–c contains a discussion of taking Greek slaves (as a result of battle). This practice is discouraged for pragmatic reasons (the weakening of the state), yet it appears that there is an uneasiness with the practice, perhaps due to the essential conflict involved in enslaving freedmen.

[15] Either the slaves must be kept from associating and organising in rebellion, or they should be granted proper treatment, *Laws*, vi. 777d.

[16] For example, the sixth century BC philosopher Zaleucus gives a typical discussion of the unilateral responsibilities of the slave's obedience, particularly doing what is "just through fear", τούς μὲν οὖν δούλους προσήκει διὰ φόβον πράττειν τι τῶν δικαίων, "Προοίμια", Stob. *Anth.*, iv. 2.19.

ruling and being ruled" outlined in *Laws*, iii. 690a. The protocol of just treatment is characterised by a list of specific duties, which are, surprisingly, *solely related to the master*. Plato cites the masters' behaviour as the primary indicator of just relations, notably omitting any corresponding observations concerning slaves. Appropriate behaviours noted above include the avoidance of violence towards the slaves,[17] as well as forbidding their ill-treatment (ἀδικεῖν). The manner in which a master treats a slave, furthermore, becomes the measure of the master's character, *Laws*, vi. 777e:

> For it is in his way of dealing with men whom it is easy for him to wrong that shows most clearly whether a man is genuine or hypocritical in his reverence for justice (σέβων τὴν δίκην) and hatred of injustice (μισῶν...τὸ ἄδικον).

It is notably the masters who are responsible for establishing just relations between themselves and the slaves, justice being the central motif of Plato's treatment. His observations include no less than eight references to the master's behaviour in terms of justice, righteousness, and holiness.[18] Significantly, this behaviour is generalised to include all relationships which involve authority over weaker subjects, implying a universal application of justice. Just treatment of slaves is incumbent upon "every master, or king, and everyone who possesses any kind of absolute authority over a person weaker than himself", *Laws*, vi. 777e.[19]

Plato and the NT *Haustafeln*

Plato's discussion of the household relations, though treated in the context of state management, illustrates, first of all, the currency of cultural debate over the regulation of subordinated pairs within and without the household. His categorical assumptions concerning the nature of these pairs in terms of

---

[17] μήτε τινα ὕβριν ὑβρίζειν εἰ τοὺς οἰκέτας should be understood as capricious, wanton violence, for Plato allows some form of punishment, *Laws*, vi. 777e: "We ought to punish slaves justly, and not to make them conceited by merely admonishing them as we would free men."

[18] *Laws*, vi.777d–e, 2x ὀρθῶς, 5x various forms of δίκαιος, as well as modifiers describing contrary behaviour in terms of defilement (ἀμίαντος) and unholiness (ἀνόσιος).

[19] It should be noted, however, that justice is understood in relation to the slave's position, not in terms of equality; hence we see here (*Laws*, vi, 777e–778a) the limitations placed upon social intercourse, as well as the principle of more severe punishment for the offending slave vis-à-vis the free citizen. Particular examples can be found in *Laws*, ix. 868a–c and 889c–d, where vastly differing punishments are allotted for murder.

ruler-ruled, though apparently static, demand, by their very nature, dynamic regulation. The presence of subordinated authority relationships, including their regulation, offers points of comparison to the NT *Haustafeln*.

Authority and Tradition. In spite of their divergent literary contexts and intentions, a comparison with the HT is merited, in that both Plato and the HT rely upon an assumed source of authority to validate the ordering of relationships. Whereas Plato makes a direct appeal to nature and traditional views of culture (written and unwritten laws) to give justification and form to authority relationships, the HT likewise relies upon distinct ontological structures to construe its relational model. Firstly, the HT assumes a relational and subordinated order, based upon the fundamental divine-human axis outlined in the theological sections found in Ephesians and Colossians. It is Christ who emerges as the ontological reference point and regulatory authority. In the Christ Hymn of Colossians 1:15–18, Christ's person and resultant authority are characterised in ultimate terms.[20] The sweeping nature of Christ's divine authority, summarised in 1:19 as πᾶν τὸ πλήρωμα, transcends time and includes both earthly authorities and the church. In Ephesians, the author expands the theme of salvation (which frames the Col. Christ Hymn, Col. 1:13; 20) and invests authority in Christ as the mediator of the restored relationship to God (Eph. 1:4–23); his soteriological work results, however, not only in reconciliation, but the reception of authority resembling those aspects found in Col. (Eph. 1:20b–23). Both descriptions of Christ's authority, it should be noted, end with a description of him as head of the church. It is this fundamental, vertical authority relationship between the church and Christ (characterised by faith) which establishes and regulates the human relations (characterised by love). In the HT mandates, then, reference to the divine axis establishes the nature of the stratified HT relations; only one verse omits direct reference to Christ, God or divine tradition.[21] Secondly, the HT makes use of tradition, both Hellenistic and Jewish, to establish the authority and nature of its commands. Weidinger is correct in calling attention to a traditional understanding of relationships contained in the HT mandates.[22] The commands to

---

[20] The Hymn of Christ is remarkable for its repetitive use of παν- and πασ- derivatives, which emphasise either the primary or absolute nature of his authority.

[21] Col. 3:18b; 20b; 22b; 23; 24; 25; 4:1 (only Col. 3:19, the instruction to the husbands, lacks reference to Christ); Eph. 5:21; 22b; 23; 24; 25; 26; 27; 28; 29; 30; 31 (appeal to theological tradition); 6:1; 2–3 (appeal to theological tradition); 4; 5; 6; 7; 8; 9.

[22] Weidinger, *Haustafeln*, 11. He suggests that Paul has made use of the "Moral des Alltags", the importance of which would have been recognised in the Hellenistic context. This

submit and obey are described in traditional terms in Col. 3:18 (ἀνῆκεν) and 3:20 (εὐρεστόν), as are the admonitions in Ephesians to obey (ὑπακούετε...τοῦτο γάρ ἐστιν δίκαιον) and honour (τίμα) in 6:1–2. Both appeal, certainly, to commonly held values; yet, the HT does so without reference to a broader ontological schema. The Ephesian HT relies on traditional Jewish material (particularly OT references in 5:31; 6:2, 4, 9) to substantiate its mandates, as well. Hence we cannot speak of a complete departure from the Platonic understanding of relationships ordered by a designated concept of authority and traditional ethics. Yet the HT reveals its distinctive and primary ethical orientation in the introduction of a christological regulation of authority relationships. Representing a figure who transcends traditional understandings, and who virtually displaces the rule of nature, it is Christ who informs the HT concept of proper behaviour. With eight direct references in the Colossian HT, it is the mediating terminology of the κύριος which alerts the reader that fitting behaviour is ultimately related to Christ, particularly so in the expanded slave-master regulations.[23] In Ephesians, Christ figures even more strongly, with no less than nineteen references linking proper behaviour to Christ or God (6:6b).[24] The christological implications for reciprocal duties become even more direct in Ephesians, where the Christ-church metaphor redefines the expanded husband-wife regulations in terms of love and care, submission and honour. It is the christological reasoning of the HT which constitutes a similar yet contrasting element to Plato's (and other Hellenistic authors') understanding of stratified relationships. Where Plato invokes the rule of nature, the HT makes an appeal to a standard beyond cultural norms, citing the personal mediation and example of the Lord Christ.

The Regulation of Stratified Relations. Plato's discussion of the husband-wife and parent-child relationships is limited to the ontological reasoning mentioned above, and organisational concerns; his observations revolve primarily around the functioning of the ideal state.[25] Though Plato expands his

---

corresponds to Dibelius' observation, *Kolosser*, 48, that the HT relies, to a degree, upon Hellenistic and Jewish moral categories.

[23] Col. 3:18, 20, 22, 23, 24 (2x); 4:1. All references are directed towards regulating the prescribed behaviour.

[24] Eph. 5:21, 22, 23 (2x), 24, 25 (2x), 27, 29, 32; 6:1, 4, 5, 6 (2x), 7, 8, 9 (2x).

[25] The husband-wife relationship is treated exclusively in the context of state control of the marriage union, childbearing and rearing, see especially *Laws*, vi. 772f. For children, see fn. 10 above.

ontological discussion elsewhere with remarkable result,[26] except for the slave-master relationship, he gives no direct treatment of household relationships. Slave-master relations, however, due to their potentially volatile nature (particularly the political-economic implications of rebellion), receive the fullest treatment in Plato. Though conceived as a political discussion, Plato's regulations reveal a remarkably high level of coincidence with HT vocabulary and concerns.

Plato's concern for justice in the slave-master relationship reflects the currency of this theme, long before it is taken up in the New Testament HT. Both contain direct, limiting instruction to the masters (an element missing in ancient literature, which typically focuses upon the duties of the servant, or perhaps the owner's responsibilities in securing optimum performance from the slave). The similarities at this point are striking, particularly the common concern to avoid inappropriate treatment of the slave, while striving towards an ethic of justice. In Ephesians 6:9, for instance, the author admonishes the slave owners to "leave off" threatening the slaves (ἀνιέντες τὴν ἀπειλήν), which corresponds to Plato's negative observation regarding actual violent behaviour (ὕβριν ὑβρίζειν...[or] ἀδικεῖν).

More significant, however, is the centrality of the slave-master justice motif in both Plato and the New Testament HT. Although Plato is addressing only the superordinated members of the slave-master relationship (the HT distinguishes itself here in terms of its direct address and clear admonitions to the slaves), the absence of direct address towards the slave does not preclude a concern for bilateral justice. Plato's treatment is remarkably similar to the HT justice motif in that it includes, though indirectly, both parties.[27] The Colossian HT reflects a similar regulating theme of righteousness,[28] with

---

[26] A close reading of Book V of the *Republic* reveals a tension in the author's mind between his natural categories and their boundaries (male-female) expressed in *Laws*, and native abilities. For the purposes of the state, Plato reasons, "no proof has been produced that the woman differs from the man", and for women who demonstrate "high-spirited" ability, he allows rule with men, since they share the same nature, εἰσιν ἱκαναὶ καὶ ζυγγενεῖς αὐτοῖς τὴν φύσιν. These women should, then, cohabit with, and serve alongside, the men in the *same* pursuits (*Republic*, V.456b). In more humorous tones, he admits that there would be "shrieks of indignation" from the women, were the men's right to rule employed, *Laws*, vi.781b–d.

[27] The stated purpose of just treatment, he says, is to "accord them the proper treatment, and that not only for their sakes, but still more for the sake of ourselves", *Laws*, vi.777d.

[28] Particularly clear in Col. 3:25–4:1; δίκαιος and ἀδικέω are prominent descriptors of the (im)proper behaviour in this relational pair.

the variation that the admonitions include *both* the slave and master.[29] As with Plato, appropriate behaviour is cast in terms of justice. Col. 3:25, serving as a transitional regulating principle for both members of the slave-master relationship, clearly warns: ὁ γὰρ ἀδικῶν κομίσεται ὃ ἠδίκησεν. Col. 4:1 resembles the Platonic pattern in addressing only the masters, insisting that they render to their slaves that which is just (τὸ δίκαιον) and equitable (τὴν ἰσότητα).[30] An additional element touching upon justice is that both HT insist that *ultimate* justice will be achieved, all behaviour being subject to divine scrutiny (Col. 3:24–4:1 and Eph. 6:8–9). Plato, though not expressly invoking the gods, expects the master to show himself, "by his character and action" blameless; this he does by the employment of religious imagery, *Laws*, vi. 777e: "undefiled by what is unholy or unjust." Here he appeals to the cultic imagination of the reader,[31] and appears to allow for a certain level of religious motivation for the master's treatment of the slave. In spite of this veiled appeal to piety, the HT motivation for justice is distinguished from Plato by a direct reliance upon the divine activity realised in Christ.

Conclusion

Plato's treatment of household relations, though quite limited in scope and contained within a larger discussion of the ideal state, provides us with an early point of comparison to the NT household code. Plato relies upon a recognised authority (rule of natural law) and tradition (unwritten laws) to justify and regulate stratified relations. Though his concept of natural law is foreign to the HT regulations,[32] the HT make a similar appeal to Christ and

---

[29] Though the duties of the slave are not outlined in Plato, they are certainly assumed; for this reason, it is possible to speak of a level of reciprocity between slave and master in Plato's treatment of justice.

[30] The tone of Col. is adopted in Eph., where masters are required to demonstrate the same pattern of behaviour as the slave, τά αὐτὰ ποιεῖτε, reward coming to the doer of good, εἴτε δοῦλος εἴτε ἐλεύθερος.

[31] ἀμίαντος...ἀνοσίου...ἀδίκου. Cf. the following *TDNT* articles: F. Hauck, "ἀμίαντος, κτλ.", Vol. iv, 644–47; the adjectival use is primarily in the cultic sense of purity, particularly in Plato, where it is understood as a spiritual matter; A. Oepke, "νόσος, κτλ.", Vol. iv, 1091–8; meaning is connected to ritual impurity, sickness and sin, often attributed to the wrath of a deity; G. Schrenk, "ἄδικος, κτλ.", Vol. i, 149–63; the term is often used to make a distinction between socially unacceptable behaviour and that which is religiously impious, where a "relationship to God is envisaged."

[32] Markus Bockmuehl, *Jewish Law in Gentile Churches: Halakhah and the Beginning of Christian Public Ethics* (Edinburgh: T&T Clark, 2000), 138, writes: "Despite the language of

the OT scriptures. In his regulation of household relationships, Plato reveals a concern for reciprocal responsibilities, concretely outlined in the just treatment of the slave. The masters, in untypical fashion, are admonished in terms of their behaviour and character, and are the sole recipients of his instruction. It is apparent from Plato that, from the early Hellenistic period, the regulation of the household involved not only economic considerations, but shared, with the HT, concerns over authority, reciprocity and justice.

Ancient Treatments: Aristotle

Aristotle receives particular attention in relation to the New Testament HT, as he is the earliest writer to name the three relations found in both Colossians and Ephesians, and limit them as a cohesive unit.[33] The coincidence is remarkable in itself, and constitutes one of the clearest points of literary similarity between the HT form and Hellenistic literature, *Politics*, 1259a:

> ...the science of household management has just three divisions (τρία μέρη τῆς οἰκονομικῆς), one the relation of master to slave (δεσποτική), of which we have spoken before, one the paternal relation (πατρική), and the third the conjugal (γαμική), for it is part of household science to rule (ἄρχειν) over wife and children.

Aristotle's three relations represent a significant organisational development over earlier discussions, in that he defines these relations in terms of their function within the *oikos*. The *oikos*, which for Aristotle constitutes the basic socio-economic unit of society,[34] establishes the fundamental tenor of the relationships in terms of household management, as well as limiting the relationships to those in its immediate sphere. This is in contrast to other Hellenistic authors who frame their discussion of proper relations in broader, political and sociological contexts, including within their scope any number of

---

propriety and decency in affirming natural orders, the moral argument of these household codes for the most part is formally based neither on convention nor nature, but on an appeal to revelation in Christ."

[33] Later writers such as Ariston, Hecaton, Seneca and Hierocles have adopted Aristotle's schema under the rubric "concerning household management". See Balch's helpful discussion, *Wives*, 51f.

[34] Like Plato, Aristotle links the household to the welfare of the state. The moral formation and education of the women and children should be undertaken to secure its future welfare, *Politics*, 1260b.

relationships not strictly belonging to the household.[35] Indeed, the *oikos* organisation constitutes a departure from the Platonic understanding of the continuity between the state and household according to ruler/ruled dichotomy. The household, isolated as a unit, is held in contrast to the broader free society, allowing for a more nuanced understanding of authority among its members.[36] Aristotle's isolation of *oikos* and its three primary relations, husband-wife, parent-child and master-slave is largely regarded as the model from which later economic discussions have taken their impulse; among New Testament scholars, it is regarded as the most probable genesis of the HT, in both form and concern.[37] In spite of Aristotle's importance in defining the sphere of household management, little attention has been given to the regulation which he actually prescribes for the three household relations.

Ontology and the Stratification of Relations

Aristotle shares a number of ontological assumptions which we have noted in Plato; in particular, he adopts Plato's deterministic ontological stratification of human relations according to nature, and applies them to the three household relations. The ruler/ruled dichotomy is adopted, albeit with allowances for differing manner of rule, *Politics*, 1260a:

> Hence there are by nature various classes of rulers and ruled. For the free rules
> the slave, the male the female, and the man the child in a different way.

This ontological stratification is, as noted above, foreign to the formal reasoning of the HT. Aristotle introduces another element, however, which serves to illustrate the propriety of the ruler/ruled dichotomy: *virtue*. It is inward virtue, distributed variously and according to nature among the

---

[35] Hierocles, for example, Stob. *Anth.*, iv. 27.23, organises relationships in three concentric circles, beginning with self, then family, then wider relations; Epictetus, *Discourses*, ii.14.8, lists the relations of father, brother, citizen, wife, neighbour, fellow traveller, ruler and subject; Plutarch, *Moralia, De Liberis Educandis*, 10, includes relations to the gods, parents, elders, laws, strangers, those in authority, friends, women, children and servants.

[36] *Politics*, 1255b, denies that all forms of rule are basically the same. Here Aristotle contrasts republican rule among free citizens, and the monarchical rule of the householder. Elsewhere, he further distinguishes between types of rule *within* the household.

[37] Dunn, *Colossians*, 243, representing common opinion, regards the question of HT origins as "settled"; it is derived from the cultural debate over household management. Gielen, *Tradition*, 546f., in her thorough treatment of origins, reaches the same conclusion.

classes,[38] which substantiates and justifies the stratified relationships within the household. In a detailed discussion of the virtues necessary to rule or be ruled, Aristotle concludes, *Politics*, 1260a:

> It is evident therefore that both [ruler and ruled] must possess virtue, but that there are differences in their virtue.

Although Aristotle's allowance for moral virtue among both ruler and ruled appears to offer a more systematic and differentiated view of stratified relations, as well as easing the tension in the Platonic dichotomy, it remains distant from the HT understanding of subordination, which neither makes use of anthropological ontological categories, nor appeals to virtue for substantiation of its mandates.[39] The introduction of virtue does not, we hope to demonstrate, introduce reciprocity or eliminate the stratification between the household relations in Aristotle; it becomes, rather, an illustration for the preservation of unilateral rule.[40]

The Household Relations

Aristotle's treatment of the household relationships found in the HT resembles, to a large degree, that which we have found in Plato. His thought, however, includes two elements which represent genuine developments over Platonic categories. Both developments (along with a number of less significant details) provide points of comparison to the NT *Haustafeln*. The first is the concept of managing the household according to the principle of reciprocal benefit; the second is the regulation of the various relations according to *differing* types of government. The latter, pragmatic diversification allows Aris-

---

[38] Virtue of ruling or being ruled is fixed in the soul as a predetermined ontological reality, where slaves' souls, for example, are defective, having no deliberative faculty, *Politics*, 1260a.

[39] The HT frames virtue in behavioural terms.

[40] T.J. Saunders, *Aristotle: Politics, Book I and II*, eds. J.C. Ackrill and L. Judson, Clarendon Aristotle Series (Oxford: Clarendon Press, 1995), 98, broaches a significant tension in Aristotle's distribution of virtue. He asks, "But why does Aristotle not scout the notion of a sliding scale of virtue ('more or less') on which a man, woman, child and slave might appear in that order, a higher point indicating a greater claim to rule? Because such claims, except in the case of the free adult male, are precisely what he cannot tolerate: the male's rule must be 'unqualified'—that is, the virtues of the other three persons must not appear on a scale implying any entitlement to rule at all."

218

totle to avoid the universal application of justice seen in Plato,[41] and, as we shall see, neglect reciprocal benefits for certain members of the household.

Husbands and Wives: Republican Government. As with Plato, women are not considered to be *essentially* equal to men. Aristotle insists that they are inferior in this relation.[42] This arises, he argues, from the soul, which is constitutionally different from that of men, who are, by nature, "fit to command".[43] The household is consequently characterised in general terms as a monarchy, due to the sole position of authority being invested in the male householder, *Politics*, 1255b. It would seem that Aristotle has, at this point, merely adopted Plato's authority schema. Aristotle's characterisation of the household as a monarchy would, then, stand in stark relief to the HT, which neither names a mediating governmental structure, nor specifically designates one member to hold sole authority over all others.[44] Just as Aristotle has expanded and differentiated the understanding of natural rule in terms of the soul and its virtues, he likewise divides the household into discrete forms of government corresponding to the three relational pairs. Each form of government should, ideally, allow the members to interact in a manner befitting their particular ontological constitutions. This is an important innovation within the Aristotelian regulation of the household, and one which allows, by virtue of its specificity, a greater similarity to the HT regulations. Other ancient writers characteristically speak of household relations in terms of an overarching principle of rule, illustrated from the perspective of the male householder only; by introducing specific governing models, Aristotle allows for variation among the *duties* of respective household relationships, as well as recognising *unique characteristics* of the individual members. This feature

---

[41] Indeed, Aristotle is critical of those who "cling to some principle of justice" in an attempt to regulate relations, *Politics*, 1255a.

[42] *Politics*, 1254b: "...the male is by nature superior and the female inferior, the male ruler and the female subject." Aristotle does note that this may not apply in marriages which are formed "contrary to nature", *Politics*, 1259b. In *Nicomachean Ethics*, 8.10.5, he explains this concession: "An heiress may rule over her husband, but in this case the authority "goes not by virtue, but by wealth and power."

[43] *Politics*, 1259b. The soul, he reasons, is made up of various parts, each member of the household possessing different parts, or the same part in varied degrees; the female, for instance, does not possess a full deliberative faculty, *Politics*, 1260a.

[44] The shared responsibility and authority of the parents, for instance, are implied in the requirements of the fifth commandment, which instructs the children to obey and honour them without distinction, Eph. 6:1–3.

of his discussion resembles the NT household code's more specific manner of regulation according to the particular relational axis.

In the husband-wife relationship, Aristotle characterises their governmental relation as "republican", which suggests a certain level of parity. This is, however, not the case.[45] Aristotle assures the reader that he does not allow for any broad principle such as justice or courage to form his argument,[46] but concentrates upon the unique characteristics of each person in the relational pair. It is the man who has the constitutional "courage of command" (ἡ...ἀρχικὴ ἀνδρεία), the woman also demonstrating courage, but that of subordination (ἡ δ' ὑπηρετική), *Politics*, 1260a. In spite of the superordinate position of the man, Aristotle's differentiated view of human nature according to virtue, as well as his resistance towards generalisation of the household governmental form, combine to form his innovative approach to regulating the household relations: reciprocal duties. Within the husband-wife relationship, their varied natures assure that neither member has control over all spheres of the household:

> ...the husband rules in virtue of fitness (κατ' ἀξίαν γὰρ ὁ ἀνὴρ ἄρχει), and in matters that belong to a man's sphere; matters suited to a woman he hands over to his wife. When the husband controls everything (ἁπάντων δὲ κυριεύων), he transforms the relationship into an oligarchy, for he governs in violation of fitness (παρὰ τὴν ἀξίαν), and not in virtue of superiority. (*Nic. Eth.* 8.10.5)

Aristotle's rationale for dividing the duties between husband and wife according to virtue cannot be found in the HT, though the result of his reasoning, discrete reciprocal duties, bear closer resemblance. The broader context of his thought, however, reveals another element which regulates the behaviour of this relational pair. Speaking of the various forms of relational government, Aristotle characterises a number of relationships, including husband and wife, in terms of friendship (φιλία). The pairs, however, are considered fundamentally unequal in terms of their nature, and are therefore liable to different degrees of affection.[47] The HT reciprocal commands, though cer-

---

[45] In *Politics*, 1259b, Aristotle concedes that republican government suggests equality as well as an interchange of rule; this he does not allow, for the male "stands in this [designated rule] relationship to the female continuously."

[46] He is critical of this approach in Socrates (in Plato, *Meno*, 74b f.) and insists that all persons within the household "have a moral virtue of their own", and that men and women, in particular, are not constitutionally the same, *Politics*, 1260a.

[47] The ontological understanding of varied natures regulates the level of reciprocity: "The affection rendered in these various unequal friendships should also be proportionate: the better

tainly framed with an understanding of the significant differences and responsibilities represented among the relational pairs, are not regulated by, nor do they appeal to, Aristotle's ontological argument. In spite of the unequal manner of their allocation, there are similar, benign elements operating in the execution of reciprocal duties:

> ...for each of these persons has a different excellence and function (ἀρετὴ καὶ τὸ ἔργον), and also different motives for their regard, and so the affection and friendship (φιλία) they feel are different. Now in these unequal friendships the benefits that one party receives and is entitled to receive are not the same on either side. (*Nic. Eth.*, 8.7.1–2)

Although Aristotle does not delineate the reciprocal duties of husband and wife in the clear form found in the HT, it is apparent that his understanding of these household responsibilities should be characterised by friendship, affection and a fitting measure of reciprocity. This concern is not unlike the broader tenor of Col. and Eph., where the members of the Christian community are to exercise a fundamental measure of love (ἀγάπη) in all relations. In terms of the HT, this affection comes closest to the behaviour expected of the husband in Col. 3:19 and Eph. 5:25–33.

Parents and Children: A Monarchy. In his discussion of the relationship between parents and children, Aristotle does not rely upon ontological differences to establish the parents' authority. Avoiding the harsh assessment of children in Plato, his reasoning is pragmatic: the child, not yet fully developed,[48] stands in need of guidance. The most appropriate form of government in such cases is monarchy:

> For the rule of the father over the children...is that of a king; for the male parent is the ruler in virtue both of affection and of seniority, which is characteristic of royal government...this is the position of the elder in relation to the younger and of the father in relation to the child. (*Politics*, 1259b)

Common to other ancient writers and the HT is Aristotle's assumption that parents and children will enjoy certain benefits; the children receive nurture

---

of the two parties, for instance, or the more useful or otherwise superior as the case may be, should receive more affection than he bestows." It is according to the individual's worth (κατ' ἀξίαν) that affection should be rendered, thus guaranteeing equity (ἰσότης [Col. 4:1!]) in relationships, *Nic. Eth.*, 8.7.2.

[48] *Politics*, 1260a.

and education, the parents honour and service.[49] The HT differs, however, at two points in its exercise of parental authority. Firstly, and perhaps less significantly, the HT makes no attempt to liken the parent-child relationship to a form of government beyond the household. Aristotle's comparison of this relationship to monarchical rule, however, introduces a second point of comparison: the male is singled out[50] for the task of rule over the children with little or no reference to the role of the mother.[51] The HT, in its instruction to the parents, singles out the father in its address to the parents as well; both forms call the πατέρες to avoid negative practices (Col.: μὴ ἐπεθίζετε; Eph.: μὴ παροργίζετε), while Eph. 6:4 includes the positive admonition to rear the children in the training and instruction of the Lord. In spite of this similarity, the HT does not allow a monarchical understanding, as the instruction to the children assumes that *both* parents are active in giving instruction which requires obedience (as well as receiving honour in the Eph. passage)[52]: ὑπακούετε τοῖς τοῖς γονεῦσιν is the common command found in both passages. The HT does not, then, envision or mandate a singular parental authority, and quite probably reflects the inclusive nature of honour which is expected in the fifth commandment (τίμα τὸν πατέρα σου καὶ τὴν μητέρα), explicitly mentioned in Eph. 6:2–3. The obedience expected of the children in the HT is given, in any event, to both parents without reference to relative authority. It also incorporates a divine component, characterising the required obedience as corresponding to the will of God: being fitting in the Lord (Col. εὐάρεστον) or righteous (Eph. δίκαιον). Ephesians connects such obedience with the Mosaic command to honour father and mother, underscoring the divinely ordained nature of the children's admonition. Aristotle does not appeal directly to divine will to secure any particular behaviour

---

[49] τροφῆς καὶ παιδείας are duties the father provides the children; the parents, conversely, are honoured, τιμῶνται οἱ γονεῖς, *Nic. Eth.*, 8.11.3.

[50] The male rules over both the woman and children as a pair, *Politics*, 1259b, 1260a; *Nic. Eth.*, 5.11.9. He is accounted sole authority over the child in the manner of a king, *Politics*, 1259b; *Nic. Eth.*, 8.10.4; as a ruler, 1260a; as a king, shepherd and the source of the child's existence, *Nic. Eth.*, 8.11.1–2.

[51] The distinction of the male as ruler over the children appears to be systematic, according to his understanding of the male's rule over all the household; the woman receives no mention in this regard. There are, however, indications that the woman, though not ruling, receives reciprocal benefits. Aristotle speaks of the children's behaviour in connection with the *parents*, *Nic. Eth.*, 8.7.2; 8.12.2; 8.12.5–6; in particular, the children should show honour to both parents, *Nic. Eth.*, 8.11.3.

[52] This resembles the benefits of reciprocity (honour) which Aristotle mentions in *Nic. Eth.*, 8.11.3, but his observations do not take imperative form.

from children; on the contrary, his interests lie in establishing the father's unique rule. To this end, he likens *divine* rule to fatherhood, thereby securing the earthly order of household rule:

> The relationship of father to sons is regal in type, since the father's first care is for the children's welfare. This is why Homer styles Zeus 'father,' for the ideal of kingship is paternal government. (*Nic. Eth.*, 8.10.4)[53]

It is remarkable, in light of Christian tradition,[54] that the HT does not attempt to make use of parallels between divine fatherhood and the structure of the household. The various relations are not brought under a unifying concept or system such as fatherhood or monarchy; it is Christ alone who *personally* regulates the HT pairs.[55] Though human relations are drawn into analogy with Christ and the church in Eph. 5:22–33, the analogy is limited to the husband-wife pair only. The HT does not allow the husband, father or master to represent or displace Christ as sole regulatory agent over the household.

Slaves and Masters: Tyrannical Rule. Aristotle affirms Plato's consigning of slaves to the realm of household property; he notes that the slaves' nature differs from other humans to such a degree, that their "usefulness diverges little from that of animals."[56] The slave is positioned at the least desirable, yet necessary, end of a broad social spectrum, which, according to his defective nature, disenfranchises him from normal social intercourse or political involvement. Aristotle draws a logical conclusion with pragmatic implications: due to nature, some humans[57] are born with minds and bodies fit for menial service; it is these who "are by nature slaves" (οὗτοι μέν εἰσι φύσει δοῦλοι, *Politics*, 1254b). This natural and openly observable state of affairs makes slavery an "institution both expedient and just."[58]

---

[53] Homeric citation from *Iliad*, i. 544. Parallel section in *Politics*, 1259b. Even the love of the children towards the parents is modelled after the love of "men for the gods", *Nic. Eth.*, 8.12.5.

[54] The common reference to God as father can be seen in Col. and Eph., as well: Col. 1:2, 3, 12; 3:17; Eph. 1:2, 3, 17; 2:18; 3:14; 4:6; 5:20; 6:23.

[55] Each pair contains at least one mention of the "lord", or alternately, "Christ"; in every case, this represents a personal and regulatory figure.

[56] *Politics*, 1254b. He consigns slaves to "one of the natural classes" of humans, *Politics*, 1260a.

[57] He resists any scheme that suggests that this corresponds to noble or low birth; the natural capabilities determine, ultimately, which form of government is to be applied, *Politics*, 1255b.

[58] Having established the general premise that slavery is a natural condition, Aristotle, it must be said, makes mention of arguments directed against his position. He admits a certain

Aristotle, being most interested in systematising the household relations, moves the discussion of the nature of the slave towards the proper form of government with which to organise the slave-master relationship. This revolves, as with the other relations, around the natural virtues of the slave. He asks:

> ...does the slave possess any other excellence besides his merits as a tool and servant...or has he no excellence besides bodily service? (*Politics*, 1259b)

After a lengthy discussion of the possible and necessary qualities for slave and master, he concludes that the virtues of master and slave are fundamentally different, the slave demonstrating defects which necessitate his subordination:[59]

> And all possess the various parts of the soul, but possess them in different ways; for the slave has not got the deliberative part at all... (*Politics*, 1260a)

> ...[the slave] participates in reason so far as to apprehend it, but not to possess it... (*Politics*, 1254b)

> And we laid down that the slave is serviceable for the mere necessities of life, so that clearly he needs only a small amount of virtue... (*Politics*, 1260a)

The fundamental differences between slave and master call for a form of government that fits the nature of both parties, and secures advantages for both. To this degree, Aristotle is interested in both parties.[60] Equity, however, is not the concern of household government, whose interests are weighted towards the free members of the household.[61] Indeed, Aristotle characterises the slave-master relationship in terms of tyranny, "since in it the master's interest is aimed at." (*Nic. Eth.*, 8.10.4). Aristotle contrasts the benign nature

---

ambiguity (with Plato) of slaves made not by nature, but law (κατὰ νόμον δοῦλος), but avoids what are for him frivolous discussions regarding slaves captured in war; both cases merely serve to underscore his contention that there are "certain persons who are essentially slaves everywhere and certain others who are so nowhere", *Politics*, 1255a.

[59] Gerard Verbecke, in *Moral Education in Aristotle* (Washington: Catholic University of America Press, 1990), 156, aptly describes the subjugation of slaves (and women) in Aristotle's schema as "natural subordination".

[60] The government must fit the natures of slave and master; to govern badly, he insists, "is to govern disadvantageously for both parties", *Politics*, 1255b.

[61] "Household management takes more interest in...its free members than in that of slaves." *Politics*, 1259b.

of the free relations of society (including the parent-child and husband-wife relations) with the strictures of tyranny, for which the slave relationship serves as primary example:

> ...there is little friendship between ruler and subjects in tyranny. For where there is nothing in common between ruler and ruled, there can be no friendship (φιλία) between them either, any more than there can be justice (δίκαιον). It is like the relation between a craftsman and his tool...all these instruments it is true are benefited by the persons who use them, but there can be no friendship, nor justice towards inanimate things; indeed not even towards a horse or an ox, nor yet towards a slave as slave. For master and slave have nothing in common: a slave is a living tool, just as a tool is an inanimate slave. Therefore there can be no friendship with a slave as slave, though there can be as human being: for there seems to be some room for justice in the relations of every human being with every other that is capable of participating in law and contract...hence even in tyrannies there is but little scope for friendship and justice between ruler and subjects. (*Nic. Eth.*, 8.11.6–7)

Interestingly, though the relationship is not characterised by justice or friendship, the slave is seen as intertwined with the master's interests to a significant degree. Aristotle employs somatic language to illustrate the symbiotic nature of the slave-master relation within the household. This is an early example of somatic language being employed, in similar manner to the Ephesian husband-wife relationship, to express the nature of household relations.[62] He reasons that both master and slave benefit from the "exercise of mastership", for:

> ...the same thing is advantageous for a part and for the whole body or the whole soul, and the slave is a part of the master – he is, as it were, a part of the body, alive yet separated from it. (*Politics*, 1255b)

In spite of this imagery, Aristotle's regulation of the slave-master relationship represents a reciprocity which envisions the advantage of the master. His notion of respective virtue, though innovative, translates into a form of subjection unknown in other ancient treatments of this relational pair.

---

[62] Aristotle uses somatic language to describe rule, "...it is possible to discern the rule of both master and of statesman: the soul rules the body with the sway of a master", *Politics*, 1254b. The soul is considered to rule over the body as "head" (κεφαλή), *Politics*, 1253b. See also *Nic. Eth.*, 8.11.6, where Aristotle likens master and slave to soul and body.

Conclusion

Aristotle, like Plato, assumes a division of household relations along the ruler/ruled ontological dichotomy, with the male householder assuming the position of authority and advantage over all relations. His political and economic concerns are similar, as well, with the exception of the distinguishing mark of insisting upon *reciprocal* benefit. The level of reciprocity attributed to Aristotle in the household regulation has been exaggerated, however, for it is essentially linked to the innovative and limiting factor of relative virtue. In this manner, the household relations incorporate reciprocity to the advantage of the superordinate (superior) member. This manner of household regulation represents a significant development over Plato, in that he rejects an overarching principle of justice in favour of rule according to the individual virtues represented upon each relational axis. The isolation and systematisation of the three household relations, coupled with his insistence upon a discrete governmental form, effects profound differences in the administration of the household as formerly understood by Plato. This, as we have seen, was especially noticeable within the slave-master relationship. This development also brings his views into conflict with the HT at several points. The HT is not concerned, for instance, with establishing relationships according to sociological concepts such as class, or appealing to particular, innate virtues based on a stratified anthropological model. The HT members, in contrast, share a common sociological context within the church. Beyond the mediating lordship of Christ, no appeal is made to establish a locus of authority or ethic of advantage. It is interesting to note that the HT operates on a surprisingly behavioural level: members are commanded to display particular *actions* such as love or obedience; no reference is made to their relative moral fitness. Secondly, the HT mandates do not attempt to identify or establish a systematic form of government which might characterise the household rule, nor do they attempt to regulate the relational pairs in individual fashion; it is, remarkably, Christ who characterises the governmental form, and unifies the administration of the axes. Lastly, the HT does not favour master over slave,[63] rather explicitly states that no favour will be shown before Christ. Rather than rejecting justice as a regulatory element, the HT anticipates present and future justice, Col. 3:22–4:1 and Eph. 6:5–9. In contrast to Aristotle,

---

[63] Saunders, *Aristotle*, 76, points out the relative administration of justice in Aristotle which he characterises as "proportionate equality" between master and slave. This is linked to their essential virtue and potential service, the master enjoying a favourable advantage in both instances.

226

the HT slave-master relation is explicit in its rejection of double-standards, as well as its expectation of justice administered, ultimately, by Christ.

Ancient Treatments: Pseudo-Aristotle

Pseudo-Aristotle,[64] writing in the latter half of the fourth century BC, was influenced by portions of Aristotle's *Πολιτικά*, as well as elements of Xenophon's *Οἰκονόμικος* in the creation of his three-part treatise on economics, the *Oeconomica*.[65] Book I and II are both extant in Greek versions, although Book II is estimated to be from a significantly later hand. Book III, extant only in Latin, is a homily on married life. It is particularly noteworthy in that it offers a less fragmentary witness to the ancient understanding of the husband wife-relationship.

The Household in Pseudo-Aristotle

The initial reading of Book I of the *Oeconomica* reveals a number of subtle differences which distinguish it from the earlier work of Plato and Aristotle. Firstly, the discussion of the State is extremely limited, the household government being held, notably, as a more ancient[66] and differentiated[67] governmental form. The treatise deals almost exclusively, then, with household concerns and its proper management. In similar manner, the treatment of the household is free from the earlier philosophical discussions concerning the ontological makeup of the relational pairs.

Pseudo-Aristotle is brief in his discussion of the nature and makeup of the household; he relies on the assumptions and familiar categories provided in earlier treatments of the household to open his discussion, yet he introduces, ultimately, new elements which indicate a subtle number of changes over antecedent regulations. He claims, for instance, that "the household has

---

[64] Philodemus, a contemporary of Cicero, attributes Book I to Theophrastus, the successor of Aristotle and the Peripatetic School.

[65] Book II, a collection of anecdotes which illustrate the various manners in which ancient rulers gathered taxes, is not of interest to our study.

[66] "...it is evident that the art of Housecraft is older than Statecraft...accordingly, we must consider what the nature of Housecraft, and the household, which it creates, actually is.", *Oeconomica* i, 1.15.

[67] They differ, firstly, in terms of the communities over which they rule, and secondly, in that the household is distinguished by its sole ruler, *Oeconomica*, i.1.1–4.

but a single ruler",[68] echoing Plato, Xenophon and Aristotle; household rule, however, is divided in his treatment, with significant authority placed in the mistress.[69] Another example of change regards the classic division of the household into its human and property ("goods and chattel") components.[70] As in previous discussions, slaves are consigned to the latter category, being "human chattel."[71] In spite of this conservative tone, the slave is character-ised as human, deserving of respect and worthy of aspirations, including freedom.[72] Pseudo-Aristotle's discussion of the household, then, is ultimately less theoretical than that of previous thinkers, and certainly not consistent with their governmental and ontological constructs. It is, in light of earlier discussions, surprisingly pragmatic, and focused upon the efficient, coopera-tive management of the household in practical, human terms. In this manner, Pseudo-Aristotle is closer to the concerns of the HT, which are concentrated, primarily, upon the household and the behaviour of its members. Because Pseudo-Aristotle is chiefly concerned with efficient household management, there are new emphases in his regulation of the household relations, which we have detected to a limited degree in Plato and Aristotle: the reciprocal good of the household members. Where earlier treatments gave clear prefer-ence to the householder's welfare, the expression of reciprocity in Ps.-Aristotle genuinely befits the word. This becomes especially clear in Book III, where the husband-wife relationship is described in unusual detail, their reciprocal duties designated to create both unity and harmony in the house-hold.

Husbands and Wives. As mentioned above, Pseudo-Aristotle appears to ad-here to the conventional paradigm of a single ruler in the household. This, however, is not the case, as he describes a household managed by the coop-erative effort of husband and wife. The ruler/ruled dichotomy no longer leads the discussion of household management; concepts such as unity, coopera-tion, love and honour are tangible values which guide the household relation-ships, and allow the author to suggest particular behaviours which advance their realisation. In this regard, the thought of Pseudo-Aristotle resembles the

---

[68] *Oeconomica,* i.1.5.

[69] Aristotle suggests this possibility in his division of virtue, but does not develop it; Pseudo-Aristotle makes clear reference to the shared rule of the household, see discussion below.

[70] *Oeconomica,* i.2.1.

[71] *Oeconomica,* i.5.1.

[72] *Oeconomica,* i.5.1–20; in this section, the slaves are given the potential of freedmen.

tenor of the HT mandates in their call to display particular behaviours, be they love, honour, or submission.

The wife enjoys a high level of honour within the household, holding "precedence" among its free associates, and having the "first claim" among its human members.[73] It is she who has primary care of the household, the duties of the man falling largely to activities of protection and provision, and not directly associated with its care. Still, Ps.-Aristotle envisions both master and mistress sharing responsibilities in the running of the household.[74] It is at this point that Ps.-Aristotle appeals to natural differences between the man and woman; their complexity, he reasons, allows for a greater degree of "mutual help, goodwill and co-operation." The differences, remarkably, do not establish a hierarchy of rule, but "contribute to the same end", a reciprocal and necessary[75] marriage partnership. The bond of marriage, as in the reasoning of Eph. 5:31, is divinely ordained:

> And so with this purpose in view [cooperative existence] Divine Providence has fashioned the nature (φύσις) of man and of woman for partnership (πρὸς τὴν κοινωνίαν). (Oeconomica, i.3.4)

This understanding of partnership includes for Ps.-Aristotle the pragmatic element of establishing the household, yet it shares with the HT the personal and ethical dimension characterised by *reciprocal* behaviours. In Book I, Ps.-Aristotle's instruction to the man and wife is terse in its formulation; the admonitions to both are expressed negatively, resembling the instruction reserved for the husbands in the HT.[76] The man, first of all, is to observe the following rule:

> We begin then with the rules that should govern a man's treatment of his wife. And the first of these forbids him to do her wrong (μὴ ἀδικεῖν); for if he observes this, he is not likely to suffer wrong at her hands. (Oeconomica, i.4.1)

---

[73] *Oeconomica*, i.2.1; i.3.1.

[74] "The master and the mistress should, therefore, give personal supervision, each to his or her special department of the household work." *Oeconomica*, i.6.4. See also *Oeconomica*, iii.1., where the wife is named mistress of the home, with only partial supervision of the man.

[75] "Neither the female, however, can effect this without the male, nor the male without the female; whence the union of the sexes has of necessity arisen." *Oeconomica*, i.3.1.

[76] The admonitions to the male are also longer, with examples and reasoning, another similarity with the HT instruction.

Wives, consequently, are admonished to support the husband's efforts on behalf of the household in a spirit of cooperation:

> Wives should neither importune their husbands, nor be restless in their absence…
> (*Oeconomica*, i.4.2)

Ps.-Aristotle's treatise on married life in Book III expands upon the basic instruction found in Book I. It is here that the concepts of reciprocity and household harmony are fully developed. Mutual love, realised in reciprocal duties, establishes "precious unity of mind."[77] The woman, being the mistress of the household, is addressed first. Her primary responsibility is to "bear an orderly rule", which, to a large degree, takes place without reference to the husband, who carries other responsibilities.[78] In the execution of her duties, two elements emerge, which resemble the HT mandates. She is, first of all, to obey her husband "in all other matters" which pertain to his rule [outside the household], and, if need be, yield him obedience in household affairs, as well.[79] The obedience required of the woman resembles the submission required by the HT mandates, and contains qualifying elements, as well: She should yield only in "fitting ways", and never to anything "base or unworthy."[80] Secondly, Ps.-Aristotle introduces fear as an appropriate posture for the wife towards her husband: "Between a free woman and her lawful spouse there should be a reverent and modest mingling of love and fear." (*Oeconomica*, iii.3). The context of the passage makes it clear that the man should exercise "right-minded" rule, which engenders appropriate fear in the woman. This fear, which is contrasted to that felt for despots, may be compared to that commanded in the summary phrase of Eph. 5:33.

Instruction to the husband is limited solely to the relation to his wife, and resembles the tenor of the HT admonitions, including their reciprocal nature. The virtues of the good wife are connected by a simple sentence, "And the rules which a good husband will follow in treatment of his wife will be similar." (*Oeconomica*, iii.2). The distinctive duties of the husband, however, are several. He is responsible for her training, which the author insists must be

---

[77] *Oeconomica*, iii.4. The couple should "strive to perform all duty…the husband towards those of his wife no less than his own, and she in turn towards his."

[78] The spheres of influence are divided between men and women; the men are active outside of the household, making it "unfitting that a man should know all that passes within the house." *Oeconomica*, iii.1.

[79] *Oeconomica*, iii.1

[80] *Oeconomica*, iii.1.

230

undertaken with "unstinting care." This care is likened to the cultivation and defense of a farmer's field; the caring husband not only tends the land, but is willing to die for it, "a death which men crown with the highest of praise."[81] These sentiments resemble the duties of the husband as found in Eph. 5:25–27, where the love of the husband should reflect Christ's willing sacrifice, as well as working to vouchsafe the wife's welfare. Indeed, the HT command to love is also incumbent upon husbands in Ps.-Aristotle: "Now a virtuous wife is best honoured when she sees that her husband…loves her and trusts her and holds her as his own."[82] This love is described in similar manner to Col. 3:18, particularly in its absence of harshness: "And if through ignorance she has done wrong, he should advise her without threatening, in a courteous and modest manner. Indifference and harsh reproof he must alike avoid."[83]

The instruction to husbands and wives found in Ps.-Aristotle evidences, then, similarities to the HT instruction at several levels, including an emphasis upon reciprocity, clear behavioural duties which are given in relational, not managerial, terms, and an ethic permeated by divine sanction, unity and love.

Parents and Children. Similar to most ancient treatments of the household, the topic of children receives considerably less attention than the other relations. In typical ancient fashion, Ps.-Aristotle points out the logic of child-rearing in terms of reciprocal benefits, though the address is limited to the proper behaviour of fathers and mothers only.[84] Unlike Aristotle, Ps.-Aristotle explicitly links *both* parents[85] to the upbringing of the child:

> Rightly reared by father and mother, children will grow up virtuous, as those who have treated them piously and righteously deserve that they should…For unless the parents have given their children an example how to live, the children will in their turn be able to offer a fair and specious excuse [for undutifulness]. (*Oeconomica*, iii.2)

This gives a reverse but corresponding image to the HT requirement of the children to obey both parents; it is particularly interesting that both Ps.-Aristotle and the HT include negative manifestations of improper child-

---

[81] *Oeconomica*, iii.2.
[82] *Oeconomica*, iii.2.
[83] *Oeconomica*, iii.3.
[84] *Oeconomica*, i.3.3.
[85] Though he divides their duties along the lines of nurture (mothers) and education (fathers), *Oeconomica*, i.3.4.

rearing (Col. 3:21; Eph. 6:4). The warnings in the HT, however, are directed towards the fathers only.

Slaves and Masters. Ps.-Aristotle does not diverge greatly from previous thinkers in that he assumes the slave to belong to a sub-category within the society, that of "human chattel."[86] He differs from earlier discussions, however, in that he does not attempt to substantiate his assumptions by ontological argument; yet his pragmatic subdivisions among the slaves, as well as their varied treatment,[87] find no echo in the HT or its reasoning. The slave, regardless of his duty in the household, should receive treatment which observes a balance between liberty and cruelty:

> In our intercourse with slaves we must neither suffer them to be insolent nor treat them with cruelty. (*Oeconomica*, i.5.1)

The slave's treatment is ultimately tied to his behaviour in the household; Ps.-Aristotle apportions to the slave three elements of life: his responsibility of work, and according to his performance, chastisement or reward:

> Slaves, again, are no exception to the rule that men become worse when better conduct is not followed by better treatment, but virtue and vice remain alike unrewarded. Accordingly we must keep watch over our workers, suiting our dispensations and indulgences to their desert (κατ᾽ ἀξίαν ἕκαστα); whether it be food or clothing, leisure or chastisement that we are apportioning. (*Oeconomica*, i.5.3)

Ps.-Aristotle's logic corresponds at this point to the HT principle of just reward for the slave as found in the slave-master instruction. Interestingly, it is applied in a broader manner in the HT, along human *and* divine axes, and to *both* parties. In Colossians, for example, the slave is promised heavenly reward (Col. 3:24), as well as punishment (Col. 3:25) for the services rendered to the earthly lord, though the phrase ὁ ἀδικῶν κομίσεται ὃ ἠδίκησεν can be understood to include both heavenly and earthly judgements for ill behaviour. The masters are admonished to afford correct and fitting benefits to the slaves, in similar manner to the instruction found in Ps.-Aristotle, τὸ δίκαιον καὶ ἰσότητα τοῖς δούλοις παρέχεσθε, Col. 4:1. In Ephesians, likewise, the slave's just reward is seen as coming from the Lord; the divine principle,

---

[86] *Oeconomica*, i.5.1.

[87] The "two types of slaves" are tied, ultimately, to their abilities, either earning "positions of trust" (ἐπίτροπος), or being common labourers (ἐργάτης). The former receive preferential treatment, *Oeconomica*, i.5.1.

however, is extended to the masters, as well.[88] The masters' duties towards
the slave are to reflect the principle of reward and punishment, as they are
instructed to imitate, in the role of master, the instruction given to the slaves:
τὰ αὐτα ποιεῖτε πρὸς αὐτους.

Though the instruction in Ps.-Aristotle does not include the element of
divine mediation, or call for the reciprocity found in the HT, there is a sense
of justice and goodwill which permeates his instruction. Indeed, Ps.-Aristotle
goes beyond the reciprocal balance of the HT, and recommends a degree of
preference for the slave's welfare. Of the earliest treatments of household
relations, this aspect represents a genuine and positive development in the
treatment of household servants. The householder should, for instance, insure
that the slaves are allowed to take part in feasts and enjoy their benefits even
more than the freedmen, since their lot in life is restricted.[89] The concept of
justice on behalf of the household servant goes even further, however. The
slave's labours are ultimately intended to benefit *more* than the householder:

> Every slave should have before his eyes a definite goal or term of his labour. To set
> a prize of freedom before him is both just and expedient (δίκαιον γὰρ καὶ
> συμφέρον); since having a prize to work for, and a time defined for its attainment,
> he will put his heart into his labours. (*Oeconomica*, i.5.5)

These sentiments stand in contrast to earlier treatments of the household relations, which see the slave in largely economic terms, and from the perspective of the householder's ultimate benefit. It surpasses the instruction and
intention of the HT, as well, which insists on just treatment, but does not address the possibility of manumission. That this subject appears so clearly in
an ancient treatment of the household allows for the assumption that the authors of the NT household codes were familiar with the discussion; it appears, however, that the HT concern is limited to the immediate behaviours
touching upon the household relations. Any penultimate considerations such
as the welfare of the house or the slave's freedom fall between the immediate
behavioural emphasis and the ultimate regulating factor of Christ's judgement.

---

[88] The term ἕκαστος (ἕκαστα [οἰκέτας]) emphasises the individual responsibility highlighted in both passages; in Eph. 6:8, this is extended to both parties, εἴτε δοῦλος εἴτε
ἐλεύθερος.

[89] Here his wording resembles the slave/free balance of Eph. 6:8, yet the kind treatment
should favour the slave, μᾶλλον *τῶν δούλων* ἕνεκα ποιεῖσθαι ἢ *τῶν ἐλευθέρων,*
Oeconomica, i.5.5.

Conclusion

Ps.-Aristotle represents a development of household management which is less systematic than earlier treatments, particularly in its attention to the household without reference to a greater political/philosophical scheme. He is, in this manner, similar to later treatments of household relations, which, as we shall see, tend to depart from theoretical constructs to the behavioural realities of household management. For this reason (and in similar manner to the HT), an emphasis upon reciprocal duties and the ethical matters of regulation of the household come to the fore. Although his treatment of the parent-child relationship is limited, the detailed admonitions to husbands and wives, as well as to slaves and masters, demonstrate similarities to the later HT mandates. The instruction to husbands and wives, for instance, emphasises unity and love under divine direction; the duties incumbent upon its members are both balanced and observable. Elements such as fear in the wife and sacrificial love on the part of the husband reflect the tenor of the New Testament HT relationship. The instruction to the slaves and masters, similarly, reflects a genuine and common concern for the slave's welfare, including the important concept of justice. The discussion of manumission, which exceeds the HT vision, is singular for this period and illustrative of the author's advanced views.

In the following section, we will turn our attention to three authors, whose regulation of the household closely corresponds to the historical period of the HT formulations. It is our hope that the discussions found in Philo, Musonius and Plutarch will contribute to a fuller picture of the philosophical and practical discussions which almost certainly contributed to the New Testament HT framework and understanding.

Contemporary Treatments: Philo

Philo represents a particularly interesting perspective for comparison with the HT regulation of the household. His writings, in similar manner to the HT, reflect the outlook of a particular first century religious community. The expected audience, like that of the HT, is not homogenous, but contains a large Hellenistic element not familiar with traditional Jewish morality or law. Philo's concern to communicate to a Hellenistic audience the profundity and relevance of Jewish Law, history and traditions has, therefore, both a didactic and distinctively apologetic tone. Though the apologetic aspect cannot be found in the Col. or Eph. HT,[90] his concern to make concrete application of moral principles corresponds with the tenor of the HT instruction. Philo makes mention of the several relationships commonly regulated in ancient treatments of societal ethics, including those of the New Testament HT.[91] His discussion of these relationships, however, is not made in the context of the household or economic theory, but surfaces in each instance in relation to numerous and varied topics touching upon Jewish law and custom.[92] The HT relations are not to be found in a single treatment; for this reason, there is not the systematic or logical cohesion between the household relations found in the HT and earlier Hellenistic writers. Household management is not, particularly in the case of the husband-wife and parent-child relationships, Philo's primary point of discussion, but serves to illustrate the broader intention of the author. The result is a sometimes unilateral and fragmentary treatment of its relationships. It is interesting and exceptional, then, that the master-slave relationship receives, as we have found with other ancient writers, a significantly more detailed analysis in Philo.

Philo and Household Relations

Husbands and Wives. Fragmentary mention of the duties of husbands and wives can be found in Philo. In his discussion of the simplicity of Jewish regulation in both private and civil matters, Philo announces the duties of the wife, with the attendant responsibility of the husband embedded within his description:

> Other rules again there are of various kinds: wives must be in servitude to their husbands (γυναῖκας ἀνδράσι δουλεύειν), a servitude not imposed by violent ill-

---

[90] The instruction contained in the parenesis and HT of 1 Peter anticipates the apologetic function of proper behaviour, including good deeds, 2:12, 15, suffering, 2:20, and submission, 3:1–2.

[91] In *De Decalogo* 165–167, he lists relations which involve honour and stratification, including old and young, rulers and subjects, benefactors and benefited, masters and slaves, parents and children. In *De Post. Caini* 181, Philo enumerates the right behaviours expected of a man, including, among others, honour towards parents, loving care of a wife, rearing children, happy and blameless relations with servants, management of the house, reverence towards elders, respect for the departed, fellowship with the living and piety towards the Deity.

[92] In a discussion of the manner of instruction in the Law, for example, Philo mentions that the householder may be the one who instructs his wife as husband, the children as father and the slave as master, *Hypothetica*, 7.14.

treatment but promoting obedience in all things (πρὸς εὐπείθειαν δ' ἐν ἅπασι).
(*Hypothetica*, 7.3)

The duty of the wife to render obedience is a common expectation in antiquity; Philo's description of her role in terms of servitude is unique, and without further elaboration of his meaning, we must conclude that his understanding of the wife's duty represents a departure from earlier Hellenistic writings, as well as being at least superficially out of concord with the HT mandates.[93] Whether the verb δουλεύειν indicates duties akin to household servants, or is intentionally hyperbolic to emphasise the traditional nature of Jewish households, cannot be discerned from this limited context. The much more complete instruction regarding the master-slave relationship may be helpful in uncovering Philo's understanding of a servant's responsibilities and proper treatment. In any event, the prescribed servitude of wives comes very close to the HT requirement in its completeness: ἐν ἅπασι mirrors the HT ἐν παντί of Eph. 5:24b.

The husband's behaviour, though not addressed directly, shares the negative, limiting element which we have encountered in the HT mandates (bitterness/hatred) concerning the husband: there should be no violent mistreatment (ὕβρεως μὲν οὐδεμιᾶς) of the wife. This common element is complemented by very few instances of expected behaviour on the part of the husband in Philo. The most notable instance can be found in his summary statements concerning the behaviour of an upright man; such a man is careful to fulfil his social responsibilities to all members of society, including his wife, to whom he should show care, ἐπιμέλειαν γυναικός.[94] This brief description of the husband's duty towards the wife resembles the caring aspect developed within the Ephesian HT (5:25–29), yet fails to fully correspond to the HT requirement of love.

Parents and Children. Unlike his treatment of the husband-wife relationship, Philo's instruction regarding parents and children is less fragmentary,

---

[93] Dorothy Sly's detailed study, *Philo's Perception of Women*, Brown Judaic Studies, vol. 209 (Atlanta: Scholars Press, 1990), is helpful at this point. She notes that Philo recognises a constitutional corruption in the woman's nature (passions/flesh, 89) which requires the man's external, reasoned control (mind, 110, 219). Women show virtue only to the degree in which they manifest male characteristics; for this reason, she concludes, 223: "The spiritual accountability he [Philo] urged upon men had no counterpart in the woman's quarter." This represents a significant contrast to the HT.

[94] *De Post. Caini*, 181.

236

yet formulated in contexts concerned with topics other than the regulation of the household. The primary texts which contain material regarding the parent-child relationship can be found in *De Decalogo*, 165–167 and *Spec. Leg.*, ii. 225f. Both texts are located in a discussion regarding the implications of the fifth commandment. Particular attention is given to relations, including parents,[95] which merit such deference. The discussion in *De Decalogo* is preliminary, and is limited to outlining the basic intention of the ten commandments; it is only in the significantly more extensive *Spec. Leg.* where Philo extrapolates the implications of the individual commandments for daily life. The citation from *De Decalogo*, 165–167 is, due to Philo's organisational strategy,[96] considerably shorter than the discussion found in *Spec. Leg.*, yet it depicts the basic assumptions found in greater detail there:

> In the fifth commandment on honouring parents (περὶ γονέων τιμῆς) we have a suggestion of many necessary laws drawn up to deal with relations of old to young, rulers to subjects, benefactors to benefited, slaves to masters. For parents belong to the superior class of the above-mentioned pairs, that which comprises seniors, rulers, benefactors and masters, while children occupy the lower position with juniors, subjects, receivers of benefits and slaves. (*De Decalogo*, 165–66)

Philo, though explicating an ancient Jewish command, resembles numerous Hellenistic sources at this point;[97] in particular the use of τιμάω as the ideal posture for children towards their parents. His reasoning, however, is quite different, and closely resembles that of the Eph. HT. The obedience required in Philo and the HT mandate in Eph. 6:2 is *explicitly* tied to the fifth commandment, so that both make similar use of the Decalogue to build a larger ethical argument. The requirement to render honour, and its reasoning, then, represent the strongest point of agreement between Philo's instruction and the HT.

Philo's discussion of the fifth commandment, however, uncovers a systematic treatment of relationships which evidences closer affinities with Hellenistic thought; in particular, the bifurcation of the duty to honour along the

---

[95] The topic of honouring parents receives mention, though no thorough treatment, elsewhere in Philo: *Quod Deus Immutab.*, 17; *De Plantatione*, 146; *De Ebrietate*, 17–18; *De Mutatione Nom.*, 40; *De Vita Mosis*, ii, 198; *De Post. Caini*, 181.

[96] Philo organises his more detailed discussions in *Spec. Leg.* after the "ten words" of the Decalogue, *Spec. Leg.* i.1.

[97] The list of stratified relations given here resembles numerous duty lists of the period.

classic ruler/ruled dichotomy.[98] Parents deserve honour, he reasons, first of all because of their seniority in relation to the children, and concomitantly, by virtue of their daily roles as benefactor, instructor and master of the children (all superordinated roles). Parental authority does not arise merely from these pragmatic considerations, however. It is nature which has endowed them with a god-like[99] authority:

> But in addition to the benefits they confer, parents have also received authority over their offspring. That authority is not attained by lot or voting…but is awarded by the most admirable and perfect judgement of nature above us which governs with justice things both human and divine. (*Spec. Leg.,* ii.231)

This reasoning, of course, corresponds to earlier philosophical ordering of relationships κατὰ φύσιν. Philo's understanding of naturally ordered relationships is at odds with the HT at this point, whose conception of relationships is ordered according to, and fully regulated by, the person of Christ. The ontological implications of this significant difference allow Philo to construe a nearly unregulated and unilateral parent-child relationship. The authority conferred by nature upon parents, for example, is nearly absolute; Philo illustrates how the parents' authority is reflected in the manner in which children may be corrected. Graduated in terms of severity, discipline may include admonishment, beatings, degradation, bonds, and ultimately, death.[100] The character of the parent-child relationship, moreover, is likened

---

[98] Philo indicates two "orders" which divide relationships, *Spec. Leg.,* ii.227: "Now parents are assigned a place in the higher of these two orders, for they are seniors and instructors and benefactors and rulers and masters: sons and daughters are placed in the lower order, for they are juniors and learners and recipients of benefits and subjects and servants."

[99] Though Philo differentiates between the divine and human commands, he organises his work, tellingly, around two sets of five commandments, linking the fifth command with the first four (having primarily divine aspect), cf. *De Decal.* 50–51, 106, 121. The fifth commandment, he reasons, is "more concerned with the divine", parental authority attaining a god-like aspect. He considers parents to be "mid-way between the natures of God and man", and having "raised not-being into being"; they are to be "to their children as God is to the world", *Spec. Leg.,* ii.225; *De Decal.,* 106. This sentiment can be seen in Iamblichus' account of Pythagoras' speech, where the philosopher exhorts young men to render honour their parents "as to the divinities", *De Vita Pythagorica,* 8.38. Hierocles, like Philo, delineates the advantages enjoyed by children as a result of their parents; the parents, he says, may be considered as earthly gods, who, due to their proximity, may be honoured more than the gods themselves, Πῶς χρηστέον τοῖς γονεῦσιν, Stob. *Anth.,* iv.25.53.

[100] The Law, as found in the Pentateuch, is critical in forming Philo's thought at this point. The significance of its authority can be seen in the numerous allusions found in the exposition of the fifth commandment. He intensifies the original Mosaic command at points (*Spec. Leg.,*

in nature to the slave-master relationship.[101] This is reflected in the tone of the duties which are incumbent upon the children. As parents are admonished to "employ more active and severe admonitions" to counteract undesirable behaviour in their children, these should "stand in awe of those who begot them, fearing them both as rulers and masters (ὡς ἄρχοντας καὶ ὡς φύσει δεσπότας)."[102] The language which Philo uses to describe the parent-child relationship is unique in its nature and harsh implications, and finds little common ground with earlier Hellenistic treatments or the HT. The concept of honour required of the Law becomes paramount, so that the regulation of the relational axis is slanted towards uncompromising rigidity and unilateral fulfilment of its demands. The parents' authority stands, as a result, in parallel relationship to the absolute nature of the command. It can be said without exaggeration, then, that Philo allows a strong parallel between the parent-child relationship and the rule of God over humanity.[103]

Both Philo and the HT understand the child's responsibility towards the parents in terms of obedience, the Eph. HT framing its command, with Philo, in light of the fifth commandment. Though the Col. HT may suggest severity in its call to obedience κατὰ πάντα, the HT tone seems, overall, less severe and more balanced in its requirements. As with the husband-wife relationship, it may be that Philo is attempting to portray the strict orderliness of the Law's demands, with little interest in examining the broader regulation of the relationship. Indeed, his treatment is limited to a discussion of how honour is to be rendered in the several societal relations, and assumes from the start that this command is unnaturally performed; other relational considerations

---

ii.239, for instance, insists that the fear required in Lev. 19:3 was intended by God to precede affection, φόβον πρὸ εἰνοίας. In Spec. Leg. 232, the parents appear to have more independence in deciding the child's fate than Dt. 21:18–21 allows!). Punishments and proper behaviour are drawn from various OT texts: Spec. Leg., ii.232, Dt. 21:18–21; Spec. Leg., ii.238, Lev. 19:32; Spec. Leg., ii.239, Lev. 19:3; Spec. Leg., ii.243f, Ex. 21:15; Spec. Leg., ii.248, Ex. 21:16f; Lev. 20:9; Dt. 27:16.

[101] Philo reasons in Spec. Leg., ii.233, that children, being born to the parents and costing them dearly, justifies their servant status: "But parents have not only been given the right of exercising authority over their children, but the power of a master corresponding to the two forms under which servants are owned, one when they are home-bred, the other when they are purchased."

[102] Spec. Leg., ii.241. Philo understands the power of rule over the children to be for their well-being, Hypothetica, 7.3: γονεῖς παῖδων ἄρχειν ἐπὶ σωτηρίᾳ καὶ πολυωρίᾳ.

[103] In Spec. Leg., ii.225, he makes this very claim: "...so they [parents] in imitation of his power, as far as they are capable, immortalise the race."

such as filial affection, he reasons, need no regulation.[104] Perhaps because of this limitation, Philo's treatment of the parent-child relationship differs significantly from the contemporary HT. It lacks, first of all, the positive admonition given to the parents in the HT; secondly, it is primarily concerned with the execution of the fifth commandment – a unilateral approach which does not coincide with the reciprocal nature of the HT mandates; and lastly, the parent-child relation, characterised solely in terms of honour rendered, becomes absolute and unregulated; this stands in particular contrast to the mediating influence granted Christ in the HT.

Slaves and Masters. Though Philo's discussion of the husband-wife and parent-child relations reveals considerable limitations when compared to the HT or other similar material, his understanding of the master-slave relationship surprises not only with its complete and reciprocal treatment of duties, but also with the extended and critical approach to the master's behaviour. The comparatively conservative tendencies we have noted above are not to be found at all; if anything, Philo demonstrates an unparalleled sense of equity and justice among Hellenistic treatments of this relational pair. Once again his discussion of household relations is not found in the context of social theory or household management, but in detailed commentary upon the implications of the OT Law. In the case of the slave-master relationship, the Law's regulation does not correspond to common Hellenistic categories, and therefore receives detailed commentary. This regulation, we hope to show, revolves around the unique implications of Sabbath rest.

Philo considers the correct regulation of the slave-master relationship to be elemental to leading a good life.[105] Slaves are included, notably, in his list of stratified relationships in *De Decalogo* 165–167, indicating, at least in this general treatment, that Philo has adopted the common ruler/ruled dichotomy in construing the duties of this relational pair.[106] The reciprocal duties of slave and master reflect Philo's recognition of their unequal status:

---

[104] In *Spec. Leg.,* ii.239–40, Philo explains that Moses commands that which is not *naturally* performed (honour); commands to love are not necessary, for they arise from nature, requiring no injunction.

[105] *De Post. Caini,* 181, delineates "the best things of life", which include "happy and blameless relations to domestic servants."

[106] On balance, Philo actually sees servants as ranking only lower in "fortune", *Spec. Leg.,* iii.137.

240

And there are many other instructions given…to servants on rendering an affection-
ate loyalty to their masters, to masters on showing gentleness and kindness *by which
inequality is equalised. (De Decalogo,* 167)

This balanced understanding of the above duties resembles the fundamental
sentiments of most Hellenistic authors, and those of the HT, with the notable
exception of the motivation δι' ὧν ἐξισοῦται τὸ ἄνισον. The general adaptation of the ontological dichotomy in most thinkers precludes this element
of motivation. The HT recognises a fundamental equality before the Lord
(Col. 3:25–4:1; Eph. 6:9), yet this fact and its motivation are primarily by-
products of the believer's standing in Christ and the equalising force of the
coming judgement. The potential abuses and inequalities of the slave-master
relationship are redressed through the mediation of Christ, yet are not treated
as an isolated category or an achievable status. For Philo, however, the notion of a slave's equality with the master,[107] as well as the potential of attaining freedom are addressed in his treatment of the relational pair, and play a
significant role in the motivation and formulation of his mandates.

The Value of the Slave

In *Spec. Leg.,* iii.137–143, Philo discusses the implications of the Law's restrictions upon slave punishment in Dt. 20:20–21. He reflects the common-
sense approach of many Hellenistic thinkers which regarded the death or in-
jury of a slave as a considerable financial loss.[108] He goes beyond the fiscal
concerns of earlier treatments, as well as the requirements of the Law itself,
however, when he requires that the master not punish severe crimes by his
own hand; justice is to be sought according to law and the courts.[109] The
slave receives, then, an unprecedented level of legal protection in Philo. The
reason for this unusual concern for the slave becomes clear:

Servants rank lower in fortune but in nature can claim equality with their masters,
and in the law of God the standard of justice (κανὼν τῶν δικαίων) is adjusted to
nature and not fortune. And therefore the masters should not make excessive use of
authority over slaves by showing arrogance and contempt and savage cruelty.
(*Spec. Leg.,* ii.137)

---

[107] Speaking of Philo's view of the slave's nature, Bockmuehl, *Law,* 109, observes: "Equality before nature implies equality before God, with resulting moral obligations."

[108] *Spec. Leg.,* iii.143, warns, typical of other slave-master treatments, that killing only in-
jures the householder, and represents considerable loss of property.

[109] *Spec. Leg.,* iii.143.

Philo extends this passage with strong criticism of masters who practice harsh treatment of slaves; such men, he suggests, have a native or acquired hatred of their fellow-men, and their behaviour indicates that they are merely "tyrants with smaller resources."[110] Such behaviour will not, he insists, escape justice, which is personified to exact retribution upon cruel masters.[111]

Philo's ethic of justice reveals similarities and differences to the HT mandates at this point. Both share, firstly, the concern that justice characterise the master-slave relationship (Col. 3:25–4:1). The concept of justice, and the citations of illicit conduct, however, are wholly aimed at the master in Philo; the HT also names the slaves as responsible members in this regard (Col. 3:25; Eph. 6:8). Secondly, both Philo and the HT give warnings of coming retribution in the case of misdeeds. Philo's personification of justice, however, can be understood to indicate human or divine agency; the HT is clear that the final resolution of justice lies with the Lord in the future process of judgement. It is important to note that Philo locates the foundation of his ethic in the law of God, which is his "standard of justice".[112] The law functions as the point of ethical orientation, much as Christ regulates the relationships within the HT. Both have, then, ethical reference points, intended to secure justice.

Philo differs from the HT, however, in his comments regarding the ontological makeup of slave and master. Where both affirm equality which is ultimately guaranteed through the administration of justice, Philo goes much further by reversing the common Hellenistic view of slaves: they are ontologically *equal* to their masters.[113] The ontological argument augments the

---

[110] *Spec. Leg.*, iii.138.

[111] In *Spec. Leg.*, iii.140, Philo notes that misconduct will not enjoy immunity, for the master "will have for his adversary justice, the hater of evil, the defender and champion of the ill-used, who will call upon him to give account for the unhappy condition of the sufferers."

[112] Bockmuehl, *Law*, 108, points out that although Philo appeals to the Stoic understanding of natural law, he links this closely with God, and in particular, the Law (cf. *De Vita Mosis*. 2.51).

[113] *Spec. Leg.*, iii.137: φύσεως δὲ τῆς αὐτῆς μεταποιοῦνται τοῖς δεσπόταις. See also *Spec. Leg.*, ii. 69 and 83, where the slave is *contrasted* with unreasoning animals, a favourite Hellenistic comparison (see also *De Virtutibus* 173). Contrary to many Hellenistic authors, who allow some races to be considered slaves by nature, Philo states in *Spec. Leg.*, ii. 69, that no man is naturally a slave, ἄνθρωπος γὰρ ἐκ φύσεως δοῦλος οὐδείς. Though freedom was a known Stoic theme in Philo's day, it was primarily concerned with the freedom achieved through wisdom and lost through foolishness or wicked behaviour. The institution of

ethical force of justice. The HT relies, notably, on the mediation of Christ alone. Philo's ontological argument, however, is never formally pressed into service towards the mediation of the slave-master relationship; it is, rather, the stipulation of the Law which provides the measure of justice and equality. In this regard, Philo resembles the reasoning to the HT, which employs the symbols and values of the faith community (in this comparison Christ or the Law) to establish ethical conduct. It is the Law, in particular the Sabbath regulations, which indicate the ultimate nature of the slave-master relationship and its responsibilities.

The Sabbath Rest

In Philo, the concept of Sabbath rest is the aspect of the Law which gives rise to his most detailed analysis of the slave-master relationship. It is treated in two sections, *Spec. Leg.*, ii.66–69 and *Spec. Leg.*, ii. 79–85. The former passage pertains to the regulation of the weekly Sabbath observance; the latter is a homily regarding the cyclical freeing of slaves recorded in Dt. 15:12–18. It is the concept of Sabbath rest which underlies Philo's strong egalitarian ethic, and gives rise to his extraordinary emphasis upon freedom:

> ...the servants are not to refuse to entertain still higher hopes, but should find in the relaxation allowed after six days an ember or spark of freedom, and look forward to their complete liberation... (*Spec. Leg.*, ii.67)

> ...when the truly sacred number of the seventh year is about to begin, grant freedom to him who is naturally free (ἐλεύθερον μεθίεσο τὸν ἐλεύθερον φύσει) and grant it without hesitation, my friend, and rejoice that you have found an opportunity of benefiting the highest of living creatures, man, in his chief interest. For a slave can have no greater boon than freedom. (*Spec. Leg.*, ii.84)

It is interesting to note that the Law, functioning in its regulatory role, contains both penultimate and ultimate aspects; the slave enjoys a degree of freedom presently, but hopes, ultimately, for the dissolution of the slave-master bond. The concept of unrealised freedom, as well as its egalitarian force, introduces a mediating influence to Philo's treatment of the slave-master relationship. Though the HT does not discuss the topic of constitutional freedom, it anticipates conduct which is similarly regulated and determined by the present reality of Christ's mediation, as well as anticipating

---

slavery was not directly addressed. In *Philo*, Vol. vii, App., 624, G.H. Whitaker declares, "there is no other which lays down the principles so explicitly as this."

ultimate justice at his coming. The hope of freedom may be compared to the hope engendered by Christ's ultimate role in judgement. Other elements of Philo's regulation of the slave-master relationship reveal similar parallels to the HT, as well.

As noted above, the instruction contained in Philo's treatment of the master-slave relationship is primarily concerned with regulating the behaviour of the master. Though concerned with positive behaviour as well, he concentrates upon negative behaviours which directly affect household servants. Like the HT, the form of address is direct, making use, however, of the second person *singular*. In contrast, the slave, who receives the majority of instruction in both HT forms, is never directly addressed in Philo. The few mentions of the slaves' behaviour are nearly always in reference to the master's, and exclude any mention of potential negative behaviour (a HT feature). The master, in contrast to the HT, carries the larger share of responsibility in Philo's treatment of this relational pair. Negative behaviours, which Philo condemns in the master, include the excessive use of authority, evidencing arrogance, contempt or cruelty, requiring oppressive loads of work, as well as hurling insults or threats.[114] These negative behaviours should, ideally, be displaced by normal care (food and shelter) and the conscious fulfilling of the Law's more particular demands. These include allowing the slave to observe the weekly Sabbath, as well as insuring his ultimate freedom. The masters should vouchsafe, then, both present and future aspects of the slave's welfare.[115]

Although the instruction to the slaves is limited and indirect, it becomes clear that Philo anticipates a reciprocal ethic much in keeping with the HT schema. The master is advised to approach the slave relationship in terms of "give and take", τὰ μὲν διδούς, τὰ δὲ καὶ λαμβάνων, which consists of the master's provision, and the slave's co-operative and swift service.[116] The combination of domestic service and reciprocal, custodial care resembles both the HT instruction, as well as earlier, philosophical treatments. Philo introduces another element, however, which reverses the discrete responsibilities of master and slave and represents an equalising force: the Law. The Sabbath requirement, he points out, is given to slave *and* free, and teaches

---

[114] The HT includes similar regulation of negative behaviours of masters in Col. 3:25, ὁ ἀδικῶν; and Eph. 6:9, ἀνιέντες τὴν ἀπειλήν. Note that the noun used for threats is identical in Philo, *Spec. Leg.*, ii.83: ἀπειλαῖς.

[115] *Spec. Leg.*, ii. 83–85. The care of the servant includes his tenure within the household, as well as securing his future through adequate provision at his dismissal.

[116] *Spec. Leg.*, ii. 83.

"both masters and men an admirable lesson." The masters, in granting the slaves Sabbath rest, must learn to

> ...work themselves without waiting for the offices and attentions of their menials...
> (*Spec. Leg.*, ii.67)

The principle introduced by the Sabbath may be compared, at least to a degree, to the mutual submission advanced in Eph. 5:21 under the "fear of Christ". The regulating element of both (Sabbath Law/Christ) allows for a surprising fluidity between community members, particularly the submission (and the reversal of roles?) of otherwise superordinated members. Both possess unique, dynamic elements; the Law and Christ each effect unexpected change in the static household roles by means of their mediation. Philo expresses this clearly:

> But the result of this occasional submission (ὑπομεῖναι) of the free to do the menial offices of the slave, together with the immunity allowed to the slave, will be a step forward in human conduct towards the perfection of virtue, when both the seemingly distinguished and the meaner sort remember equality and repay to each other (ἀλλήλοις) the debt incumbent on them. (*Spec. Leg.*, ii.68)

Conclusion

Philo represents a unique point of comparison to the HT in that his regulations reflect those of a religious community. His treatment of the household relations resemble, at points, the ontological reasoning of his Hellenistic contemporaries, and equal even the harshest, unilateral treatments of both the husband-wife and parent-child relational pairs. Though Philo relies on the Decalogue to provide regulation of the parent-child relationship, these two pairs reveal only superficial similarities to the HT in their actual mandates. The employment of the OT law in regulating these relationships takes on an absolute character which is reserved, in the HT, for Christ. The apologetic tone which characterises Philo may have influenced him at this point to portray an overly conservative and rigid picture of household regulation; the reality within his faith community may have been considerably different. This is certainly the case in his regulation of the slave-master relationship. Philo is unparalleled in his call to reciprocity and equity, and stands in contrast to the contemporary, utilitarian view of slaves. The elements of present and future divine justice, as well as the regulating authority of Mosaic Law found here, draw him close to the motivation and regulation of the HT slave-master relationship. Philo extends the implications of his OT exegesis (constitutional equality) beyond the limited HT regulatory concerns of equality before the Lord. The present aspect of equality explicitly calls for freedom for the slave.

Contemporary Treatments: Musonius Rufus

Caius Musonius Rufus was an energetic proponent of Stoic ideas in the first century, probably best known as the teacher of Epictetus. His thought, extant only in fragmentary form, was not collected into any systematic order until the early nineteenth century. The present collection[117] consists of conversations (diatribes) and moral discourses. Though Musonius does not attempt to discuss the household as an economic or political unit, it is clear that he sees the home in terms of the welfare of society, and upholds its integrity.[118] His essays are primarily concerned with the relationship of philosophy and its practical expression in societal ethics; in this manner they touch upon household relations. As a Stoic philosopher, Musonius promotes a positive and egalitarian view of human nature,[119] which is discernible in his advice to the various household relations.

Household Relations

Masters and Slaves. In contrast to other ancient and contemporary thinkers, little has survived of Musonius' thought regarding master-slave relations. Though his universal appeal to philosophy would have doubtless included the slave, we can only suppose what regulations he might have suggested. It is clear, however, that he includes the slaves among those relations which fall under the rule of propriety and justice. In his essay concerning sexual

---

[117] The original collection of I.V. Peerlkamp (1822) has been published more recently with the translation of Cora Lutz, *Musonius Rufus: "The Roman Socrates"*, ed. G. Cumberledge, Yale Classical Studies, vol. 10 (London: Oxford University Press, 1947). Citations from Musonius will be taken from this volume, including the essay number, e.g., iii.20, and page in Lutz' volume.

[118] In xiv, 30–35, 92, Musonius insists that each man "take thought of his own city, and to make his home a rampart for its protection." Society is built upon and grows out of marriage, the home and the city.

[119] Musonius, discussing the nature of the soul, assumes that all men, strong or weak, young or old, can take hold of the discipline of philosophy, and thereby attain to virtue. The soul is innately good, and man is fashioned by nature to be able to live "free of error and nobly", ii, 36–39.

indulgence, he is quick to point out that licence can lead to manifestations of corruption and injustice (ἀδικίαν); his unflattering characterisation of the individual yielding to such temptation as a "swine rejoicing in his own vileness" is related to the master-slave relationship:

> In this category belongs the man who has relations with his own slave-maid; a thing which some people consider quite without blame, since every master is held to have in his power to use his slave as he wishes. (xii, "Περὶ Ἀφροδισίων", 25–40, 86)

Musonius' sentiments that the slave not be treated as an object of indulgence correspond to the injunction of Col. 3:25–4:1, where the warning to the master (and slave) is characterised in similar terms of unrighteousness; the master, further, is reminded in Colossians to grant the slave that which is right and fair (τὸ δίκαιον καὶ ἰσότητα). The HT mandates agree with Musonius' critique of absolute power over the slave; both insist upon authority modulated by the Lord in heaven (Col. 4:1; Eph. 6:9).

Parents and Children. Musonius' advice regarding the rearing of children is limited in its scope, and closely tied to the role of philosophy in forming virtue. He insists that the children, both male and female, receive the same instruction in matters pertaining to the formation of character.[120] This loosely corresponds to the inclusive Ephesian HT command to rear the children "in the training and instruction of the Lord"; Musonius' philosophical principles and Christian instruction provide a similar basis for general household instruction of children. Both encourage a positive model of development.

Musonius also warns, as with the HT, against inappropriate behaviour in rearing the children. Whereas the HT mentions specific parental failings in Col. 3:21 and Eph. 6:4, Musonius is less specific. He simply alerts the parents to be just – under the watchful eye of Zeus:

> ...so whoever is unjust to his own family sins against the gods of his fathers and against Zeus, guardian of the family, from whom wrongs done against the family are not hidden... (xv, 29–31, 96)

Zeus plays, then, a similarly regulatory role to that of Christ in the HT. This can be seen most clearly in Musonius' treatment of the requirement of obedience.[121] We have noted that, in the HT commands, obedience of the children

---

[120] His essay "Should Daughters Receive the Same Education as Sons?", iv, p.42–49, lists numerous qualities such as courage and self control, which transcend gender.

[121] Essay xvi, 100, is titled "Must One Obey One's Parents Under All Circumstances?"

is required in both Col. and Eph., yet with different modifying phrases. The Col. command is unmitigated, ὑπακούετε τοῖς γονεῦσιν κατὰ πάντα, while Eph. introduces a more direct and moderating influence of Christ in the formulation, ὑπακούετε τοῖς γονεῦσιν ὑμῶν ἐν κυρίῳ. What appears to be a modulating development in the HT schema, is treated, interestingly, in Musonius' discussion of obedience, as well. A young mans asks the philosopher, "Tell me, Musonius, must one obey one's parents in all things (χρὴ πάντα πείθεσθαι τοῖς γονεῦσιν), or are there circumstances under which one need not heed them?"[122] The question represents the ethical tension raised by the adverbial modifier πάντα in both this query and the Col. HT formulation. As discussed earlier, it appears that the author of Ephesians has deleted this feature of the Col. formulation in order to enhance the mediating influence of Christ; this is precisely the pattern we find in Musonius. After discussing the nature of obedience (and generally upholding it in most matters), he does allow for disobedience in requirements which run contrary to the good. Ultimately, the good is associated with Zeus himself; obedience is rendered to man or God, as in the following example:

> Your father forbids you to study philosophy, but the common father of all men and gods, Zeus, bids you and exhorts you to do so. His command and law is to be just and honest, beneficent, temperate, high-minded, superior to pain, superior to pleasure, free from all envy and all malice; to put it briefly, the law of Zeus bids man to be good. But being good is the same as being a philosopher. If you obey your father, you will follow the will of man; if you choose the philosopher's life, the will of God. (xvi, 30f., 104–106)

Musonius' instruction to children and parents, then, evidences similarities to the HT in its common requirement of obedience, and the expectation of just parental behaviour; the Ephesian HT shows further similarities in that both adopt a positive approach to education. Most striking, however, is the concern of both Musonius and the Eph. HT, that the required obedience be divinely regulated.

Husbands and Wives. Musonius' treatment of the husband-wife relationship is distinguished by two characteristics: firstly, it concentrates on philosophical and ontological categories attached to the learning of philosophy, with

---

[122] Musonius, xvi, 100. That this is current thinking is shown in Epictetus' discussion in *Encheiridion,* 30, where children are to yield, even to bad fathers, at all times (παραχωεῖν ἁπάντων); also in *Discourses,* ii.1..7, a son should always yield and obey in all things (πάντα ὑπακούειν).

little attention granted to the pragmatic (household) concerns of earlier authors;[123] secondly, it reveals a remarkable degree of shared responsibility and reciprocity between husband and wife, which flow from an emphasis upon marital union.

The first characteristic is due, perhaps, to the limited scope of much of Musonius' discussion. He is attempting to convince the reader of the indispensable nature of philosophy in regulating human relations. To this end, he argues for what seems to be a total break with the traditional, bifurcated understanding of male and female duty κατὰ φύσιν. In the realms of reason, the senses and inclination towards virtue, he insists that no humans are to be distinguished in terms of natural ability.[124] These natural abilities are the gifts of the gods, apportioned, notably, to both men and women:

> Καὶ οἰκείωσις φύσει πρὸς ἀρετὴν οὐ μόνον γίνεται τοῖς ἀνδράσιν, ἀλλα καὶ γυναιξίν. (iii. 1–2, 40)

Musonius further insists that there are no human tasks, either in public life or the household, which might be isolated as unique duties of either man or woman. In anticipation of the objections of his opponents, however, he makes a critical concession concerning their physical natures:

> But I do say that, since in the human race man's constitution is stronger and woman's weaker, tasks should be assigned which are suited to the nature of each; that is, heavier tasks should be given to the stronger and lighter ones to the weaker.[125] For all human tasks, I am inclined to believe, are a common obligation and are common to men and women, and none is necessarily appointed for either

---

[123] Musonius does discuss the woman's character in Stoic terms, as well as duties within the household, including housekeeping, the tending of slaves and frugality (see iii, 9–25, 40f.). These examples are given, however, to illustrate the necessity and propriety of her philosophical training, and are without reciprocal duties of the husband. In this manner he mentions a number of characteristics, three of which are of note in relation to the HT. Where the woman is in charge of the household, she should be just, iv, 14, 44, probably in conjunction with her direction of the servants. The love for her children is to be above the love of life, and takes the verb ἀγαπάω, unusual in this context, and reminiscent of the husband's posture in Eph. 5:25. The wife is characterised as one who helps and serves (ὑπηρετέω) her husband, even performing work considered that of a slave, iii, 7–9, 42, perhaps an acknowledgement of the woman's submission. His discussion of marriage in xii a, b and xiv, on the other hand, contains only common and reciprocal duties.

[124] See especially ii. 15–30, 36; iii. 25f., 38–41; iv. 7–17, 44; iv. 1–5, 46.

[125] Musonius' characterisation of the women as weaker (ἀσθενέστεροςα) parallels that of 1 Peter 3:7. His reasoning is mirrored in Hierocles' discussion, *Οἰκονομικός*, Stob. *Anth.*, iv.28.21.

one exclusively, but some pursuits are more suited to the nature of one, some to the other (τὰ [ἔργα] μὲν τῆδε τῇ φύσει, τὰ δὲ τῆδε), and for this reason some are called men's work and some women's. (iv, 15–31, 46)

This concession may appear at first glance to be a simple revision of the common schemes of labour division known throughout antiquity. Musonius' argument does indeed resemble the pragmatic reasoning of earlier thinkers at this point, yet his reluctance to divide duties κατὰ φύσιν on ontological grounds is indicative of an important element of his thinking regarding the husband-wife relationship: common, natural abilities distinguish and define the union of two humans, as well as their reciprocal duties. In his treatment of husband-wife relations, Musonius shifts the traditional perspective of discussion from the disparity formed by ontological differences (and their resultant, distinctive duties) to a paradigm of parity and union. This distinctive perspective and its emphases reveal interesting similarities and contrasts to the contemporary HT form and message.

Marriage as Divinely Appointed Union

Musonius' emphasis upon marital union not only distinguishes his perspective from earlier authors, it provides a point of comparison to the HT mandates, as well. As might be expected, the similarities are closest to the more extensive husband-wife instruction of the Eph. HT. Musonius claims, first of all, that the philosopher is the "teacher and leader of men", from whom we learn how to live appropriately, or κατὰ φύσιν. He enumerates several prominent philosophers,[126] who, despite handicaps such as poverty or homelessness, lived in the state of marriage. Their lives provide testimony, then, that the marriage union itself may be regarded as being in accordance with nature.[127] Musonius elevates the traditionally pragmatic understanding of marriage union to that of a supremely desirable good, as well as making it an indispensable cornerstone of traditional societal structures. In marriage, for example, man and woman maintain the stability of the state.[128] This strong claim is further substantiated with an argument of divine example. Musonius

---

[126] Pythagoras, Socrates and Crates, xiv. 25f., 90.

[127] He concludes, xiv.8, 92, κατὰ φύσιν δ', εἴ τι ἄλλο, καὶ τὸ γαμεῖν φαίνεται ὄν.

[128] The marriage union is both "pleasant and necessary"; both home and city do not "depend upon woman alone or upon men alone, but upon their union with each other"; "Whoever destroys human marriage", he reasons, "destroys the home [οἶκον], the city [πόλιν] and the whole human race", xiv. 35, 92.

illustrates how the gods themselves, functioning as patrons, guards and help-ers, tend to the needs of the marriage union.[129] Their example, however, sim-ply reflects the design of creation:

> ...marriage, if anything, is manifestly in accord with nature. For to what other purpose did the creator of mankind first divide our human race into two sexes, male and female, then implant in each a strong desire for association and union with the other, the male for the female and the female for the male? Is it not plain that he wished the two to be united and to live together, and by their joint efforts to devise a way of life in common...? (iv, 8–14, 92)

The marriage union is, ultimately, created by the design of God; this assump-tion underlies Musonius' argument, and comes close to approximating the reasoning of Ephesians 5:31, which summarises the account of woman's creation in terms of God's ultimate intention of union, Gen. 2:24, οἱ δύο εἰς σάρκα μίαν. The created order, then, is understood in terms of establishing and justifying the marriage bond in both authors.

Reciprocity is the hallmark of the marriage union within Musonius' dis-cussion. Though the reciprocal form of the HT commands is missing in Mu-sonius, emphasis upon reciprocal duty is especially strong in his formula-tions, nonetheless. His understanding of the marital duties, however, is dis-similar from that of the HT in that it does not delineate distinct tasks for each member. Instead, he insists upon *common* responsibilities, and makes use of vocabulary which emphasises the cooperative nature of the marriage un-ion.[130] This union is complete in its compass, again approximating the sense "one flesh" found in Ephesians:

> The husband and wife...should come together for the purpose of making a life in common and of procreating children, and furthermore of regarding all things in common between them, and nothing peculiar or private to one or the other, not even their bodies. (xiii a, 11–13, 88)

With the exception of child-rearing, Musonius emphasises only one neces-sary and distinctive characteristic of the marriage bond, which is conspicuous in its detail and prominence—mutual love:

---

[129] In particular, he mentions three θεοὶ μεγάλοι, Hera, Eros and Aphrodite, iv. 20–21, 94.

[130] In the two short essays related to marriage, the following forms are employed to under-score and describe the manner and nature of duties: the reciprocal pronoun ἀλλήλ- (8x) as well as numerous verbal συν-formulations emphasise mutuality of duty (15x), while κοιν-ωνία (8x) and ὁμόνοια (5x) describe marriage in terms of commonality.

But in marriage there must be above all perfect companionship and mutual love of husband and wife, both in health and in sickness and under all conditions, since it was with the desire for this as well as for having children that both entered upon marriage. Where, then, this love for each other is perfect and the two share it completely, each striving to outdo the other in devotion, the marriage is ideal and worthy of envy, for such a union is beautiful. (xii a, 17–23, 88)

The element of love is the only aspect of marriage to which Musonius accords significant detail; married love is elevated above all others in a lengthy comparison of relationships, including brothers, friends and children. He concludes that marriage is unlike any other affection in its union of body, soul and possessions.[131] Musonius illustrates the supremacy of married love[132] by means of a familiar story, which, interestingly, bears similarities to the Ephesian HT understanding of married love, as seen in the instruction to the husbands. Musonius recounts the tale of Admetus and his young wife, Alcestis.[133] Admetus, by obtaining favour from the gods, had the privilege of living two life-spans. The dramatic proviso of this grant was that someone else must die in his place. His parents, though old, were unwilling to do so. It was his young wife, Alcestis, who gladly accepted death in her husband's stead, ἐδέξατα ἑτοίμως τὸν θάνατον πρὸ τοῦ ἀνδρός. In similar manner to the Ephesian HT reference to Christ, Musonius makes use of a familiar and moving human event to lend substance to the nature of sacrificial, married love. Its highest expression is found, as with the instruction to the husbands in Eph. 5:25, in the self-sacrifice of the marriage partner.

Conclusion

Musonius reflects a tendency in later philosophical treatments of household relations to abandon a systematic approach of regulation in terms of a political scheme or ontological category. He relies, however, on the vocabulary of earlier discussions, and employs these concepts with innovative results. In the slave-master relationship, for instance, he appropriates the language of propriety and justice, yet does not define them; his observations are limited to behaviour only. Similarly, in the parent-child relationship, he follows the traditional call to total child obedience, yet mediates this mandate by means of an appeal to the laws of Zeus. In both relationships, Musonius demon-

---

[131] Musonius, xiv, 8–9, 94.

[132] In contrast to the HT, the wife is the member who embodies love in his illustration; the context, however, implies that both members should share this characteristic.

[133] As found in Euripides' *Alcestis*, 328–342.

strates familiarity with philosophical discussion, yet remains pragmatic in his approach. Both his concerns and behavioural approach resemble the tenor of the HT. It is in the husband-wife relationship, however, where he displays the greatest innovation and detail, as well as similarities with the HT. His use of κατὰ φύσιν, clearly extricated from earlier discussions of human onto-logical makeup, is generalised to refer to the institution of marriage. It is the will of Zeus, accordingly, which has established the marriage bond (he him-self existing in marriage), making it central to the welfare of household and state. This reasoning resembles the divine sanction apportioned to marriage in Eph., and offers a parallel to the model of divine example found in the Eph. HT. Musonius expands his instruction regarding the marriage union with a strong emphasis upon parity and reciprocity. Though this particular emphasis cannot be construed as being central to the HT reasoning, Mu-sonius' understanding of its execution certainly is: the clear call for mutual love and co-operation corresponds closely with the tenor of the Eph. HT in-struction. In particular, the ideal of self-sacrificial love within marriage pre-sents us with a strikingly similar aspect of the Eph. HT sacrifice-model and motivation.

Contemporary Treatments: Plutarch

Plutarch's *Moralia* represents a late first century attempt to distil a large body of ancient philosophical reflection[134] into a broad collection of practical treatises. Among the many topics discussed in the *Moralia*, societal and household relationships find mention in his treatise, *De Liberis Educandis*. Philosophy stands, for Plutarch, as the "head and font" of all education, a discipline without which it is impossible to discern the good from the shame-ful, the just from the unjust. It provides the framework, he says, for:

> …how a man must bear himself in his relations with the gods, with his parents, with his elders, with the laws, with strangers, with those in authority, with friends, with women, with children, with servants; that one ought to reverence the gods, to hon-

---

[134] Plutarch is eclectic in his approach; in *Con. Praec.*, 48, he outlines a programme of study to aid the couple in forming their relationship: "I beg you that you beautify your character with the aid of discourses which are attended by logical demonstration and mature delibera-tion, seeking the company and instruction of teachers who will help you. And for your wife you must collect from every source what is useful…and carrying it within your own self im-part it to her, and then discuss it with her, and make the best of these doctrines her favourite and familiar themes."

our one's parents (τιμᾶν), to respect one's elders, to be obedient to the laws, to
yield to those in authority, to love one's friends, to be chaste with women, to be af-
fectionate with children, and not to be overbearing with slaves; (*Moralia, De Liberis
Educandis* 10)

Though Plutarch mentions the three household pairs among the relationships
governed by philosophical reflection, it is remarkable that he does not develop a full treatment of the parent-child and master-slave relationships, either here or elsewhere in the *Moralia*. Instead, we find Plutarch concentrat-
ing solely upon the marriage relation in his treatise, *Coniugalia Praecepta*.

Husbands and Wives

The first impression the reader receives when reading the *Moralia*, and in
particular his treatise *Coniugalia Praecepta*, is that Plutarch lacks the analytical rigour of Plato and Aristotle. The instruction is not based upon stated
ontological presuppositions rooted in nature, nor does it attempt to establish
a general principle of rule. The absence of dramatic dialogue seen in Plato
removes the element of philosophical contention (normally regarding the
ideal state and how can it be justly and efficiently managed), and strengthens
the impression that Plutarch's concern lies firmly within the limits of the
husband-wife relationship. What we find in *Coniugalia Praecepta* is much
more akin to monologue or the personal letter format surrounding the HT;
indeed, Plutarch makes use of the latter literary device in addressing his treatise to a young couple, Pollianus and Eurydice. Discussion of the household
theory, therefore, is minimal; economic concerns give way in Plutarch to the
personal, relational dynamics of the husband-wife relationship. This relational emphasis is common to the HT instruction, and gives rise to other
common features. The admonitions given to the couple, for instance, share
the HT characteristic of direct address, and even more importantly, the address is distinguished by including *both* members of the relational pair. At
this point Plutarch can be held in contrast to earlier, unilateral treatments of
the husband-wife relationship, while demonstrating distinctive similarities to
the HT instruction. These, of course, are formal similarities; a closer investigation of *Coniugalia Praecepta* is necessary to determine if this contemporary treatise betrays more significant coincidence with the HT.

Though Plutarch does not enjoin ontological argument to establish hierarchy and duties within the husband-wife relationship, he envisions a stratified relationship, nonetheless. The man is characterised as the ruler, the
woman as the obedient member. Deviation from this ideal is deemed im-

proper, and an indication of relational incongruity; either one finds women ruling over fools, or weak men attempting to rule over women of stature. The former, a marriage in which the woman has usurped rule by clever means, is likened to a catch of fish, which, having been landed by the introduction of poison, is useless to all.[135] The latter scenario, the exceptional marriage of a high-born woman to a common man (encountered in Plato and Aristotle), is equally distasteful for Plutarch; his rejection of the reversal of marriage roles is evident in the following citations:[136]

> Women who prefer to have power (κρατεῖν) over fools rather than hearken (ἀκούειν) to sensible men, are like persons who prefer to guide the blind on the road rather than follow persons of knowledge and insight. (*Con. Praec.*, 6)

> Men who through weakness or effeminacy are unable to vault upon their horses teach the horses to kneel of themselves and crouch down. In like manner, some who have won wives of noble birth or wealth, instead of making themselves better, try to humble their wives, with the idea that they shall have more authority (ὡς μᾶλλον ἄρξοντες) over their wives if these are reduced to a state of humility. (*Con. Praec.*, 8)

Having discussed inappropriate manifestations of the husband-wife relationship, Plutarch describes to the reader an ideal marriage characterised by a combination of submission and rule. He dedicates most of his discussion to the errant behaviour of the wives, however,[137] demonstrating a strong prejudice towards securing the rule and welfare of the husband. This particular feature of Plutarch's instruction is at odds with the balance found in the HT commands. In spite of this imbalance, his summary of the husband-wife roles in *Con. Praec.* reflects an understanding of marriage as a complementary joining of submission and benevolent rule. Plutarch once again relies upon contrasting, inappropriate behaviour to illustrate his point; here the instruction to the *husbands* finds its fullest expression within the treatise, and, being

---

[135] *Con. Praec.*, 5. Such wives, employing either magic spells or their fleshly charms, find themselves "the consorts of dull-witted, degenerate fools."

[136] See also *Moralia, Amatorius*, 174, where Plutarch contrasts unbalanced relationships. Ideally, the man rules and enjoys honour, without diminishing or dominating the wife, τιμώμενα καὶ πρατοῦντες μετ᾽ εὐνοίας.

[137] Plutarch concentrates on the potential failings of the wife, including peevishness, impatience, moodiness, jealousy, as well as untoward conduct towards husbands and in public affairs, among others. Instruction countering shows of outward adornment or the immodesty of self-exposure through public appearance or speech *Con. Praec.* 26, 30–31 reveals similarities to the vocabulary found in 1 Peter 3:3–4 and 1 Tim. 2:9–11.

more extensive than the woman's instruction, represents an important exception to our previous observation. The language offers a number of interesting parallels with the HT mandates, as well, *Con. Praec.*, 33:

> So it is with women also; if they subordinate themselves to their husbands (ὑποτάττουσαι[138] μὲν γὰρ ἑαυτὰς τοῖς ἀνδράσιν), they are commended, but if they want to have control (κρατεῖν δὲ βουλόμεναι μᾶλλον τῶν κρατουμένων), they cut a sorrier figure than the subjects of their control. And control ought to be exercised by the man over the woman (κρατεῖν δὲ δεῖ τὸν ἄνδρα τῆς γυναικός), not as the owner (οὐχ ὡς δεσπότην κτήματος) has control of a piece of property, but as the soul controls the body, by entering into her feelings and being knit to her through goodwill (ἀλλ᾽ ὡς ψυχὴν σώματος, συμπαθοῦντα καὶ συμπεφυκότα τῇ εὐνοίᾳ). As, therefore, it is possible to exercise care over the body (σώματος ἔστι κήδεσθαι) without being a slave to its pleasures and desires, so it is possible to govern (ἄρχειν) a wife, and at the same time delight and gratify her.

This brief instruction reveals several similarities to the HT form. Plutarch addresses, first of all, the husband and wife in coincidental order with the HT. Both members receive instruction which is complementary in nature, and which conveys appropriate and reciprocal behaviours. The instruction to the women, further, is similarly characterised by its comparative brevity to that given to the men. More significant, however, is the literary form which frames Plutarch's instruction. Though this segment of instruction is expressed in the third person, the broader letter contains direct address as found in a personal letter; these admonitions are therefore *similar* in force to the direct address and command forms found in the HT. As with the HT, general admonitions become specific for each member; Plutarch characterises the nature of the husband-wife relationship, likewise, by means of its attendant duties. The author intends, as with the HT, that the addressees adopt the pattern of instruction given, in this case, the submission-rule dynamic.

While Plutarch's instruction demonstrates similarities to the HT mandates, it is missing an important element which we have observed in both New Testament and other manifestations of household instruction. Rule and submission are given as a critical starting point in construing the husband-wife relationship, though without significant introduction or reference to broader theory. Plutarch introduces no mediating principle for their employment, nor does he make an appeal to authority, other than the general witness

---

[138] This form derived from Attic, ὑποτάττω.

256

of philosophy, for their justification.[139] Plutarch's motivation resembles, then, neither the more systematic philosophers before him, nor the more contemporary HT, which contains the qualifying element of the *Begründungssatz*. The witness of philosophy, in all its varied manifestations, stands in contrast to the unifying and regulating rule of Christ in the New Testament HT.

Beyond similarities and differences in form, the content of Plutarch's summary provides interesting points of contrast and comparison to the HT mandates. His advice to the woman, for instance, consists of a positive-negative contrast between submission and desire for control; this contrasting element is missing in the HT instruction to the woman, though it is notably present elsewhere throughout the HT.[140] The HT instruction to the women consists exclusively of positive commands, including submission (Col. 3:18; Eph. 5:22, 24) and fear (Eph. 5:33b). The positive element of Plutarch's instruction, however, reveals a striking similarity: the expected behaviour of the woman contains the identical verb, ὑποτάσσω. This is a particularly interesting connection, since this is a rare example in non-Christian Greek literature of ὑποτάσσω being used to describe the woman's posture towards the man.[141] The verbal coincidence of ὑποτάσσω is even more remarkable in that it is employed at a point in the essay where Plutarch is summarising the fundamental nature of the husband-wife relationship, in similar manner to the contemporary HT. The question must then be asked if this verbal coincidence and summarising function indicate a similar understanding of the husband-wife relationship vis-à-vis the HT mandates. Much like the HT instruction found in Ephesians, Plutarch's understanding of the husband-wife relationship is more fully explicated in the instruction to the man, and it is here that we find an answer.

In similar form to the NT household code, more attention is directed towards the man's duties in Plutarch's summary in *Con. Praec.*, 33 (which is, as noted above, a departure from the broader tendency of the treatise). In par-

---

[139] He cites examples of philosophers who support his contentions in theory and deed, as well as making good use of legendary and historical figures, i.e., Theano, *Con. Praec.*, 48.

[140] Men's potentially negative behaviour serves as contrast in the HT husband-wife instruction (Col. 3:19; Eph. 5:29); similarly, in the instruction to parents and children, it is the men who are warned against negative behaviour (Col. 3:21; Eph. 6:4). In the slave-master relationship, both slave (Col. 3:22, 23, 25; Eph. 6:6, 7) and master (Col. 3:25; Eph. 6:9) are warned of inappropriate, negative behaviour.

[141] The other known instance is Ps. Callisthenes, *Hist. Alex. Magni* i. 22.4. In most instances, also elsewhere in Plutarch, the woman is called upon to obey (ὑπακούειν) the man.

ticular, both the HT and Plutarch illustrate the correct behaviour of the man by means of contrasting desirable/undesirable behaviours. Plutarch contrasts the normal use of rule (κρατεῖν) with its abuse, despotic ownership (οὐχ ὡς δεσπότην κτήματος). Likewise, the HT contrasts the command to love (ἀγαπᾶτε τὰς γυναῖκας, Col.3:19; Eph.5:25) with bitterness (μὴ πικραίνεσθεπρὸς αὐτάς, Col. 3:19) and hatred (τὴν ἑαυτοῦ σάρκα ἐμίσησεν, Eph. 5:29). The similarity between the two forms draws attention to their most visible contrast, however: the husbands, though similarly enjoying the submissive posture of their wives, are called to a dissimilar primary duty. Although both household codes envision a stratified husband-wife relationship, the HT command to love (ἀγαπᾶτε) is a requirement of the man unique[142] to the HT; it cannot be logically construed to fully correspond to rule (κρατεῖν). Both Plutarch and the HT are similarly and genuinely concerned with promoting equitable husband-wife relationships as well as the establishment of authority; yet Plutarch adopts, at least at the formal level, the classical approach of understanding the relationship primarily in terms of rule. The HT, in contrast, reflects the broader theological tendencies of the larger letters, which promote the benevolent, loving rule of Christ in all relations. It is the person of Christ who establishes and mediates all relations, as well as providing an ethical model of the HT. It appears that the christological emphasis of the HT lies at the root of this very significant difference.

Though Plutarch's instruction to the husband is characterised by rule, it must be added that this rule is depicted in a humane and sympathetic manner. His extended admonition to the husband reveals several features which bear remarkable similarities to the instruction to the husbands found in the Ephesian HT, and reveal the common concern to establish the husband-wife relationship through a *differentiated* understanding of rule. This Plutarch achieves by means of an emphasis upon the *unity* found in the marriage bond. The *Coniugalia Praecepta* are full of references which insist that the couple be bound in a life of common goals and duties, although leadership rests, ultimately, with the man.[143] The marital bond is understood as a coop-

---

[142] Wives, however, are expected to fear and love their husbands (φοβηθῆμε καὶ ἀγαπάζαι τὸν αὐταυτᾶς ἄνδρα) in Callicratidas, "Περὶ οἴκου εὐδαμονίας", Stob. *Anth.*, iv.28.16–18. Berger, *ANRW*, 26.2, 1086, cites possible correspondence between Eph. 5:25–33 (ἀγαπᾶν, ἐκτρέφει καὶ θάλει) and Sosiades, Stob. *Anth.*, iii.1.173, where husbands are to care for their wives, Οὓς τρέφεις ἀγάπα.

[143] Terms such as common life, harmony and concord characterise living together (συμβίωσιν), and dominate the language of the introduction and first section; Plutarch sums up in *Con. Praec.*, 11: "Whenever two notes are sounded in accord the tune is carried by the

258

erative and interdependent association, characterised by reciprocity and gentle care; the idea of union is depicted, further, in somatic terms.[144] These concerns and language are especially evident in Plutarch's summary of the husband-wife relationship in *Con. Praec.*, 33. The elements of the husband's responsibility share several features with the HT admonitions in Ephesians: Firstly, both sets of instruction include negative, contrasting behaviours which are intended to highlight appropriate marital conduct. In Plutarch, the husband's control is contrasted with that exercised over inanimate property; the contrast is categorical, and draws attention to the uniqueness of the marriage relation. In Colossians and Ephesians, the undesirable behaviours of bitterness or hatred are associated with, and emphasise, the realm of marital relations. Both contrasts, however, serve to enhance the critical nature of the attendant, positive material which follows. Further, Ephesians and Plutarch conclude their treatments of the husband-wife relationship with an authoritative affirmation of the intimate union found in marriage. Both authors, interestingly, choose to liken this union to the body. In Ephesians, the author cites Gen. 2:24, καὶ ἔσονται οἱ δύο εἰς σάρκα μίαν to authenticate the reality of union between husband and wife, as well as between Christ and the church. Plutarch makes a similar observation, yet supports his contention with other traditional material. He cites the reflections of the philosophers, which for him constitute a similar authority to the scriptures:

> Philosophers say of bodies (σωμάτων) that some are composed of separate elements, as a fleet or an army, others of elements joined together, as a house or a ship, and still others form together an intimate union (συμφυής), as in the case of every living creature. In about the same way, the marriage of a couple in love with each other is an intimate union. (*Con. Praec.*, 34)

By employing somatic language to express the intimate nature of the marriage union, it serves as a model for illustrating the desired behaviour of the

---

bass; and in like manner every activity in a virtuous household is carried on by both parties in agreement, but discloses the husband's leadership and preferences." See also *Moralia, Amatorius*, 769a, where physical union is characterised as the beginning of friendship, as the sharing of great mysteries [ὥσπερ ἱερῶν μεγάλων κοινωνήματα].

[144] In marriage, Plutarch argues, the bond is so intimate, that individual self-interest should be excluded; he takes his example from science: "...physicians tell us that blows to the left side of the body record the sensation on the right side, so in the same way, it is a lovely thing for the wife to sympathise with her husband's concerns and the husband with the wife's, so that each, as ropes, being intertwined, get strength from eachother, thus, by the due contribution of goodwill in corresponding measure by each member, the partnership (κοινωνία) may be preserved by the joint action of both."

husband, as well. In Ephesians, intimacy and responsibility are implicated as the husbands are admonished to love their wives as their own bodies (ὡς τὰ ἑαυτῶν σώματα, 5:28). The woman's interests, well-being and vitality are closely connected to the husband's own welfare (ὁ ἀγαπῶν ἑαυτοῦ γυναῖκα ἑαυτὸν ἀγαπᾷ, 5:28b). In similar manner, Plutarch conjoins the welfare of husband and wife by designating to them complementary portions of a single human being in *Con. Praec.*, 33. The husband is considered to be the soul of the union, the woman the body; his control over her follows the normal human relation of the soul to the body (ὡς ψυχὴν σώματος). The manner in which the soul [husband] is to control the body [wife] is wholly positive and humane: "by entering into her feelings and being knit to her through goodwill" (συμπαθοῦντα καὶ συμπεφυκότα τῇ εὐνοίᾳ). If the husband's exercise of care does not degenerate into a servile expression of the body's (wife's) needs (ὥσπερ οὖν σώματος ἐστι κηδεσθαι μὴ δουλεύοντα ταῖς ἡδοναῖς αὐτοῦ καὶ ταῖς ἐπιθυμίαις), his rule will serve to "delight and gratify her" (οὔπω γυναικὸς ἄρχειν εὐφραίνοντα καὶ χαριζόμενον). Plutarch's instruction, placed in contrast to despotic ownership and punctuated with ἀλλ', resembles the tone of the HT instruction in Ephesians 5:29: Οὐδεὶς γάρ ποτε τὴν ἑαυτοῦ σάρκα ἐμίσησεν ἀλλὰ ἐκτρέφει καὶ θάλπει αὐτήν. The HT emphasis is equally upon the welfare of the wife, yet the wife's association with the husband is made even more direct and intimate. There is no bifurcation of the marriage union into body and soul; the husband is not disassociated from the wife, but characterised as sharing the same essence of flesh and self (Eph. 5:28). The result is clear: the husband is to love the wife as himself (Eph. 5:33a). Though the tenor of the two authors is similar, the HT joins the welfare of husband and wife in a more intimate, direct manner. To this observation it should be noted that the HT modifies the somatic imagery by introducing the person of Christ in Ephesians 5:29b. The care of the husbands for the wives (ἐκτρέφει καὶ θάλπει) is to be modelled after the example of Christ and the church, καθὼς καὶ ὁ Χριστὸς τὴν ἐκκλησίαν. The spiritual, mediating influence of Christ is thereby introduced to the somatic ethical model. It is Christ, then, who ultimately determines the appropriate behaviour of the husband towards the wife.

Conclusion

Plutarch's regulation of the household relations provides one of the most detailed analyses of the husband-wife pair contemporary to the New Testament HT. His eclectic approach to traditional material avoids the systematic divisions of earlier authors, as well as their reliance upon an authoritative point of ethical reference. His observations are given in the context of direct address, which makes them both personal and immediate. These features of his treatment facilitate a tone and behavioural aspect which resemble the HT. In particular, his admonitions rely upon negative examples to highlight the desired behaviour, and are given to both members in turn. The desired behaviour is, notably, similar in content and tone to the HT, especially with its emphasis upon unity, submission and love. Though Plutarch understands the husband's role in terms of rule, his sympathetic advice, replete with somatic metaphors and calls to gentle care, approaches the HT understanding of love, and stands as testimony to a non-Christian marriage regulation of remarkable depth and sensitivity.

Conclusion

From our analysis of ancient and first century treatments of household relations, several broad observations can be made. Firstly, there appears to be a discernible progression, however uneven, in the development of household regulation. The earlier attempts to substantiate the household regulation by means of ontological categories or a political schema have been largely abandoned by the first century. In its place we find an emphasis upon reciprocal behaviour, with references to justice and mutual benefit. It appears that these elements, found in the weave of the earlier discussions, have been distilled from their systematic frameworks by the later authors.

In spite of this general development towards de-systematisation of household regulations, the various thinkers tend to display an otherwise surprising degree of independence of thought, which interrupts any notion of *seamless* progression. There is neither a consensus of thought which might be attributed to either period (cf. the significant differences in slave ontology and regulation in Plato and Aristotle), nor can it be said that individual authors necessarily evidence uniformity in their concerns and manner of regulation (cf. Philo). The picture of household regulation which develops is one of immense complexity. Various elements of the discussion, including political intention, ontological assumptions, general principles and traditions, when present, create significant differences in the outcome of the regulation. For this reason it would be difficult, if not impossible, to attribute elements of the New Testament household code to a particular author, context or period. Instead, it seems more probable that the HT authors were familiar with the broad brush-strokes of the contemporary discussion, which likely exercised a certain level of influence.

The extent of borrowing, and points at which the New Testament HT *has* been influenced by the Hellenistic authors is, then, difficult to ascertain. From our discussion, it has become apparent that numerous elements of the Hellenistic treatments of the household have no counterpart in the HT regulation, or more, were in conflict with its ethic and reasoning. Similarly, certain aspects of the HT had currency in Hellenistic and Jewish thought, be it the principle of justice, the concept of reciprocity, divine supervision or any number of coincidences in thought and vocabulary discussed above. The HT could conceivably be, as some have maintained, a borrowing of numerous elements of the contemporary, regulatory posture. The question arises, then, to what degree might the HT be understood as uniquely Christian? The formal characteristics of the HT outlined in chapter one[145] suggest that the HT is indeed a parenetic form which had no direct parallel, yet these elements, of themselves, do not convey a particular Christian meaning. The answer must lie elsewhere.

Our thesis has maintained that the central impulses of the HT, and ultimately its regulation, are dependent upon, and related to, the theological message of the respective letter. The expanded sections in both the Col. and Eph. HT were shown to evidence affinities with the theology of their respective letters. This aspect of the HT is not substantially different, it must be granted, to theological regulation such as divine justice in other, Hellenistic, authors. The uniquely Christian element of the HT is not, then, its supervision by the divine offices of Christ (though this is both prominent and essential). It lies, rather, in the nature of his person (as appertained in the events of salvation: his incarnation, suffering, resurrection and pending return in glory and judgement) and the believer's intimate union with him. The New Testament HT and their regulation cannot be understood as uniquely Christian without the mediation of Christ, and all that this may imply. Each household relationship, then, is construed in reference to Christ and his work in the church. Elements such as sacrificial love and divine retribution differ from their Hellenistic counterparts only insofar as they are *Christ's* love and *Christ's* justice. The Christian HT does not introduce unheard of principles to the regulation of the household, as we have seen. It only introduces Christ.

---

[145] These characteristics, tabulated by Gielen, *Tradition*, 3f., are as follows: a closed parenetic unit which stands out from its context; subjects which are addressed in pairs and sequentially; relationships characterised by superordination/subordination; subordination is the cohesive theme of the unit; the subordinated party is addressed first; direct address is employed with definite article and nominative plural; the address is followed by imperative admonition; the admonition is followed by an explanation (*Begründungssatz*).

Far from being an unflattering estimation of the church's contribution to household regulation, its simplicity may hold the key to understanding the thorny aspects of HT instruction. The common matters of obedience, love, submission and honour might, perhaps, find their Christian meaning and *Verwertbarkeit* to the degree in which they are Christ's.

Conclusion

We began our study by asking "What's in a name?", with the observation that the New Testament household codes, having been identified as a cohesive parenetic unit, had received treatment as a discrete literary phenomenon within their larger letter contexts. The scholarly scrutiny devoted to the HT form has led to the demarcation of the household code as a genre, evidencing a number of characteristics unique to its New Testament expression. A survey of form-critical investigations regarding its provenance and adoption as Christian parenesis illustrated the remarkable diversity of opinion regarding the HT's original form and function. The location of this traditional *Urtafel*, however, whether conceived as Christian catechism, Jewish tradition or Hellenistic economic theory, was shown to be unanimous: it lies somewhere *outside* of the composition and concerns of the New Testament text. The HT, then, as we find it in Colossian and Ephesians, has been regarded as a profane or lightly christianised import; any connection to the style and theological concerns of the larger letter has been assumed to be insignificant. The resultant isolation from its New Testament context has led, inadvertently, to the disenfranchisement of the HT as a vehicle of genuine Christian ethics. Without diminishing the importance of form-critical findings, this result is quite likely due, in part, to the methodological limitations of diachronic analysis. In concert with the tendency of form-critical studies to isolate the HT from its context, the nature of the admonitions present further difficulty. The HT commands requiring obedience and submission appear to be out of step with our times and certain declarations of Scripture, and are, perhaps, fundamentally inconsonant with the Christian faith. A palpable undercurrent of discomfort with the HT message is easily recognised in many studies. Our study, then, has considered two aspects of the HT and its regulation: it is an attempt, firstly, to augment the form-critical investigations of the last century by ascertaining to what degree, if any, the HT intentionally promotes the theological and ethical perspective of the respective letter. Secondly, if the HT can be shown to evidence theological impulses within its mandates, we hope to isolate any uniquely Christian elements of their regulation and motivation.

In order to establish a relationship between the HT form and the broader letter, we undertook a thorough investigation of the theology of Colossians and Ephesians. Each treatment included an analysis of the extraordinary features of the respective letter's household code. Particular attention was given to the expanded material in each HT, under the assumption that the expansion represented the most developed expression of the author's ethical reasoning. In both instances, we found coincidence in the theological concerns and vocabulary of the larger letter. In chapter two, we began with an analysis of Colossians. The letter's emphasis upon Christ's universal dominion was shown to regulate human behaviour. Expressed in terms of his matchless power, this dominion was shown to have its focal point in the process of redemption. The believer, rescued and reconstituted in terms of Christ's redemptive work, now serves a new, heavenly master. A heavenly-earthly axis, servant-master, is established. By means of a series of soteriological movements, the author joins the reality of Christ's achievements to the believers' lives and ethics, bringing the effects of the vertical relationship to bear upon horizontal behaviour. The last of these soteriological events, Christ's return in glory and judgement, precedes the instruction contained in the HT; we found that the expanded instruction to the slaves and masters derives its motivation and regulation from the eschatological hope embodied in Christ's expected appearing. The instruction to the slave and masters also demonstrated an affinity with the tenor of the broader letter, particularly the view of the believer as a servant of Christ. This, combined with the coming of Christ in glory and judgement, established an uniquely Christian aspect for the regulation of the slave-master relationship. It is Christ himself, we concluded, who modulates the relationships of the HT with a surprising level of authority, fulfilling his roles as generous redeemer, Lord over all relations, and the coming judge.

Chapter three investigated the literary relationship between Colossians and Ephesians, with particular attention given to the HT form. Here we attempted to demonstrate that the letter of Ephesians is dependent upon the Colossian *Vorlage*, while highlighting the remarkable independence of thought in his adaptation of the original material. In the HT, the largest segment of coincidental material between the letters, we noted numerous modifications, which suggested intentional theological reflection. The largest expansion, found in the instruction to husband and wife, appeared to us to be central to the author's regulation of household relations. Here the author demonstrated the highest degree of independence and creativity. If our thesis is correct, we argued, it would be this segment of the HT which would display the closest relationship to the theology of the letter.

In chapter four, Ephesians was analysed in similar manner to Colossians. We set out to determine the central theological themes of the letter, with the intention of tracing them, if present, in the Ephesian HT. As anticipated, the redaction of the Colossian material brought with it numerous changes, especially in theological perspective. We noted several stylistic features employed by the author, which found expression in the HT, as well. More important, however, was the new perspective which the author of Ephesians developed. The vertical axis which regulated the Colossian ethical instruction, influenced by the eschatological force of Christ's judgement, underwent a significant shift from lord-servant to Christ-church. Though appearing as a slight change, it corresponds to a general, present-oriented ecclesiastical emphasis found in Ephesians. It is precisely this ecclesiastical emphasis which finds strong representation within the husband-wife instruction of the HT. Christ is depicted in relation to the church, a relationship which in turn becomes the idealised pattern of human relations. The instruction to man and wife is intertwined with the ecclesiastical motif to such a degree, that the use of analogy becomes, at points, unclear; we found that the HT served as human regulation *and* theological instruction regarding the church. This subtle use of analogy enables the author of Ephesians to introduce a profound degree of theological reasoning in his HT form, particularly the mediation of love in divine and human relations. As with Colossians, the motivation and regulation of the HT relations are superintended by the person of Christ; here the focus falls upon his role as redeemer, while his present relationship with God as the beloved, and the church as her bridegroom, serve as exemplar of relationships characterised by love.

Our last chapter returned to the form-critical discussion. Here we selected six significant Hellenistic texts which deal with household relationships. Our intention was to offer a comparison of the reasoning and motivation behind these texts and the HT, a feature absent in previous studies. We found that the HT cannot be assigned to any particular period or author; the evidence suggests an uneven development of ideas. The similarities and differences between the various forms were equally stark. The HT, though displaying undeniably unique features in form, was shown to share numerous *concerns* of the Hellenistic authors' regulation. Particular aspects of its message, including reciprocity, submission, justice, honour, divine retribution and love can be found attested among the Hellenistic thinkers. The singular aspect of its reasoning and motivation, however, which may be isolated as uniquely Christian, is the person of Christ. This finding underscores the importance of the HT's manner of regulation, which is dependent upon the mediation of Christ in all relations. The person of Christ represents both the central and unique element of the HT ethic.

Our study, being necessarily limited in scope, leaves several interesting and important aspects of the New Testament HT development and message unanswered. How has the HT developed in its related forms (including *Gemeinetafeln* and *Ständetafeln*) within the canon and the Apostolic Fathers? Does the reasoning, motivation and authority structure (i.e., Christ) remain the same? Is there a relationship between the theology of these related parenetic forms and that of the larger letter? The HT in 1 Peter, for instance, seems to indicate this possibility; the HT form is coloured by the letter's concerns regarding suffering and the apologetic benefits of just living. It appears that this would be a fruitful extension of our study.

Although we have found that the HT found in Colossians and Ephesians do indeed find their theological reasoning in the broader letter, we have not attempted to suggest ways in which the mandates of the HT can be (if at all) extricated from the unpopular reputation they have garnered in our modern time. Certainly it has become apparent from our study that the commands find a significant amount of regulation via the mediation of Christ; the interpretation and execution of the HT commands *must* incorporate this modifying element. Any conception of obedience, for example, which is known to be dissonant with Christ's character, would be objectionable. For this reason, criticism aimed at the HT ethic, which suggests unsavoury motivation or cruel excesses, can be rejected, it seems, as being inconsistent with its essential message. Another help for understanding may be in the intimate identification of Christ found in the HT commands. The obedience, love, submission and honour to be rendered are all modified in terms of Christ. Without dodging the implications of these weighty imperatives, it may be possible and legitimate to find a less "offensive" understanding of them as *Christ's* love, submission, etc. If the identification and union of the believer with Christ is indeed as complete as our analysis has shown, any independent understanding of these terms would, it seems, be inappropriate, and contrary to the HT ethic. In the end, it appears that the *Haustafeln* cannot be rightly understood (or executed) without an informed application of the letter's theology; in both the Colossian and Ephesian examples, we have found this to be the centrality of Christ as the unique mediator of the divine and human axes.

Bibliography

Lexical and Grammatical Works

Bauer, W. *A Greek-English Lexicon of the New Testament and Other Early Christian Literature*. Trans. W.F. Arndt and F.W. Gingrich. 2nd ed., Rev. F.W. Gingrich and F. Danker. Chicago: University of Chicago, 1979.

Balz, H. and Schneider, G., eds. *Exegetical Dictionary of the New Testament*. Grand Rapids: Eerdmans, 1990–1993.

Blass, F. and Debrunner, A. *A Greek Grammar of the New Testament and Other Early Christian Literature*. Trans. R.W. Funk. Cambridge: CUP, 1961.

Blass, F. and Debrunner, A., rev. F. Rehkopf. *Grammatik des neutestamentlichen Griechisch*. 15th ed. Göttingen: Vandenhoeck & Ruprecht, 1979.

Kittel, G. and Friedrich, G., eds. *Theological Dictionary of the New Testament*. Grand Rapids: Eerdmans, 1964–1976.

Klauser, T., ed. *Reallexikon für Antike und Christentum*. Stuttgart: Anton Hiersemann, 1959.

Kohlenberger III, J.R., Goodrick, E.W. and Swanson, J.A., eds. *The Exhaustive Concordance of the Greek New Testament*. Grand Rapids: Zondervan, 1995.

Louw, E.A. Nida, J.P., et al., eds. *Greek-English Lexicon of the New Testament Based on Semantic Domains*. New York: United Bible Societies, 1989.

Metzger, Bruce. *A Textual Commentary on the Greek New Testament*. Stuttgart: United Bible Societies, 1975.

Robertson, J.A.T. *A Grammar of the Greek New Testament in Light of Historical Research*. 4th ed. Nashville: Broadman, 1934.

Strack, H.L. and Billerbeck, P. *Kommentar zum Neuen Testament aus Talmud und Midrasch*. 8th ed. München: C.H. Beck'sche Verlagsbuchhandlung, 1982.

Texts and Translations

Aristotle. *Nicomachean Ethics*. Trans. H. Rackham. LCL, London: William Heinemann, 1962.

Aristotle. *Politics*. Vol. 21 Trans. H. Rackham. LCL. London: William Heinemann, 1977.

Aristotle, (Pseudo). *Oeconomica*. Vol. II Trans. G.C. Armstrong. LCL. London: William Heinemann, 1935.

Cicero. *De Officiis: On Moral Obligation*. Trans. John Higginbotham. London: Faber and Faber, Ltd., 1967.

Diogenes Laertius, 2 Vols. Trans. R.D. Hicks. LCL. London: William Heinemann, 1925.

Dionysius of Halicarnassus. *Roman Antiquities*. 7 Vols. Trans. E. Cary. LCL. London: William Heinemann, 1938.

Epictetus. *Discourses, Manuals and Fragments*. 2 Vols. Trans. W.A. Oldfather. LCL. London: Heinemann, 1928.

Eusebius. *Church History*. Vol. 1 Nicene and Post-Nicene Fathers, eds. H. Wace and P. Schaff. Oxford: Parker and Company, 1890.

Heinrichs, J. and Eck, W., eds. *Sklaven und Freigelassene in der Gesellschaft der römischen Kaiserzeit*. Vol. 61, Texte zur Forschung. Darmstadt: Wissenschaftliche Buchgesellschaft, 1993.

Horace. *Epistles*. In The Works of Horace. Trans. J. Connington. London: G. Bell and Sons, 1922.

Irenaeus. *Against Heresies*. Vol. 5 Ante-Nicene Christian Library, eds. A. Alexander and J. Donaldson. Edinburgh: T&T Clark, 1868.

Josephus. *Against Apion*. 2 Vols. Trans. J. Thackeray. LCL. London: Willian Heinemann, 1926.

Klein, L., ed. *Iamblichi: De Vita Pythagorica Liber*, Bibliotheca Scriptorum Graecorum et Romanorum Teubneriana. Stuttgart: B.G. Teubner, 1975.

Lake, K. *The Apostolic Fathers*. 2 Vols. LCL. London and Cambridge, MA: Harvard University Press, 1998.

Latyschev, Basilius, ed. *Inscriptiones Tyrae, Obliae, Chersonesi Tauricae, Aliorum Locorum a Danubio Usque ad Regnum Bosporum*. Vol. 1, Inscriptiones Antiquae, Orae Septentrionalis Ponti Euxini, Graecae et Latinae. Petropoli: Societatis Archaeologicae Imperii Russici, 1885.

Lutz, Cora E. *Musonius Rufus: "The Roman Socrates"*. Vol. 10 Yale Classical Studies, ed. G. Cumberledge. London: Oxford University Press, 1947.

Martínez, F.G. *The Dead Sea Scrolls Translated: The Qumran Texts in English*. Trans. W.G.E. Watson. 2nd ed. Leiden: E.J. Brill, 1996.

Nestle, Eberhard, Nestle, Erwin, Aland, K., et.al. *Novum Testamentum Graece*. Stuttgart: Deutsche Bibelgesellschaft, 1986.

Origen. *Contra Celsum*. Trans. and ed. Henry Chadwick. Cambridge: CUP, 1953.

Philo. 12 Vols. Trans. F.H. Colson, G.H. Whitaker, et. al. LCL. London: William Heinemann, 1929–1962.

Plato. 12 Vols. Trans. H.N. Fowler, et. al. LCL. London: William Heinemann, 1914–1927.

Pliny. *Epistulae English: The Letters of the Younger Pliny*. Trans. and ed. B. Radice. The Penguin Classics. Harmondsworth: Penguin, 1969.

Plutarch. *Moralia*. 17 Vols. Trans. F.C. Babbitt, et. al. LCL. London: William Heinemann, 1927–1976.

Polybius. *Histories*. Vol. 5 LCL. London: William Heinemann, 1927.

Pseudo-Phocylides. *Sentences*. In Pseudo-Phocylide, ed. Pascale Derron. Paris: Société D'Édition "Les Belles Lettres", 1986.

Rahlfs, A., ed. *Septuaginta*. Stuttgart: Deutsche Bibelgesellschaft, 1979.

Rufus, C. Musonius. *Reliquiae*. In Bibliotheca Scriptorum Graecorum et Romanorum, ed. O. Hense. Leipzig: B.G. Teubner, 1905.

Schaff, Philip. *The Oldest Church Manual, Called the Teaching of the Twelve Apostles, The Didache and Kindred Documents*. 2nd ed. New York: Funk & Wagnalls, 1886.

Seneca. *Moral Essays*. 3 Vols. Trans. J.W. Basore. LCL. London: William Heinemann, 1928–1935.

Städele, Alfons. *Die Briefe des Pythagoras und der Pythagoreer*. Vol. 115 Beiträge zur klassischen Philologie, eds. R. Merkelbach, C. Zintzen and E. Heitsch. Meisenheim: Anton Hain, 1980.

Thesleff, Holger. *The Pythagorean Texts of the Hellenistic Period*. Humaniora XXX.1 Acta Academiae Aboensis, Series A. Åbo: Åbo Akademi, 1965.

Wachsmuth, C. and Hense, O., eds. *Ioannis Stobaei. Anthologium*. 5 Vols. Berlin: Weidmann, 1958.

Tov, Emanuel, ed. *Discoveries in the Judaean Desert*. Oxford: Clarendon, 1961–2000.

Weinreich, Otto. *Stiftung und Kultsatzungen eines Privatheiligtums in Philadelphia in Lydien.* Vol. 10 Sitzungsberichte der Heidelberger Akademie der Wissenschaften, Philosophisch-Historische Klasse. Heidelberg: Carl Winters Universitätsbuchhandlung, 1919.

Wengst, Klaus, ed. *Didache (Apostellehre): Barnabasbrief, Zweiter Klemensbrief, Schrift an Diognet.* München: Kösel-Verlag, 1984.

Xenophon. *Memorabilia and Oeconomicus.* Trans. E.C. Merchant. LCL. London: William Heinemann, 1923.

Commentaries and Studies

Abbott, T.K. *A Critical and Exegetical Commentary on the Epistles to the Ephesians and to the Colossians.* Vol. 45 International Critical Commentary, eds. A. Plummer, S.R. Driver and C.A. Briggs. Edinburgh: T&T Clark, 1897.

Achtemeier, Paul J. "Omne verbum sonat: The New Testament and the Oral Environment of Late Western Antiquity." *JBL* 109 (1990): 3–27.

Ackrill, J.C. *Aristotle's Ethics.* London: Faber & Faber, 1973.

Aland, Kurt and Barbara. *Der Text des Neuen Testaments.* 2nd ed. Stuttgart: Deutsche Bibelgesellschaft, 1989.

Alkier, Stefan. *Urchristentum: Zur Geschichte und Theologie einer exegetischen Disziplin.* Vol. 83 Beiträge zur Historischen Theologie, ed. J. Wallmann. Tübingen: J.C.B. Mohr, 1990.

Annas, Julia. *An Introduction to Plato's Republic.* Oxford: Clarendon Press, 1981.

———. "Plato's Republic and Feminism." In *Plato*, ed. Gail Fine, 747–761. Oxford: Oxford University Press, 2000.

Arnold, C.E. *Ephesians: Power and Magic.* Vol. 63 Society for New Testament Studies Monograph Series, ed. G.N. Stanton. Cambridge: CUP, 1989.

———. *The Colossian Syncretism.* Vol. 77. 2nd ed. WUNT, eds. M. Hengel and O. Hofius. Tübingen: Mohr, 1995.

Aune, D. E., ed. *Greco-Roman Literature and the New Testament: Selected Forms and Genres.* Vol. 21, SBL: Sources of Biblical Study. Atlanta: Scholars Press, 1988.

Bacht, Herbert. "Einfalt." In *Reallexikon für Antike und Christentum*, ed. Theodor Klauser, Vol. 4, 821–840. Stuttgart: Anton Hiersemann, 1959.

Balch, David. "Household Codes." In *Greco-Roman Literature in the New Testament: Selected Forms and Genres*, ed. D.E. Aune, Vol. 21, 25–50. Atlanta: Scholars Press, 1988.

———. *Let Wives Be Submissive: The Domestic Code in I Peter.* Vol. 26 SBL Monograph Series, ed. James Crenshaw. Chico: Scholars Press, 1981.

———. "Neopythagorean Moralists and the New Testament Household Codes." In *ANRW*, ed. W. Haase and H. Temporini, 2.26.1, 380–411. Berlin: Walter De Gryter, 1992.

Baltensweiler, H. *Die Ehe im Neuen Testament.* Zürich: Zwingli Verlag, 1967.

Barclay, John M.G. *Colossians and Philemon.* New Testament Guides, ed. A.T. Lincoln. Sheffield: Sheffield Academic Press, 1997.

———. "Ordinary but Different: Colossians and Hidden Moral Identity." *Australian Biblical Review* 49 (2001): 34–52.

———. "Paul, Philemon and Christian Slave-ownership." *NTS* 37 (1991): 161–186.

Barnes, J., ed. *The Cambridge Companion to Aristotle.* Cambridge: CUP, 1995.

Bartchy, S. Scott. *ΜΑΛΛΟΝ ΧΡΗΣΑΙ: First-Century Slavery and the Interpretation of 1 Cor. 7:21.* Vol. 11 SBL Dissertation Series. Missoula: SBL, 1973.

270

Barth, M. *The Broken Wall: A Study of the Epistle to the Ephesians*. London: Collins, 1960.
———. *Ephesians*. 2 Vols. Anchor Bible, ed. R.E. Brown. Garden City: Doubleday, 1974.
———. "Traditions in Ephesians." *NTS* 30 (1984): 3–25.
——— and Becke, H. *Colossians: A New Translation with Introduction and Commentary*. Trans. A. Beck. Vol. 34B Anchor Bible Series. London: Doubleday, 1994.
Batey, R. "Jewish Gnosticism and the 'Heiros Gamos' of Eph. V. 21–33." *NTS* 10 (1963): 121–127.
———. "The mia sarx Union of Christ and the Church." *NTS* 13 (1967): 270–281.
———. *New Testament Nuptial Imagery*. Leiden: E.J. Brill, 1971.
Baumert, N. *Antifeminismus bei Paulus?* Vol. 68 Forschung zur Bibel, eds. R. Schnackenburg and J. Schreiner. Würzburg: Echter Verlag, 1992.
———. *Frau und Mann bei Paulus: Überwindung eines Mißverständnisses*. 2. Auflage. Würzburg: Echter Verlag, 1993.
Bedale, S. "The Meaning of κεφαλή in the Pauline Epistles." *JTS* 5 (1954): 211–215.
Bellen, H. *Studien zur Sklavenflucht im römischen Kaiserreich*. Vol. 4 Forschungen zur antiken Sklaverei, eds. J. Vogt and U. Instinsky. Wiesbaden: Franz Steiner, 1971.
Berger, Klaus. *Formgeschichte des Neuen Testaments*. Heidelberg: Quelle & Meyer, 1984.
———. "Hellenistische Gattungen im Neuen Testament." In *ANRW*, eds. Wolfgang Haase and Hildegard Temporini, 25.2, 1031–1432. Berlin: Walter de Gruyter, 1984.
———. "Zu den sogenannten Sätzen Heiligen Rechts." *NTS* 17 (1970–71): 10–40.
———. "Zum Traditionsgeschichtlichen Hintergrund Christologischer Hoheitstitel." *NTS* 17 (1970–71b): 391–425.
Bertram, G. "παιδεύω κτλ." In *TDNT*, eds. G. Kittel and G. Friedrich, 5, 596–625. Grand Rapids: Eerdmans, 1964.
Best, E. *A Critical and Exegetical Commentary on Ephesians*. The International Critical Commentary, eds. C.E.B. Cranfield, J.A. Emerton and G.N. Stanton. Edinburgh: T&T Clark, 1998.
———. *One Body in Christ*. London: S.P.C.K., 1955.
———. *Ephesians*. New Testament Guides. Sheffield: JSOT Press, 1993.
———. "Who Used Whom? The Relationship of Ephesians and Colossians." *NTS* 43 (1997): 72–96.
Betz, Hans Dieter, ed. *Plutarch's Theological Writings and Early Christian Literature*. Vol. 3, Studia ad Corpus Hellenisticum Novi Testamenti. Leiden: E.J. Brill, 1975.
Beyer, H.W. "διακονέω, διακονία, διάκονος." In *Theological Dictionary of the New Testament*, 2, 81–93. Grand Rapids: Eerdmans, 1964.
Bieberstein, Sabine. "Disrupting the Normal Reality of Slavery: A Feminist Reading of the Letter to Philemon." *JSNT* 79 (2000): 105–116.
Bockmuehl, Markus. *Jewish Law in Gentile Churches: Halakhah and the Beginning of Christian Public Ethics*. Edinburgh: T&T Clark, 2000.
Borgen, Peder. *Philo, John and Paul: New Perspectives on Judaism and Early Christianity*. Vol. 131 Brown Judaic Studies. Atlanta: Scholars Press, 1987.
Bornkamm, G. "Die Hoffnung im Kolosserbrief. Zugleich ein Beitrag zur Frage der Echtheit des Briefes." In *Studien zum Neuen Testament und Patristik*, 77, 56–64. Berlin: Academie, 1961.
Bosanquet, Bernard. *A Companion to Plato's Republic*. 2nd ed. London: Rivington, Parcival & Co., 1895.
Bouttier, Michel. *L'Épître de Saint Paul aux Éphésiens*. Vol. IXb Commentaire du Nouveau Testament, ed. J. Zumstein. Geneva: Labor et Fides, 1991.

Bradley, D.G. "The Origins of the Horatory Materials in the Letters of Paul." Dissertation, Yale University, 1947.

―――. "The Topos as a Form in Pauline Paraenesis." *Journal of Biblical Literature* 72 (1953): 238–246.

Brown, R.E. "The Semitic Background of the NT Mysterion, II." *Biblica* 40 (1959): 70–87.

Bruce, F.F. *The Epistles to the Colossians, to Philemon and to the Ephesians.* New International Commentary on the New Testament. Grand Rapids: Eerdmans, 1984.

Bujard, Walter. *Stilanalytische Untersuchungen zum Kolosserbrief als Beitrag zur Methodik von Sprachvergleichen.* Vol. 11 Studien zur Umwelt des Neuen Testaments, ed. H.G. Kuhn. Göttingen: Vandenhoeck & Ruprecht, 1972.

Bultmann, R. *Primitive Christianity in its Contemporary Setting.* New York: Meridian Publishing, 1956.

Butting, Klara. "Pauline Variations on Genesis 2:24: Speaking of the Body of Christ in the Context of the Discussion of Lifestyles." *JSNT* 79 (2000): 79–90.

Cadbury, H.J. "The Dilemma of Ephesians." *NTS* 5 (1958–59): 91–102.

Caird, G. B. *Paul's Letters from Prison.* New Clarendon Bible, ed. H.F.D. Sparks. Oxford: Oxford University Press, 1976.

Cameron, A. *Christianity and the Rhetoric of Empire: The Development of Christian Discourse.* Vol. 45 Sather Classical Lectures. Berkeley: University of California Press, 1991.

Cannon, G.E. *The Use of Traditional Materials in Colossians.* Macon: Mercer University Press, 1983.

Caragounis, C.C. *The Ephesian Mysterion: Meaning and Content.* Vol. 8 Coniectanea Biblica, New Testament Series, eds. L. Hartman, H. Riesenfeld and B. Gerhardsson. Lund: CWK Gleerup, 1977.

Carrington, P. *The Primitive Christian Catechism.* Cambridge: CUP, 1940.

Casey, R.P. "Gnosis, Gnosticism and the New Testament." In *The Background of the New Testament and Its Eschatology*, eds. W.D. Davies and D. Daube. Cambridge: CUP, 1956.

Clark, S.B. *Man and Woman in Christ: An Examination of the Roles of Men and Women in Light of Scripture and the Social Sciences.* Ann Arbor: Servant Books, 1980.

Clarke, Andrew. *Serve the Community of the Church: Christians as Leaders and Ministers.* First-Century Christians in the Graeco-Roman World, ed. A.D. Clarke. Grand Rapids/Cambridge: Eerdmans, 2000.

Coleman-Norton, P.R. *Roman State & Christian Church.* 3 Vols. London: SPCK, 1966.

Collins, J.N. *Diakonia: Re-interpreting the Ancient Sources.* Oxford: Oxford University Press, 1990.

Coutts, J. "Ephesians 1:3–4 and 1Peter 1:3–12." *NTS* 3 (1956–1957): 115–127.

―――. "The Relationship of Ephesians and Colossians." *NTS* 4 (1957–58): 201–207.

de Ste. Croix, G.E.M. "Early Christian Attitudes to Property and Slavery." In *Studies in Church History*, ed. D. Baker, 12, 1–38. Oxford: Blackwell, 1975.

Crombie, I.M. *An Examination of Plato's Doctrines.* Vol. 1. London: Routledge & Paul, 1962.

Crouch, J.E. *The Origin and Intention of the Colossian Haustafel.* Vol. 109 Forschungen zur Religion und Literatur des Alten und Neuen Testaments, eds. E. Käsemann and E. Würthwein. Göttingen: Vandenhoeck & Ruprecht, 1972.

Dahl, N.A. *Studies in Ephesians.* Vol. 131 WUNT, eds. M. Hengel and O. Hofius. Tübingen: Mohr Siebeck, 2000.

D'Angelo, M.R. "Colossians." In *Searching the Scriptures: A Feminist Commentary*, ed. E. Schüssler Fiorenza, Vol. 2, 313–324. New York: Crossroad Publishing, 1994.

Daube, D. "Haustafeln." In *The New Testament and Rabbinic Judaism*, Jordan Lectures in Comparative Religion, Vol. 2, 90–105. London: Athlone Press, 1956.

Dawes, G.W. *The Body in Question: Metaphor and Meaning in the Interpretation of Ephesians 5:21–33*. Vol. 30 Biblical Interpretation Series, eds. R.A. Culpepper and R. Rendtorff. Leiden: Brill, 1998.

Deichgräber, Reinhard. *Gotteshymnus und Christushymnus in der frühen Christenheit: Untersuchungen zur Form, Sprache und Stil der frühchristlichen Hymnen*. Vol. 5 Studien zur Umwelt des Neuen Testaments, ed. K.G. Kuhn. Göttingen: Vandenhoeck & Ruprecht, 1967.

DeMaris, Richard E. *The Colossian Controversy: Wisdom in Dispute in Colossians*. Vol. Sup. 96 JSNT. Sheffield: JSOT Press, 1994.

DeSilva, David A. *Honor, Patronage, Kinship and Purity: Unlocking New Testament Culture*. Downers Grove: InterVarsity Press, 2000.

Dibelius, M. *An die Kolosser, Epheser, an Philemon*. 3 ed. Handbuch zum Neuen Testament, ed. H. Greeven. Tübingen: J.C.B. Mohr, 1953.

———. "Zur Formgeschichte des Urchristentums." *Theologische Revue* 3 (1931): 207–242.

Dodd, C.H. *Gospel and Law: The Relation of Faith and Ethics in Early Christianity*. Cambridge: CUP, 1951.

Donelson, L.R. *Colossians, Ephesians, 1 and 2 Timothy, and Titus*. Westminister Bible Companion. Louisville: Westminister John Knox Press, 1996.

Dunn, James. *The Epistles to the Colossians and to Philemon*. The New International Greek Testament Commentary, eds. W.W. Gasque, I.H. Marshall and D.A. Hagner. Grand Rapids: Eerdmans, 1996.

———. "The Household Rules in the New Testament." In *The Family in Theological Perspective*, ed. S.C. Barton. Edinburgh: T&T Clark, 1996.

Ernst, J. *Die Briefe an die Philipper, an Philemon, an die Kolosser, an die Epheser*. Regensburg: Pustet, 1974.

Evans, J.D.G. *Aristotle*. Sussex: Harvester Press, 1987.

Faust, Eberhard. *Pax Christi et Pax Caesaris: religionsgeschichtliche,traditionsgeschichtliche und sozialgeschichtliche Studien zum Epheserbrief*. Vol. 24 Novum Testamentum et orbis antiquus. Freiburg: Universitätsverlag, 1993.

Ferguson, Everett. *Backgrounds of Early Christianity*. Grand Rapids: Eerdmans, 1993.

Fielder, Peter. "Haustafel." In *Reallexikon für Antike und Christentum*, ed. T. Klauser, 13, 1063–1074. Stuttgart: Anton Hiersemann, 1986.

Filson, F.V. "The Significance of the Early House Churches." *JBL* 58 (1939): 105–112.

Finley, M.I. *Ancient Slavery and Modern Ideology*. London: Chatto & Windus, 1980.

———, ed. *Slavery in Classical Antiquity: Views and Controversies*. Cambridge: W. Heffer & Sons, 1960.

Fischer, K.M. *Tendenz und Absicht des Epheserbriefes*. Vol. 111 Forschung zur Religion und Literatur des Alten und Neuen Testaments, eds. E. Käsemann and E. Würthwein. Göttingen: Vandenhoeck & Ruprecht, 1973.

Fitzgerald, John T. "The Catalogue in Ancient Greek Literature." *Journal for the Study of the New Testament* 146, Supplement Series (1997): 245–260.

Foerster, W. "Die Irrlehrer des Kolosserbriefes." In *Studia Biblica et Semitica, FS T.C. Vriezen*, 71–80. Wageningen: Veenman, 1966.

——— and Herrmann, J. "κληρονομία κτλ." In *TDNT*, ed. G. Kittel, 3, 758–785. Grand Rapids: Eerdmans, 1965.

273

Fossum, C.E. *The Image of the Invisible God: Essays on the Influence of Jewish Mysticism on Early Christianity.* Novum Testamentum et orbis antiquus. Freiburg: Vandenhoeck & Ruprecht, 1995.

Francis, F.O. "The Christological Argument in Colossians." In *God's Christ and His People, FS N.A. Dahl*, eds. W.A Meeks and J. Jervell, 192–208. Oslo: Universitetsforlaget, 1977.

Freund, Julien. *The Sociology of Max Weber.* Translated by Mary Ilford. London: Penguin Press, 1970.

Friedrich, J.H. "κληρονομία κτλ." In *EDNT,* eds. H. Balz and G. Schneider, 2, 298–301. Grand Rapids: Eerdmans, 1993.

Funk, A. *Status und Rollen in den Paulusbriefen: Ein inhaltsanalytische Untersuchung zur Religionssoziologie.* Innsbruck: Tyrolia-Verlag, 1980.

Furnish, Victor Paul. *Theology and Ethics in Paul.* Nashville: Abingdon Press, 1982.

Gammie, John G. "Paraenetic Literature: Toward a Morphology of a Secondary Genre." *Semeia* 50, Paraenesis: Act and Form (1990): 41–77.

Garland, David E. *Colossians and Philemon.* NIV Application Commentary Series, ed. T. Muck. Grand Rapids: Zondervan, 1998.

Gerstenberger, E.S., and Schrage, W. *Man and Woman.* Trans. D.W. Stott. Nashville: Abingdon, 1980.

Gese, M. *Das Vermächtnis des Apostels: Die Rezeption der paulinischen Theologie im Epheserbrief.* Vol. 99 WUNT, eds. M. Hengel and O. Hofius. Tübingen: Mohr Siebeck, 1997.

Gibbard, S.M. "The Christian Mystery." In *Studies in Ephesians,* ed. F.L. Cross, 97–120. London: A.R. Mowbray, 1956.

Gielen, M. "Haustafel." In *Lexikon für Theologie und Kirche,* ed. W. Kasper, Vol. 4, 1219–1220. Freiberg: Herder, 1993–2001.

———. *Tradition und Theologie neutestamentlicher Haustafelethik.* Vol. 75 Athenaeums Monografien: Bonner Biblische Beiträge, eds. Frank-Lothar Hossfeld and Helmut Merklein. Frankfurt: Anton Hain, 1990.

Gnilka, J. "Das Paulusbild im Kolosser- und Epheserbrief." In *Kontinuität und Einheit,* eds. P.-G. Müller and W. Stenger, 178–193. Freiburg: Herder, 1981.

———. *Der Epheserbrief.* Vol. 10 Herders Theologischer Kommentar zum Neuen Testament, eds. A. Vögtle, R. Schnackenburg and A. Wikenhauser. Freiburg: Herder, 1971.

———. *Der Kolosserbrief.* Vol. 10 Herders Theologischer Kommentar zum Neuen Testament, eds. A. Vögtle, A. Wikenhauser and R. Schnackenburg. Freiburg: Herder, 1980.

———. *Die frühen Christen: Ursprünge und Anfang der Kirche.* Vol. Supp. 7 Herders Theologischer Kommentar zum Neuen Testament, eds. J. Gnilka and L. Oberlinner. Freiburg: Herder, 1999.

———. "Paränetische Tradition im Epheserbrief." In *Mélanges Bibliques: en hommage au R.P. Béda Rigaux,* eds. A. Descamps and A. de Halleux, 397–410. Gembloux: Duculot, 1970.

———. *Paulus von Tarsus: Apostel und Zeuge.* Vol. Supp. 6 Herders Theologischer Kommentar zum Neuen Testament, eds. J. Gnilka and L. Oberlinner. Freiburg: Herder, 1996.

———. *Theologie des Neuen Testaments.* Vol. Supp. 5 Herders Theologischer Kommentar zum Neuen Testament, eds. J. Gnilka and L. Oberlinner. Freiburg: Herder, 1994.

274

Goppelt, Leonhard. *Der Erste Petrusbrief.* Vol. 12. 8th ed. Kritisch-exegetischer Kommentar über das Neue Testament, ed. Ferdinand Hahn. Göttingen: Vandenhoeck & Ruprecht, 1978.

Grabner-Haider, A. *Paraklese und Eschatologie bei Paulus.* Vol. 4 Neutestamentliche Abhandlungen, ed. J. Gnilka. Münster: Verlag Aschendorff, 1967.

Grant, R. M. "Early Christians and Gnostics in Graeco-Roman Society." In *The New Testament and Gnosis. FS R. McL. Wilson,* eds. A.H.B. Logan and A.J.M. Wedderburn. Edinburgh: T&T Clark, 1982.

Greeven, H. "Ehe nach dem Neuen Testament." *NTS* 15 (1968): 365–388.

Grundmann, W. "Das palästinische Judentum." In *Umwelt des Urchristentums,* eds. J. Leipoldt and W. Grundmann, 143–291. Berlin: Evangelische Verlagsanstalt, 1965.

Hahn, Ferdinand. *Christologische Hoheitstitel: Ihre Geschichte im frühen Christentum.* Vol. 83. 2nd ed. Forschungen zur Religion und Literatur des Alten und Neuen Testamentes, eds. E. Käsemann and E. Würthwein. Göttingen: Vandenhoeck & Ruprecht, 1964.

———. "Die Christologische Begründung urchristlicher Paränese." *Zeitschrift für die neutestamentliche Wissenschaft* 72 (1981): 88–99.

———. "Paulus und der Sklave Onesimus: Ein betrachtenswerter Kommentar zum Philemonbrief." *Evangelische Theologie* 37 (1977): 179–185.

Harnack, Adolf von. "Der Vorwurf des Atheismus in den drei ersten Jahrhunderten." *Texte und Untersuchungen zur Geschichte der altchristlichen Literatur* 28.4 (1905): 1–16.

Harris, Murray J. *Colossians and Philemon.* Grand Rapids: Eerdmans, 1991.

———. *Slave of Christ: A New Testament Metaphor for Total Devotion to Christ.* Vol. 8 New Studies in Biblical Theology, ed. D.A. Carson. Leicester: Apollos, 1999.

Hartman, Lars. "Code and Context: A Few Reflections on the Parenesis of Colossians 3:6–4:1." In *Understanding Paul's Ethics,* ed. B.S. Rosner, 177–191. Grand Rapids: Eerdmans, 1995.

———. "Some Unorthodox Thoughts on the "Household Code Form"." In *The Social World of Formative Christianity and Judaism, FS Howard Clark Kee,* ed. J. Neusner. Philadelphia: Fortress Press, 1988.

———. "Universal Reconciliation (Col. 1:20)." *Studien zum Neuen Testament und seiner Umwelt* 10 (1985): 109–21.

Harvey, A.E. "The Use of Mystery Language in the Bible." *JTS* 31 (1980): 320–336.

Hasenstab, Rudolf. *Modelle paulinischer Ethik: Beiträge zu einem Autonomie-Modell aus paulinischem Geist.* Vol. 11 Tübinger Theologische Studien, eds. W. Kasper A. Auer, H. Küng and M. Seckler. Mainz: Matthias-Grünewald-Verlag, 1977.

Hay, David M. *Colossians.* Abingdon New Testament Commentaries. Nashville: Abingdon Press, 2000.

Heine, Susanne. *Christianity and the Goddess: Systematic Criticism of a Feminist Theology.* London: SCM Press, 1988.

Hendricks, W.L. "All in All: Theological Themes in Colossians." *SWJT* 16 (1985): 23–35.

Hendriksen, W. *Ephesians.* London: Banner of Truth, 1967.

Hengel, Martin. *Crucifixion in the Ancient World and the Folly of the Message of the Cross.* Trans. J. Bowden. London: SCM Press, 1977.

———. "Die Ursprünge der christlichen Mission." *New Testament Studies* 18 (1971): 184–219.

———. *Studies in Early Christology.* Edinburgh: T&T Clark, 1995.

Hinson, E.G. "The Christian Household in Colossians 3:18–4:1." *Review and Expositor* 70 (1973): 495–506.

275

Holtzmann, H.J. *Kritik der Epheser- und Kolosserbriefe auf Grund einer Analyse ihres Verwandschaftsverhältnisses.* Leipzig: Wilhelm Engelmann, 1872.

Hoppe, R. "Das Mysterium und die Ekklesia: Aspekte zum Mysterium-Verhältnis im Kolosser- und Epheserbrief." In *Gottes Weisheit im Mysterium,* ed. A. Schilson, 81–101. Mainz: Matthias-Grünewald Verlag, 1989.

———. *Epheserbrief-Kolosserbrief.* Stuttgarter Kleiner Kommentar: Neues Testament 10. Stuttgart: A. Hiersemann, 1987.

——— and Busse, U., eds. *Von Jesus zum Christus: Christologische Studien: Festgabe für Paul Hoffmann zum 65. Geburtstag.* Ed. E. Gräßer. Beiheft 93, Zeitschrift für die neutestamentliche Wissenschaft. Berlin: Walter de Gruyter, 1998.

Horst, van der, P.W. "Observations on a Pauline Expression." *NTS* 19 (1972–73): 181–187.

———. "Pseudo-Phocylides and the New Testament." In *Zeitschrift für neutestamentliche Wissenschaft* 69 (1978): 187–202.

Houlden, J.L. *Paul's Letters from Prison: Philippians, Colossians, Philemon and Ephesians.* Westminster Pelican Commentaries. Philadelphia: Westminster Press, 1977.

House, H.W. "The Doctrine of Christ in Colossians." *BS* 149 (1992): 180–192.

Huebner, Hans. *Law in Paul's Thought.* Trans. J.C.G. Greig. Studies of the New Testament and its World, ed. J. Riches. Edinburgh: T&T Clark, 1984.

Hughes, G.J. *Aristotle: On Ethics.* Routledge Philosophy Guidebooks. London: Routledge, 2001.

Jonas, Hans. *Gnosis und spätantiker Geist.* Göttingen: Vandenhoeck & Ruprecht, 1934.

———. *The Gnostic Religion.* Boston: Beacon Press, 1963.

Juncker, Alfred. *Die Ethik des Apostels Paulus,* Vol. 2, Die Konkrete Ethik. Halle, 1919.

Kähler, E. *Die Frau in den paulinischen Briefen. Unter besonderer Berücksichtigung des Begriffs Unterordnung.* Zurich: Gotthelf Verlag, 1960.

———. "Zur 'Unterordnung' der Frau im Neuen Testament." *Zeitschrift für Evangelische Ethik* 3 (1959): 1–13.

Kahl, Joachim. *Das Elend des Christentums oder Plädoyer für eine Humanität ohne Gott.* Vol. 1093 Rororo aktuell. Hamburg: Rororo, 1977.

Kamlah, E. *Die Form der katalogischen Paränese im Neuen Testament.* Vol. 7 WUNT, eds. J. Jeremias and O. Michel. Tübingen: J.C.B. Mohr (Paul Siebeck), 1964.

———. "Philos Beitrag zur Aufhellung der Geschichte der Haustafeln." In *Wort and Wirklichkeit: Studien zur Afrikanistik und Orientalistik, FS E.L. Rapp zum 70. Geburtstag. Teil 1: Geschichte und Religionswissenschaft,* 90–95. Meisenheim/Glan: Anton Hain, 1976.

———. " Ὑποτάσσεσθαι in den NT Haustafeln." In *Verborum Veritas: FS Stählin,* eds. O. Böcher and K. Haacker. Wuppertal: R. Brockhaus, 1970.

Kasch, W. F. " ῥύομαι." In *TDNT,* ed. G. Kittel, 6, 998–1003. Grand Rapids: Eerdmans, 1965.

Käsemann, Ernst. *Paulinische Perspektiven.* 2nd ed. Tübingen: J.C.B. Mohr (Paul Siebeck), 1972.

———. "Sätze Heiligen Rechtes im Neuen Testament." *NTS* 1 (1954–55): 248–260.

Kehl, Nikolaus. *Der Christushymnus im Kolosserbrief: Eine motivgeschichtliche Untersuchung zu Kol. 1,12–20.* Vol. 1 Stuttgarter Biblische Monographien. Stuttgart: Verlag Katholisches Bibelwerk, 1967.

Kidd, Reggie M. *Wealth and Beneficence in the Pastoral Epistles.* Vol. 122 SBL Dissertation Series, eds. David Petersen and Charles Talbert. Atlanta: Scholars Press, 1990.

276

Kiley, Mark. *Colossians as Pseudepigraphy.* The Biblical Seminar. Sheffield: JSOT Press, 1986.

Kitchen, Martin. *Ephesians.* New Testament Readings, ed. J. Court. London: Routledge, 1994.

Klauck, H.-J. *Die religiöse Umwelt des Urchristentums II: Herrscher- und Kaiserkult, Philosophie, Gnosis.* Kohlhammer Studienbücher Theologie 9.2., eds. G. Bitter, et al. Stuttgart: Kohlhammer, 1996.

―――. *Gemeinde zwischen Haus und Staat: Kirche bei Paulus.* Freiburg: Herder, 1992.

―――. *Hausgemeinde und Hauskirche im frühen Christentum.* Vol. 103 Stuttgarter Bibelstudien, eds. H. Merklein and E. Zenger. Stuttgart: Katholisches Bibelwerk, 1981.

―――. *Religion und Gesellschaft im frühen Christentum.* Vol. 152 WUNT, eds. M. Hengel and O. Hofius. Tübingen: Mohr Siebeck, 2003.

Knox, John. *Philemon among the Letters of Paul: A New View of Its Place and Importance.* 2nd ed. New York: Abingdon, 1959.

Koschorke, K. "Die Polemik der Gnostiker gegen das kirchliche Christentum." In *Gnosis and Gnosticism,* ed. Martin Krause. Leiden: E.J. Brill, 1977.

Kramer, Werner. *Christ, Lord, Son of God.* Trans. Brian Hardy. Vol. 50 Studies in Biblical Theology. London: SCM Press, 1966.

Krause, M. "Christlich-gnostische Texte als Quellen für die Auseinandersetzung von Gnosis und Christentum." In *Gnosis and Gnosticism,* ed. Martin Krause. Leiden: E.J. Brill, 1981.

Kraut, Richard, ed. *Plato's Republic: Critical Essays.* Ed. S.M. Cahn, Critical Essays on the Classics. Lanham: Rowman & Littlefield, 1997.

Kreitzer, L.J. *The Epistle to the Ephesians.* Epworth Commentaries, ed. I.H. Jones. Peterborough: Epworth Press, 1997.

Kümmel, W. G. *Introduction to the New Testament.* London: SCM Press, 1984.

Lähnemann, Johannes. *Der Kolosserbrief: Komposition, Situation und Argumentation.* Vol. 3 Studien zum Neuen Testament, eds. W. Marxsen, G. Klein and W. Schrage. Gütersloh: Gütersloher Verlagshaus Gerd Mohn, 1971.

Lampe, Peter. "Keine 'Sklavenflucht' des Onesimus." *Zeitschrift für Neutestamentliche Wissenschaft* 76 (1985): 135–137.

Laub, Franz. *Die Begegnung des frühen Christentums mit der antiken Sklaverei.* Vol. 107 Stuttgarter Bibelstudien, eds. H. Merklein and E. Zenger. Stuttgart: Verlag Katholisches Bibelwerk, 1982.

―――. "Sozialgeschichtlicher Hintergrund und ekklesiologische Relevanz der neutestamentlich-frühchristlich Haus- und Gemeinde-Tafelparänese—ein Beitrag zur Soziologie des Frühchristentums." *Münchener Theologische Zeitschrift* 37 (1986): 249–271.

Leyden, W., von. *Aristotle on Equity and Justice: His Political Argument.* London: Macmillan, 1985.

Lightfoot, J.B. *St. Paul's Epistles to the Colossians and to Philemon.* The Epistles of St. Paul. London: Macmillan, 1904.

―――. *The Apostolic Fathers.* London: Macmillan, 1898.

Lillie, William. "The Pauline House-Tables." *Expository Times* 86 (1974–75): 179–183.

Lincoln, A.T. "A Re-Examination of 'the Heavenlies' in Ephesians." *NTS* 19 (1972–73): 468–483.

―――. *Ephesians.* Vol. 42 Word Biblical Commentary, ed. Ralph P. Martin. Dallas: Word Books, 1990.

―――. *Paradise Now and Not Yet: Studies in the Role of the Heavenly Dimension in Paul's Thought with Special Reference to His Eschatology.* Vol. 43 Society for New Testament Studies: Monograph Series. Cambridge: CUP, 1981.

277

———. "The Household Code and Wisdom Modes of Colossians." *JSNT* 74 (1999): 93–112.

———. "The Theology of Ephesians." In *The Theology of the Later Pauline Letters*, ed. J.D.G. Dunn. Cambridge: CUP, 1993.

———. "The Use of the OT in Ephesians." *JSNT* 14 (1982): 16–57.

Lindemann, A. "Die Gemeinde von 'Kolossä'. Erwägungen zum 'Sitz im Leben' eines deuteropaulinischen Briefes." *Wort und Dienst* 16 (1981): 111–134.

———. *Der Epheserbrief.* Vol. NT8 Zürcher Bibelkommentare, eds. H.H. Schmid and S. Schulz. Zürich: Theologischer Verlag, 1985.

———. *Paulus im ältesten Christentum.* Tübingen: J.C.B. Mohr, 1979.

Lips, Hermann, von. "Die Haustafel als 'Topos' im Rahmen der Urchristlichen Paränese, Beobachtungen anhand des 1. Petrusbriefes und des Titusbriefes." *NTS* 40 (1994): 261–280.

Lohmeyer, Ernst. *Die Briefe an die Philipper, an die Kolosser und an Philemon.* Vol. 9. 13th ed. Kritisch-exegetischer Kommentar über das Neue Testament, ed. H.A.W. Meyer. Göttingen: Vandenhoeck & Ruprecht, 1964.

Lohse, Eduard. "Christusherrschaft und Kirche im Kolosserbrief." *NTS* 11 (1964–1965): 203–216.

———. *Colossians and Philemon.* Trans. W.R. Poehlmann and R.J. Karris. Hermeneia - A Critical and Historical Commentary on the Bible, ed. H. Koester. Philadelphia: Fortress Press, 1971.

———. *Die Einheit des Neuen Testaments: Exegetische Studien zur Theologie des Neuen Testaments.* Göttingen: Vandenhoeck & Ruprecht, 1973.

———. "προσωπολημψία." In *TDNT*, ed. G. Kittel, 6, 779–780. Grand Rapids: Eerdmans, 1965.

———. *Theologische Ethik des Neuen Testaments.* Vol. 5.2 Theologische Wissenschaft, eds. W. Jetter, C. Andresen, W. Joest, O. Kaiser, E. Lohse and A.M. Ritter. Stuttgart: Verlag W. Kohlhammer, 1988.

Lona, H. E. *Die Eschatologie im Kolosser- und Epheserbrief.* Vol. 48 Forschung zur Bibel, eds. R. Schnackenburg and J. Schreiner. Würzburg: Echter Verlag, 1984.

Lührmann, Dieter. "Neutestamentliche Haustafeln und Antike Ökonomie." *New Testament Studies* 27 (1981): 83–97.

———. "Wo man nicht mehr Sklave oder Freier ist." *Wort und Dienst* 13 (1975): 55–83.

Luther, Martin. "Der kleine Katechismus von 1529." In *Luthers Werke, Volksausgabe in acht Bänden*, Vol. 3. Berlin: C.A. Schwetschke und Sohn, 1898.

Luz, Ulrich. "Überlegungen zum Epheserbrief und seiner Paränese." In *Neues Testament und Ethik, FS für R. Schnackenburg*, ed. H. Merklein, 376–396. Freiburg: Herder, 1989.

MacDonald, M.Y. *The Pauline Churches. A Socio-historical Study of Institutionalization in the Pauline and Deutero-Pauline Writings.* Society for New Testament Studies: Monograph Series 60. Cambridge: CUP, 1988.

MacRae, G.W. "Nag Hammadi and the New Testament." In *Gnosis. FS Hans Jonas*, ed. Barbara Aland. Göttingen: Vandenhoeck & Ruprecht, 1978.

Malherbe, A.J. "Hellenistic Moralists and the New Testament." In *ANRW*, eds. W. Haase and H. Temporini, 2.26.1, 267–333. Berlin: Walter de Gruyter, 1992.

———. *Moral Exhortation: A Greco-Roman Sourcebook.* Library of Early Christianity, ed. W.A. Meeks. Philadelphia: Westminster Press, 1986.

———. *Paul and the Popular Philosophers.* Minneapolis: Fortress Press, 1989.

———. *Social Aspects of Early Christianity.* Baton Rouge: LSU Press, 1977.

Martin, Ralph P. *Colossians: The Church's Lord and the Christian's Liberty.* Exeter: Paternoster Press, 1972.

———. *Colossians and Philemon.* New Century Bible, eds. R.E. Clements and M. Black. London: Oliphants, 1974.

Martin, Troy W. *By Philosophy and Empty Deceit: Colossians as a Response to a Cynic Critique.* Vol. Sup. 118 JSNTS. Sheffield: Sheffield Academic Press, 1996.

Meeks, W.A. and Francis, F.O., eds. *Conflict at Colossae: a Problem in the Interpretation of Early Christianity.* Vol. 4, Sources for Biblical Study. Missoula: SBL, 1973.

———. "The 'Haustafeln' and American Slavery: The Hermeneutical Challenge." In *Theology and Ethics in Paul and his Interpreters,* eds. E.H. Lovering and J.L. Sumney, 232–253. Nashville: Abingdon Press, 1996.

———. "In one Body: The Unity of Humankind in Colossians and Ephesians." In *God's Christ and His People, FS N.A. Dahl,* eds. W.A. Meeks and J. Jervell. Oslo: Universitetsforlaget, 1977.

Merk, O. *Handeln und Glauben: Die Motivierung der paulinischen Ethik.* Marburger Theologische Studien 5. Marburg: N.G. Elwert, 1968.

Merklein, H. *Christus und die Kirche: Die theologische Grundstruktur des Epheserbriefs nach 2,11–18.* Vol. 66 Stuttgarter Bibelstudien, eds. R. Kilian, H. Haag and W. Pesch. Stuttgart: Katholisches Bibelwerk, 1973.

———. *Das Kirchliche Amt nach dem Epheserbrief.* Vol. 33 Studien zum Alten und Neuen Testament, eds. V. Hamp and J. Schmid. München: Kösel-Verlag, 1973.

———. "Eph 4,1–5,20 als Rezeption von Kol 3,1–17 (zugleich ein Beitrag zur Problematik des Epheserbriefes)." In *Kontinuität und Einheit FS F. Mußner,* eds. P.-G. Müller and W. Stenger, 194–210. Freiburg: Herder, 1981.

———, ed. *Neues Testament und Ethik, FS für R. Schnackenburg.* Freiburg: Herder, 1989.

———. "Paulinische Theologie in der Rezeption des Kolosser- und Epheserbriefes." In *Paulus in den neutestamentlichen Spätschriften,* ed. K. Kertelge, 89, 25–69. Freiburg: Herder, 1981.

Merz, Anette. "Why Did the Pure Bride of Christ (2 Cor 11:2) Become a Wedded Wife (Eph. 5:22–33)? Theses about the Intertextual Transformation of an Ecclesiastical Metaphor." *JSNT* 79 (2000): 131–147.

Meyer, R.P. *Kirche und Mission im Epheserbrief.* Vol. 86 Stuttgarter Bibelstudien. Stuttgart: Katholisches Bibelwerk, 1977.

Michel, O. "Σκύθης." In *TDNT,* ed. G. Kittel, 7, 447–450. Grand Rapids: Eerdmans, 1965.

Mitton, C.L. *Ephesians.* New Century Bible Commentary, eds. R. Clements and M. Black. Grand Rapids: Eerdmans, 1983.

———. *The Epistle to the Ephesians.* Oxford: Clarendon Press, 1951.

Moritz, T. *A Profound Mystery: The Use of the Old Testament in Ephesians.* Vol. 85 Supplements to Novum Testamentum, eds. A.J. Malherbe and D.P. Mössner. Leiden: E.J. Brill, 1996.

Moule, C.F.D. *The Epistles of Paul the Apostle to the Colossians and to Philemon.* Cambridge Greek Testament Commentary, ed. C.F.D. Moule. Cambridge: CUP, 1968.

———. "The Nature and Purpose of 1 Peter." *NTS* 3 (1956–57): 1–11.

Moule, H.C.G. *The Epistle to the Ephesians.* Cambridge: CUP, 1902.

Moxnes, Halvor, ed. *Constructing Early Christian Families: Families as Social Reality and Metaphor.* London: Routledge, 1997.

Muddiman, J. *The Epistle to the Ephesians.* Black's New Testament Commentaries, ed. M.D. Hooker. London: Continuum, 2001.

Müller, K.-H. "Die Haustafel des Kolosserbriefs und das antike Frauenthema. Eine Rückschau auf alte Ergebnisse." In *Die Frau im Urchristentum*, eds. H. Merklein, K. Müller and G. Dautzenberg, 95, 263–319. Freiburg: Herder, 1983.

Munro, W. *Authority in Paul and Peter: The Identification of a Pastoral Stratum in the Pauline Corpus and 1 Peter*. Vol. 45 Society for New Testament Studies: Monograph Series. Cambridge: CUP, 1983.

———. "Col. 3:18–4:1 and Eph. 5:21–6:9: Evidences of a Late Literary Stratum?" *NTS* 18 (1972): 434–47.

Mußner, F. "Contributions made by Qumran to the Understanding of the Epistle to the Ephesians." In *Paul and Qumran*, ed. J. Murphy-O'Connor, 164–7. London: Chapman, 1968.

———. *Der Brief an die Epheser*. Vol. 10 Ökumenischer Taschenbuchkommentar zum Neuen Testament, eds. E. Gräßer and K. Kertelge. Würzburg: Echter Verlag, 1982.

Nash, R.S. "Heuristic Haustafeln: Domestic Codes as Entrance to the Social World of Early Christianity: The Case of Colossians." In *Religious Writings and Religious Systems*, eds. E.S. Frerichs, A.J. Levine and J. Neusner, 2. Atlanta: Scholars Press, 1989.

Newman, Carey C. *Paul's Glory-Christology: Tradition and Rhetoric*. Vol. 69 Supplements to Novum Testamentum, eds. A.J. Malherbe and D.P. Mössner. Leiden: Brill, 1992.

Niederwimmer, Kurt. *Die Didache*. Vol. 1 Kommentar zu den Apostolischen Vätern, eds. G. Kretschmar, K. Niederwimmer and N. Brox. Göttingen: Vandenhoeck & Ruprecht, 1989.

Nordling, J. G. "Onesimus Fugitivus: A Defense of the Runaway Slave Hypothesis in Philemon." *JSNT* 41 (1991): 97–119.

O'Brien, Peter T. *Colossians and Philemon*. Vol. 44 Word Biblical Commentary, ed. R.P. Martin. Waco: Word Books, 1982.

———. *The Letter to the Ephesians*. The Pillar New Testament Commentary, ed. D.A. Carson. Grand Rapids: Eerdmans, 1999.

Ochel, W. *Die Annahme einer Bearbeitung des Kolosserbriefes im Epheserbrief*. Würzburg: Konrad Triltsch, 1934.

O'Neill, J.C. "The Source of Christology in Colossians." *NTS* 26 (1979–1980): 87–100.

Pagels, E. "Adam and Eve: Christ and the Church." In *The New Testament and Gnosis, FS R. McL. Wilson*, eds. A. H. B. Logan and A. J. M. Wedderburn. Edinburgh: T&T Clark, 1983.

———. *The Gnostic Gospels*. London: Weidenfeld and Nicolson, 1980.

———. *The Gnostic Paul*. Philadelphia: Fortress Press, 1975.

Pangle, T.L. *The Laws of Plato*. Chicago: University of Chicago Press, 1980.

Pakaluk, Michael. *Aristotle: Nicomachean Ethics, Books VIII and IX*. Clarendon Aristotle Series, eds. J.C. Ackrill and L. Judson. Oxford: Clarendon Press, 1998.

Pape, D.R. *God and Woman: A Fresh Look at what the New Testament says about Women*. London: Mowbrays, 1977.

Percy, Ernst. *Die Probleme der Kolosser- und Epheserbriefe*. Lund: C.W.K. Gleerup, 1946.

Perdue, Leo G. "The Social Character of Paraenesis and Paraenetic Literature." *Semeia* 50, Paraenesis: Act and Form (1990): 5–39.

Perkins, Pheme. *Ephesians*. Abingdon New Testament Commentaries, ed. V.P. Furnish. Nashville: Abingdon Press, 1997.

———. *The Gnostic Dialogue*. New York: Paulist Press, 1980.

Petersen, N.R. *Rediscovering Paul: Philemon and the Sociology of Paul's Narrative World*. Philadelphia: Fortress Press, 1985.

280

Phillips, W.D. *Slavery from Roman Times to the Early Transatlantic Trade.* Manchester: University Press, 1985.

Plessner, Martin. *Der OIKONOMIKOΣ des Neupythagoreers 'Bryson' und sein Einfluss auf die islamische Wissenschaft.* Orient und Antike, eds. G. Bergsträsser and O. Regenbogen. Heidelberg: Carl Winter's Universitätsbuchhandlung, 1928.

Pokorný, P. *Der Brief des Paulus an die Epheser.* Theologischer Handkommentar zum Neuen Testament 10/II, eds. J. Rohde, E. Fascher and C. Wolff. Leipzig: Evangelische Verlagsanstalt, 1992.

———. *Der Brief des Paulus an die Kolosser.* Vol. X/1 Theologischer Handkommentar zum Neuen Testament, eds. J. Rohde, E. Fascher and C. Wolff. Berlin: Evangelische Verlagsanstalt, 1987.

———. *Der Epheserbrief und die Gnosis: Die Bedeutung des Haupt-Glieder-Gedankens in der entstehenden Kirche.* Berlin: Evangelische Verlagsanstalt, 1965.

Polhill, J.B. "The Relationship between Ephesians and Colossians." *Review and Expositor* 70 (1973): 439–50.

Porter, S.E. and Clarke, K.D. "Canonical-Critical Perspective and the Relationship of Colossians and Ephesians." *Biblica* 78 (1997): 58–86.

Praechter, Karl. *Hierokles der Stoiker.* Leipzig: Dieterich'sche Verlags-Buchhandlung, 1901.

Quinn, Jerome D. "Paraenesis and the Pastoral Epistles: Lexical Observations Bearing on the Nature of the Sub-genre and the Soundings on its Role in Socialization and Liturgies." *Semeia* 50, Paraenesis: Act and Form (1990): 189–210.

Rapske, B.M. "The Prisoner Paul in the Eyes of Onesimus." *NTS* 37 (1991): 187–203.

Reeve, C.D.C. *Aristotle: Politics.* Cambridge: Hackett Publishing, 1998.

Reitzenstein, R. *Die Hellenistischen Mysterienreligionen.* Leipzig: B.G. Teubner, 1927.

Rengstorf, K.H. *Die neutestamentlichen Mahnungen an die Frau, sich dem Manne unterzuordnen.* FS für O. Schmitz Verbum Dei manet in Aeternum, ed. W. Förster. Witten: Luther Verlag, 1953.

———. *Mann und Frau im Urchristentum.* Vol. 12 Arbeitsgemeinschaft für Forschung des Landes Nordrhein-Westfalen. Köln-Opladen: Westdeutscher Verlag, 1954.

Richards, E. Randolph. *The Secretary in the Letters of Paul.* Vol. 42 WUNT, eds. M. Hengel and O. Hofius. Tübingen: J.C.B. Mohr, 1991.

Robinson, J.A. *St. Paul's Epistle to the Ephesians.* London: Macmillan, 1903.

Robinson, James M. "Gnosticism and the New Testament." In *Gnosis. FS Hans Jonas,* ed. Barbara Aland. Göttingen: Vandenhoeck & Ruprecht, 1978.

Roon, A., Van. *The Authenticity of Ephesians.* Vol. 39 Supplements to Novum Testamentum, ed. W.C. van Unnik. Leiden: Brill, 1974.

Rorty, A.O., ed. *Essays on Aristotle's Ethics.* Berkeley: University of California Press, 1980.

Rowe, C. and Brodie, S. *Aristotle: Nicomachean Ethics.* Oxford: Oxford University Press, 2002.

Runia, David T. *Philo in Early Christian Literature: A Survey.* Vol. 3 Compendia Rerum Iudaicarum ad Novum Testamentum, Section 3: Jewish Traditions in Early Christian Literature. Assen: Van Gorcum, 1993.

Russell, D.A. *Plutarch.* London: Duckworth, 1973.

Sampley, J.P. *"And the Two Shall Become One Flesh": A Study of Traditions in Eph. 5:21–33.* Cambridge: CUP, 1971.

Sanders, E.P. "Literary Dependence in Colossians." *JBL* 85 (1966): 28–45.

Sanders, J.T. *Ethics in the New Testament: Change and Development.* London: SCM, 1986.

Sandmel, Samuel. *Philo of Alexandria: An Introduction.* Oxford: Oxford University Press, 1979.

Sappington, Thomas J. *Revelation and Redemption at Colossae.* Sup. Vol. 53 JSNT. Sheffield: JSOT Press, 1991.

Saunders, T.J. *Aristotle: Politics, Book I and II.* Clarendon Aristotle Series, eds. J.C. Ackrill and L. Judson. Oxford: Clarendon Press, 1995.

Sayers, Sean. *Plato's Republic: An Introduction.* Edinburgh: Edinburgh University Press, 1999.

Schenk, W. and Quell, G. "δίκη, κτλ." In *TDNT,* eds. G. Kittel and G. Friedrich, 2, 174–225. Grand Rapids: Eerdmans, 1964–76.

———. "Christus, das Geheimnis der Welt, als dogmatisches und ethisches Grundprinzip des Kolosserbriefes." *Evangelische Theologie* 43 (1983): 138–155.

———. "Der Brief des Paulus an Philemon in der neueren Forschung (1945–1987)." In *ANRW,* eds. W. Haase and H. Temporini, 2.25.4, 3439–95. Berlin: Walter De Gryter, 1987.

———. "Der Kolosserbrief in der neueren Forschung (1945–1985)." In *ANRW,* eds. W. Haase and H. Temporini, 2.25.4, 3327–3364. Berlin: Walter De Gryter, 1987.

Schillebeeckx, E. *Marriage: Human Reality and Saving Mystery.* London: Sheed and Ward, 1965.

Schlier, H. *Christus und die Kirche im Epheserbrief.* Vol. 6 Beiträge zur Historischen Theologie. Tübingen: J.C.B. Mohr, 1930.

———. *Der Brief an die Epheser.* Düsseldorf: Patmos, 1957.

Schmidt, J. *Der Epheserbrief des Apostels Paulus: Seine Adresse, Sprache und literarischen Beziehungen.* Freiburg: Herder, 1928.

Schmithals, Walter. *Neues Testament und Gnosis.* Vol. 208 Erträge der Forschung. Darmstadt: Wissenschaftliche Buchgesellschaft, 1984.

———. "The Corpus Paulinum and Gnosis." In *The New Testament and Gnosis: FS R. McL. Wilson,* eds. A.H.B. Logan and A.J.M. Wedderburn. Edinburgh: T&T Clark, 1983.

Schnackenburg, R. *Der Brief an die Epheser.* Vol. 10 Evangelisch-Katholischer Kommentar zum Neuen Testament, eds. E. Schweizer and U. Wilckens. Zürich: Benziger Verlag, 1982.

Schneider, Gerhard. *Jesusüberlieferung und Christologie, neutestamentliche Aufsätze, 1970–1990.* Vol. 67 Supplements to Novum Testamentum, eds. A.J. Malherbe and D.P. Mössner. Leiden: Brill, 1992.

Schöllgen, Georg. "Hausgemeinden, οἶκος-Ekklesiologie und monarchischer Episkopat, Überlegungen zu einer neuen Forschungsrichtung." *Jahrbuch für Antike und Christentum* 31 (1988): 74–90.

———. "Ökonomik und Hauswirtschaft." In *Reallexikon für Antike und Christentum,* ed. T. Klauser, 13, 815–830. Stuttgart: Anton Hiersemann, 1986.

———. "Was wissen wir über die Sozialstruktur der paulinischen Gemeinden?" *NTS* 34 (1988): 71–83.

Schrage, Wolfgang. *Ethik des Neuen Testaments.* Vol. 4 Grundrisse zum Neuen Testament, ed. G. Friedrich. Göttingen: Vandenhoeck & Ruprecht, 1982.

———. "Zur Ethik der neutestamentlichen Haustafeln." *NTS* 21 (1975): 1–22.

Schroeder, David. *Die Haustafeln des Neuen Testaments* (dissertation). Hamburg, 1959.

———. "Lists, Ethical." In *Interpreter's Dictionary of the Bible,* ed. G.A. Buttrick, Supp. Vol., 546–547. Nashville: Abingdon, 1976.

Schulz, Siegfried. *Neutestamentliche Ethik.* Zürcher Grundrisse zur Bibel, eds. H.H.Schmidt and S. Schulz. Zürich: Theologischer Verlag Zürich, 1987.

Schüssler Fiorenza, E. *A Critical Feminist Ekklesia-logy of Liberation.* London: SCM Press, 1993.

———. *In Memory of Her: A Feminist Theological Reconstruction of Christian Origins.* London: SCM Press, 1983.

Schweizer, E. *Church Order in the New Testament.* London: SCM Press, 1961.

———. *Der Brief an die Kolosser.* Evangelisch-Katholischer Kommentar zum Neuen Testament, eds. R. Schnackenburg, J. Blank, E. Schweizer and U. Wilckens. Zürich: Benziger Verlag, 1976.

———. *Der erste Petrusbrief.* Zürcher Bibelkommentare. Zürich: Theologischer Verlag, 1972.

———. "Die Weltlichkeit des Neuen Testaments: Die Haustafeln." In *Beiträge zur alttestamentlichen Theologie, FS für W. Zimmerli zum 70. Geburtstag,* eds. R. Hanhart, R. Smend and H. Donner. Göttingen: Vandenhoeck & Ruprecht, 1977.

———. "Traditional Ethical Patterns in Pauline and post-Pauline Letters." In *Text and Interpretation: Studies in the New Testament, FS Matthew Black,* eds. Ernest Best and R. McLachlan Wilson. Cambridge: CUP, 1979.

———. "Zum Sklavenproblem im Neuen Testament." *Evangelische Theologie* 32 (1972): 502–506.

Seeberg, A. *Der Katechismus der Urchristenheit.* Leipzig: A. Deichert, 1903.

Sellin, Gerhard. "Die Paränese des Epheserbriefes." In *Gemeinschaft am Evangelium, FS für Wiard Popkes,* eds. P. Fiddes, J. Molthagen and E. Brandt. Leipzig: Evangelische Verlagsanstalt, 1996.

Selwyn, E.G. *The First Epistle of St. Peter.* London: Macmillan & Co., Ltd., 1946.

Shellrude, G.M. "The Apocalypse of Adam: Evidence for a Christian Gnostic Provenance." In *Gnosis and Gnosticism,* ed. Martin Krause. Leiden: E.J. Brill, 1981.

Simpson, E.K. and Bruce, F.F. *Commentary on the Epistles to the Ephesians and the Colossians.* New International Comentary on the New Testament. Grand Rapids: Eerdmans, 1973.

Sly, Dorothy. *Philo's Perception of Women.* Vol. 209 Brown Judaic Studies. Atlanta: Scholars Press, 1990.

Snodgrass, K.R. *Ephesians.* The NIV Application Commentary, ed. T. Muck. Grand Rapids: Zondervan, 1996.

Stählin, G. "ἰσότης κτλ." In *TDNT,* ed. G. Kittel, 3, 343–355. Grand Rapids: Eerdmans, 1965.

Stalley, R.F. *An Introduction to Plato's Laws.* Oxford: Blackwell, 1983.

Standhartinger, Angela. *Studien zur Entstehungsgeschichte und Intention des Kolosserbriefs.* Vol. 94 Supplements to Novum Testamentum, eds. A.J. Malherbe and D.P. Mössner. Leiden: Brill, 1999.

———. "The Origin and Intention of the Household Code in the Letter to the Colossians." *JSNT* 79 (2000): 117–130.

Steinmetz, F. "Protologische Heils-Zuversicht: Die Strukturen des soteriologischen und christologischen Denkens im Kolosser- und Epheserbrief." *Frankfurter Theologische Studien* 2 (1969).

Strecker, Georg. "Die neutestamentlichen Haustafeln." In *Neues Testament und Ethik: FS für R. Schnackenburg,* ed. H. Merklein, 349–375. Freiburg: Herder, 1989.

———. "Ziele und Ergebnisse einer neutestamentlichen Ethik." *New Testament Studies* 25 (1979): 1–15.

283

Stuhlmacher, P. "Christliche Verantwortung bei Paulus und seinen Schülern." In *Evangelische Theologie* 28 (1968), 165–186.

―――. *Der Brief an Philemon.* Evangelisch-Katholischer Kommentar zum Neuen Testament, eds. R. Schnackenburg, J. Blank, E. Schweizer and U. Wilckens. Zürich: Benziger Verlag, 1975.

Suhl, Alfred. *Der Brief an Philemon.* Vol. NT 13 Zürcher Bibelkommentare, eds. H.H. Schmid, G. Fohrer, S. Schulz. Zürich: Theologischer Verlag, 1981.

―――. "Der Philemonbrief als Beispiel paulinischer Paränese." *Kairos* 15 (1973): 267–279.

Sumney, Jerry L. *"Servants of Satan", "False Brothers" and Other Opponents of Paul.* Vol. Sup. 188 Journal for the Study of the New Testament, ed. S.E. Porter. Sheffield: Sheffield Academic Press, 1999.

Tanzer, S.J. "Submerged Traditions of Sophia: Ephesians." In *Searching the Scriptures: A Feminist Commentary*, ed. E. Schüssler Fiorenza, 2. New York: Crossroad Publishing Company, 1994.

Terrien, S. *Till the Heart Sings: A Biblical Theology of Manhood and Womanhood.* Philadelphia: Fortress Press, 1985.

Thiessen, W. *Christen in Ephesus: Die historische und theologische Situation in vorpaulinischer und paulinischer Zeit und zur Zeit der Apostelgeschichte und der Pastoralbriefe.* Vol. 12 Texte und Arbeiten zum neutestamentlichen Zeitalter. Tübingen: Franke Verlag, 1995.

Thraede, Klaus. "Ärger mit der Freiheit. Die Bedeutung von Frauen in Theorie und Praxis der alten Kirche." In *"Freunde in Christus werden..." Die Beziehung von Mann und Frau als Frage an Theologie und Kirche*, ed. Gerta Scharffenroth, 31–182. Berlin: Gelnhausen, 1977.

―――. "Zum historischen Hintergrund der Haustafeln des Neuen Testaments." *Pietas* Sup. Vol. 1980, FS B. Kötting (1980): 359–368.

Towner, P.H. "Households and Household Codes." In *Dictionary of Paul and His Letters*, eds. G.F. Hawthorne, et. al., 417–419. Downers Grove: InterVarsity Press, 1993.

Trench, R.C. *Synonyms of the New Testament.* Grand Rapids: Eerdmans, 1953.

Trompf, G.W. "On Attitudes toward Women in Paul and Paulinist Literature: 1 Cor. 11: 3–6 and Its Context." *Catholic Biblical Quarterly* 42 (1980): 196–215.

Urassa, W.M. *Psalm 8 and its Christological Re-Interpretations in the New Testament Context: An Inter-Contextual Study in Biblical Hermeneutics.* Vol. 577 European University Studies, Theology XXIII. Frankfurt a.M.: Peter Lang, 1998.

Urmson, J.O. *Aristotle's Ethics.* Oxford: Blackwell, 1988.

Usami, Koshi. *Somatic Comprehension of Unity.* Vol. 101 Analecta Biblica. Rome: Biblical Institute Press, 1983.

Verbecke, Gerard. *Moral Education in Aristotle.* Washington: Catholic University of America Press, 1990.

Verner, David Carl. *The Household of God: The Social World of the Pastoral Epistles.* Vol. 71 SBL Dissertation Series, ed. William Baird. Chico: Scholars Press, 1983.

Vogt, Joseph. *Ancient Slavery and the Ideal of Man.* Trans. Thomas Wiedemann. Blackwell's Classical Studies, ed. Oswyn Murray. Oxford: Basil Blackwell, 1974.

Wagener, Ulrike. *Die Ordnung des "Hauses Gottes".* Vol. 65. 2nd ed. WUNT, eds. M. Hengel and O. Hofius. Tübingen: J.C.B. Mohr, 1994.

Walker, W.O. "The 'Theology of Woman's Place' and the 'Paulinist' Tradition." *Semeia* 28 (1983): 101–112.

284

Walsh, J.J. and Shapiro, H.L., eds. *Aritotle's Ethics: Issues and Interpretations*. Wadsworth Series in Philosophical Criticism. Belmont: Wadsworth Publishing, 1967.

Wanke, G. and Balz, H. "φοβέω κτλ." In *TDNT*, eds. G. Kittel and G. Friedrich, 9, 189–219. Grand Rapids: Eerdmans, 1964.

Watson, F.B. *Agape, Eros, Gender: Towards a Pauline Sexual Ethic*. Cambridge: CUP, 2000.

Weber, Max. *Wirtschaft und Gesellschaft: Grundriß der Verstehenden Soziologie*. 5th ed. Tübingen: J.C.B. Mohr (Paul Siebeck), 1972.

Wedderburn, A.J.M. and Lincoln, A.T. *The Theology of the Later Pauline Letters*. New Testament Theology, ed. J. D.G. Dunn. Cambridge: CUP, 1993.

Wegenast, K. *Das Verständnis der Tradition bei Paulus in den Deuteropaulinen*. Vol. 8 Wissenschaftliche Monographien zum Alten und Neuen Testament, eds. G. Bornkamm and G. von Rad. Neukirchen: Neukirchener Verlag, 1962.

Weidinger, Karl. *Die Haustafeln, ein Stück urchristlicher Paränese*. Vol. 14 Untersuchungen zum Neuen Testament, ed. H. Windisch. Leipzig: J.C. Heinrichs'sche Buchhandlung, 1928.

Weiser, A. "Titus 2 als Gemeindeparänese." In *Neues Testament und Ethik: FS für R. Schnackenburg*, ed. H. Merklein, 397–414. Freiburg: Herder, 1989.

Wendland, H.D. *Ethik des Neuen Testaments: eine Einführung*. Vol. 4. 2nd ed. Grundrisse zum Neuen Testament, ed. G. Friedrich. Göttingen: Vandenhoeck & Ruprecht, 1975.

———. "Zur sozialethischen Bedeutung der neutestamentlichen Haustafeln." *Studien zur evangelischen Sozialtheologie und Sozialethik* 5 (1959): 104–114.

Wendland, Paul. *Die hellenistisch-römische Kultur in ihren Beziehungen zum Judentum und Christentum: Die urchristlichen Literaturformen*. Vol. 2. 4th ed. Handbuch zum Neuen Testament. Tübingen: Mohr, 1912.

Wengst, Klaus. *Christologische Formeln und Lieder des Urchristentums*. Vol. 7 Studien zum Neuen Testament. Gütersloh: Mohn, 1972.

———. *Tradition und Theologie des Barnabasbriefes*. Vol. 42 Arbeiten zur Kirchengeschichte. Berlin: Walter de Gruyter, 1971.

———. "Versöhnung und Befreiung: Ein Aspekt des Themas 'Schuld und Vergebung' im Lichte des Kolosserbriefes." *Evangelische Theologie* 36 (1976): 14–26.

Wescott, B.F. *St. Paul's Epistle to the Ephesians*. London: Macmillan, 1906.

Wessels, G.F. "The Eschatology of Colossians and Ephesians." *Neotestamentica* 21 (1987): 183–202.

Wickert, U. "Der Philemonbrief - Privatbrief oder apostolisches Schreiben?" *Zeitschrift für neutestamentliche Wissenschaft* 52 (1961): 230–238.

Wiedemann, Thomas. *Greek and Roman Slavery*. London: Croom Helm, 1981.

Wild, R.A. "'Be Imitators of God': Discipleship in the Letter to the Ephesians." In *Discipleship in the New Testament*, ed. F.F. Segovia, 127–143. Philadelphia: Fortress, 1985.

Wilhelm, Friedrich. "Die Oeconomica der Neupythagoreer Bryson, Kallikratidas, Periktione, Phintys." *Rheinisches Museum für Philologie* 70 (1915): 161–223.

Wilson, Andrew. "The Pragmatics of Politeness and Pauline Epistolography: A Case Study of the Letter of Philemon." *JSNT* 48 (1992): 107–119.

Wilson, Walter T. *The Hope of Glory: Education and Exhortation in the Epistle to the Colossians*. Vol. 88 Supplements to Novum Testamentum, eds. A.J. Malherbe and D.P. Mössner. Leiden: Brill, 1997.

Winter, Bruce W. *Philo and Paul Among the Sophists*. Vol. 96 Society for New Testament Studies: Monograph Series. Cambridge: CUP, 1997.

Winter, S. C. "Paul's Letter to Philemon." *NTS* 33 (1987): 1–15.

Wisse, Frederik. "Prolegomena to the Study of the New Testament and Gnosis." In *The New Testament and Gnosis. FS R. McL. Wilson*, eds. A.H.D. Logan and A.J.M. Wedderburn. Edinburgh: T&T Clark, 1983.

Witherington, B. *Women in the Earliest Churches*. Vol. 59 Society for New Testament Studies: Monograph Series, ed. G.N. Stanton. Cambridge: CUP, 1988.

Wolter, Michael. *Der Brief an die Kolosser, Der Brief an Philemon*. Vol. 12 Ökumenischer Taschenbuchkommentar zum Neuen Testament, eds. E. Gräßer and K. Kertelge. Gütersloh: Gütersloher Verlagshaus Gerd Mohn, 1993.

Woyke, Johannes. *Die neutestamentlichen Haustafeln: ein kritischer und konstruktiver Forschungsüberblick*. Vol. 184 Stuttgarter Bibelstudien. Stuttgart: Verlag Katholisches Bibelwerk, 2000.

Wright, N.T. *The Epistles of Paul to the Colossians and to Philemon*. Vol. 12 The Tyndale New Testament Commentaries, ed. L. Morris. Leicester: Inter-Varsity Press, 1986.

———. "Poetry and Theology in Colossians 1:15–20." *NTS* 36 (1990): 444–468.

Wuellner, William. "Greek Rhetoric and Pauline Argumentation." In *Early Christian Literature and the Classical Intellectual Tradition*, ed. W.R. Schoedel and R.L. Wilken, 53, 177–188. Paris: Éditions Beauchesne, 1979.

Yamauchi, Paul. *Pre-Christian Gnosticism: A Survey of the Proposed Evidences*. London: Tyndale, 1975.

Yarbrough, O. Larry. *Not Like the Gentiles: Marriage Roles in the Letters of Paul*. Vol. 80 Society of Biblical Literature: Dissertation Series. Atlanta: Scholars Press, 1985.

Yates, R. *The Epistle to the Colossians*. Epworth Commentary. London: Epworth, 1993.

Yorke, G. *The Church as the Body of Christ in the Pauline Corpus: A Re-examination*. London: University Press of America, 1991.

Zeilinger, F. *Der Erstgeborene der Schöpfung: Untersuchungen zur Formalstruktur und Theologie des Kolosserbriefes*. Wien: Herder, 1974.